The Psychologies in Religion
Working With the Religious Client

About the Editors

E. THOMAS DOWD, PHD, ABPP, is professor of psychology at Kent State University and previously taught at Florida State University and the University of Nebraska. His area of interest is in cognitive behavior therapy, its theoretical and conceptual development and its applications. He has served as president of the International Association for Cognitive Psychotherapy, the American Board of Cognitive and Behavioral Psychology, and the American Academy of Cognitive and Behavioral Psychology. He has also served over the years on many professional and university governance boards and committees. He is the author of numerous books, book chapters, and journal articles, and he has made numerous national and international presentations.

STEVAN LARS NIELSEN, PHD, is clinical professor of student development at Brigham Young University. His area of interest is rational-emotive-behavior therapy, including its religious applications. He is adjunct professor with the Department of Psychology, where he teaches graduate and undergraduate courses. He is the co-author of a book integrating religious material with rational-emotive-behavior therapy, author of four chapters, and 18 journal articles. One of his chapters focuses on using the Qur'an during treatment of a Muslim client.

The Psychologies in Religion

Working With the Religious Client

Edited by

E. Thomas Dowd, PhD, ABPP
Stevan Lars Nielsen, PhD

SPRINGER PUBLISHING COMPANY
NEW YORK

To Therese, my wife, Kathleen and Jon, my daughter and son-in-law,
and Michael, my son. They are most of the reasons behind all my activities.
And above all to the Deity, by whatever name (s)he is called,
who inspired this book and continues to inspire us.

—E. Thomas Dowd

To Allen Bergin: Your enthusiasm for science and religion launched my career
in psychology. Your courage and dedication to both inspire me still.

—Stevan Lars Nielsen

Springer Publishing Company, Inc.
11 West 42nd Street
New York, NY 10036

Acquisitions Editor: Sheri W. Sussman
Production Editor: Jeanne Libby
Cover design by Joanne Honigman
Typeset by Daily Information Processing, Churchville, PA

06 07 08 09 10 / 5 4 3 2 1

Library of Congress Cataloging-in-Publication Data

The psychologies in religion : working with the religious client /
E. Thomas Dowd, Stevan Lars Nielsen, editors.
        p. ; cm.
    Includes bibliographical references and index.
    ISBN 0-8261-2856-4
    1. Psychology and religion. 2. Psychotherapy—Religious aspects.
    [DNLM: 1. Psychotherapy—methods. 2. Religion and Psychology.
3. Models, Psychological. WM 460.5.R3 P9747 2006] I. Dowd,
E. Thomas. II. Nielsen, Stevan Lars.
    BF51.P735 2006
    200.1'9—dc22
                                                        2005031315

Printed in the United States of America by Maple-Vail Book
Manufacturing Group.

Contents

Contributors

SABA RASHEED ALI, PHD, is an assistant professor of counseling psychology at the University of Iowa in the Division of Psychological and Quantitative Foundations. She received her doctoral degree in counseling psychology from the University of Oregon in 2001. Her research interests include women and Islam and the intersections between multiculturalism and feminism. Additional research interests include vocational development of underserved youth, especially vocational and educational development of rural youth.

PAUL ASHBY, MDIV, DDIV, did his doctoral work at Colgate Rochester Divinity School. Ashby has served as senior minister of Mainline churches in Ohio, Connecticut, and California. He has received a "Friends of Tibet" award for his work with Tibetan refugees in Connecticut and a Merrill Fellowship to Harvard University to conduct research in world religions.

THE REV. DR. JAMES R. BEEBE, D.MIN, is a retired Air Force pilot and associate rector at St. Paul's Episcopal Church. He received his doctor of ministry from Drew University in 21st Century Church Leadership, specializing in classical Christian spirituality in a postmodern age. He is soon to be the rector of St. Patrick's Episcopal Church in Incline Village, Nevada.

JOHN R. BELCHER, MDIV, PHD, LCSW-C, received a masters of social work from the University of Kentucky in 1981 and masters of divinity from Lexington Theological Seminary in 1982. He served as pastor of a small rural Kentucky congregation for three years. He then worked for two years as a therapist at a community mental health center in Wyoming before pursuing a PhD in social welfare. Since 1987, he has taught for the University of Maryland School of Social Work. He is an active therapist and pastoral counselor. He also teaches for the Ecumenical Institute at St. Mary's Seminary and University.

RABBI AMY RUTH BOLTON, MA, is a conservative rabbi in Highland Park, New Jersey. She received a BA in psychology and an MA in rabbinic studies. Rabbi Bolton has worked as a hospice chaplain and has taught both youth and adults in a variety of settings.

DONALD L. BUBENZER, MDIV, PHD, is department chair and professor of counseling and human development services at Kent State University. He scholarly interests are in couple and family counseling from a narrative–constructionist perspective, the study of leadership, and the measurement of the subjective.

NEHARIKA CHAWLA, MA, is a graduate student in the Addictive Behaviors Research Center where she conducts research on mindfulness meditation and its role in promoting well-being and in preventing and treating addictive behavior problems. She received her MA in psychology from Brandeis University.

THE REV. DR. DAVID E. FARLEY, PHD, received his BA from Midland College, master of divinity from Hamma Divinity School, MA in psychology from Fairleigh Dickinson University, and PhD from Oxford University in the UK. He is currently the pastor of the Lutheran Church of the Holy Communion in Philadelphia, Pennsylvania, and served in past parishes in New York, Indiana, and Rhode Island. He has been a faculty member at University of Texas M.D. Anderson Cancer Center and Cornell Medical Center.

ELIZABETH A. GASSIN, PHD, is an associate professor of psychology at Olivet Nazarene University. She received her PhD in educational psychology at the University of Wisconsin, studying the psychology of interpersonal forgiveness with Dr. Robert Enright. She continues to write about forgiveness, as well as about integration of psychology and Orthodox theology. She has spent several years teaching in various places in Russia, including one year as a Fulbright scholar.

REV. KEVIN GILLESPIE, SJ, PHD, is an associate professor in the Department of Pastoral Counseling at Loyola College in Baltimore, Maryland. Having received his doctorate in pastoral psychology from Boston University in 1998, Fr. Gillespie has written and presented internationally on topics relating to psychology and religion. In 2001, he published *Psychology and American Catholicism; From Confession to Therapy?*. Fr. Gillespie is a member of Division 36 of the American Psychological Association.

IRA S. HALPER, MD, is an assistant professor of psychiatry at Rush Medical College and director of the Cognitive Therapy Center at Rush University Medical Center in Chicago, Illinois. Dr. Halper's interests include both biological psychiatry and cognitive behavioral therapy.

DANIEL K. JUDD, PHD, was reared in Southern Utah and Northern Arizona, where he worked on the family ranch and as a river guide on the Colorado River. He holds an MS in family science and a PhD in counseling psychology from Brigham Young University (BYU). Dr. Judd is presently a professor of Ancient Scripture at BYU, where he has also served as a department chair. He is the author of numerous books and articles on various aspects of religion and mental health and has served in numerous leadership positions in his church. Dr. Judd and his wife Kaye are the parents of four children and live in Orem, Utah.

KATE MIRIAM LOEWENTHAL, PHD, is professor of psychology at Royal Holloway, University of London, UK. She has published several books and a number of articles on mental health and religion in minority groups, and other topics. She is currently involved in research and service provision, particularly in the Orthodox Jewish community.

AMINIA MAHMOOD, BA, is currently a doctoral student in the counseling psychology program at the University of Iowa and anticipates graduating in summer of 2008. Her research and scholarly interests include Multicultural issues, religion and spirituality, feminism, social class and social justice issues. She is particularly interested in conducting research on the American Muslim population. She self-identifies as Just a Muslim.

G. ALAN MARLATT, PHD, is professor of psychology and director of the Addictive Behaviors Research Center, University of Washington, where he conducts training and research on the prevention and treatment of alcohol and other addictive behavior problems in college students and Native American Youth, as well as on the effects of Vipassana meditation on relapse and general well-being. He received his PhD in psychology from Indiana University.

REBECCA MURRAY, PHD, earned her doctorate in clinical psychology from Georgia State University. She is associate professor in the Department of Psychology at Georgia Southern University, where she teaches a number of undergraduate and graduate courses, publishes clinically relevant research, and maintains a part-time private practice.

ARTHUR M. NEZU, PHD, ABPP, received his PhD in clinical psychology from the State University of New York at Stony Brook in 1979. At present, he is professor of psychology, medicine, and public health at Drexel University in Philadelphia, Pennsylvania, where he serves as Director of the Center for Behavioral Medicine and Mind/Body Studies. Dr. Nezu was previously president of the Association for Advancement of Behavior Therapy and is current president of the American Board of Cognitive and Behavioral Psychology.

CHRISTINE MAGUTH NEZU, PHD, ABPP, received her PhD from Fairleigh Dickinson University and completed her psychology residency training at Beth Israel Medical Center. She is currently a professor of psychology and associate professor of medicine at Drexel University in Philadelphia, Pennsylvania. She is the founding co-director for the Center for Behavioral Medicine and Mind/Body Studies at Drexel, and is also the director for Assessment and Treatment Services for sexual aggression.

DIANNE LINDLEY NIELSEN, PHD, earned the doctorate in clinical psychology at Brigham Young University. She is an assistant clinical professor of Student Development at the Brigham Young University Counseling and Career Center. She and her husband, Stevan Lars Nielsen, are the parents of four sons. Both are clinical psychologists and practicing Mormons. They hold positions giving them responsibility to teach the teenagers in their congregation. Her interests include the treatment of personality disorders and the use of self-help materials.

MICHAEL E. NIELSEN, PHD, is associate professor of psychology at Georgia Southern University. He has written widely on psychological aspects of religion and has presented his research internationally. He also writes for the general public through his award-winning Psychology of Religion web pages and a regular column on religion for Sunstone magazine.

AMY B. QUILLIN, PHD, is a disability specialist and acting director of Disability Services at Kent State University. Her dissertation focused perceptions of the spiritual among master's level students in counseling. She has an interest in the integration of counseling and spirituality.

STEPHEN R. RUSSELL, MA, is a pre-doctoral intern in clinical psychology at the University of Tennessee, Health Sciences Center in Memphis, Tennessee. His clinical and research interests include marriage and family therapy, acute psychopathology, and religious and spiritual integration and training.

DR. SARA SAVAGE, PHD, a social psychologist, is senior research associate with the Pyschology and Christianity Project, Faculty of Divinity, University of Cambridge, UK, and lectures in pastoral psychology at the Cambridge Theological Federation. Savage has recently produced the Beta Course, a multi-media, video-based pastoral care course for churches and theological colleges (www.beta-course.org). Research areas pertain to fundamentalism and moral reasoning, young people and world view, the arts and spirituality. Prior to her academic career, Savage danced full-time for 12 years with a Christian dance group, touring widely in 17 different countries.

MARK A. YARHOUSE, PsyD, is an associate professor of psychology in the Doctoral Program in clinical psychology at Regent University, Virginia Beach, Virginia. Dr. Yarhouse serves on the editorial boards of *Journal of Psychology and Theology, Journal of Family Violence, and Marriage & Family: A Christian Journal.* He is director of the Institute for the Study of Sexual Identity and co-author of *Sexual Identity Synthesis: Attributions, Meaning-Making and the Search for Congruence.*

Preface

Psychologists and other mental health therapists have only recently discovered religion! Yes, some writers and therapists, such as Allen Bergin, have written on religious topics for years. On the other hand, well-known therapists such as Sigmund Freud and Albert Ellis openly disparaged religion and considered it to be at best worthless and at worst destructive. For them, it was a form of childish superstition and neuroticism, to be outgrown as soon as possible. Even more contemporary therapists have all too often covertly treated religion and by implication religious people with condescension or scorn. It was simply a topic not discussed in therapy. In part, this may have been caused by the fact that psychologists as a group are much less religious than the general population. Religious clients returned the favor by avoiding secular therapists, sometimes considering therapy as potentially destructive to their faith. For example, one advertisement of a Christian therapist stated, "No psychology is needed."

However, within the last 5 or 6 years, there have been a number of books on psychology and various aspects of religion, several published by the American Psychological Association. In a sense, one might say that psychologists have discovered religion and are beginning to see knowledge of religious beliefs and attitudes as an aspect of cultural competence. These books, however, have largely consisted of a description of the belief structures of people in different religious denominations or, in some instances, a consideration of aspects of religious practice, such as coping. They can be seen as looking from the outside in and are valuable because they provide therapists with information about the values and religious practices of their clients.

However, what has been missing is a look from the inside out; that is, an examination of the thinking, personality, and development processes, as well as clinical concerns of clients who are members of particular religious groups. Religious upbringing influences people in ways that are difficult or impossible to describe, and this book provides a "window on their world," as it were. In addition, it examines possible future religious development as spiritualism begins to replace institutional religion and as religious choice replaces religious constraint. This book will be helpful to all therapists who want to understand how religious people "really think."

Foreword

Psychologists often claim to take great pride in their neutrality or indifference about the religious faith of their patients. While espousing neutrality, psychologists have been far from neutral at times. Indeed, for many years, psychologists have often taken the lead in ridiculing or dismissing religious beliefs—as if religion is to be equated with some kind of shared paranoid ideation or repressive personality disorder. Contrary to these secular prejudices held by some psychologists, there is now growing evidence that individuals who participate in their faith are less likely to be depressed, more likely to report higher psychological well-being, and more likely to experience their marriages as rewarding and happy.

As a practicing clinician in New York City, I have provided psychotherapy for Jews, Christians, Muslims, Buddhists and atheists. Having been raised Roman Catholic, I have come to understand that each individual—even those claiming to be "secular humanists"—often bring to their experience in therapy a set of assumptions, values, life-narratives, and cultural perspectives that may differ from my own. It is because of this cultural value-context of my patients that I have sought out more reading in Judaism, Protestantism (of various denominations), Buddhism, Islam, and Sufiism. I have made it a point to re-read sections of the Bible on a regular basis and to learn from patients from different faiths how meaning is made in their religion. I have gotten more out of understanding the human dilemma from reading Abraham Joshua Heschel than from reading almost any book in psychoanalysis. As a result, I have found the current edited volume, *The Psychologies in Religion,* to be a valuable source of information.

E. Thomas Dowd and Stevan Lars Nielsen have brought together experts from a wide range of religious faiths to provide the reader with an overview of what we, as psychologists, need to know about the individual faith and cultural context of our patients. Psychotherapy has often been viewed by more "fundamental" religions—such as Orthodox Judaism, Roman Catholicism, and Fundamental Christianity—as anti-thetical to their faith. This, of course, need not be the case, but psychoanalysis and its tendency to pathologize religious faith has not been helpful. Nor has Albert Ellis' earlier diatribes been encouraging.

It is my view that religion is often a projective technique—that is, if one is a judgmental person, one will focus on the judgmental and intolerant views within a religion. On the other hand, if one is loving and kind, she will find a compassionate voice. For example, it is easy for Western Christians to view Islam as an intolerant religion—when it is unfairly equated with terrorism. But a reading of the Koran—and a reading of history during the Spanish Inquisition—will reveal that Islam has a long history of tolerance, diversity, mutual support, and a loving God. Religion in the hands of the wrong person can yield unfortunate results. But this point is also true for democracy.

Different religious faiths vary in their tendency to view "truth" as a culturally-relative construct. For example, more "foundational" religions attest to a truth that is derived from a direct, unchanging interpretation of the Bible. These more foundational or fundamental belief systems may hold to tenets that seem inimical to the modern mind—such as the belief that homosexuality or masturbation are sins. Indeed, even the idea of "sin" may strike contemporary psychologists as overly judgmental, intolerant, and mean-spirited.

Yet, within these religious systems, there is also another view that is encouraging—the view that God is not only the voice of justice, but also of mercy. For example, the devout Christian—regardless of which church one belongs to—can view his religion as justifying intolerance, guilt and shame. Or one can focus on the message of Jesus who was loving, kind, compassionate, and forgiving. In fact, the Christian who uses his religion to hate himself presents himself with the extraordinary irony—that he is unable to forgive himself, but his God is able to forgive him. Indeed, for Christians, the refusal to accept the Holy Spirit that brings one close to God and to His Forgiveness is the one "sin" that is not forgiven. It is, in a sense, a turning away from Grace.

Let us take "humility"—one of the virtues that is not fashionable in this highly achieved, materialistic world. Some time ago a rather dysphoric divorced man came to me for counsel, reporting a series of relationships with women in which he seemed to dominate and devalue. Once again he was beginning another relationship on the same shaky terms. I told him our goal would be to seek out humility and acceptance—along with appreciation. Seeing my Irish surname, he quickly equated this with Catholicism—the more easily to devalue my point. But we then examined the advantages to him of taking this new approach—since his old approach had been a chronic failure. Indeed, noting that he had been raised Jewish, I pointed out to him that these were values inherent in the prayers of an observant Jew each day. They were prayers of humility and appreciation. We finally settled on Buddhism as a common ground, drawing on loving kindness and compassionate mind. Apparently, these are values that work for everyone.

In recent years, there has been a growing emphasis on "positive psychology"—with its emphasis on acceptance, gratitude, compassion, and forgiveness. These, of course, have been the primary ideas of all the major religions. Religion—just as the Stoic philosophers thousands of years ago—has been the major "self-help" movement. All religions provide a context for determining meaning, connectedness, redemption, appreciation, and value. Where religions utilize rituals, it is ultimately for the purpose of making memorable and publicly shared the meanings that hold together one's faith. One can take a secular humanist view and cynically dismiss these—or one can take another view—that these symbolic, emotionally intense, and culturally based systems give solace, stability, and belongingness.

More people seek out counsel from their religious leaders than from psychotherapists. As psychologists, we will gain a great deal from the insights and ideas reflected in this valuable book. As we learn about the wisdom that is inherent in each of these religions, we will not only help our patients find their way out of the traps in their lives, but we may also help ourselves—as human beings who need to know where wisdom shall be found.

ROBERT L. LEAHY, PHD
American Institute for Cognitive Therapy
New York City

Religion for Psychotherapists: The Psychologies *in* Religion versus the Psychology *of* Religion

Stevan Lars Nielsen and E. Thomas Dowd

Religion is undoubtedly the oldest and most ubiquitous social institution in all of human history. Religious expressions go back to the dawn of humanity, and there has never been a wholly agnostic or atheistic culture. (Communist governments have claimed official atheism, but religious expression has survived in all communist-run societies to date.) Throughout history, religion has been simultaneously the source of humanity's greatest consolation and greatest divisiveness. Yet, until very recently, psychotherapists have largely ignored or denigrated this phenomenon. Indeed, certain influential figures such as Freud and Ellis considered religion to be intrinsically a form of neurosis, although in his latter years Ellis has changed his mind considerably. It is possible that one reason for this state of affairs is that religion and psychotherapy are competing systems for the creation of meaning—and few people take competition lightly. In addition, different brands of psychotherapy and religion differ among themselves, and even within themselves, about appropriate forms of ultimate meaning. The purpose of this book is to examine the psychological assumptions, both tacit and explicit, that lie behind different religions. In doing so, the authors hope to provide psychotherapists with a greater understanding of their religious clients, who after all constitute a sizable number of people, especially in the United States. In this, the book also differs from others on the topic of religion and psychotherapy or psychology, which have largely been descriptions of the history and beliefs of various groups.

The goals and practices most evident in the psychology of religion are briefly summarized at the website maintained by the American Psychological Association (APA) for its many divisions:

> Division 36, Psychology of Religion, promotes the application of psychological research methods and interpretive frameworks to diverse forms of religion and spirituality; encourages the incorporation of the results of such work into clinical and other applied settings; and fosters constructive dialogue and interchange between psychological study and practice on the one hand and between religious perspectives and institutions on the other. The Division is strictly nonsectarian and welcomes the participation of all persons who view religion as a significant factor in human functioning (American Psychological Association, 2005).

The title, *The Psychologies in Religion,* was chosen because the authors believe that religions imbue their adherents with distinct psychological world views. Psychology's "research methods and interpretive frameworks" are fully legitimate, scholarly, and scientific to be sure, yielding significant benefit to the world of knowledge through the disciplined (i.e., the discipline of psychology) study of religion. However, studying religions as if they are a source of their own unique psychologies can further prepare psychologists, especially applied psychologists, to better accommodate religious differences encountered among those with whom they work.

The authors do not assert that every religion has its own "*science* of the nature, functions, and phenomena of the human mind (formerly of the soul)" (italics added); this is definition 1.a. of psychology from the *Oxford English Dictionary (OED)*. However, almost every religion includes "a treatise on, or system of, psychology"; this is *OED* definition 1.b. for psychology. A particular religion's psychology may be formal, informal, or some combination of both. The authors further propose that religions imbue their adherents with tacit psychological models that subsequently exert significant influence in the adherents' lives. Each religion has (returning to the *OED*) a "*Psychologie* [that] is a doctrine which searches out man's [sic] Soul, and the effects of it" (italics original); this excerpt from a 1653 book on anatomy provides the earliest English exemplar of *psychology* found by the *OED*'s editors. This earliest documented appearance of *psychology* in English may have been what prompted the *OED*'s editors to include "(formerly of the soul)" in their 1.a. definition of *psychology* that it is the "*science* of the nature, functions, and phenomena of the human mind (formerly of the soul)."

Because *psychology* first described a discipline for studying the soul, it is little surprise that religions, which give considerable attention to doctrines of the soul, have developed certain models of thinking, emotion, behavior, personality, and so forth in their theologies, creeds, traditions, and doctrines of the soul. Such religious psychologies may be tacit and informal or explicit and systematic. Religions also enact, maintain, and promulgate in their doctrines, sacraments, traditions, and customs, religious practices that sometimes parallel, intersect, impede, counter, and augment psychological interventions. The authors propose that an examination of these religious psychologies will yield insights distinct from what has been learned in the psychology of religion and may help prepare psychologists to better work with religious individuals.

A FRAMEWORK FOR STUDYING
THE PSYCHOLOGIES IN RELIGIONS

This volume uses some different religious categories than those used in previous books, which tend to be derivations of the specific groups that arose from the 16th century European Reformation. As Wuthnow (1988) notes, there has been a decline in the significance of the traditional denominations and a corresponding rise in religious special interest groups as well as a liberal or conservative split, which often sunders different subgroups within traditional denominations. The chapter grouping within Christianity better reflects the restructuring of American religion to which Wuthnow refers. In addition, non-Christian, and even non-western, religions are included in recognition of the fact that American society is more religiously diverse than ever before. The authors apologize in advance if certain traditional groups are combined in ways to which certain readers object, or if groups are omitted that readers consider important. Choices had to be made to prevent the book from becoming excessively long. American religion is extremely diverse and complex.

Chapter contributors were sought who could bring dual expertise to their chapters, expertise about a particular religion as well as psychological sophistication. Authors were sought who were themselves committed members of their respective faith tradition, in order to provide an insider's view of the faith, which was accomplished in all but two instances. Authors were sought who could tell at least something about eight topics, including seven psychological themes, in order to explain elements of the religion about which they wrote:

1. An Introduction, including some history
2. Epistemologic tools accepted by the religion
3. Any theory of personality implicitly or explicitly inherent to the religion's theology and customs
4. Any religious model of psychological development
5. The religion's view of psychological health and illness
6. The religion's view of how behavior, emotions, thinking, personality, and status with God change
7. Moral issues common to the religion's commandments
8. Emotional or psychological problems to which members of the religion may be more prone.

They were asked to provide a balanced overview, including as much information as page limitations allowed for each of these eight domains. The following are examples of questions they were asked to answer.

Introduction to the religion. Authors were asked to provide what they consider the minimum information, including historical facts, necessary to define and explicate the religion. For example, what defines a Mormon, so that most Mormons would agree that a particular person is a Mormon? What makes Sunni and Shia Muslims different from one another? What makes Roman and Orthodox Catholics different from one another? What parts of the history of a religion make a difference to our understanding models of the mind adherents of the religion carry with them?

Epistemological tools. What do the doctrines and traditions of the religion consider valid sources of knowledge and valid ways of knowing? For example, how does the theology treat scholarship and science? How do lay members of a religion think about scholarship and science? Do popular ways of knowing for members of the religion conflict with the scholarship and science most mental health professionals find familiar and probative?

Theory of personality. Do the doctrines, creeds, and traditions of a religion describe or imply a particular model of personality functioning? For example, does the religion account for traits? How does the religion account for human agency, learning, or motivation?

Theory of human development. Is there a systematic or implied account of how humans become functioning responsible adults in the theology, traditions, or customs of the religion? How can a human fall short of full functioning? Does this reduce responsibility or sinfulness of misbehavior? What does the theology tell about how humans became human (as in the creation of humans) or about what it means to be human? Is there something in the theology that explains what is unique about humans, making them different from animals?

Theory of psychological health and pathology. Does the religion's theology clarify what causes humans to be psychologically healthy or have psychological problems (e.g., does the religion have an explicit view about when psychological illness removes culpability?). Does the theology of a religion view sin as a kind of illness? Does the theology imply that illness is a sin or that righteous living is sufficient to prevent mental illness?

Theory of human change. Religions almost always have models of sin and repentance. Does a religion's model of misbehavior and correction provide insights into how humans might change other undesirable features of their thoughts or behavior? How much independence is it assumed that humans have in making changes? To what degree is it possible for humans to lose their agency through illness or sin?

Common moral issues. Religions prescribe some behaviors, forbid others, and declare yet others problematic. The worst of these behaviors usually are called sins. What behaviors or states might be treated as sin in this religion? What religious mechanisms are available for obtaining forgiveness or expiation or purification from sin in this religion?

Common clinical issues. Are there extra propensities to suffer guilt about particular events or behaviors because of particular doctrines or traditions within a particular religion? Are there overt or tacit influences that may lead to extra guilt about sex, eating, drinking, or recreation? Are marriage and divorce treated with a particularity that might exacerbate adherents' response to marital difficulties?

PSYCHOLOGICAL INTEREST IN RELIGION

Judging by frequency of words appearing in scholarly citations and abstracts, psychology has given about 2% of its attention to religion and spirituality. As of January 1, 2005, 40,975 of the 1,988,575 (2.05%) scholarly works catalogued in *Psychological Abstracts (PA)* include *religion, religious, spirit, spiritual,* or related words. For comparison purposes, consider that the name *Freud* and related words such as *Freudian* appear in 19,819 *PA* citations and abstracts (0.99% of materials catalogued by *PA*); *empathy* and related words appear 10,532 times (0.53%); *self-esteem* and related words appear 23,255 times (1.16%); *Pavlov, Skinner, classical conditioning, operant conditioning,* and related words appear 24,753 times (1.24%); *psychoanalysis* and related words appear 68,261 times (3.42%); *counseling* and related words appear 78,772 times (3.94%); *psychotherapy* and related words appear 110,950 times (5.55%); *cognition* and related words appear 216,326 times (10.82%);

brain and words including *neuro-* as a root (e.g., neuropsychology) appear 298,979 times (14.96%); and *behavior* and related words (e.g., behaviorism) appear 532,384 times (26.64% of the *PA* catalogue).

Appearance rates for *religion, spiritual,* and related words have remained fairly consistent over the 12 decades catalogued in *PA* (Table 1.1), ranging between 1.44% and 3.81%. Also note in Table 1.1 that the proportion of citations including religion-related words and the words *psychotherapy, counseling,* or related words increased from the 1930s through the 1950s. Since the 1950s, 15% to 20% of *PA* citations, including references to religion or spirituality, also have included words related to psychotherapy or counseling. Assuming that frequency of appearance in the *PA* catalogue yields an index of scholarly interest, it seems clear that relationships among religion, counseling, and psychotherapy have become a significant element of psychological interest in religion.

REDUCTIONISM IN THE
PSYCHOLOGY OF RELIGION

Wulff (1997) notes that inherent to scholarly attention, including the psychology of religion's scholarly attention, is a probability of tension between this scholarship and its object, between religion and the psychology of religion. This tension probably arises because a degree of reductionism is inherent to the hermeneutics of most scholarly or scientific inquiry. The "psychological research and interpretive frameworks" noted in the Division 36 website appropriately describe psychology's tools, which themselves are appropriate. However, by the nature of their technical elements of measurement, modeling, prediction, testing, experimentation, analysis, and so forth, they explain religion to psychologists in reduced psychological terms. Even if born of sympathetic intent, psychological explanations of religious phenomena inevitably yield alternative, nonreligious explanations. Such reduced explanations then may seem disrespectful of religion as an object of psychological attention.

REDUCTIONISM AS ATTACK

Experiencing this psychological reductionism as attack is perhaps most famously apparent in Freud's psychoanalytic interpretations of religious phenomena. Religion was explained as (was psychoanalytically reduced to) some variety of psychosexual developmental conflict or the form of

TABLE 1.1 Occurrences and Percentages of Occurrence of Citations and Abstracts Including Words Related to Religion or Spirituality and Words Related to Psychotherapy or Counseling in *Psychological Abstracts* by Decade of Citation

Decades	Total citations and abstracts	Word occurrences and percentages of occurrences in citations and abstracts			
		Citations with words related to religion or spirituality	Religion and spirituality words as % of all citations	Citations with religion, spirituality and counseling or psychotherapy words	Counseling and psychotherapy words as % of citations with religion or spirituality words
Before 1900	4,122	64	1.55%	0	0.00%
1900 to 1909	8,216	265	3.23%	2	0.75%
1910 to 1919	12,929	223	1.72%	1	0.45%
1920 to 1929	31,792	1,210	3.81%	35	2.89%
1930 to 1939	65,095	1,894	2.91%	133	7.02%
1940 to 1949	53,107	1,318	2.48%	138	10.47%
1950 to 1959	86,007	1,729	2.01%	317	18.33%
1960 to 1969	133,167	2,069	1.55%	299	14.45%
1970 to 1979	270,388	4,000	1.48%	707	17.68%
1980 to 1989	427,740	7,023	1.64%	1,315	18.72%
1990 to 1999	552,035	11,830	2.14%	2,340	19.78%
2000 through 2004	353,977	9,350	2.64%	1,065	11.39%
All citations	1,998,575	40,975	2.05%	7,089	17.30%

Note. Citations and abstracts tallied on January 1, 2005.

its resolution. Many religious individuals have had difficulty with such psychosexual developmental models of religiosity. For example, hearing that one's religious devotions are manifestations of oedipal castration anxiety is quite jarring even to religious psychologists familiar with psychosexual developmental theory. Taking offense from such explanations is perhaps less likely if one remembers that virtually all human cognition and socialization similarly has been reduced to psychosexual developmental explanations, and a wide range of socially responsible behaviors have been explicitly linked to castration anxiety. Offense is not intended in psychoanalytic analyses.

Perhaps because Freud's voluminous scholarly work included so many references to religion, and perhaps because his works can be said to have concluded with focused considerations of religion in *The Future of an Illusion* (1927), *Discontent in Civilization* (1930), and *Moses and Monotheism* (1939), his psychoanalytic treatments of religion have become somewhat emblematic of the psychology of religion. For example, in his widely used text book, *Psychology of Religion: Classic and Contemporary,* Wulff (1997) cites Freud more than any other author; Freud is cited on 86 of his 645 pages, Carl Jung on 80 pages, and William James on 76 pages.

Reductionism as attack probably can be considered an accidental consequence of the hermeneutic disconnect between psychology's tools and religious epistemology. However, psychologists also have more overtly attacked religion. The best example of such an attack is from Albert Ellis, who, although not identified with the psychology of religion, is probably the most overt and famous (or infamous) of psychology's critics of religion. He is probably as famous for attacking religion as a mentally unhealthy neurosis as for developing Rational Emotive Behavior Therapy (REBT), the first of the cognitive behavioral therapies. Ellis's criticisms of religion have prompted ongoing controversy and debate within the psychological community for more than 40 years, including 18 published exchanges since 1960; that is, 36 articles divided between Ellis's attacks and other psychologists' defenses of religion (see Johnson, 1994). His criticisms were most concisely presented in *The Case Against Religion: A Psychotherapist's View* (1971):

> If religion is defined as man's dependence on a power above and beyond the human, then as a psychotherapist, I find it to be exceptionally pernicious. For the psychotherapist is normally dedicated to helping human beings in general, and his patients in particular, to achieve certain goals of mental health, and virtually all these goals are antithetical to a truly religious viewpoint. . . . Religiosity, to a large degree, essentially is masochism; and both are forms of mental sickness.

RAPPROCHEMENT AND ACCOMMODATION

At least two influences were responsible for shifting psychology toward accommodating rather than attacking religion. One was a general emphasis on broadening its scope with regard to cultural differences. The other was a more specific exhortation aimed at getting psychotherapists and counselors to respect, accommodate, and integrate their clients' values, especially their religious values, during treatment.

One exhortation was both dramatic and rather controversial to some psychologists because of its venue. In his 1980 article "Psychotherapy and Religious Values," in the *Journal of Consulting and Clinical Psychology (JCCP)*, Allen Bergin averred that psychotherapy and counseling clients, a large majority of whom are religious, are likely to experience their psychotherapists, a majority of whom are agnostic or atheist, as somewhat critical of their core religious values. Bergin, who was already well known for promulgating psychotherapy effectiveness research, argued that psychotherapeutic effectiveness will suffer "until the theistic belief systems of a large percentage of the population are sincerely considered and conceptually integrated" in therapeutic formulations (p. 95).

JCCP's editor at the time, Bergin's long-time collaborator and friend, Sol Garfield, reported that he had received many responses to Bergin's article, but had chosen to publish two that were characteristic of the others. Both were quite critical: Walls (1980) wrote, "Bergin's (1980) proposal that we broaden clinical psychology's scope by integrating religious values . . . *is a potentially dangerous notion* that could result in the assertion of absolutes without justification" (italics added, p. 641). Ellis echoed views presented in *The Case Against Religion:*

> Devout, orthodox, or dogmatic religion (or what might be called religiosity) is significantly correlated with emotional disturbance. . . . The elegant therapeutic solution to emotional problems is to be quite unreligious and have no degree of dogmatic faith that is unfounded or unfoundable in fact (1980, p. 637).

Bergin and Ellis subsequently debated these points twice at annual meetings of the APA and a reprise of their debates appeared about 12 years after Bergin's *JCCP* article in the *American Psychologist* (Bergin, 1991; Ellis, 1992).

Many psychotherapists—too many to review for this chapter—have since described how religiosity and psychotherapy might be integrated (for reviews see Hall & Hall, 1997; Worthington, Kurusu, McCullough, & Sandage, 1996; Worthington & Sandage, 2001). Ironically, one of the first suggestions for integrating religion with psychotherapy was published under the title, "Strange Bedfellows? Rational-Emotive Therapy and Pastoral Counseling," wherein Lawrence and Huber (1982) proposed frequent use of Christian scripture to energize and strengthen rational-emotive interventions. Suggestions for religion-integrative REBT were subsequently repeated many times over (DiGiuseppe, Robin, & Dryden, 1990; Ellis, 1994; Johnson & Nielsen, 1998; Johnson, Ridley, & Nielsen, 2000; Maurits & Ellis, 1998; Nielsen, 1994; Robb, 2001, 2002; Warnock, 1989). Examples of such religious REBT have been described in numerous case excerpts and case studies (Johnson, 2004; Nielsen, 2004; Nielsen, Ridley, & Johnson, 2000; Young, 1984). A book length treatment manual for religiously oriented REBT has been published (Nielsen, Johnson, & Ellis, 2001). The efficacy of integrating Christian scripture with REBT has been supported in two controlled clinical trials (Johnson, Devries, & Ridley, 1994; Johnson & Ridley, 1992). Four controlled clinical trials have supported Christian-oriented cognitive-behavioral therapy (CBT) (Hawkins, Tan, & Turk, 1999; Pecheur & Edwards, 1984; Propst, 1980; Propst, Ostrom, Watkins, Dean, & Mashburn, 1992), and three controlled clinical trials have supported Islamic CBT (Azhar & Varma, 1995a,b; Azhar, Varma, & Dharap, 1994). These nine CBT and REBT studies are the only tests of religion integrative therapy of which the authors are aware so far.

In addition to these developments has been a rather striking shift in Ellis's approach to religion. Ellis contributed the following during a discussion of the ethics of therapy with religious clients:

NIELSEN: Are religious beliefs themselves fair targets for disputation? You've noted that it's important to be sensitive to your client's ethnic background and religious beliefs. . . .

ELLIS: Most of the time I don't question a client's dogmas. I'm a therapist, and my concern is whether their beliefs are self-defeating. If I were having a debate with them, I might question their rigid views. However, during therapy I'm very selective. So I very rarely question whether they hold Jewish, Muslim, Christian, or any other religious values. . . .

NIELSEN: You've made an important distinction between, say, a public debate and psychotherapy.

ELLIS: Oh, yes, that's right. In psychotherapy I would be unethical if I didn't pretty much try to limit my focus to the clients' problems, their goals, and their self-fulfillment. Now every once in a while we may get into some philosophical discussion, and we may be having a good time doing so. However, then I remind them, "You know, the time is passing. We'd better get back to your specific problems." I enjoy this kind of discussion, but that's not what therapy is for (Nielsen & Ellis, 1994, p. 330).

Twenty years after his critical response to Bergin's *JCCP* article, Ellis wrote:

> Although I have, in the past, taken a negative attitude toward religion, and especially toward people who devoutly hold religious views, I now see that absolutistic religious views can sometimes lead to emotionally healthy behavior. . . . Accordingly, I have attempted . . . to describe some of the basic constructive philosophies of REBT and to indicate how they are similar to and compatible with basic religious philosophies. This appears to be particularly true of some of the REBT and benevolent religious philosophies of self-control and change, unconditional self-acceptance, high frustration tolerance, unconditional acceptance of others, the desire rather than the dire need for achievement and for approval, the acceptance of responsibility, the acceptance of self-direction, the acceptance of life's dangers, the philosophy of nonperfectionism, and the philosophy of accepting disturbance. There are many remarkable similarities in some of the major religious and REBT attitudes (2000, p. 31).

RELIGIOUS COMPETENCY AS A SUBSET OF CULTURAL COMPETENCY

In 1973, directors of graduate programs in psychology met in Vail, Colorado, to review and fine tune models for training professional psychologists. Among the conclusions of their meeting was a resolution asserting that competent psychological treatment requires awareness and consideration of cultural uniqueness in those receiving treatment (Korman, 1974). Standards for ethical practice have increasingly emphasized development of skills and competencies for accommodating ethnically and culturally diverse clients (Ridley & Kleiner, 2003; Sue, Arredondo, & McDavis, 1972; Sue & Sue, 1977). This emphasis is evident in General Principle E among the APA's Ethical Principles of Psychologists and Code of Conduct (2002):

> Psychologists respect the dignity and worth of all people, and the rights of individuals to privacy, confidentiality, and self-determination. Psychologists are aware that special safeguards may be necessary to protect the rights and welfare of persons or communities whose vulnerabilities impair autonomous decision making. Psychologists are aware of and respect cultural, individual, and role differences, including those based on age, gender, gender identity, race, ethnicity, culture, national origin, *religion,* sexual orientation, disability, language, and socioeconomic status and consider these factors when working with members of such groups. Psychologists try to eliminate the effect on their work of biases based on those factors, and they do not knowingly participate in or condone activities of others based upon such prejudices (p. 4, italics added).

General Principle E imposes on psychologists, at least on applied psychologists, responsibilities for accommodating individual differences, including individual differences tied to religiosity.

Four kinds of competencies are apparent in General Principle E: First, psychologists are responsible for becoming aware of religious differences, presumably by educating themselves about religion and its manifestations among the individuals whom they study or work. Second, psychologists are responsible for considering the effects of religious differences during their psychological work. At a minimum, this seems to require making some adjustments or accommodations for the religious differences about which they have learned. Third, psychologists are responsible for decontaminating their psychological work by detecting and correcting biases about religious differences. Presumably this is done by distrusting unsubstantiated generalizations about religious differences while investigating and attempting to validate presumptions about relationships between religion and psychological constructs. Fourth, psychologists have a responsibility to challenge and change effects arising because of invalid information about religious differences.

THE DEVIL IS IN THE DETAILS OF INTEGRATING RELIGION WITH TREATMENT

Treating religious clients, especially when one is unfamiliar with clients' religious backgrounds, can present challenges apparent only in the details of conducting therapy. Consider one author's (S.L.N.) experience while attempting to treat a Muslim student using REBT. (This case was, by the way, the proximal prompt for formulating this book. A full case study is available in Nielsen, 2004, which is in Richards & Bergin, 2004.)

A devout young Sunni Muslim woman, raised as a U.S. citizen in a predominantly Muslim country, was studying a scientific discipline at Brigham Young University (BYU). She sought treatment at the BYU Counseling and Career Center where I practice. Early in the first session, she noticed and commented on a copy of the Qur'an sitting next to copies of the Bible, Book of Mormon, Dhammapada, Bhagavad-Gita, and other religious books on the shelves above my desk. She wondered if I knew the Qur'an and seemed quite pleased when I told her I had read it. She laughed when I told that I knew, "just enough to be a really dangerous infidel!" We agreed that we two, both "people of the book" (referring to our joint belief in the prophets of the Hebrew and Christian Bibles), could likely work together. She had already been a student at BYU for about a year, and had familiarized herself with the Church of Jesus Christ of Latter-Day Saints by attending some church services and enrolling in a class designed to familiarize nonmember students with the church, and its principles and customs.

About 2 years before our meeting, this unfortunate young woman had been the victim of an acquaintance rape. Like many of my religious clients, she was filled with self-blame and guilt about the circumstances that preceded the rape, exacerbated by a cultural tradition in the country where she was raised, which treated women as guilty in a rape unless they suffered some severe injury through their resistance to physical attack. Although our religious beliefs and backgrounds were quite different, it became clear that like others of my religious clients she was much more demanding of herself and much more self-condemnatory than seemed warranted from what the Qur'an says about sin. Like my devout Mormon clients, she benefitted greatly from our searching for and integrating teachings from the Qur'an in the REBT interventions we tried. She had to (and was happy to) teach me what could be found in the Qur'an concerning promises of forgiveness for the repentant sinner. These verses helped her to challenge her pervasive self-blame and catastrophizing. As she searched, it also became increasingly clear to her that her feelings of guilt were based on beliefs founded in culture-centric biases against women more than on rules from the Qur'an. She found she strongly favored the Qur'an over the cultural view.

As part of our discussion of sin and redemption, I asked if there was a mechanism for confession to clergy in order to obtain expiation. She again educated me about the more democratic approach of the Sunni Muslims, who hold that all are equal in God's eyes. Her confessions would be to God alone, she told me.

As is usual during my treatment of religious clients, I also attempted to have this young woman remind herself that God is a loving father in heaven. She quickly stopped the conversation, telling me that to imagine that humans are children of God was an arrogant conceit. As had become a pattern, I suggested that this was yet another lapse from an infidel. She was not offended but laughed at what had become a joke. Perhaps our collaborative relationship had proceeded enough that little would have offended her. However, she told me that some Muslims could find the idea offensive.

How could I have discovered that Sunni Muslims would not confess to clergy? How could I have learned that Muslims might find the idea that God is our father in heaven insulting to God? Perhaps these are pieces of knowledge too specialized to obtain except through comprehensive study of comparative theology. Therapy arguably was not the best place or time for these discoveries, but perhaps it was inevitable that integrating Islam with CBT or REBT would brush up against these issues. It seems doubtful that it would be possible to learn these things about the Sunni

Muslims by reading broadly or deeply in the psychology of religion. It does not seem as doubtful that a study of the psychological assumptions embedded in Sunni Islam would reveal what the Sunni Muslims believe about repentance or their relationships with the deity. Such an understanding would have had immediate pragmatic consequences for my sessions with this young woman and deeper philosophical implications for our therapeutic goals.

Reflecting upon this case example, I (E.T.D.) was struck by two aspects that I think are extremely important in working cross culturally with religious clients; respect for the client's beliefs and an openness and willingness to learn. Dr. Nielsen demonstrated both characteristics in addition to a sense of humor. Too often client religious beliefs may be interpreted as examples of neurosis or distorted thinking processes that should be overcome, rather than a valuable client meaning structure with which the therapist should work.

The chapters in this book cannot provide a comprehensive response to the questions asked of each author. There is certainly more to say about any religion and its psychological implications than can be captured in either a chapter or book length volume. However, we hope that this volume provides fresh insights, suggests directions for further study, and prepares our readers to better accommodate their religious clients. Finally, we will be pleased if it raises further questions.

REFERENCES

American Psychological Association. (2002). *Ethical principles of psychologists and code of conduct*. Retrieved December 10, 2004, from http://www.apa.org/ethics/code2002.pdf

American Psychological Association. (2005). APA Divisions, Division 36 section. Retrieved March 20, 2005, from http://www.apa.org/about/division/div36.html.

Azhar, M. Z., & Varma, S. L. (1995a). Religious psychotherapy as management of bereavement. *Acta Psychiatrica Scandinavia, 91*, 223–235.

Azhar, M. Z., & Varma, S. L. (1995b). Religious psychotherapy in depressive patients. *Psychotherapy and Psychosomatics, 63*, 165–168.

Azhar, M. Z., Varma, S. L., & Dharap, A. S. (1994). Religious psychotherapy in anxiety disorder patients. *Acta Psychiatrica Scandinavica, 90*, 1–2.

Bergin, A. E. (1980). Psychotherapy and religious values. *Journal of Consulting and Clinical Psychology, 48*, 95–105.

Bergin, A. E. (1991). Values and religious issues in psychotherapy and mental health. *American Psychologist, 46*, 394–403.

DiGiuseppe, R. A., Robin, M. W., & Dryden, W. (1990). On the compatibility of Rational-Emotive Therapy and Judeo-Christian philosophy: A focus on clinical strategies. *Journal of Cognitive Psychotherapy, 4*, 355–368.

Ellis, A. (1971). *The case against religion: A psychotherapist's view.* New York: Albert Ellis Institute for Rational Emotive Behavior Therapy. Retrieved December 1, 2004, from http://www.geocities.com/bororissa/rel.html

Ellis, A. (1980). Psychotherapy and atheistic values: A response to A. E. Bergin's "Psychotherapy and religious values." *Journal of Consulting and Clinical Psychology, 48,* 635–639.

Ellis, A. (1992). Do I really hold that religiousness is irrational and equivalent to emotional disturbance? *American Psychologist, 47,* 428–429.

Ellis, A. (1994). My response to "Don't throw the therapeutic baby out with the holy water": Helpful and hurtful elements of religion. *Journal of Psychology & Christianity, 13,* 323–326.

Ellis, A. (2000). Can rational emotive behavior therapy (REBT) be effectively used with people who have devout beliefs in God and religion? *Professional Psychology: Research and Practice, 31,* 29–33.

Hall, M. E. L., & Hall, T. W. (1997). Integration in the therapy room: An overview of the literature. *Journal of Psychology and Theology, 25,* 86–101.

Hawkins, R. S., Tan, S. Y., & Turk, A. A. (1999). Secular versus Christian inpatient cognitive-behavioral therapy programs: Impact on depression and spiritual well-being. *Journal of Psychology & Theology, 27,* 309–318.

Johnson, W. B. (1994). Albert Ellis and the "religionists": A history of the dialogue. *Journal of Psychology and Christianity, 13,* 301–311.

Johnson, W. B. (2004). Rational emotive behavior therapy for disturbance about sexual orientation. In P.S. Richards & A.E. Bergin (Eds), *Casebook for a spiritual strategy in counseling and psychotherapy* (pp. 247–265). Washington, DC: American Psychological Association.

Johnson, W. B., Devries, R., & Ridley, C. R. (1994). The comparative efficacy of Christian and secular rational-emotive therapy with Christian clients. *Journal of Psychology & Theology, 22,* 130–140.

Johnson, W. B., & Nielsen, S. L. (1998). Rational-emotive assessment with religious clients. *Journal of Rational-Emotive & Cognitive Behavior Therapy, 16,* 101–124.

Johnson, W. B., & Ridley, C. R. (1992). Brief Christian and non-Christian rational-emotive therapy with depressed Christian clients: An exploratory study. *Counseling & Values, 36,* 220–229.

Johnson, W. B., Ridley, C. R., & Nielsen, S. L. (2000). Religiously sensitive rational emotive behavior therapy: Elegant solutions and ethical risks. *Professional Psychology: Research & Practice, 31,* 14–20.

Korman, M. (1974). National conference on levels and patterns of professional training in psychology: Major themes. *American Psychologist, 29,* 301–313.

Lawrence, C., & Huber, C. H. (1982). Strange bedfellows? Rational-emotive therapy and pastoral counseling. *Personnel & Guidance Journal, 61,* 210–212.

Maurits, K., & Ellis, A. (1998). The interface between rational emotive behavior therapy (REBT) and Zen. *Journal of Rational-Emotive & Cognitive Behavior Therapy, 16,* 5–43.

Nielsen, S. L. (1994). Rational-Emotive Behavior Therapy and religion: Don't throw the therapeutic baby out with the holy water. *Journal of Psychology and Christianity, 13,* 312–322.

Nielsen, S. L. (2004). A Mormon rational emotive behavior therapist attempts Qur'anic rational emotive behavior therapy. In P. S. Richards & A. E. Bergin (Eds.), *Casebook for a spiritual strategy in counseling and psychotherapy* (pp. 213–230). Washington, DC: American Psychological Association.

Nielsen, S. L., & Ellis, A. (1994). A discussion with Albert Ellis: Reason, emotion and religion. *Journal of Psychology and Christianity, 13,* 327–341.

Nielsen, S. L., Johnson, W. B., & Ellis, A. (2001). *Counseling and psychotherapy with religious persons: A rational emotive behavior therapy approach.* Mahwah, NJ: LEA.

Nielsen, S. L., Ridley, C. R., & Johnson, W. B. (2000). Religiously sensitive rational emotive behavior therapy: Theory, techniques, and brief excerpts from a case. *Professional Psychology: Research & Practice, 31,* 21–28.

Pecheur, D. R., & Edwards, K. J. (1984). A comparison of secular and religious versions of cognitive therapy with depressed Christian college students. *Journal of Psychology & Theology, 12,* 45–54.

Propst, L. R. (1980). The comparative efficacy of religious and nonreligious imagery for the treatment of mild depression in religious individuals. *Cognitive Therapy & Research, 4,* 167–178.

Propst, L. R., Ostrom, R., Watkins, P., Dean, T., & Mashburn, D. (1992). Comparative efficacy of religious and nonreligious cognitive-behavioral therapy for the treatment of clinical depression in religious individuals. *Journal of Consulting & Clinical Psychology, 60,* 94–103.

Richards, P. S., & Bergin, A. E. (Eds.). (2004). *Spiritual strategy case studies.* Washington, DC: American Psychological Association.

Ridley, C. R., & Kleiner, A. J. (2003). Multicultural counseling competences: History, themes, and issues. In D. B. Pope-Davis, H. L. K. Coleman, W. M. Liu, & R. L. Toporek (Eds.), *Handbook of multicultural competencies in counseling and psychology* (pp. 3–20). Thousand Oaks, CA: Sage.

Robb, H. R. (2001). Facilitating rational emotive behavior therapy by including religious beliefs. *Cognitive & Behavioral Practice, 8,* 29–34.

Robb, H. R. (2002). Practicing rational emotive behavior therapy and religious clients. *Journal of Rational-Emotive & Cognitive Behavior Therapy, 20,* 169–200.

Sue, D. W., Arredondo, P., & McDavis, R. J. (1992). Multicultural counseling competencies and standards: A call to the profession. *Journal of Counseling & Development, 70,* 477–486.

Sue, D. W., & Sue, D. (1977). Barriers to effective cross-cultural counseling. *Journal of Counseling Psychology, 24,* 420–429.

Warnock, S. D. (1989). Rational-emotive therapy and the Christian client. *Journal of Rational-Emotive & Cognitive Behavior Therapy, 7,* 263–274.

Worthingon, E. L., Jr., Kurusu, T. A., McCullough, M. E., & Sandage, S. J. (1996). Empirical research on religion and psychotherapeutic processes and outcomes. A 10-year-review and research prospectus. *Psychological Bulletin, 119,* 448–487.

Worthington, E. L., Jr., & Sandage, S. J. (2001). Religion and spirituality. *Psychotherapy: Theory, Research, Practice, Training, 38,* 473–478.

Wulff, D. M. (1997). *Psychology of religion: Classic and contemporary* (2nd ed.). New York: John Wiley & Sons.

Wuthnow, R. (1988). *The restructuring of American religion.* Princeton, NJ: Princeton University Press.

Young, H. (1984). Practising RET with Bible Belt Christians. *British Journal of Cognitive Psychotherapy, 2,* 60–76.

CHAPTER TWO

Bricolage:
The Postmodern Eclectic
Identifying Syncretistic Religious Cosmologies

James R. Beebe

THE RISE OF RELIGIOUS PLURALISM

According to the American Religious Identity Survey conducted in 2001 (Kosmin & Lachman, 2001), 76.5% of the U.S. population identified themselves as Christian. Although that seems like an overwhelming percentage, it reflects a 10% *decrease* from a similar survey conducted 10 years earlier. Some Christian groups recorded modest gains (Episcopalians/Anglicans increased 13%; Presbyterians increased 12%; the Church of Jesus Christ of Latter-Day Saints increased 8%; Baptists and United Methodists remained the same). Hindus, on the other hand, exploded from 227,000 to 766,000 (an increase of 237%) in that same period. Muslims increased about 109%, and Buddhists 170%. This is all to say, of course, that the clear trend within the U.S. population is toward religious pluralism.

Even within established Christian denominations there seems to be a blending of theologies, with denominational boundaries much weaker now than they were 50 years ago. Roman Catholics are marrying Methodists and Baptists are marrying the Eastern Orthodox, and as young couples begin to decide in which tradition they should raise their children, doctrinal considerations seem to be taking a back seat to family practicalities. As sociologist Peter Berger notes, American culture has shifted "from fate to choice" (Carroll & Roof, 2002).

Some suggest that this trend toward pluralism began as a series of religious disestablishments (Carroll & Roof, 2002). The opening volley, of course, was the U.S. Constitution, which both forbade the establishment of a national religion and protected the free exercise thereof. A sort of demographic disestablishment then took place in the mid-19th century with the immigration of hundreds of thousands of European Roman Catholics and Jews. Will Herberg codified this trend with his seminal work in 1960, Protestant-Catholic-Jew.

A more subtle disestablishment occurred during the late 1960s, when the Baby Boomers began to draw clear distinctions between spirituality and organized religion, and the Vietnam debacle led them to recognize the self-serving inclinations of institutions in general. This distinction between spirit and institution suggested that spiritual authenticity resided in inner experience rather than outward form and polity.

The upshot of this series of disestablishments was a radically different approach toward religion. Gone were the days when children inherited their parents' faith tradition; one's spirituality became a matter of choices ("thereby creating an eclectic mix suitable to one's taste") (Carroll & Roof, 2002). Add to the mix the liberalizing of immigration statutes in the 1960s—with a resulting influx of Jainists, Buddhists, Muslims, and Confucianists—and the American religious landscape began to become kaleidoscopic.

Carroll and Roof (2002) contend that pluralism did more than diversify the population; it actually changed the way in which people viewed religion itself. They suggest that pluralism encouraged the privatizing of faith (i.e., just as the public religious arena became unrecognizable, so the spirituality of one's inner world became paramount). In turn, religious pluralism and the privatization of faith have led to a posttraditional society in which the locus of religious authority has migrated from Holy See and pulpit to individual choice and experience. In this posttraditional, postmodern society, truth itself has become a contentious issue. Grand meta-narratives (universal stories that determine the meaning of creation and humanity) are increasingly rejected as overreaching and imperialistic.

Even language became suspect because (as Michel Foucault suggested) language and power are inseparable in many different ways. Hence, if people use language as a tool of domination, then interpreters must begin their analysis of that language with the "hermeneutics of suspicion," in the words of higher education. So the claims of the grand historical meta-narratives of Judaism, Christianity, and Islam as normative for the lives of Americans have become at least malleable, if not suspect.

Contingency and interpretation have replaced objective certainty in the postmodern world. Culture itself is seen as constructed. Berger and

Luckmann (1995) describe this process as reification, or "the apprehension of the product of human activity as if they were something else than human products." The upshot of all this is that ultimate importance is not being placed in societal structures and institutions (including the church).

Therefore, it should not be surprising how easy it is to shape-shift one's beliefs—and even one's identity—from one value system, one religious institution, or one set of colleagues to another. Lifton (1993) calls this phenomenon the emergence of the protean self (from the peculiar morphing activities of Proteus as told in the Greek myth).

Further complicating the picture is a movement away from a purely cognitive approach to faith (e.g., the catechism) and toward other legitimate ways of knowing (e.g., intuition, imagination, feelings, experience). Now people seem to be seeking the authenticity of a genuine spiritual experience that transcends the arid, external ethical systems and dogmas associated with organized religion (Carroll & Roof, 2002).

Paradoxically, a renewed interest in the natural world and the place of humanity in it often conflicts with the longing for corporate belonging. One often hears the sentiment, "I can worship God just as easily, perhaps even more so, in nature as in church." This individualistic, mystical approach to inner spirituality contrasts markedly with a concurrent desire to establish oneself in the midst of a caring anchor community. In the fragmentation of a postmodern world, people yearn for koinonia (the New Testament Koine Greek expression that loosely translates as fellowship, although it is meant in the deeper sense of sharing one another's burdens).

What we seem to have, then, is an increasingly pluralistic society that has been formed by the gradual disestablishment of religion and the displacement of the locus of authority from institution to individual. Denominational boundaries have weakened, faith has become a matter of choice rather than inheritance, religion has been privatized, and people increasingly view truth claims and meta-narratives with a hermeneutic of suspicion. There is easy movement into and out of religious establishments and an unprecedented intermarriage among those holding quite different belief systems. The protean human has emerged, with the ability to reinvent one's identity through serial religious identifications and a mix-and-match syncretism.

Wuthnow summarizes the situation as one in which "dwellers" have become "seekers":

> A traditional spirituality of inhabiting sacred places has given way to a new spirituality of seeking . . . people have been losing faith in a metaphysic that can make them feel at home in the universe and [now] increasingly negotiate among competing glimpses of the sacred, seeking partial knowledge and practical wisdom (Carroll & Roof, 2002, p. 56).

THE PROBLEM OF IDENTIFYING VALUE SYSTEMS

These long-term trends are making it increasingly difficult for psychotherapists to accurately identify any traditional and clearly delineated belief systems that motivate their clients. Moreover, an accurate assessment of core religious values must also have a predictive value if therapy is to have both a starting place and a direction. Philosophers of religion may be somewhat helpful because they are not limited to narrow, traditional definitions. Instead, they attempt to deal with the ineffability of religion by describing its main attributes (attributes, incidentally, that must apply across the board).

This is more difficult than it seems. Is religion a cognitive phenomenon? Those who define religion as belief in God, for example, may exclude Buddhists, who strive toward a state of being rather than a deity. Is religion primarily a matter of the emotions? Defining religion in affective terms is similarly unhelpful, as Pentecostalists and Hindus have a widely divergent understanding of what constitutes true religious feeling. In an attempt to circumvent this dilemma, theologian Paul Tillich has made a more inclusive attempt to define religion as one's "ultimate concern": "a concern which qualifies all other concerns as preliminary and which itself contains the answer to the questions of the meaning of our life" (Schmidt, 1988).

There are other broad ways of identifying belief systems. Roger Schmidt, for example, suggests that all religions have certain characteristics in common. He lists these in the categories of functional, formal, and substantive (Schmidt, 1988). Religion functions, for example in important emotional, social, and intellectual ways. Emotionally, religion promotes hope in the midst of despair and serves as a moral compass to prevent or control natural human impulses such as acquisitiveness, sexuality, and anger.

Socially, religions are powerful instruments that define appropriate human interactions and chains of command. Predictable rituals, ceremonies, and rites of passage offer human beings a template for living. Intellectually, religion offers explanations for three universal religious questions: "Who am I?" "What is my purpose?" and "What is my destiny?" In fact, Victor Frankl's entire approach to psychotherapy, something he calls logotherapy, is based on the assumption that the will-to-meaning is a primary human motivator.

Rodney Stark has further classified the human experiences of transcendence in several archetypal ways (Schmidt, 1988). One is the confirming type of religious experience (i.e., religious experiences that reinforce one's sense of the sacred). Confirming experiences usually are characterized by the sense that one has, indeed, apprehended truth, an event that may be accompanied by a sense of peace, joy, satisfaction, or awe.

Stark calls another typology saving religious experience. These experiences are usually found in belief systems that allow for a misuse of human freedom vis-à-vis divine intention. In saving experiences, one is restored to a former (or improved) state, usually involving forgiveness, integration, and health. Commissioning experiences, on the other hand, are those in which a person is convinced that the sacred has contacted him or her directly and with a specific purpose. The prophets (e.g., Samuel, Isaiah, Muhammad) who figure so dramatically in the Islamic and Judao-Christian tradition are examples.

Stark calls another type of religious experience possessional, in which one undergoes an altered state of consciousness (e.g., visions, speaking in tongues, automatic writing). Possessional experiences occur regularly, for example, within Pentecostal Christian groups or Native American shamanism. Stark also describes another category of religious experience, the mystical. Common to the experiences of Buddhists, Sufis, and Jewish and Christian mystics is a sense of oneness with the sacred whereby, for a brief interlude, the mystic no longer experiences the world (and, more importantly, the self) as fragmented and differentiated.

For the therapist, those broader classifications might be more helpful than traditional, cognitive-based approaches to their clients' religious beliefs. They might even represent analytical improvements over assumptions that could be made about, say, a practicing American Roman Catholic (e.g., does the Vatican's prohibition of birth control and abortion determine the client's choices and outlook on sexuality, or has the client selectively chosen which doctrines to which to adhere?).

Unfortunately, Stark's classifications may be too broad to have practical value during therapy. For example, the therapist might spend a good deal of time exploring a client's religious experiences, but not *why* they happened and how they affect the client's life. Similarly, using Schmidt's paradigm, the therapist has to determine what the client's religious beliefs are before learning how they function in the client's life.

One also could use a moral or ethical approach. Although they differ dramatically in terms of what the object of worship properly is, the world's religious traditions share amazingly similar attitudinal norms and standards of behavior. Confucianism, Shintoism, Judaism, and Islam all emphasize obedience to a higher law (whether it be the way of the ancients, a respect for ubiquitous spirit, or following God's commandments). Virtually all world religions are inclusive, at least to the extent that all of humanity is invited into participation in the holy.

However, a purely moral or ethical approach is not comprehensive enough because, in their eclectic approach to spirituality, many postmodern people also borrow from popular culture. It is not surprising that an increasing acceptance of gay and lesbian persons has been as a direct result of sitcoms and night-time television. Furthermore, media and marketing have created various "consumer virtues" (e.g., one uses the same sets of skills to select both margarine and a church home). The point is, of course, that the values inherent in popular culture often find their way into the eclectic person's belief system.

This process is much swifter than the gradual acculturation of the past. Brasher (2001) estimates that there are more than 1 million fully functional, religiously oriented websites on the World Wide Web. Therefore, web surfers seeking spiritually like-minded people not only have immediate access to millions in their own culture, but also instant access to Confucianists in China and Sikhs in Pakistan.

How, then, in the midst of an increasingly pluralistic and diverse religious milieu, do therapists discover their clients' belief systems? Merely researching the Westminster Confession or the Roman Catholic Catechism or the Upanishads is not a realistic option. Is there some evaluative instrument to help therapists determine their clients' world views?

FINDING AN ACCURATE EVALUATIVE INSTRUMENT

In 1992, vexed by the increasingly complicated belief patterns of many, even within mainstream Christian churches, Jones published what he called "The Theological Worlds Inventory." The information that follows is a summary of Jones' theoretical framework for this instrument. The assumption with which Jones approached it is that there is a gap between one's unmet, but nonetheless lived needs, and the events, insights, or persons who have illuminated and ministered to those needs in an incomplete way. Therefore, one's theological world consists mainly of unmet (perhaps unconscious) longings for which traditional catechisms are only marginally useful.

Realizing this, Jones has assembled a 63-question inventory, the results of which identify five familiar theological themes: separation and reunion, conflict and vindication, emptiness and fulfillment, condemnation and forgiveness, and suffering and endurance. Notice that none of the theological worlds relies on the doctrinal positions of any of the world's religions. Instead, in a much more practical vein, emphasis is placed on lived faith and experience.

Obviously, people do not fall exclusively into one camp; rather, they exhibit varying characteristics of all of them. Nevertheless, Jones' paradigm is a useful (and perhaps more accurate) approach to the evaluation of clients' religious beliefs and world views. The following is a brief description of each theological world. Common characteristics, behaviors, and attitudes are presented for clients inhabiting each world, and suggestions for further exploration during therapy are offered.

Separation and Reunion

Those who experience life as separation and reunion often feel a sense of abandonment and of being an insignificant organism in a vast universe. What is longed for in this theological world is coming home, a regaining of the harmony that has been lost in this life. Nevertheless, the person for whom separation and reunion are recurrent themes does experience meaningful, although episodic, moments of sacramental wonder. They are mystical moments where the person feels somehow at one with God and the world.

One of the (perhaps unconscious) understandings of this person is that life is transient, home lies elsewhere, and human beings are visitors on a strange planet. Spiritual harmony is achieved in this theological world by finding one's true self and having that true self become a beacon that points to the divine.

One avenue for therapeutic exploration is to discern the factors that have led to this person's sense of alienation (perhaps from family, colleagues, self, or God). Another avenue is to discover to what extent the client's emphasis on achieving an inner state of being or social "belonging" has obviated taking the necessary actions to make those things possible. A third avenue is behavioral, with the learning of certain appropriate social or professional skills.

Conflict and Vindication

According to Jones, people who inhabit this world understand the self-interest that is evident in all human interactions. They look around and see institutionalized racism or sexism. They see a world of nations and international cartels in which only winners and losers emerge. Life is conflict and a zero-sum game. This world cries out for reform, perhaps even revolution. Adherents to this world view are motivated by the vision of Revelation's "new heaven and earth," one in which the world's ills have been set aright.

It is not surprising that residents in this world are motivated by social issues and causes such peace, justice, and freedom. They have a well-developed social conscience and are willing to set aside personal comfort and safety to minister to the general welfare. Unfortunately, they also tend to be very serious and unwilling or unable to enjoy the moment. They exist for a future they will not live to see, so life becomes a battleground.

One avenue for therapy in this world view is to determine to what extent the individual is motivated by self-righteousness (perhaps as projection). Ironically, because this person is so motivated by altruism toward oppressed-people-as-abstraction, he or she might lack empathy for individuals actually encountered. Likewise, the inhabitant of this conflict and vindication world is a prime candidate for exhaustion and burnout, given the impossibility of his or her utopian dreams. Another avenue might be to help the client initiate an exploration of his or her inner world, because that is probably a neglected area. One possible outcome is the embracing of ambiguity as part of the human condition (rather than the immature demand that things be either good or evil).

Emptiness and Fulfillment

Those who are motivated by the themes of emptiness and fulfillment have a very difficult time accepting themselves. A typical fear is that of being an imposter: "If people really knew me, they wouldn't like me." That theme varies, of course, and may have to do with the issue of competency. This client often feels inadequate or overwhelmed and fears losing his or her identity, of being nothing. (This may be manifested by a fear of death.) Life in the world of emptiness and fulfillment usually is resolved through the instrumentality of belonging, of being accepted by a group or family.

One avenue for therapy for the inhabitant of the world of emptiness and fulfillment is to explore the client's family of origin or significant early experiences that may have led the client to feel marginalized. This reframing may emphasize becoming as opposed to being; that is, stressing the client's potential to become, rather than the client's resignation to a certain state or condition. Another therapeutic avenue might be to explore the client's illusions (to borrow the Eastern word) about what is needed for his or her happiness and fulfillment.

Condemnation and Forgiveness

In the world of condemnation and forgiveness, the client emphasizes his or her shortcomings vis-à-vis a superior behavioral or attitudinal model. This person is likely to experience much guilt and shame and be haunted by the fear of being judged. Life for this person is difficult, and self-acceptance is unlikely except through exterior agency. People in this world experience redemption, salvation, and enlightenment through the grace of God. These are people of second birth who are likely to view life after redemption as one lived in obedience to God's will.

It is likely that the citizen of this world will deprecate his or her good deeds or special talents as not being worthy of divine acceptance. They are skilled at seeing hidden and self-centered motivations behind every action and hold the virtue of humility in high regard. They see the world in which people need to repent and believe to receive forgiveness for their manifold sins.

One avenue for therapy for a client in this world is to explore his or her rigid understandings of good and evil, of before and after, as if life were a problem to be solved. There is a tendency for this client to treat his or her postsalvation actions and attitudes as being rather better than they actually are. Accordingly, he or she might use manipulative guilt-trips on others and hold to unrealistic, even damaging us-against-them stances. Another therapeutic avenue is to explore the whole issue of worthiness and how this person's exaggerated self-censure developed in the first place. Persons in fundamentalist religious groups are particularly at risk.

Suffering and Endurance

Clients who inhabit this world experience life as a burden. They are resigned to the inevitability of bad things happening, and the best they can expect is to be able to meet these trials and disappointments with courage and determination. They have the sense of being victimized in many ways and are tempted to be cynical. They distrust hope-filled attitudes, but acknowledge that suffering, rightly endured, may result in redemptive human qualities such as patience, empathy, and acceptance. The client in this world does not believe that we can change the way things are and values perseverance. He or she might, indeed, look forward to a time in which there is no more suffering, but not expect to find it in this life.

One avenue for therapy for the citizen of the suffering and endurance world is Frankl's logotherapy (or meaning-centered) approach. Frankl, a survivor of Auschwitz, believed that if one understood the reason, then any experience of life could be endured. Accordingly, he believed that meaning in life could be found through: (a) loving something or someone, (b) creating something, or (c) creating a redemptive attitude if in the midst of an intractable problem. Of course, a logical therapeutic alternative might be an exploration of the client's nurture, or lack thereof, in his or her family of origin, with an eye to accepting what has been and starting over as an initiator of life rather than a victim of it.

REFERENCES

Berger, P. L., & Luckmann, T. (1995). The dehumanized world. In W.T. Anderson (Ed.), *The truth about the truth.* New York: Penguin.

Brasher, B. E. (2001). *Give me that online religion.* San Francisco: Jossey-Bass.

Carroll, J. W., & Roof, W. C. (2002). *Bridging divided worlds: Generational cultures in congregations.* San Francisco: Jossey-Bass.

Jones, W. P. (1992). *Worlds within a congregation.* Nashville, TN: Abingdon Press.

Kosmin, B. A., & Lachman, S. P. (2001). *American Religious Identity Survey (ARIS)*. New York: School of the City University of New York.

Lifton, R. J. (1993). *The protean self: Human resilience in an age of fragmentation*. New York: Basic Books.

Schmidt, R. (1988). *Exploring religion*. Belmont, CA: Wadsworth.

SECTION I

The Sacramental Traditions

CHAPTER THREE

Catholicism and Psychology

Kevin Gillespie

A client walks through your door and mentions that she is Catholic. As you learn of her denominational identity, you find yourself developing a series of associations. They may include thoughts about the church, the pope, the bishops, or Catholic approaches to social issues such as abortion, birth control, or the scandal of clergy abuse. Her ethnicity, moreover, may make you ask yourself, what kind of Catholic? As part of a pluralistic universe, you might also be led to wonder what difference does being a Roman Catholic make?

This chapter offers a brief overview of some of the more salient features of Roman Catholicism that are relevant for the treatment of clients. Such an attempt is addressed by means of definitions, distinctions, and descriptions of a multiplicity of beliefs, concepts, and historical events that have shaped Catholicism and its adherents. Given the limited parameters of the chapter, there is no attempt to address the differences among Catholics according to ethnic backgrounds. Indeed, from African to Asian, Irish to Italian, Hispanic to Polish, many expressions of the Catholic faith are conditioned by cultural variables. Such diversity reflects the Catholic Church's belief in the mandate of Christ to go out and teach all nations (Mt. 28:19). In this respect, Catholic *qua* Catholic sees itself as a faith that is multicultural in scope and historical in depth.

With its vast diversity the Catholic Church, as a web of peoples and international institutions, nevertheless promotes some common elements of belief. It should be noted that Catholic clients as individuals may, in a cafeterialike fashion, accept some beliefs and not accept others. Such decisions and doubts may suggest a congruent sense of belonging or an alienated sense of marginalization. Moreover, because Roman

Catholicism possesses a plethora of principles of faith and promotes a vast array of devotions (often with culturally determined rituals), one needs to be careful when making generalizations. Consequently, what a client says about his or her faith needs to be heard and understood from the context and culture of the client's perspective. However, such a perspective may not necessarily reflect what Roman Catholic tradition understands what a principle of faith denotes or devotion connotes. As discussed later, the Catholic Church (especially since the Second Vatican Council) does not simply expect its followers to believe or act just because a priest, or even a pope, says they should. With a wider breadth for communication among cultures and enhanced scholarship that has explored the depths of its long history, Catholicism's institutions, intellects, and individual believers have sought to adapt themselves culturally and respond critically to what the Second Vatican Council referred to as "the signs of the times."

It should be noted also that recent concerns about sexual abuse by Catholic priests and religious authorities are not explicitly addressed in this chapter. It seems obvious, however, that such abuses have produced many victims and have seriously damaged the confidence many Catholics have in their religious authorities and the church's sacred structures. As a result, many Catholics are seeking elsewhere for meaning and spiritual sustenance. Wuthnow's (2000) categories of *dwellers* and *seekers* may be useful for the clinician in distinguishing to what extent a Catholic client is one whose faith "dwells" within the piety and practices of the institutional church, in contrast to a Catholic client who although raised Catholic is seeking outside the institutional church for meanings. The present chapter may prove helpful in working with Catholic clients who fit either category.

IMPORTANT ASPECTS OF ROMAN CATHOLICISM

The chances are good that your Catholic client has little if any sophisticated understanding of the intricacies of the Catholic faith. Indeed he or she may be a Catholic by and large because he or she grew up within a Catholic subculture consisting of a parish, and perhaps had some Catholic education. The client may even have married a Catholic and is raising the children Catholic. For the greater part of the 20th century, at least within an American urban context, one could have assumed that Catholic clients developed their denominational identity by means of a strong parish–school structure. However, then again, up until the 1960s Catholics were hesitant to see psychologists, and they especially avoided psychoanalysts. Confession was viewed as the means whereby Catholics could express their moral, and to some extent, their emotional problems. Often little distinction was made between emotional and moral problems.

To appreciate the social and symbolic world of the Catholic client, it is helpful to have a sense of some of the overall statistics of Catholics and their institutions in the Untied States. According to the 2003 Catholic Almanac, there are 62,018,436 Catholics in the United States. This includes 47,199 priests; 85,034 religious sisters; and 5,970 religious brothers. Catholic institutions include 19,584 parishes; 6,745 elementary schools; 1,358 high schools; 238 colleges and universities; and 586 hospitals. The sheer volume of Catholic institutions indicates that Catholics, at least in the United States, influence the mainstream American way of life. At the same time, many Catholic institutions, especially parishes have a hierarchical governance structure that uses a system that can be efficient in its centralization but authoritarian in its decision making. Catholic institutions also can create an atmosphere where so much stress is placed upon individuals conforming to rules and regulations that creativity and individual thought is de-emphasized and even difficult.

In attempting to understand how a Catholic institutional background can influence the Catholic client from a psychological perspective, it is important to realize that Roman Catholicism in the past has had a somewhat contentious relationship with psychology. It has only been since the 1960s that Catholics were generally encouraged to see a clinical psychologist for emotional issues. Much of the prohibition had to do with the ways that the Catholic Church has viewed one of its central missions as the care of the soul *(cura animarum),* and has used its seven sacraments as means of so caring. This was especially the case with the sacrament of penance.

The Second Vatican Council held in Rome between 1962 and 1965 represents a major shift in the way Catholics engaged the modern world. Convened under Pope John XXIII and concluded by Pope Paul VI, the Council produced a series of documents whose effects are still reverberating throughout Catholicism today. So significant was the Council's initial impact that distinct responses among Catholics have developed so that it has become common to speak sociologically of pre- and post-Vatican II Catholics. One can presume, for instance, that Catholics over 50 grew up with meatless Fridays, regular confession, and mandatory Sunday mass. Moreover, their parents were strongly encouraged to send them to a Catholic school. Furthermore, they were most likely to be exposed to such devotions as May processions and stations of the cross. Many Catholics over 50 were trained to have consciences in which the phrase "under pain of mortal sin" was mantralike. To deliberately miss mass on Sunday might be viewed as a mortal sin, as was premarital sex.

Catholic children, especially those religiously trained in Catholic grade schools by means of question-and-answer catechisms, developed a Catholic casuistry whereby they could readily distinguish the subtleties of moral actions. They also strove to be compliant to the various representatives of authority. In this respect, this older Catholic cohort had a faith that had the strength of being intelligent and thoughtful, but the weakness of tending toward rigidity and fear. Clients with such a background fit into what Kennedy (1995) describes as Culture I Catholics (external locus of religious authority). Such practice of the Catholic faith tends to be rooted in faith structured around authority and compliance and is less open to exploration and valuing personal experiences.

On the other hand, Catholic children whose early formative years occurred during or after the Second Vatican Council tend to have a less formal faith. Raised at a time when one's experience of faith was emphasized and when it was normal to experiment with one's beliefs and actions, such Catholics tend to pay less attention to Catholic rules and devotions. They tend to seek out various psychological literatures as a means of self-understanding. The primacy of one's individual conscience represents a central principle for these Catholics. Such a group fits into what Kennedy (1995) describes as a Culture II Catholic, one having a more internal locus of authority.

It should be noted, however, that the style and substance of the pontificate of Pope John Paul II has had a major impact on Catholics of both groups, leading some Catholics to become more compliant with the church's authority, whereas other Catholics are more alienated from Catholicism's structures of authority. Moreover, many younger Catholics have sought the security of the pre-Vatican II style and structures.

DISTINCT CATHOLIC DOCTRINES
AND DEVOTIONS

Many Roman Catholics continue the traditions of their ethnic faith heritage. This is visible in various devotions and the use of cultural-specific sacraments, including saying the rosary; praying novenas (nine days of prayer); and engaging in processions honoring Mary, the mother of Jesus, or a specific saint (e.g., St. Patrick).

In its doctrinal identity, the Catholic Church defines itself as "one, holy, catholic and apostolic." It identifies itself as "one" through its identification with the oneness of the trinity (the Father, Son, and Holy Spirit) (*Catechism of the Catholic Church*, No. 813). The Catholic Church identifies itself as "holy" because it is in communion with Christ, who is holy, and because, as a community of faith, it is sanctified through Christ

(*Catechism*, No. 823). The church identifies itself as "catholic" in two ways: first, through its identification with the universal Christ and second because Christ has given it the mission to "go out to the whole world" (Mt. 28:19) (*Catechism*, Nos. 830–831). Finally, the church is "apostolic" because it remains faithful through the successors of St. Peter to the origin founded upon the 12 apostles (*Catechism*, No. 863). Catholicism's detailed dogmatic tradition is based on interpretations of the bible. Doctrines, in turn, represent explanations whereby divinely revealed truths or dogma may be understood.

A principal doctrine of the Catholic faith is its devotion to Jesus' mother, known as the "blessed mother." As the mother of Jesus, Mary assumes a unique place because she represents the bridge between the divine and the human. This has led to some confusion; Catholics have been perceived as worshipping Mary as a goddess. Although Catholic doctrine has been clear about Mary's human and nondivine identity, the various images of Mary through the centuries and in the cathedrals, churches, and educational institutions named in her honor might lead one to believe otherwise.

Mary's role in Catholicism is inseparable from her union with Christ and flows directly from it (*Catechism* No. 964). For Catholics, this belief is expressed in the doctrine of the immaculate conception that essentially points to her relationship with the Christ. Mary's motherhood, then, is the reason for her being given special devotion above all other saints. Catholicism has highlighted this role through special feasts that celebrate the significant moments in her life. The most significant universal devotion that Catholics have toward Mary is the rosary, which consists of a series of five decades using the "hail Mary" prayer. Using the rosary, a believer meditates over various events or "mysteries" of the life of Christ and his mother.

Roman Catholic women who are pregnant or who are mothers often have a special devotion to Mary and pray for her intercession. Here again, some confusion between belief and doctrine may occur. To pray before a statue of Mary may suggest that a person is worshipping the statue and believing Mary to be a goddess. Piety does not necessarily follow doctrine, however; Mary is not meant to be worshiped, but to serve as a human intercessor between God and humanity. In other words, the doctrine of the Catholic Church believes that one can offer prayers to God through Mary. This same belief characterizes Catholic devotions to the saints. Men and women who have lived lives of heroic virtue are seen after their deaths as helping the living draw closer to God.

Another distinct characteristic of Catholicism is the role of authority. Roman Catholicism *qua* Roman places a great deal of significance upon authority both for symbolic as well as structural reasons. Catholicism traces its sense of authority from Jesus' injunction to Peter, "You are Peter and upon this rock I will build my church" (Mt. 16:18). Thus, Catholicism believes its authority to have been divinely inspired through the call and mission of Peter. Because Peter traveled to Rome where he was martyred, the church sees its center there, literally at the tomb of Peter over which the Vatican was built. In this respect, Roman Catholicism identifies itself as Roman because of what it views as the primacy of the Petrine ministry that the pope embodies symbolically.

Structurally Catholicism's authority revolves around Rome as well. With the pope as the head of a centralized hierarchy, Catholicism seeks to coordinate its many institutional layers. The basic layer is the community of faith that gathers around a geographic region known as a parish. Many parishes are centralized under a diocese, and several dioceses in a geographical area combine to form an archdiocese. The Archdiocese of Denver, for example, also consists of the dioceses of Colorado Springs and Pueblo. Within Catholicism's ecclesiological structure, the bishops are appointed and generally serve until they reach 75, when they are required by the church's code of canon law to submit their resignation to the pope. The pope is seen as the first bishop among all other bishops. Periodically, the bishops gather to form a synod, from which come their teachings about faith and morals. Often the pope issues statements on various moral and religious matters, some of which have more of an impact on the church than others. Such was the case with the encyclical *Humanae Vitae,* in which the pope forbade Catholics to use artificial birth control.

Recently, more emphasis has been given to those men and women trained in theology as having some teaching authority in Catholicism, and as such are informal members of the church's magisterium. Catholicism's authority seeks to form the conscience of every individual in a way that one's capacity to choose and make moral decisions will be done within the context of faith. This "sense of the faithful" *(sensus fidelium),* although often deemphasized, plays an important part in Catholicism's promotion of teachings. For example, it has been argued that because the position forbidding artificial contraception was widely rejected by the faithful, it did not carry the moral authority that church documents have had.

The principle of infallibility represents a unique belief that has been controversial both inside and outside Catholicism. There are two types of infallibility, ordinary and extraordinary. Ordinary infallible statements pertain to those arrived at by the college of bishops at a council. Extraordinary infallible statements pertain to those issued by the pope when he speaks *ex cathedra* (from the "chair of Peter"). There have been only two occasions: (a) in 1854, the bull of Pope Pius IX defined as infallible, the belief or dogma of Mary's Immaculate Conception as a dogma; and (b) in 1950 when Pope Pius XII declared as infallible the Assumption of Mary, which asserts that as the mother of Jesus, Mary at her death was "assumed" into heaven. It should be noted that what makes such statements infallible is not that the pope as a single human being believed this position of faith to be absolutely true. Instead, the pope by virtue of his office confirms the common and historic sense of the faithful that the teachings are true and without error.

EPISTEMOLOGICAL TOOLS ACKNOWLEDGED AND SUPPORTED BY ROMAN CATHOLICS

Throughout its long intellectual tradition Catholicism has placed a great deal of emphasis on balancing faith and reason. Catholic dogmas of faith are expressed sacramentally and thought through systematically. Unity in the midst of diversity is crucial in the organization of the Catholic mind and structures. Inconsistency is eschewed. In this respect the Catholic Church places a high value on reason. The writings of Augustine and Aquinas, whose thought inspired the scholastic tradition, have been most notable in this respect. These writers, along with Catholic thinkers in general, relied heavily upon deductive logic to develop systematic ways of understanding God, nature, and humanity. Such a method led Aquinas, for instance, to view theology as the "queen of the sciences" and all disciplines were embraced and subservient to its principles. As shown historically, the deductive approach was later challenged by the inductive methods of empirical sciences. Instead of arguments derived from established philosophic principles, induction through observation and experiment became the means for scientific knowledge. The break from deductive methods and the emergence of scientific paradigms through inductive methods served to fracture the systematic knowledge of Catholic thinkers that it time led to deep divisions between faith and reason, theology and science, and eventually religion and psychology.

Catholic tradition, however, in its epistemological efforts has developed other methods, most notably its emphasis on the analogic imagination, more precisely the sacramental imagination. As McDargh (1985), Greeley (1990), and Tracy (1998) describe it, the analogic imagination suggests an approach to reality in terms of both/and, which contrasts with the dialectic either/or approach that is more typical of Protestantism. Through the analogic imagination, then, the Catholic mind seeks to connect the human with the divine, the temporal with the eternal, the immanent with the transcendent, and grace with nature. Such an imagination is most commonly used in the symbols and rituals of the Catholic sacramental system, which serve to help one to imagine and thus believe in the presence of Jesus Christ.

Pope John Paul II's encyclical *Fides et Ratio* (Pope John Paul II, 1998) stressed the need for striking a balance between knowing and believing. In speaking of how one believes so as to understand *(credo ut intellegam)* and how one seeks understanding in order to believe *(intellego ut credam)*, the pope stated:

> Faith and reason are like two wings on which the human spirit rises to the contemplation of truth; and God has placed in the human heart a desire to know the truth—in a word, to know himself—so that, by knowing and loving God, men and women may also come to the fullness of truth about themselves (Pope John Paul II, 1998, p. 4).

This balance between faith and reason carries for the Catholic over into the worlds of theology and science and by the same token with spirituality and psychology. Any Christian faith implies the revelation found. In this respect, it should be noted that one of the most significant changes that the 20th century brought to Roman Catholicism was a new emphasis upon the bible. Spurred on by ecumenical efforts in biblical scholarship and endorsed by the documents of the Second Vatican Council, the church gave the study of and praying over scripture a new emphasis. Previously, Catholicism relied primarily upon the sacraments and sacramentals to inspire. Moreover, it relied heavily upon the interpretations of scripture provided through its long intellectual tradition and large institutional systems and structures. Unlike many Protestant denominations, whereby believers may be encouraged to interpret scripture according to the way a passage may speak to them as individuals *(sola scriptura)*, Catholics are taught to interpret the bible through the lenses of revelation and reason provided through commentaries, sermons, and teachings.

As noted, Catholicism relies heavily upon the analogic imagination as a means of knowing and believing. Although at times perceived as fostering magic and superstition, the sacramental imagination serves for the believer as a primary modality to experience Christ. The central constituent of such a system of beliefs is the Paschal Mystery—the birth, life, death, and resurrection of Jesus revealed through the Holy Spirit. The Catholic liturgical year revolves around the various mysteries so that time is seen as sacred (e.g., Christmas, Good Friday, Easter, and Pentecost). It should be noted that one misuse of the sacramental imagination was manifested in the phenomenon of clergy abuse. Catholic figures such as priests and religious men and women had often almost iconic status among Catholics. As a result, they were less likely to be held accountable for their immoral and even illicit behaviors.

THEORY OF PERSONALITY

For Roman Catholicism, the person represents an image of God *(an imago Dei)*. Because every person is a creature loved into existence in the image of the loving Creator, we are all worthy of dignity. Each person is seen as a composite unity of body, mind, and soul. Such a synthesis emerged as an extension of believing in the resurrection of Jesus of Nazareth. Belief in his resurrection led to the doctrine that a person's soul has the potential of eternal life after death. Moreover, Catholic tradition, with varying emphases, has incorporated the mind–body and matter–spirit relationships first formulated by Plato and Aristotle. Catholicism eschews an emphasis upon one without the other. A person is neither just matter nor simply spirit. Consequently, reductionistic theories of materialism or idealism are unacceptable. By the same token, Catholicism espouses that every individual has a free will that is situationally influenced but not determined. In this respect Catholicism opposed deterministic theories of behavior. The capacity of an individual to make free but informed moral choices lies at the basis of Catholicism's theological anthropology, which sees God in all creation as well as the dignity of every human being.

Catholicism places a great emphasis upon the formation of one's conscience. This capacity to make judgments of reason is seen to be at the heart of the person (*Catechism*, No. 1777). It is "an individual's most secret core and his sanctuary. There he is alone with God whose voice echoes in his depths" (Abbott, 1966, p. 213). Through conscience, the individual creates and assumes responsibility for actions that enhances self-understanding, and virtue that develops character. In this respect, Catholics, through the church's system of sacraments, are encouraged to appropriate and live out the four cardinal virtues of prudence, justice, fortitude, and temperance.

Catholicism's views on morality derive from its emphasis on moral conscience, which, in turn, derives from its belief and understanding of human freedom. As such the individual must endeavor to have an informed conscience, one whereby decisions are made on information and sound judgment. The ten commandments, the tenets of faith expressed by Jesus Christ in the beatitudes, and the principles of natural law serve as the matrix for the formation of one's conscience. Catholicism's intellectual and institutional cultures serve as means for promoting such formation. These include the seven sacraments that individually and collectively provide ritualistic ways for shaping and strengthening one's capacity to make prudent judgments of love. The sacrament of penance with the confession of sins (offenses against reason, truth, and right conscience) requires an "examination of conscience." The mass (the celebration of the Eucharist), begins with an examination of conscience. Homilies at mass, meanwhile, are meant to guide and inspire listeners toward right action.

Human freedom serves as a key constituent of the Catholic faith. With freedom comes responsibility for one's actions. Because humans possess freedom and responsibility, actions are conceived as moral, amoral, or immoral. The latter actions are deemed sinful. Sin is viewed as a misuse of such freedom. Whether through deliberate and intentional actions (sins of commission) or neglect or ignorance (sins of omission), every person has the capacity to use his or her freedom wisely or unwisely.

Traditionally Catholic moral theologians have distinguished three types of sins: (a) Original sin, seen as the first sin of Adam and Eve; (b) mortal sin, which "destroys charity in the heart of man by a grave violation of God's law" (*Catechism*, No. 1854); and venial sin, which "allows charity to subsist, even though it offends and wounds it" (*Catechism*, No. 1855). In recent years, theologians have spoken of mortal sin in terms of a *fundamental option*. That is to say, the gravity of mortal sin requires a radical choice against the principles of love and life. Rather than emphasis being placed upon whether or not an individual conforms to a set of laws, Catholics moral theologians and pastoral ministers seek to help a person understand how sinful behaviors are not congruent with their deeper and truer self, and how God wishes them to be loved and to love.

Finally, Catholicism asserts that the human personality should not be limited to the understandings of psychology or any science. Although much is to be learned and understood about human nature through sciences such as psychology, Catholicism believes that there is a mystery of human existence that can never be fully comprehended by science. Religious faith provides ways of understanding the personality (i.e., the soul) that transcends the human condition and provides a wider connection to the meaning of being human; that is, a creature loved into life and embraced at death by a loving Creator.

HUMAN DEVELOPMENT

Although there is no specific Roman Catholic psychological theory of human development, Catholic theologians have for centuries subscribed to the medieval axiom of Thomas Aquinas that grace perfects or builds on nature *(gratia perfectit naturam)*. A contemporary understanding of this axiom would hold that God's presence may be seen in how a human being develops physiologically, psychologically, and socially. In this respect, the biopsychosocial model whereby a person is understood for diagnostic purposes is congruent with Catholic belief.

By means of its vast array of educational institutions, Catholicism has sought to promote a person's physiologic, psychological, and social development, for such are the areas where Catholics believe that the spirit of God communicates with an individual. By promoting a person's development by means of education it is more likely that a person's awareness of God's presence (because presumably one understands of the world of creation) is enhanced. Hence, Catholicism has placed a great emphasis on creating opportunities through educational institutions for Catholics and others, to know about the life and the teachings of Christ and the values that belief in Christ implies.

It has been through educational institutions that Catholicism theologic and philosophic tradition has developed. Dating back to the Middle Ages with the teachings of Anselm (d. 1109), Thomas Aquinas (d. 1274), and Bonaventure (d. 1274) through the battles with the modern era, some of whose thinkers, such as Descartes and Rousseau had been trained in Catholic institutions, Catholic perspectives on human development, both individually and collectively had been seen in terms of the development of soul more than self. The great spiritual classics such as Augustine's *Confessions* and Teresa of Avila's *Interior Castle* illustrate such an emphasis.

With the emergence of psychology as a formal discipline in the late 19th century, Catholicism in Europe and in North America adapted a defensive stance toward the study of the mind apart from the soul. Toward the end of the century, the "new psychology" of the laboratory challenged the relevance of the "soul." Then, at the birth of the 20th century, Freud's psychoanalytic theory confronted the Catholic understanding of the mind. For a religious system long dominated by a scholastic and rational psychology, the empiric and clinical findings of the "new psychology" seemed to rob psychology first of its soul and then of its mind. During the twentieth century as Gillespie (2001) describes, Catholicism's resistance toward psychological theories of human development gradually waned such that most contemporary theories of human development have been adapted in varying degrees by Roman Catholic thinkers. It should be noted, however, that the key criteria for such acceptance are the freedom and dignity of every individual.

THE THEORY OF PSYCHOLOGICAL
HEALTH AND PATHOLOGY

Roman Catholicism in adhering to the principle that charity involves not only love for one's neighbor, but also that the love of oneself necessarily encourages one to care for one's body and mind as well as one's soul. However, in Roman Catholic tradition, there have been saints whose physical and even mental health may be seen by some as neurotic. Moreover, there are some who view the celibate lifestyles of Catholic religious men and women as unwise at best and delusional at worst.

From an historical perspective, Catholicism's emphasis upon grace and sin has been more pronounced than its views toward sanity and mental illness. Alcoholism, for instance, was traditionally understood as resulting from an individual's immoral actions and vices. It was only during the later part of the 20th century that alcoholism, as well as other addictions, was seen in terms of disease that limits a person's freedom and hence moral responsibility.

Throughout its history and among a plethora of cultures and subcultures, Catholics have seen themselves as members of a community. In this respect, a catholic is a member of a parish community, which in turn is part of a diocese that connects it to other communities in the wider church. Such a series of relationships are meant to manifest one's connection to the body of Christ. Seen in these terms, then the health of Catholicism traditionally has been viewed in terms of his or her relationship to the community of faith, which, in turn, reflects one's connection to Christ. As a result, the worst illness a Catholic could suffer is to be excommunicated from the community of faith.

THE THEORY OF HUMAN CHANGE INHERENT IN ROMAN CATHOLICISM

For Catholicism, the seven sacraments and the various sacramentals serve a dual function of supporting a person's faith as well as inspiring change. Catholic belief holds that change occurs in and through the grace of God (i.e., God's communication of Self to the self of an individual). For the Catholic, the challenge is to live a life made up of choices and virtues whereby one is open to such communication. For more than 40 years Meissner has pursued the significance of grace perfecting nature from psychoanalytic perspectives (Meissner, 1961, 1964, 1973, 1984, 1987, 1992, 2000, 2003). Meissner, for example, sees the perfecting of nature through grace as "reflected on the psychological level in the parallel development of the ego in autonomy, control, freedom, and maturity of function, together with thee emergence of spiritual identity" (Meissner, 1987, p. 58).

Catholicism promotes spiritual change through the seven sacraments, which for Martos (1982) replicates common human rituals. In the sacrament of baptism, a person, usually an infant, is welcomed into the Christian family through a rite of initiation. Later, in childhood or early adolescence, this initiation process becomes broadened and deepened through the sacrament of confirmation. The sacrament of matrimony expresses the marriage rite while ritualizing the sharing of food, and the ritual of sacrifice are represented in the sacrament of the Eucharist, a sacrament that takes place during a Catholic mass. Rituals of atonement and healing are embedded in the sacraments of penance and the sacrament of the sick. Finally, the sacrament of ordination (holy orders) uses a variety of consecration rituals. For the Catholic, then, the seven sacraments represent the principal means of faith formation, because how one prays is how one believes *(lex orandi, lex credendi)*.

The sacrament of penance or reconciliation had for centuries been a means for Catholics to discuss emotional as well as spiritual problems in a confidential setting with another human being (i.e., a priest). Indeed, many Catholics would not receive communion (i.e., the Eucharist) at mass unless they had been to confession recently. With the increased availability of psychotherapists and counselors, as well as new understandings of confession that emerged from post-Vatican II Catholicism, the regular use of the sacrament by Catholics has declined significantly.

Besides the seven sacraments, there are other rituals and symbols that serve as conduits to encounter Christ. These are known as sacramentals. Less formal than sacraments, sacramentals are likewise products of the analogic imagination. They help believers to imagine that God can be encountered through blessings over ashes, holy water, religious medals, and the images of God conveyed by means of icons, holy cards, stained glass windows, and statues. As rituals, sacraments and sacramentals serve to intensify one's experience of God's encounter with human beings, and indeed with all creation. Such an encounter, it should be noted, is not limited to sacraments and sacramentals because the sacramental imagination of Catholicism is pantheistic in scope (i.e., that God exists in all creation). Such a belief contrasts with pantheism, in which God is believed to be everything.

COMMON MORAL ISSUES ENCOUNTERED

Among the myriad of moral issues, it has been the Catholic Church's stance on sexuality that has most led to emotional conflict among Catholics. Roman Catholicism's view of sexuality has been influenced by an Augustinian notion that the body is to be overcome and its urges to be suspected. Such a view, in turn, led many Catholics to associate sexuality with sin. Even acts of masturbation were for centuries deemed seriously sinful. In more recent years aided by the insights of developmental theorists,

Catholicism's approach to sexuality has become less apodeictic. For example, the Catholic *Catechism* in its approach to masturbation states that "one must take into account the affective immaturity, force of acquired habit, conditions of anxiety, or other psychological or social factors that lessen or even extenuate moral culpability" (*Catechism*, No. 2352). However, fornication, whether in adultery or premarital sex, is still considered a grave sin.

Abortion in all forms, even to save the life of a mother, is seen as intrinsically wrong. In addition, Catholicism opposes all forms of artificial contraception, only allowing for birth control that involves rhythm or natural planning method. Catholicism faced one of its most significant crises of credibility around the issue of contraception. In the summer of 1968, Pope Paul VI issued the encyclical *Humanae Vitae*, which went against the recommendations of the majority of members of the committee the pope had formed to investigate the matter. Instead, the pope reasserted Catholicism's long held opposition to the use of contraceptive devices. Interestingly enough, Archbishop Karl Woytyla, the future Pope John Paul II, was a major figure in supporting the position taken by Pope Paul VI.

Controversies and considerable opposition soon followed the issuance of the encyclical. Studies, such as those conducted by the sociologist Andrew Greeley, have found that the encyclical became a major source of dissension within the church, as Catholics began to question the credibility of Catholic leaders and teachings. Indeed, at the 1968 annual meeting of the American Catholic Psychological Association, members, in questioning the encyclical's opposition to artificial contraception, raised serious questions about the encyclical's psychological understanding of the human person and its overall approach to psychology (Gillespie, 2001). What's more, the enthusiastic acceptance of the Documents of the Second Vatican Council dissipated, and there occurred a wave of alienation among Catholic clergy and laity alike.

As Greeley states:

> *Humanae Vitae* canceled out the positive results of Vatican II and sent the church into a sudden and dramatic decline; priests refused to endorse the teaching in the confessional; Sunday church attendance dropped off sharply; church collections diminished; resignations from the priesthood increased, while those who remained diminished their efforts to recruit young men for the vocation, and family support for religious vocations eroded. Acceptance of papal authority declined dramatically (Greeley, 1982, p. 36).

The Catholic approach to homosexuality has been another area that has been a source of considerable controversy. Throughout its tradition

Catholicism has maintained the position that homosexual acts are "intrinsically disordered." In this respect, Catholicism has opposed gay marriages and the adoption of children by gay couples. More recently, Catholic bishops have issued pastoral statements supporting the dignity and human rights of those with such an orientation. The Catholic *Catechism* asserts: "They must be accepted with respect, compassion and sensitivity. Every sign of unjust discrimination in their regard should be avoided" (*Catechism,* No. 2358). However, a great deal of controversy remains within the Catholic community about the place of homosexuals in Catholicism. For some, it seems inconsistent for Catholicism to support the dignity of those men and women who have a homosexual orientation, yet at the same time criticize homosexual genital activity. As a consequence of such criticism, many homosexual Catholics have become alienated and have left the church.

As noted in the discussion of the encyclical *Humane Vitae,* Catholics, even those who take their faith seriously, experience considerable conflict between believing what Catholicism says about contraception or homosexuality, and what they themselves believe to be healthy sexual practices. Indeed, a credibility gap has developed, and has led many Catholics in recent years to question Catholic moral stances on these and other issues such as euthanasia, and its ecclesiastical opposition to women's ordination. Moreover, the scandal of clerical sexual abuse has further weakened Catholicism's moral authority and widened its credibility gap.

At the same time, the Catholic Church has taken very liberal positions on social issues such as capital punishment, social welfare, and human rights in general. A psychological dissonance has developed in which Catholicism has become identified as conservative when it comes to sexual issues, yet liberal and even radical on many social issues. Catholic leaders believe these moral positions of opposition and promotion of sensitive personal and social moral issues reflect a congruent system of morality that can be weaved into what the late Joseph Cardinal Bernadin referred to as a "seamless garment" of morality. By this Bernadin believed that the Catholic Church should promote a consistent ethic for life that challenged not only abortion but other social concerns such as capital punishment, euthanasia, and war.

Another dimension of sexuality and Catholicism involves the role of women. Women, especially religious women, over the centuries have been leaders within some church structures (e.g., hospitals and schools). Nevertheless, only since Vatican II have women been given responsibilities within Catholicism's system of governance. Because Catholicism does not permit women to be ordained, they are prevented from entering into the higher church structures of the *magisterium.* At the same time, given the shortage of ordained Catholic clergy, a greater number of women are serving as the principal parish administrators. Also, a large number of doctorates in Catholic theology are being obtained by women, many of whose doctorates take a feminist approach to Catholicism's ecclesiastical concerns.

COMMON CLINICAL ISSUES ENCOUNTERED

This chapter has presented an historical and conceptual overview of the major beliefs of the Catholic faith. As noted, it is difficult to characterize the vast variety of Catholics. It was shown, for example, that there are distinct differences between pre- and post-Vatican II Catholics. The role that authority has in the Catholic system of faith also was shown. Such authority, when misapplied or misinterpreted, can lead some Catholics toward compliancy and even dependency. Also, given the significance of sin in the Catholic framework, some Catholics, especially elder ones, may be more vulnerable to obsessions and scrupulous behaviors. Then there is the phenomenon of "Catholic guilt," particularly when it comes to sexual issues. Catholic patients may at times become obsessed with a belief that a violation of Catholicism's moral sexual guidelines will lead one to eternal damnation. This belief can, in turn, create a great deal of anxiety and depression.

In concluding this chapter, it may be helpful to present several cases so as to exemplify the relevance of some concepts. A brief comment is provided after each case.

Client A

Jane is a middle-aged woman who grew up Roman Catholic. Her presenting problem has to do with her anxious relationships with her elderly parents and two brothers, all of whom are faithful Catholics. She sees that some of the issues between them have to do with her remarriage. She informs you that 5 years ago she and her husband of 20 years divorced. A year ago she remarried without obtaining an annulment. She informs you that as a result she has been excommunicated from the church. She states that she did not want to go through the Catholic bureaucracy to obtain an annulment. She believes that her second marriage to a Catholic man is a good one, except that she feels guilty when she goes to church with her two teenage children from her first marriage. They go up for communion while she and her husband do not, and she feels guilty about not receiving.

Comment: Contrary to popular belief a Catholic who divorces and remarries without an annulment is not excommunicated. Although the official Catholic position prohibits her from receiving communion, some pastoral theologians advise her that if she is faced with circumstances where she could not obtain an annulment in good conscience, then she could receive the Eucharist.

Client B

Bruce is a 28-year-old gay man whose presenting symptoms indicate a mild depression. He went to a Catholic grade school, Catholic high school, and state university. When he was 20, he "came out of the closet." Since then he has had several homosexual relationships. Presently, Bruce has been involved in a homosexual relationship for about 1 year. They are talking about obtaining a marriage license in one American state, although he knows that the pastor of the Catholic Church that he attends would disapprove. He feels conflicted and depressed over the matter.

Comment: As noted, Catholicism calls for a compassionate understanding of homosexuality, but disapproves of a gay lifestyle. Bruce's conflict and potential alienation are well founded. Although there are Catholic support groups, sadly he may need to find support elsewhere other than in his community of faith.

Client C

You have been seeing a Catholic woman for several months. During one session, she reveals that several years earlier she had had an abortion. One of the consequences of the abortion was her belief that she has committed a mortal sin and has been excommunicated from the Catholic Church. She relates that she used to enjoy going to mass on Sundays because it helped her to pray and cope with some emotional issues. She also enjoyed seeing friends there.

Comment: Although Catholicism sees an abortion as intrinsically evil, a woman who chooses to have one is not excommunicated. Whether an action constitutes a mortal sin or not depends on how much freedom and reflection went into the choice. It often is the case that such a choice is made under extreme duress and desperation, and hence, one's freedom may be limited. In any event, the sacrament of penance (confession) should restore her fully to the church community.

CONCLUSION

This chapter has provided an overview that represents a church whose long and complex tradition is well known. Through a series of definitions, descriptions, and a detailed history of several issues pertaining to

Catholicism's relationship to clinical psychology, it is hoped that a better understanding of the religious background of a Catholic client may be appreciated. At times a client may bring various forms of "baggage" from her faith tradition, whereas there may be other times when a client's Catholic faith may serve to help one cope and hope. Some psychologists may perceive all Catholics as having similar values, but as this chapter has tried to show, the complexity of the faith, its long tradition, the recent changes in Catholicism, not to mention the cultural appropriation of one's faith, make every Catholic client a unique individual.

Finally, there are many texts on Roman Catholicism, books that clinicians may find helpful, including: *What Makes Us Catholic: Eight Gifts for Life,* by Thomas Groome (2003), a noted religious educator; *A People Adrift: The Crisis of the Roman Catholic Church in America* (2003) by *New York Times* columnist Peter Steinfels; *The Catholic Revolution: New Wine and Old Wineskins and the Second Vatican Council* (2004) by sociologist Andrew Greeley; and *The Coming Catholic Church: How the Faithful Are Shaping a New Catholicism* (2003) by David Gibson.

REFERENCES

Abbott, W. M. (Ed.) (1966). *The documents of Vatican II.* New York: America Press.

Bunson, M. (Ed.) (2003). *The Catholic almanac.* Huntington, IN: Our Sunday Visitor Books.

Catechism of the Catholic Church. (English translation.) (1994). Liguori, MO: Liguori Publications.

Gibson, D. (2003). *The coming Catholic Church: How the faithful are shaping a new Catholicism.* New York: HarperSanFrancisco.

Gillespie, C. K. (2001). *Psychology and American Catholicism: From confession to therapy?* New York: Crossroads.

Glazier, M., & Hellwig, M. K. (1994). *The modern Catholic encyclopedia.* Collegeville, MN: The Liturgical Press.

Greeley, A. (1982). Going their own way. *New York Times Sunday Magazine* October 10, 1982, In J. Dolan (Ed.). (1985). *The American Catholic experience* (p. 435). Garden City, NY: Doubleday.

Greeley, A. (1990). *Catholic myth: The behavior and beliefs of American Catholics.* New York: Scribner's.

Greeley, A. (2001). *The Catholic imagination.* Berkeley, CA: University of California Press.

Greeley, A. (2004). *The Catholic revolution: New wine and old wineskins and the Second Vatican Council.* Berkeley, CA: University of California Press.

Groome, T. (2003). *What makes us Catholic: Eight gifts for life.* New York: HarperSanFrancisco.

Kennedy, E. (1995). *Tomorrow's Catholic, yesterday's church: The two cultures of American Catholicism.* New York: Triumph.

Martos, J. (1982). *Doors to the sacred: A historical introduction to sacraments in the Catholic church*. Garden City, NY: Image.

McBrien, R. P. (1994). *Catholicism: New Edition*. San Francisco: HarperSanFrancisco.

McDargh, J. (1985). Theological use of psychology: Retrospective and prospective. *Horizons 12*, 247–264.

Meissner, W. W. (1961). *Annotated bibliography in religion and psychology*. New York: Academy of Religion and Mental Health.

Meissner, W. W. (1964). Prolegomena to a psychology of grace. *Journal of Religion and Mental Health, 3*, 209–240.

Meissner, W. W. (1973). Notes on the psychology of hope. *Journal of Religion and Mental Health, 12*, 120–139.

Meissner, W. W. (1984). *Psychoanalysis and religious experience*. New Haven, CT: Yale University Press.

Meissner, W. W. (1987). *Life and faith: Psychological perspectives on religious experience*. Washington, DC: Georgetown University Press.

Meissner, W. W. (1992). *Ignatius of Loyola: The psychology of a saint*. New Haven, CT: Yale University Press.

Meissner, W. W. (2000). *The cultic origins of Christianity: The dynamics of religious development*. Collegeville, MN: Liturgical Press.

Meissner, W. W. (2003). Transformative processes in the spiritual exercises. In W. W. Meissner & C. R. Schlauch (Eds.), *Psyche and spirit: Dialectics of transformation* (pp. 119–152). New York: University Press of America.

Pope John Paul II. (1998). *Fides et Ratio*. Retrieved June 3, 2004, from http://www.cin.org/jp2/fides.html

Pope Pius XII. (1953). Psychotherapy and religion: An address to the fifth international congress of psychotherapy and clinical psychology. *Catholic Mind, 435*.

Shafranske, E. P. (1996). Psychotherapy with Roman Catholics. In P. S. Richards & A. E. Bergin (Eds.), *Handbook of psychotherapy and religious diversity* (pp. 59–88). Washington, DC: American Psychologic Association.

Steinfels, P. (2003). *A people adrift: The crisis of the Roman Catholic Church in America*. New York: Simon & Schuster.

Tracy, D. (1998). *The analogic imagination*. New York: Crossroads.

Wuthnow, R. (2000). *After heaven: Spirituality in America after the 1950s*. Berkeley, CA: University of California Press.

CHAPTER FOUR

Beloved to God:
An Eastern Orthodox
Anthropology

Elizabeth A. Gassin and J. Stephen Muse

OVERVIEW AND HISTORY
OF EASTERN CHRISTIANITY

The Eastern Orthodox Church consists of a family of self-governing national bodies, such as the Greek, Russian, and Serbian Orthodox Churches. A common misunderstanding is that each local church (Serbian, Romanian, etc.) is a separate denomination, but this is not the case; these national communities are united through a common theological and liturgical tradition and maintain full Eucharistic communion with one another. There are about 300 million Orthodox Christians worldwide, about four million of whom reside in the United States.

Because many in the West assume that Roman Catholicism and Eastern Orthodoxy are similar, in reviewing the history and theological foundations of Orthodox Christianity, we emphasize some of the salient differences between these two traditions. Although the two arose from the same Apostolic root in the first century, differing cultural patterns and theological emphases slowly emerged in the two geographic areas, dividing them into separate streams before their official split in 1054 AD. This is the date of formal ecclesial separation when the pope's emissaries from Rome arrived in Constantinople to serve Patriarch Michael Cerularius with notice of excommunication; the Patriarch then excommunicated the emissaries. A further blow to unity resulted from the Crusaders' sack of Constantinople in 1204, leaving it vulnerable to invasion from the Turks, who eventually ended a thousand years of a flourishing Byzantine Empire.

The theological tenor of the Eastern Christian tradition, which emerged from a cultural context that did not undergo a Dark Age, Renaissance, Enlightenment, or Reformation, is quite different from that of the West. With its emphasis on liturgy, icons, continual prayer, watchfulness, purification of the heart, and the vision of the Uncreated Light, scholars sometimes refer to the Orthodox Church as the "mystical" Christian tradition (Lossky, 1973).

The Eastern view of personhood, articulated by the Cappadocian fathers of the 4th century in light of the Church's understanding of the Holy Trinity, also has its unique aspects. While the Orthodox Church—like the Western Christian tradition—maintains that humanity was created in the image and likeness of God, Adam and Eve are not viewed as being fully mature individuals before the fall. The view of St. Irenaeus of Lyon is typical of the Eastern tradition, which understands Adam to be childlike with the potential for growth, but not fully developed. Orthodox doctrine (following St. Athanasius more so than St. Augustine) teaches that before the fall, grace and gifts of the Spirit were given to the first man from outside; therefore, it was possible for them to be lost. Through the fall, humanity also became subject to natural law of decay and death.

From the Eastern perspective, sin is a break in communion with God and others. We do not inherit the guilt for Adam's sin genetically, but rather are subject to the existential conditions inherent to the fall. In contrast to the Western focus on total depravity, the Orthodox viewpoint is characterized by the perspective of St. Gregory Palamas: "All layers of the human self are by nature good, and it is only the misuse of free choice which creates havoc within the human person" (1995, p. 53). Moreover, sin is not seen as an individual, legalistic concept relating to juridical transgression that requires substitutionary atonement, but rather as a sickness and developmental arrest that is "cured" by entering into the fullness of life opened up in Christ.

For the Orthodox Christian, salvation is made possible by the life of Christ in its *entirety* (Incarnation, Baptism, Crucifixion, Resurrection). The seal of salvation is, in the words of St. Seraphim of Sarov, the acquisition of the Holy Spirit. Salvation is possible because Christ "takes on himself the renewal of creation" that had become subject to decay and unites persons in loving union with the Holy Trinity through His mystical body. The Orthodox doctrine of redemption, as formulated by St. Athanasius in the 4th century, holds that "repentance does not lead man out of his natural condition, but only stops sin" (cited in Florovsky, 1987, p. 42). For *deification* (or *theosis*),[1] the restoration of immortality, completion of development in Christ is required. As distinct from most

---

[1]All foreign words are Greek unless otherwise noted.

Western theologies, the experience of this completion or salvation is not limited to a point in time but is a lifetime synergistic process, involving not only God's presence and activity, but also one's own personal struggle *(ascesis)* to be open to and cooperate with the energies of Grace.[2] Through this grace-infused effort, as St. Anthony observed, you "become yourself."

Despite the overtones in modern English idiom, the word *deification* does not mean that the person becomes what God is in the Divine *essence,* nor that he or she is dissolved into God as a drop in an ocean, as in some non-Christian Eastern philosophies. Nevertheless, as St. Athanasius maintained, it is true that in Christ "God became man, so that man might become God." The deified person becomes a partaker of the divine nature (2 Peter 1:4) *and* his or her personhood is kept intact: The I–Thou relationship between Creator and creature is not violated (Ware, 1998). This has important implications for the understanding of community (*sobornost'* [Slavonic]) in Eastern Orthodoxy, whose ontological ground is rooted in the mystery of the Holy Trinity whose three persons share one essence, but are also three separate Persons, just as each person remains uniquely his or her own essential self while dwelling in oneness with God.

EPISTEMOLOGICAL TOOLS

The Eastern Orthodox approach to knowledge of God, articulated by St. Gregory Palamas,[3] is that one does not learn about God from studying books alone or merely by using rational and logical faculties. Knowledge of God comes from direct, personal I–Thou experience in and through the act of repenting, continual prayer, guarding the heart, participation in the Church's mysteries,[4] and loving obedience. The end result is not

---

[2]The Orthodox tradition makes a distinction between God's *essence* (which is unknowable) and *energies* (which are uncreated and therefore divine, but knowable). The divine energies are often equated with the concept of *grace.*

[3]In the 14th century, a debate arose around Eastern and Western approaches to knowledge of God. The Roman Catholic philosopher, Barlaam, attacked the age-old Eastern Christian practice of the *hesychasts* of Mount Athos (those monks who practice interior silence, watchfulness and continual prayer following St. Paul's injunction to pray continuously) calling them *omfaloskopoi;* that is, men who have their souls in their navels, or in modern parlance, "navel gazers"! The unity between mind and body and the possibility of experiential, direct knowledge of God—in contrast to a mere scholastic "knowing about" God as Barlaam advocated—was articulated definitively by St. Gregory Palamas and subsequently ratified by a church council that condemned Barlaam's viewpoint. In so doing, the Eastern Church avoided the problems affecting spiritual growth resulting from a split between mind and body that developed in and through the spirit of the Renaissance, and leading eventually in the West to the impoverishment of prayer to a form of discursive thinking.

[4]The word *mysteries* refers to what Christians in the West call sacraments. Mystery *(mysterion)* is the more ancient appellation for these rites.

developing a systematic theology, but rather maintaining an existential stance in the world from moment to moment, as Florovksy (cited in Ware, 1986) points out:

> The Church gives us not a system, but a key; not a plan of God's City, but the means of entering it. Perhaps someone will lose his way because he has no plan. But all that he will see, he will see without a mediator, he will see it directly, it will be real for him; while he who has studied only the plan risks remaining outside and not really finding anything (p. 7).

Two organs of knowledge that are foundational in an Orthodox anthropology are the heart *(kardia)* and the intellect *(nous)*. The heart is not limited to either a physical organ of the body or to a person's emotional life, but rather it is the integrating totality of a person, where body, soul, and spirit, and all their attendant powers, meet. It is a place where both the conscious and unconscious reside, a place of wisdom, direct intuition (Evdokimov, 1994; Ware, 1998). The heart, being the spiritual center of the person (Ware, 1998), should have primacy in determining a person's way of being in the world, but in our unnatural fallen states, this is not the case. Developmentally, Eastern Orthodox Christianity begins with recognition that we do not live from the heart in this way; nevertheless, it is not only possible, but it alone is the *truly human* way of being toward which we strive.[5]

The Orthodox understanding of *intellect* differs from what we might commonly think upon hearing the word; it is not the activity of rational and logical thinking *(dianous),* although it is reduced to this when operating in isolation from the heart. The intellect or nous is the faculty of direct seeing and its true place is in the heart. The Buddhist concept of *mindfulness* is a close equivalent; this attentiveness is a precursor to and necessary component of prayer and repentance that eventually leads from the "drunkenness" and fragmentation of the fallen condition to what is called "mental sobriety" and unity of "having the mind in the heart." Although this submission of mind to heart has been experientially defined in different ways by those who have experienced it (cf. Chirban, 1996), Staniloae (2000) gives a representative description, stating that direct knowledge of God is possible only to the degree that conditions of the fall have begun to be reversed and the heart purified or freed from domination of worldly attachments (including attachments to its own rational thinking skills). The Orthodox tradition also refers to this as

---

[5]Space does not permit a full discussion of the Eastern patristic understanding of these crucial topics. The interested reader is encouraged to consult Archimandrite Sophrony (1991), Chirban (1996, 2001), Kadloubovsky and Palmer (1975), and Vlachos (1994).

watchfulness (nepsis), or guarding the heart from "infection" by movements of the mind extraneous to it.

As the heart and mind are purified and united in constant attentive prayer, a person becomes capable not only of more fully knowing God but also of more accurately discerning the essence of the created world around him or her. St. Maximus the Confessor referred to this process as being able to see the *logos* of each created things (including other people) (Thunberg, 1985). Archimandrite Sophrony notes the role of this type of insight in our interpersonal relations, stating that while praying, the one with a pure heart is able to see the state of the soul of the other and offer an appropriate word to him or her. Therefore, according to Eastern Christian anthropology, the accuracy of a person's understanding of the world is related directly to his or her spiritual development.

Another key epistemological issue to keep in mind when working with Orthodox Christians is that the hermeneutic used to understand "God's Word" is not *sola scriptura,* as it is commonly understood in Protestantism. Orthodoxy starts from the experience of God's word made flesh among them *prior to* the setting down of the writings of the New Testament. It is the experience of the community living life infused with the Holy Spirit that inspires both the writing and the understanding of Holy Scripture. No one person, on his or her own, apart from the communal witness of the church and the Holy Spirit is competent to interpret the scriptures. Rather, the tradition of the church (including oral tradition, scripture, decisions of the councils, the writings of the church fathers, liturgical services, the sacramental mysteries, and obedience), and the guidance of one's elder (spiritual father or mother) together elucidate scripture. Otherwise deception arises that distorts its meaning.[6]

Although one might refer to the preceding as *primary* sources of knowledge, this does not rule out an appreciation for the scientific method and modern scholarship as important resources, but only places them in a larger context. This is important to remember, especially in the field of psychology and counseling, because as Ware (1998) notes, the human person ultimately is a mystery, just as God Himself is a mystery, and both are best approached accordingly. This is particularly instructive for any counseling approach as well, because it denies any frame of reference that assumes an "expertise" toward another that is diagnostically reductionistic.

---

[6]St. Irenaeus commented on this in the early 2nd century. A certain person had defended his heretical interpretations by observing that everything was based on the Scriptures. St. Irenaeus conceded this to be true but objected that the result was a picture of a dog made out of the genuine jewels of the Holy Scripture, when in fact, those same jewels of Holy Scripture, if arranged correctly, should reveal the face of a king!

THEORY OF NORMAL PERSONALITY

Perhaps the most fundamental truth about the human person is that he or she is created in the image and likeness of God. The Eastern Christian tradition usually views *image* and *likeness* as being distinct but related concepts. The image of God includes those human capacities that reflect God; although they can be dimmed or distorted by sin, they are never lost completely. These capacities include, but are not limited to, freedom of choice, creativity, rational thought and language, the yearning to be in I–Thou relationship, displaying self-sacrificial love, and the possibility of participating in the Divine energies. Some have understood the image to be an inner impulse directed toward God (Staniloae, 2000).

The likeness of God refers to the completeness of human beings as God meant them to be (cf. Matthew 5:48: "Be perfect [or "complete"] as your Father in Heaven is perfect"). It is the fulfillment of the image that requires constant attention and effort on the part of the person over a lifetime, but cannot be attained apart from the grace of God. The person who has made strides on the path to achieving the likeness of God (i.e., on the path of salvation) begins to incarnate in his or her person many of the godly virtues mentioned in the New Testament: the Beatitudes (Matthew 5:1-12), the fruit of the Spirit (Galatians 5:21-23), and the new command given by Christ (John 13:34). In fact, it is only the person who attains this likeliness who can be said to have a "normal" personality; all who fall short are displaying various degrees of abnormality (or sin).[7]

Orthodox tradition admits both the dichotomous (body and soul/spirit) and trichotomous (body, soul, and spirit) view of the human person. Importantly, the body is viewed as an integral part of the person, as much a bearer of God's image as the soul or spirit. The body is the temple of the spirit and one of the places that God's presence becomes incarnate in this world. It is intimately involved in worship: fasting and feasting, making the sign of the cross, and experiencing the sensory festival that is Orthodox worship. The Orthodox tradition of venerating relics (bones and personal belongings) of those persons whose sanctity the church has recognized and proclaimed as saints is rooted in this belief. God's grace inhabits the body of a living saint, and it does not necessarily depart immediately after the saint has died. Further, the intimate relationship between body and soul is evident in the miraculous fragrance that is present after death in the remains of some saints, which often do not decay according to usual processes, but remain without odor and evidence of ordinary decomposition for days and sometimes up to centuries later.

---

[7]The reader interested in the practicalities of this process is encouraged to read Kontzevich (1988) and St. Theophan the Recluse (2001).

The soul *(psyche)* in Eastern Christianity is typically seen as encompassing all psychological functions and the vitality of the body. And even in trichotomous views of the person, one's spirit is usually defined in relation to the soul. Spirit includes the higher functions of the soul that are dedicated to the kind of perceiving that is capable of entering into communion with the spiritual world (Staniloae, 2000). Some conceive of the spirit not so much as a structure of the person but as the principle (Evdokimov, 1994) that enlivens both the soul and the body, opening them up to the transcendent as *person*. Ideally, there is a close connection between a person's spirit and God as spirit.

How is the human soul constructed? We have already mentioned the centrality of the heart and the intellect. A representative theologian in the Orthodox tradition, St. Maximus the Confessor (7th century AD), maintains the human soul has three powers: reason *(logos)*, desire *(epithumia)*, and temper *(thumos)*.[8] When these powers are ordered and directed aright, they promote the development of virtue in one's life—above all, the virtue of love, the presence of which is a testimony to the person's deepening union with a God, Who is love. However, when they are perverted by sin, they lose their organic connection with one another and drive the person into vice. These processes are explored more thoroughly in the following.

In the Eastern Christian context, abnormality is viewed as an indication of the ubiquitous illness of sin that touches all members of the human race. In contrast to many Western Christian approaches, the East tends to view sin in the context of what might be called a relational-medical, rather than juridical, model. Sin is the broken relationship with God, the source of life; its primary consequences are death and a distortion of the image of God in each person. This separation and distortion give rise to certain symptoms (some of which would fall into the category of personality abnormality), yet the path toward healing these symptoms and the attendant underlying illness can be had by availing oneself of the epistemological tools discussed in the preceding.

THEORY OF NORMAL HUMAN DEVELOPMENT

The Eastern Christian world view is that children begin life in a qualitatively different state than the Western tradition maintains. As noted above, the Eastern concept of original sin does *not* include the notion of

[8]Readers interested in the variety of approaches to the Orthodox understanding of the soul may consult the following works: Chirban (2001), Evdokimov (1994), Sakharov (2002), Staniloae (2000), and Vlachos (1998).

original guilt (that we all share in the guilt of Adam's sin). Therefore, although children come into the fallen world as mortals bearing the marks of fallenness in their souls (and sometimes on their bodies, in the case of disability), infants are in no way born guilty.

In general, children are seen as having a level of purity that exceeds most adults. Therefore, although adults usually are expected to be engaged in the practices of the Church (profession of faith, confession of sins, prayer, fasting) to prepare for partaking of the Eucharist, infants are admitted to the chalice as soon as they are baptized. The Orthodox Church recognizes the cognitive and moral change that takes place somewhere around 6 or 8 years old in children by encouraging them to make their first confession at that time. This reflects children's qualitatively new understanding of right, wrong, and personal responsibility.

As far as the authors know, there are no generally accepted stages of normative development across the life span in Orthodox anthropology. Psychological growth, however, is seen as teleological: *Theosis* is always held out as the goal of normative development, and it is expected that people will work toward this goal in community with others (seen most clearly by the fact that the only two "states" of adulthood that are blessed by sacramental action are marriage and monasticism).

Although the Orthodox tradition does not use the popular modern psychological term *self-actualization,* there may be a way to understand this term that is consonant with Eastern Christianity. Theologians have used different terminology to express the idea that there is a unique, organic connection between God and the person: There is a *commensurability* between the divine and human (Sakharov, 2002), each human person is endowed with a *logos* that stems from the Logos of God (St. Maximus the Confessor in Thunberg, 1985), the person is a "particle" of God (St. Gregory Nazianzen in Staniloae [2000]). God Himself is a self-giving relationship of love among the persons of the trinity. Therefore, a person finds "self"-fulfillment by entering into loving, self-sacrificial relationship, seeking union with both the Divine and other persons. In contrast to Descartes's observation, "I think; therefore I am," which leaves completion of human development in a relational vacuum, the Orthodox perspective is more aptly put as *I am loved and I love; therefore I am.* Self-actualization cannot be conceived of apart from relationship with God and others. Given the emphases on asceticism, obedience and the relational context highlighted here, we see the paradox: one finds oneself only in battling one's individual self-will while emptying oneself through the Holy Spirit in love for God and others. This happens in community, whether for a solitary monk struggling with God for salvation in the desert or in the mêlée of the city.

Development continues even after physical death; because God is endless, union with Him is always in progress. Therefore, the Orthodox pray for those who have died, that they (the deceased) may experience a more complete union with God. The eternal fate of a person is in the hands of God; therefore, a final pronouncement cannot be made about any given deceased person's standing before Him.[9] However, the Orthodox Church does make some general statements about fate beyond the grave. Because God is love, those who have striven to love Him and His creation experience Him as paradise, whereas those who do not love Him or His creation experience His eternal presence as torturous. Hell is essentially self-inflicted.

Orthodox anthropology acknowledges the role of both genes and environment in shaping an individual's development. To the extent that the illness of sin has "infected" a person's biology and environment, that person's developmental trajectory is distorted. Ultimately, for most people, free will is just as—if not more—important as genes and environment in determining one's path.[10] Persons choosing to work synergistically with God's Grace find themselves on the path of salvation.

PSYCHOLOGICAL HEALTH AND PATHOLOGY

As mentioned, there are various lenses through which the Orthodox tradition views the person; therefore, there are different ways to define health of soul. We will take up views here that follow from our preceding discussion.

One approach to psychological health and pathology is the right ordering of the three aspects of the person (body, soul, and spirit). The unhealthy person, whose darkened *nous* and heart give rise to a life of self-indulgence, allows unpurified desires to dominate the soul without discrimination. This results in a way of being that is not centered in the heart of love and as such is characterized by depersonalized and compulsive indulgence, shame, fear, aggression, and other untransformed passions that indicate division and fallen conditions. The souls of such people, in turn, dominate their spirits: Emotions or rigidity may dictate one's prayer life, a desire for rational explanation of things may turn one away from God, anger may chase out love, and fear and shame may distort the joy of eros, limiting it to compulsive genitality, energy-depleting negative emotions, and self-calming fantasies.

---

[9]The exception to this is glorified saints, whom the church formally acknowledges as standing before the throne of God in blessedness.

[10]There are probably cases where free will is limited, such as in persons with severe intellectual disability.

In contrast, the *healthy* person's spirit (surrendered in love to God) is the "executive" of this hierarchy; the soul, in turn, is willingly submitted to the spirit, which expresses itself in the body. Asceticism becomes limits assumed freely and for the sake of love; these limits foster health (of body, soul, and community) rather than a harsh antihuman stance that both punishes the body as if it were evil and endangers the larger community's well-being. Fasting, prayer vigils, almsgiving, and other forms of ascetic restraint—engaged in according to the measure of one's strength—help not only to purify the body, but to create conditions for offering the struggle between self-giving (on the one hand) and self-will and self-indulgence (on the other) to God in prayer. One bears the cross of being responsible for these contradictions in order to allow an infusion of God's Grace, so that the body becomes the temple of the Holy Spirit and the heart, its "holy of holies." Such asceticism must be practiced in the context of worship,[11] humility, personal and communal faith, and accountability, lest one fall prey to pride and end up as the Pharisee in Luke 18:9-14, who in hubris extolled his own fasting and tithing before God and judged his "lesser" brother, the tax collector.

The soul's powers (reason, desire, and temper) also have their proper hierarchy and need to be purified. In a healthy person, reason (which dwells in the purified *nous* and should be the director of the soul) is directed at establishing relationship with God, desire is channeled toward loving God, and temper becomes a constructive force to actively work for justice and display charity to others. When the illness of sin has its way, desire and temper rule reason, and each power is distorted: Desire is turned to self-love, temper is turned to hatred and destruction of others, and reason degenerates into ignorance, especially ignorance of God. The chaos resulting from this situation shatters the internal coherence within and between persons: Thoughts and emotions become disjointed from one another, relationships turn sour, and faith is lost. As Florovsky notes:

> Man turned away from the contemplation of God . . . and became shut up in himself. It was then that passion and desires flared up . . . and his life disintegrated and became fragmented (1987, p. 45).

The ascetic life in cooperation with God is also the means that move us toward healing from this pathology.

Because the person bears the image of a relational God, psychological health comes in the context of relationship with God and others. The epitome of these relationships is the mysteriologic Body of Christ, the church. Conversely, psychopathology results from and leads to isolation

---

[11]As St. Basil reminds us, "Worship without asceticism is blasphemy; asceticism without worship makes you a demon."

(or *excommunication* in its broadest sense, removing oneself from the communal life of the church). For many, the most difficult (and therefore, most healing) aspects of the ascetic lifestyle are the interpersonal ones, such as generous self-sacrifice for others and loving one's enemies, the latter of which has been termed by St. Silouan of Mt. Athos as "the surest sign of a Christian."

The astute reader has noticed that this description of psychological health is comparable with the Eastern definition of salvation. This is not coincidental, because these concepts are basically equivalent. The Greek verb σωζω has various meanings, among them *to save* and *to heal*. Salvation is indeed the healing of our souls.

Although relationships are the primary arena for human growth and development, it is being demonstrated increasingly that the relationship between biology and psychology is a seamless one, more like ancient views than those of Descartes. For example, Candace Pert, former chief of brain chemistry at the National Institute of Mental Health, maintains she can no longer make a strong distinction between the brain and the body, but sees it as *bodymind*. She notes:

> For Freud and Jung, the unconscious was still a hypothetical construct. For us, the unconscious more definitely means psychobiological levels of functioning below consciousness. Deep, deep unconscious processes are expressed at all physiological levels, down to individual organs such as the heart, lungs, or pancreas. Our work is demonstrating that all the cells of the nervous system and endocrine system are functionally integrated by networks of peptides and their receptors (cited in Siegel, 1989, pp. 36–37).

The Eastern Christian tradition, following early Hebraic idea of *nephesh* (psyche-soma) that did not distinguish between body and soul and thus linked physical and spiritual health in one whole, can affirm these modern scientific conclusions. Nevertheless, it is also noted that physical health need not be seen as indicating spiritual health, nor vice versa, as the relationship is not a linear one but more synthetic in relationship to the Divine.

THEORY OF HUMAN CHANGE

Much of the material presented in the preceding deals directly with the issue of change, because the Orthodox Church views salvation as a *dynamic* and constant striving for more complete union with God. A key concept in this process is *metanoia,* or repentance. While the Greek word literally means *a renewal of mind,* repentance is commonly viewed as change in the direction of one's life, working in synergy with God to be healed of sin in one's life and become like Him. Because sin is viewed ultimately as illness and broken relationship more so than a breaking of the law, guilt is not the primary motivating factor in this process. This is not to say that Orthodox Christians do not feel guilty: Certainly many do, and there are times when feelings of guilt are appropriate and provide motivation for positive change. The Eastern tradition does not deny that there is a "law" to be followed (the ten commandments, the new commandment of love, etc.); however, these are seen as part of the path one travels toward wholeness and union with God, rather than as laws that are ends in themselves, the transgression of which must be punished.

Repentance is hampered most of all by one's passions, or the powers of the soul in their unpurified state. Humility and self-awareness are the soil from which true repentance grows. Echoing St. Paul's admonition to judge oneself to avoid being judged (1 Corinthians 11:31), the Orthodox Church calls each of her children to *nepsis,* or attentiveness to the movements of one's soul, so that the powers of the soul can be cleansed through confession, partaking of the Eucharist, and living a prayerful life of love in communion with God and others. The high regard with which Orthodoxy views such self-awareness is demonstrated in quotes by some of its most beloved saints. For example, St. Anthony the Great observed, "who does not know himself cannot know God." St. Isaac the Syrian extends this idea, saying, "one who knows himself is greater than one who raises the dead." These quotes echo a main theme of this chapter: The hard work of purifying one's heart leads to union with God, who by His Grace resides within such a heart.

Although true repentance, renewing the relationship between God and penitent, takes place deep in the heart of a person, for the Orthodox Christian this is not a completely intrapersonal experience. The Orthodox Church views confession in the presence of a priest as a formal sacrament of the Church. At confession, an "acceptable sacrifice" is not simply a list of sins, but that combined with an admission of the passions that underlie the transgressions and a firm commitment to struggle to purify those passions and stop the behavior, attachments, and attitudes that stem from them. Here the priest does not stand in the place of God but serves as a representative both of the community (being a witness of the person's confession) and of God (by confirming God's forgiveness through the laying on of hands and reading of the prayer of absolution). Although there is a juridical element to confession (Orthodox Christians do confess transgressions of commandments), the mystery is typically viewed as part of the medicinal treasury of the church. If penance is assigned, it is not as a punishment or a "balancing of scales" but as a balm designed to heal the effects of the illness of sin.

One's relationship with a spiritual father or mother is also important in striving for repentance. This person may or may not be the one with whom one formally confesses. Ideally, this person is one to whom he or she can regularly reveal one's thoughts, feelings, sins, and struggles; the spiritual father or mother, then, is able to guide the person further along the path of salvation, giving directives for spiritual growth, offering advice for practical problems, and generally holding the person accountable in his or her quest for union with God. Unfortunately, finding a true spiritual father or mother is a relatively rare occurrence in the life of an Orthodox layperson.

COMMON MORAL ISSUES ENCOUNTERED

The Eastern Christian tradition is guided in struggles with concrete moral issues by the convictions we have already noted, such as a maximalist anthropology that sees each person related to one another in Christ and respecting human freedom. Most local Orthodox Churches have produced statements on various moral issues.[12] For brevity's sake only a select group of issues are reviewed here; the interested reader may consult the websites listed in footnote 12 and books by Harakas (1999) and Yannaras (1984).

The Eastern Christian culture tends to defend life in all arenas possible; therefore, it is not uncommon to find the Orthodox Church standing against capital punishment, abortion, and active euthanasia. This is not to say that each individual Orthodox Christian holds such views, but statements issued by various councils of Orthodox bishops tend to follow life-affirming principles. Adherence to such a perspective is rooted in the conviction that body and soul are fully integrated from the moment of conception until the moment of death (and, then, will be reunited at the resurrection; see 1 Corinthians 15). Therefore, to actively deprive any human being of life—before he is born, after she has committed a capital crime, or while he is in an apparently hopeless state of health—is at some level a denial of God: In killing His image-bearer, one's animosity toward Him is conveyed clearly (albeit perhaps unknowingly).

Issues of marriage and sexuality also are viewed through a traditional lens. Sexuality can be a blessed result of the desiring power of the soul expressed through the body. It is an inherently interpersonal activity (which has implications for the appropriateness of masturbation). To be blessed, however, sexual activity must take place in a sanctified relationship, and in the Orthodox tradition, only marriage between a man and woman is classified as such a relationship. Divorce usually is

[12]See, for example, the following websites: www.orthodoxeurope.org/page/3/14.aspx, www.oca.org/pages/ocaadmin/documents/index.html, www.goarch.org/en/ourfaith/ethics/, and www.ocampr.org

permitted (albeit reluctantly), but the church limits the number of times ecclesiastically blessed remarriage is allowed. Although one can find varying perspectives on the use of birth control, its use to completely avoid having children for reasons of personal convenience is disavowed.

A typical Orthodox layperson's theological understanding may not be as detailed as presented here, and because he has likely been raised in an essentially secular culture, it may be difficult for him to understand his church's perspective on the preceding questions. Clinicians should be prepared to assist Orthodox clients with the psychological ramifications of the conflict between the secular and sacred understandings of the person.

There is a temptation to categorize the Orthodox Church with politically conservative movements in our society; however, note that not all stances of the Eastern Church are traditionally conservative (e.g., capital punishment). In addition, note well the fact that any moral position of the Eastern Church is based not on a political philosophy or even a particular reading of specific passages of scripture, but on: (a) the theological and anthropological presuppositions elucidated in the preceding and (b) a conciliar approach to seeking the mind of Christ confirmed in the experience of the God-bearing theologians of the church, whose work constitutes 2,000 years of unbroken empiric tradition enlivened by the Holy Spirit.

Although perhaps not a moral issue (at least in all cases), clinicians should be aware of the important role ethnicity plays in the identity and faith of some Orthodox Christians. Indeed, some seem to be unable to separate their ethnic identity from their Christian faith. This melding of culture and faith is a result of what is perhaps one of Orthodoxy's greatest strengths: a philosophy of evangelism that seeks to confirm and sanctify as many aspects of the host culture as possible. In addition, the administrative divisions within the Orthodox Church are organized along national lines, supporting the connection between ethnicity and faith. Also note that most Orthodox cultures have not gone through the philosophical and political movements as in the West (e.g., the transition from understanding national leadership as divine kingship to seeing it as popular sovereignty) that broke the bond between ethnicity and religion that existed from Old Testament times. Although they need not and should not support ethnocentrism or nationalism, clinicians should be encouraged to respect and find the strengths in this deep connection between ethnicity and faith.

COMMON CLINICAL ISSUES ENCOUNTERED

Many of the issues Orthodox Christians present with necessitate an appreciation not only for the differences in ethos, theology, and world view of Eastern Christianity, but also the impact of varying cultures upon the issues involved. Therapists who work with Orthodox Christians should attend to all these arenas.

Intermarriage is a key area. Given the relatively few numbers of Orthodox Christians in the United States, as many has half of the marriages are with someone outside the person's faith and culture. Joanides (2002, 2004) has produced valuable resources for the practitioner seeking to understand the major areas of conflict that are inherent to approaching the Orthodox Christian marital system.

Although not limited to the Eastern tradition, religion in service of the ego is another area to consider. Given the Orthodox emphasis on lifelong repentance, and the numerous examples of spiritual sanctity in Orthodox Church history, there are those persons who seek prematurely to approach sanctity as a means of protecting themselves against being responsible to and for life. This can take the form of seeking to become monks out of fear of sexuality or trying to practice ascetical feats beyond one's capacities and then falling to despair and spiritual deception as a result. Jack Engler, a psychologist who studied the phenomenon of persons with borderline or narcissistic personality organization grasping on to the mystical literature and recasting their incomplete personality development as a form of "freedom from attachment to the world," coined a phrase to describe this: "You have to be somebody before you can be nobody." It is not far off from one early Desert Father's diagnostic observation: "If you see a young man climbing up to heaven on his own, yank him down; it will be good for him."

Another variant of the preceding are those persons who fear seeing a psychotherapist because they want the guarantee they feel comes with the input of a discerning Orthodox elder (e.g., one who has the ability to see the essence of persons, as described in *Epistemological Tools*). Fear and rigidity often underlie such a position; therefore, the therapist should be sensitive both to the person's desire for an approach that respects and is congruent with the Eastern tradition, and also to the importance of an approach that recognizes the psychodynamics of idealization/devaluation and possible developmental arrests that may be associated with the hesitancy to trust self and another in the immediacy and intimacy of the psychotherapeutic encounter.

It is also appropriate for the therapist working with Orthodox Christians to keep in mind the difference between *God-esteem* and *self-esteem* and the tension inherent to anthropocentric and Theocentric orientations. To those unfamiliar with it, Orthodox Christian piety may outwardly appear as low-self esteem. It is not. When St. Paul refers to himself as the "chief of sinners," he is not evidencing low-self esteem, but rather that his heart is so full of God's spirit that the smallest deviation from it is for him like a great weight upon him. Rather:

It is this humbling involved in the true recognition that we are fallen beings, or have major evil in our inward parts, that causes the Desert Fathers to pronounce such sayings as "Only I am a sinner," or "Only I am lost," or "Only I will end in hell." This is not reverse narcissistic grandiosity, etc. It is truthful self knowledge, the kind of self knowledge needed if salvational power is to reach us from God, and our own greater heart be roused from its slumber, lethargy, despair. Metropolitan Anthony of Sourozh once said, God can save and divinise the fallen being we acknowledge we are, but not the saint we pretend to be (Moran, in press).

Finally, there are those so-called "cradle" Orthodox who have grown up with the ritual of their faith without having consciously and intentionally embraced its fullness. Its influence in their lives is more subtle and may appear taken for granted, but the clinician should not miss the opportunity to help these persons awaken to their "inheritance," so that it can be an asset and resource to their further growth and healing.

CONCLUDING THOUGHTS

The Apostle of Love penned this directive to his flock:

> Beloved, let us love one another, because love is from God. . . . In this is love, not that we loved God but that he loved us . . . [and] since God loved us so much, we also ought to love one another . . . if we love one another, God lives in us, and his love is perfected in us (1 John 4:7a, 10b-12, NRSV).

Perhaps it is this *perechoresis* (interpenetration) of a loving God and human persons that encapsulates the heart of Orthodox Christian Faith: rooted in *ortho* (correct) *doxy* (glory), the Orthodox Christian is healed by finding God at the center of life, both one's own and that of the human community. All sickness and health—intrapsychic and systemic—are related to this. Understanding this Theocentric (in contrast to humanistic or anthropocentric) world view both at the content and process levels can assist the therapist in approaching a therapeutic encounter with an Orthodox Christian attentively and with humility, knowing that this encounter is truly Holy Ground and that the person encountered (however he or she may be diagnosed) will remain an unfathomable mystery. A therapist does well to seek before all else to discover how God, who is love, is already at work seeking to heal the person, His beloved, and empower him or her to love others more fully in return.

AUTHOR NOTE

Elizabeth A. Gassin, Department of Psychology, Olivet Nazarene University; J. Stephen Muse, Director of Pastoral Counseling Training, Pastoral Institute, Inc.

Correspondence concerning this chapter should be addressed to Elizabeth A. Gassin, Department of Psychology, Olivet Nazarene University, 1 University Avenue, Bourbonnais, IL 60914. Email: lgassin@olivet.edu.

REFERENCES

Chirban, J. (Ed.). (1996). *Personhood: Orthodox Christianity and the connection between body, mind, and soul.* London: Bergin and Garvey.

Chirban, J. (Ed.) (2001). *Sickness or sin: Spiritual discernment and differential diagnosis.* Brookline, MA: Holy Cross Orthodox Press.

Evdokimov, P. (1994). *Woman and the salvation of the world* (A. Gythiel, Trans.). Crestwood, NY: St. Vladimir's Seminary Press.

Florovsky, G. (1987). *The Eastern Fathers of the fourth century* (C. Edmonds, Trans.). Vaduz, Lichtenstein: Buchervvertriebsanstalt.

Palamas G. (1995). *Treatise on the spiritual life* (D. Rogich, Trans.). Minneapolis, MN: Light and Life.

Joanides, C. (2002). *When you intermarry: A resource for inter-Christian, intercultural couples, parents and families.* New York: Greek Orthodox Archdiocese of America Press.

Joanides, C. (2004). *Ministering to intermarried couples; A resource for clergy and lay workers.* New York: Greek Orthodox Archdiocese of America Press.

Harakas, S. S. (1999). *Wholeness of faith and life: Orthodox Christian ethics.* Brookline, MA: Holy Cross Orthodox Press.

Kadloubovsky, E., & Palmer, G. E. H. (1975). *Writings from the Philokalia on the prayer of the heart.* London: Faber & Faber.

Kontsevich, I. M. (1988). *The acquisition of the Holy Spirit in ancient Russia.* Platina, CA: St. Herman Press.

Lossky, V. (1973). *The mystical theology of the Eastern Church.* London: James Clarke and Co. Ltd.

Moran, J. (in press). Spiritual war: The relevance to modern therapy of the ancient Eastern Orthodox Christian path of ascetical practice. In S. Muse (Ed.), *Raising Lazarus: Integral healing in Orthodox Christianity.* Brookline, MA: Holy Cross Orthodox Press.

Sakharov, N. (2002). *I love therefore I am: The theological legacy of Archimandrite Sophrony.* Crestwood, NY: St. Vladimir's Seminary Press.

Siegel, B. S. (1989). *Peace, love, and healing: The bodymind and the path to self-healing.* New York: Harper.

Sophrony, A. (1988). *We shall see Him as He is.* Essex, England: Stavropegic Monastery of St. John the Baptist.

Sophrony, A. (1991). *Saint Silhouan the Athonite* (R. Edmonds, Trans.). Essex, England: Stavropegic Monastery of St. John the Baptist.

Staniloae, D. (2000). *The experience of God. Vol 2: The world: Creation and deification* (I. Ioanita & R. Barringer, Trans.). Brookline, MA: Holy Cross Orthodox Press.

Theophan the Recluse. (2001). *Turning the heart to God* (K. Kaisch & I. Zhiltsov, Trans.). Ben Lomand, CA: Conciliar Press.

Thunberg, L. (1985). *Man and the cosmos: The vision of St Maximus the Confessor.* Crestwood, NY: St. Vladimir's Seminary Press.

Vlachos, H. (1994). *Orthodox psychotherapy: The illness and cure of the soul in Orthodox tradition* (E. Williams, Trans.). Levadia, Greece: Birth of the Theotokos Monastery.

Vlachos, H. (1998). *The person in the Orthodox tradition* (E. Williams, Trans.). Levadia, Greece: Birth of the Theotokos Monastery.

Ware, K. (1986). *The Orthodox way.* Crestwood, NY: St. Vladimir's Seminary Press.

Ware, K. (1998, August). *The human person in Orthodox spirituality.* Presented at the Institute of Orthodox Christian Studies, Eagle River, AK.

Yannaras, C. (1984). *The freedom of morality* (E. Briere, Trans.). Crestwood, NY: St. Vladimir's Seminary Press.

CHAPTER FIVE

Lutherans

Christine Maguth Nezu, David E. Farley,
and Arthur M. Nezu

As part of the celebration of the millennium in 2000, several lists were published citing the most influential people of the past 1,000 years. Martin Luther, founder of Lutheran theology, was among the top 10 on nearly all such lists. The most frequent rationale for including his name involved the idea that he provided people a different way of relating to God—salvation no longer had to be earned, but was a gift. Prior to the 16th century, the Roman Catholic Church prescribed that strict adherence to its teachings was the only way a person was able to obtain a "correct" relationship with what many people believed to be an angry God. In other words, the church was a necessary intermediary between God and humans. However, Luther taught that Christians no longer had to go through the church to receive absolution. Rather, the path to salvation was faith in Jesus Christ. Moreover, Luther suggested that faith is a gift from God that is created by the Holy Spirit and not shaped by people's actions.

The Lutheran Church is one of several Protestant churches that grew out of the Reformation, which began in Europe during the 15th century. The word "protestant" describes a member of any of several church denominations that deny the universal authority of the pope and affirm the Reformation principles of justification by faith alone, the priesthood of all believers, and the primacy of the Bible as the only source of revealed truth.

IMPORTANT ASPECTS OF LUTHERANISM

Who are Lutherans? Since the Reformation, the Lutheran Church has grown considerably. Today, there are close to 66 million followers of Lutheranism around the world (www.religioscope.info). In the United States, there are more than 19,000 Lutheran churches, ministered by close to 29,000 clergy, and including approximately 8.5 million members. The number of Lutherans in the world is close to twice the number of individuals who identify themselves within other Protestant churches. As Noll (2003) suggests, "this is a lot of Lutherans."

American Lutherans are divided into three distinctive subgroups— the Lutheran Church-Missouri Synod, the Wisconsin Evangelical Lutheran Synod, and the Evangelical Lutheran Church of America (ELCA), with other smaller groups. Because the ELCA is the largest of these groups, this chapter focuses on this constituency. ELCA members tend to be White and consider their German or Scandinavian background to be an important part of their identity (Inskeep, 2001). Fewer than 3% are members of other ethnic minority groups. Parenthetically, the membership in the Lutheran churches in both Africa and Asia is actually increasing, whereas the rolls in Lutheran churches in Europe, including Germany, are decreasing. Overall, the number of individuals residing in Latin America and the Caribbean region who identify themselves as Lutheran remains steady.

The majority of ELCA members are middle class; 60% are women and 20% are older than 65 years. The majority live in middle America (e.g., Pennsylvania, the Great Lakes region, Minnesota, North and South Dakota). With regard to their religious commitment, a recent "Faith Practices" survey of ELCA Lutherans found that 75% of the respondents accepted "most or all" of what the Lutheran church teaches (Inskeep, 2001). Further, 25% indicated that they were "very active" within their congregation, whereas 41% were "moderately active," and 34% were "slightly active" or "inactive." Thirty-one percent attend religious services every week, whereas 42% attend almost every week and 20% once or twice a year.

HISTORICAL BEGINNINGS

During the early part of 16th century Europe, the Roman Catholic Church was the preeminent Christian institution. It exerted great influence over the lives of people and society in general. Martin Luther (1483–1546), an ordained priest, Doctor of Theology, and Professor of the Old Testament at Wittenberg University in Germany, thought the church often blurred the relationship between God and people. He further believed that the church strayed from the teachings of God as contained in the scriptures and often abused its power. One such abuse was the practice of indulgences. A person could purchase an indulgence in order to have a sin pardoned. The church at that time suggested that the saints had "stored up goodness," which it could then transfer to sinners for forgiveness of their sins by purchasing the indulgence.

Luther was greatly disturbed by the selling of indulgences because it was a clear illustration of trying to earn or pay for God's favor. On October 31, 1517, he nailed 95 theses, or items for public debate, on the door of Wittenberg University. Whereas the 95 theses concentrated on indulgences, it also raised several additional concerns about the church in general. In generating this public challenge, Luther hoped that the church would reform its practices to be more in keeping with the Bible. However, what started as an academic debate led to a religious war. Rather than the Roman Catholic Church engaging in reforms, an actual separation by Luther and his followers ensued. Whereas the term "Lutheran" originally was applied to this group in a derogatory manner, it soon became a "badge of honor." This started the Reformation and the Protestant movement. In fact, Luther is considered to be the father of Protestantism.

ACCEPTED DOCTRINES
OF THE LUTHERAN CHURCH

For the therapist wishing to learn more about where Lutherans obtain knowledge and what the Lutheran church teaches, the following section includes descriptions of several of its basic tenets and doctrines.

Jesus Christ

Lutherans generally believe that Jesus Christ is the Son of God, who was sent to become human in order to provide salvation and grace to humankind. Through his life, death, and subsequent resurrection, Jesus is thought to have overcome the "prison of sinfulness" that characterizes human nature. In this manner, it is believed that Christ restored the relationship between humans and God; one that God intended to be characterized by love and trust. Because he was with God from the beginning of time and is eternal, but also was born on earth of a virgin, Lutherans believe that Jesus was both "fully God" and "fully human."

In essence, Jesus is viewed as the bridge between God and humans and that his resurrection from the dead fostered reconciliation with God. Faith in the existence and meaning of Jesus Christ is an essential tenet of the Lutheran perspective. The "quote" contained in John 11 (verses 25–26) frequently is invoked to convey that message: "Those who believe in me, even though they die, will live, and everyone who lives and believes in me will never die."

Sacraments

Lutherans believe that two sacraments, or sacred rituals, were established by Jesus Christ—Baptism and Holy Communion. Baptism is the process by which people first become members of "Christ's body on earth;" that is, the church. It is connected to a command by Christ to those who follow him: "Go, then, to all peoples everywhere and make them my disciples; baptize them in the name of the Father, the Son, and the Holy Spirit" (Matthew 28). Baptism is believed to contain the promise of initial salvation from God and emphasizes the faith of the believer.

Holy Communion, also known as the Eucharist, the Lord's Supper, and the Sacrament of the Altar, is a celebration of the last supper that Jesus observed with his disciples before he was arrested and eventually crucified. In this sacrament, the promise of salvation is tied to earthly elements of bread and wine. These represent the body and blood of Jesus, respectively. Lutherans believe in the "real presence" (that Christ is actually present in the bread and wine), but practice "open communion" wherein all people of faith are welcome to receive the sacrament.

Sin

According to the Lutheran faith, God always intended that people live in a close relationship with him. As such, sin is not viewed as individual acts of wrongdoing, but rather the brokenness and separation that all people experience in their relationship with God. In essence, people are given freedom of choice in their lives, but all misuse that freedom. The definition of sin has less to do with the things individuals fail to do or acts they perform, but more concerned with their separation from God. The ten commandments is viewed as God's expression of his "just and loving expectations for all of creation." Falling short of these expectations is not cause for punishment, but an example of people's "need for God's mercy and forgiveness."

Justification by Faith

The doctrine of justification was the cornerstone of the Lutheran Reformation during the 16th century and was espoused as the "ruler and judge over all other Christian doctrines." In biblical times, the concept of justification meant for one to be declared guiltless or to be accounted righteous. To be justified by God indicated that one was in a saving relationship with him, whereby one's sins would be forgiven. Lutherans believe that sinners are justified by faith in the saving action of God's grace through Christ, not as a function of indulgences, as in the time prior to the Reformation, nor by one's actions. Further, Lutheran doctrine suggests that such faith, being active in love and the basis for a relationship with God, engenders people to engage in "good acts" or lead "a moral life," rather than positing that "good works" cause salvation or a relationship with God.

Within this context, Lutheran doctrine further suggests that people do not strive for salvation through their actions, but because of their justification through their faith in Christ (whose grace is the source for such salvation), they are free to "discern the deeper meanings of the structures involved in daily life" (Nairn, 2001), such as family, ministry, and the secular government. All of these structures are created and ordained by God, whereby Lutheran ethics advocate that it is within such structures that people are to live responsible lives.

Priesthood of All Believers

This doctrine suggests that all people stand before God as priests. As such, Lutherans are taught that they can approach God in prayer without going through an intermediary. Each Christian in baptism is called as a priest in order to minister in the name of Christ and is empowered by the Holy Spirit to proclaim the promise of God in the world.

Saint and Sinner

The phrase "saint and sinner" is often used by Lutherans to denote that they are simultaneously both "righteous" and "sinful." Christians are righteous as a result of both God's forgiveness of their sins and through their faith in Jesus Christ. However, through the law, they also remain sinners (i.e., disconnected from God).

Law and Gospel

Lutherans believe that they live in two "realities" at the same time—a secular one and a Christian one. Both are governed by God, but the first is governed by God as a function of the law, whereas the second is governed by God by means of the gospel. These two lives often create tensions within individuals and the church regarding various social issues, such as accepting homosexuality. Such tension can be further viewed within the two perspectives espoused in the official ELCA (1991) social statement on the interplay between church and society. On one hand, "the gospel does not take the church out of the world but instead calls it to affirm and to enter more deeply into the world." On the other hand, this statement further posits that "the gospel does not allow the church to accommodate to the ways of the world." Collectively, this Lutheran position concludes that the church must "discern when to support and when to confront society's cultural patterns, values, powers."

Spiritual Gifts

In recent years, the concept of spiritual gifts has become an increased focus for Lutherans. Previously, spiritual gifts meant "speaking in tongues," an experience that occurred on Pentecost when people of different races and tongues could understand each other. In today's world, Lutherans believe that God has given each baptized person various spiritual gifts. These may include the ability to teach, lead, counsel, sing, play football, or write a poem; that is, almost any gift that encompasses human experience. It is the responsibility of people in concert with others of the church to discern what their specific gifts are and to employ them in service to God and the community at large.

Death and Life after Death

Death in the Lutheran faith has several different themes. For example, death is frequently seen simply as a part of the life cycle—human beings have a limited life span. This limitation reminds people that they are finite. For Lutherans, each Ash Wednesday reminds them that they are "dust" and to "dust they shall return." However, both living and dying are part of the process of creation which the Bible affirms as being good.

Death also may be seen as tragic; for example, at times when it appears particularly untimely, as in the case of a child's death. It also can be seen as tragic simply because of one's desire to continue living rather than depart life. Sometimes the unwillingness to die comes from the fear of suffering that may accompany the dying process. Others see death as an enemy because of fear about what lies beyond the grave. To Lutherans, the message of Christ's victory over death (i.e., his resurrection) speaks to this fear. The promise of the resurrection of the body and eternal life are offered as comfort and reassurance. Does this mean that Lutherans believe that there is life after death? The ELCA answers this question as follows:

> Lutherans do believe that life with God persist even after death. . . .
> This of course is a great mystery, and no description of what life may
> be like in any dimension beyond history is possible. Anxiety for the

future is not a mark of faith. Christians should go about their daily tasks, trusting in God's grace and living a life of service in his name (www.elca.org-a).

EPISTEMOLOGICAL TOOLS OF THE LUTHERAN FAITH

The Lutheran Paradox

As noted, the recent "Faith Practices" survey of Lutherans found that 75% of the respondents accept "most or all" of the Lutheran church's teachings. This education is partially contained in their doctrines, as described. However, how such doctrine actually influences Lutherans' behavior, sense of Lutheran identity, and view of secular issues is in part a function of what the current Bishop of the ELCA, Mark Hanson, identifies as "the mystery of paradox" within the Lutheran faith. This paradox can be viewed in many writings that describe faith in the Lutheran context— the creation is good *and* fallen; Lutherans are justified, *yet* sinners; Jesus is human, *but* divine; the Word is both law *and* gospel; God is hidden, *yet* revealed, and Lutherans experience faith *and* reason in healthy tension.

Living out faith for a Lutheran within the context of this paradox can be seen in the manner in which the church, as an institution, addresses issues of social and ecumenical concern. The "Lutheran way" initially fosters education about an issue and then allows individual members to make an informed decision for themselves. Specifically, if the church is faced with a concern, the leaders first study it from a theological perspective; they pray for insight, consider what if anything the Bible has to say about the issue, discuss it with the broadest and most diverse base possible, and then come to a consensus statement or decision. Once a decision is made within the national or synod level, it is then passed on to various congregations. At the congregational level, there may be diverse reactions to such decisions, especially about controversial social issues. However, much of the Lutheran faith, as promulgated by this approach to addressing issues of concern, allows for a wide expression of ideas and practice of faith, rather than dictating specific behaviors, beliefs, attitudes, and morals. For example, of five differing Christian dominations (Assemblies of God, Southern Baptist, Catholic, ELCA Lutheran, and Presbyterian), Olson and Perl (2001) found the Lutheran church to be the "least strict" in dictating lifestyle behaviors.

Individual Lutherans often use the preceding approach when facing ethical or religious decisions in their own lives. As a result, not only does this lead to a situation where many Lutheran congregations have people with diverse views, but also sets the stage for individual Lutherans to interpret church doctrine in divergent ways.

The following section focuses on select issues of potential concern to the psychotherapist regarding a Lutheran perspective. These include Lutheran views on: (a) interpreting the Bible, (b) science, (c) psychological health and psychopathology, and (d) human sexuality.

Lutheran Views on Scriptural Authority

Lutherans accept the Bible as the word of God. They view the written words of both the old and new testaments as God's spirit speaking through the inspiration of the various authors (ELCA, 2003). As such, church doctrine accepts the scriptures as an authoritative source and a moral heuristic for Lutherans to proclaim their faith and manage their lives. There is a strong consensus among Lutherans that God's message to humankind is revealed through central scriptural messages such as the creation of the world, the concepts of law and mercy, and the work and teachings of Jesus Christ. What is less clear and subject to more diverse interpretations among Lutherans concerns the question of whether God's message is revealed as central overarching insights, or whether each word is to be taken literally as infallible fact that can stand outside of its cultural and historic context (www.elca.org-a).

This difference of opinion is a continual source of discourse that occurs as part of many educational, social, behavioral, scientific, and political pursuits among its members. What is characteristic of Lutherans is that there exists a cultural acceptance, tending to actual pride, in these differences and resulting discussions as important intrapersonal and interpersonal spiritual exercises. Despite the presence of some differences of opinion among Lutherans, there is a collective consensus that the Bible is not a definitive record of history or science, but rather a profound, dramatic, and compelling account of God's saving care for creation (www.elca.org-a). For example, many Lutherans have wrestled with the message of creation and concept of original sin in the stories of Adam and Eve. It is common to hear Lutherans reason that they accept God's creation of the world and original sin as a revelation they acquired through the scriptures. However, they also accept current scientific knowledge and development that questions the possibility of a literal, 6-day creation of the world and humankind, where a day equals 24 hours. In this context, the "turning away from God" that took place in the Garden of Eden can serve as a useful and insightful metaphor, rather than historical fact. As a result, Lutherans may occasionally appear to be taking both sides of an issue when it involves discussions of scriptural authority versus scriptural interpretation. However, as noted, Lutherans view this ambivalence as strength rather than weakness. In other words, they are not trying to pacify two sides of the issue, but actually view the scriptures as a way to continually attempt to understand God's message, with awareness that the Bible has been written and transcribed by many authors over a period of centuries and within specific cultural contexts.

A LUTHERAN VIEW OF PERSONALITY DEVELOPMENT

Although no explicit theory of personality is part of the Lutheran Church teachings, the tenets of its collective knowledge base do provide an implicit theory of human psychological and spiritual development. Because of the "mystery of paradox" previously described, tension and internal conflict are predictable and important aspect of each individual's emerging personality. As indicated, people are viewed as both righteous through their faith and at the same time falling short of God's expectations. People do not strive for salvation through their actions, but are expected to live responsible lives, and each person is viewed as both saint and sinner. Acceptance of these ambiguities and questioning the meaning of scripture and doctrine are viewed as important aspects of human maturation. Such experiences culminate in one's active participation in activities of discussion and dialogue with other individuals. An example of this process of faith actualization, consider how Lutherans may view the development of a child referred to in this text as "Caroline."

Caroline is likely to be baptized in infancy as an indication God's "promise" of salvation through a faith relationship. Because she is an infant, members of her family or the church congregation assume responsibility for her participation in the ritual. Over time she receives instruction in the basic tenets and doctrine of the church that is referred to as a catechism, with instructional material often presented in the form of questions and answers. Over a 2-year period during preadolescence, Caroline participates in classes that prepare her to repeat the baptism ritual during a ceremony of "confirmation," in which she affirms and acknowledges the relationship with God that was made on her behalf by others when she was an infant. This ceremony serves as an important developmental landmark for her to assume responsibility for managing the paradoxes inherent in the teachings of the church. Many churches support a collective view of one's postcommunion years of adolescence as a provocative time of personal exploration, questioning, and even possible absence from the church. During this developmental period, Caroline will face important decisions about how she will use her personal gifts, discover her purpose, and serve the human community at large. Eventually, it is hoped that she will return to the church community as a young adult to assume responsibility for her own faith and live a purposeful life. Fear and detachment from God are considered the major roadblocks or obstacles that will periodically serve to retard Caroline's actualization process.

HOW LUTHERAN DOCTRINE INFLUENCES BEHAVIOR, INDIVIDUAL BELIEFS, AND PEOPLE'S IDENTITIES AS LUTHERANS

Therapists working with Lutheran clients who embrace this acceptance of ongoing scriptural discourse may find it useful to recognize that intellectual struggles and desire for spiritual actualization consistent with God's scriptural message can have both a positive and negative impact on therapy. In those religions that have much less ambiguity concerning scriptural authority, strict adherence to biblical wording and concrete interpretation of all passages might lessen confusion and engender a clear set of guidelines for how people should live their lives, change their behavior, and cope with problems. However, Lutherans are more likely to look at different possible interpretations and meanings of these same biblical passages. This can lead to significant introspection that results in psychological conflict, or alternatively, as a catalyst for positive self-growth and new insights.

Given this context, counseling techniques that involve a supportive challenge to examine the different scriptural messages that may apply to a given situation may help activate a Lutheran client's willingness to take different perspectives in order to better understand the problem he or she is facing. For example, consider marital counseling in which a couple is dealing with one partner's extramarital affair. A more literal Bible-adherent belief orientation might focus on the sins of the adulterous spouse and the forgiveness of his or her partner. Lutheran clients, on the other hand, may be more willing to explore the various relationship problems that contributed to their estrangement and the resulting affair. Such problems may include the cheating partner's low self-esteem, distrust, or avoidance, which served as triggers for approval-seeking behavior from others. As such, it is possible for each partner to understand the many ways in which they both behaved that were alienated from their spiritual goals or the person each wanted to be. In such a case, there is a therapeutic opportunity to explore many different biblical messages about relationships, including trust, love, hope, kindness, sacrifice, and loyalty, over and above the admonition of adultery. Forgiveness continues to remain an important issue but may have more facets than one that is focused on a single sinful act.

On the other hand, a Lutheran's flexibility of thought also can have a negative impact, particularly when a given interpretation serves to reinforce his or her problem thoughts, feelings, or actions. For example, the person who engages in high-risk or offensive sexual acts may rationalize this behavior by interpreting messages of love and sexuality as "gifts from God." Another example involves the individual who engages in authoritarian or controlling behavior and interprets various biblical passages as supporting the subservience of women or various racial groups. In such cases, it may be useful for a therapist to seek additional assistance from Lutheran clergy, who may provide advice for applying biblical messages in a more accurate modern-day context, or help introduce competing egalitarian scriptural messages that can serve to reduce behavior that is destructive toward others.

The Lutheran View of Science

In terms of science as a world view, whereas supposed "conventional wisdom" suggests that "science and religion do not mix," in fact, given the flexibility of thought noted in the preceding, a scientific perspective is very compatible for Lutherans. Consider part of a dialogue between the *Journal of Lutheran Ethics* and James Houck, an atomic physicist and Lutheran. The journal posed the following question: "Do you find that your faith and your science support each other or clash—or both? How does one influence the other?" Houck's answer indicates the possibility that they can relate in a synergistic manner, rather than being simply compartmentalized:

> For me, faith and science interrelate across a full spectrum from integration to tension. At those rare moments when I am able to open my mind to the possibilities of the Universe, faith and science are indistinguishable. On most days, though, faith and science complement each other. Science grounds me in reality and faith inspires me to act (*Journal of Lutheran Ethics*, 2002).

The Lutheran View of Psychological Health and Pathology

The Lutheran view of psychological health, like physical health, has a long and varied history within the church teachings and doctrine. Early biblical accounts and descriptions of mental and behavioral disorders include suggestions of the causal influences of evil spirits, absence or withdrawal of connection to God, and sinful behavior. On the other hand, there are descriptions of provocative and strange behavior patterns, particularly among the prophets, that are described as divine visions and inspiration, which would almost surely be interpreted today as pathological. Examples include circumstances in which someone is willing to commit human sacrifice or descriptions of individuals who have strange visual experiences or speak "in tongues." This varied history and lack of clear scriptural description or interpretation of what defines and differentiates psychological health and psychopathology has resulted in many different interpretations or definitions of such concepts over the years.

The current Lutheran view of psychological health and illness, developed through repeated study, discussion, and awareness of scientific advancements in health and medicine, is one that views scientific advancement as one of God's most precious gifts. The work of scientists and professionals in the healing arts is accepted as important ways to help people to heal mental and physical problems, as well as to improve the church community's collective understanding of mental and physical illness. The charge or call of the church membership is to provide support and help to people experiencing psychological or behavioral problems (ELCA, 2001).

It is clear that most Lutherans currently view mental illness as treatable through the care provided by trained professionals. Hence, they are more likely to focus prayers on healing people's lives and providing support throughout the duration of the treatment process, rather than believing one's faith to be the sole cure.

It is unlikely that proponents of the Lutheran faith would blame or project God's punishment or wrath as the source of behavioral, emotional, or psychological disorders. Instead, there is recognition among Lutherans of a long tradition (and comfort) with integrating information from both the health sciences and religion to provide optimal support to church members with illness. A partial explanation for this perspective may be found in the traditional Lutheran view of health from a holistic and interactionist perspective. The view is holistic because it takes into account the whole person, including his or her genetic and biological characteristics, physiologic functioning, learning environment, and faith. Examples of possible contributions of an individual's learning environment can include both the personal environment (e.g., history of abuse, lack of opportunity to learn coping skills), as well as contributions of the social environment (e.g., racism, poverty, lack of access to professional care). Possible contributions of faith or spiritual strengths may include spiritual activities, such as placing oneself in God's care; hope, trust, confidence in professionals to respond to their calling to heal; and accepting support from the church community.

A holistic view of medicine is part of the church's more recent history. Over three decades ago, Granger Westberg, a Lutheran pastor and faculty member at several universities, established holistic centers and authored several books emphasizing the relationship between religion and medicine. His writings and efforts to develop holistic centers for health focused on fostering an increased understanding of the connections among the physical, emotional, spiritual, and interpersonal dimensions of life left a lasting legacy for the church with regard to an interactionist philosophy of health (Solari-Twadell, 1999).

In addition, Lutherans generally accept that states of psychological health and well-being are related to a combination of scientific knowledge and spiritual awareness, physical and mental functioning, and biological processes; how a person has learned to function in everyday life; and the ability of the person to realize his or her goals in the local community. Total well-being is viewed as the integration of each person's spiritual, psychological, and physical dimensions that result from the interrelationship of environmental, nutritional, cultural, social, and all other aspects of life. For example, perusal of the curricula offered by the psychology departments at various universities sponsored by the ELCA (e.g., Pacific Lutheran University, Luther College, Muhlenberg College) identified course offerings and descriptions identical to those offered at universities with no religious affiliation.

A study paper disseminated by the ELCA describes the "psycho-spiritually whole person" as one who has a strong faith, an ability to resist pressures to conform, a few close or intimate relationships, an appreciation of God's gifts, creative and effective problem-solving skills, self-acceptance, self-efficacy, openness toward others, an ability to directly and honestly communicate, an ability to balance the rational and emotional, involvement in charitable activities, and acceptance and tolerance of the ambiguities in life (www.elca.org-b). This definition, credited to Butman (1999), suggests a focus in counseling on building positive psychological coping skills. The counselor working with a Lutheran client who is acculturated in this perspective can find support for a treatment that requires that the individual accept problems as part of life, assume personal responsibility for seeking help to change his or her behavior to be more consistent with his or her moral beliefs and spiritual goals, and focus on positive skill-building activities. As an example, a cognitive–behavioral perspective can be viewed as particularly in sync with this framework (e.g., Nezu & Nezu, 2003) and can include mindfulness training (Kabat-Zinn, 1994), increasing pleasant events (Lewinsohn & Munoz, 1992); cognitive therapy techniques (Beck, 1995); rational emotive therapy (Nielson, Johnson, & Ellis, 2001); assertiveness training (Paterson, 2000); problem-solving therapy (A.M. Nezu, 2004); anger management (Novaco, 1975); forgiveness training (Enright, 2001); emotional tolerance training (Linehan, 1993); and acceptance and commitment therapy (Hayes, Strosahl, & Wilson, 1999).

With regard to the role of church clergy and lay persons, activities related to mental health care largely support and encourage clients to work on these goals in therapy and improve their life rather than viewing the church as the central cure (e.g., responsible to cast out demons or cure the patient). This does not mean that religiously active Lutherans find integration of religious material in counseling inappropriate, but rather that they tend to seek counseling to provide them with additional knowledge and skills from psychological science. A consensus in the literature is put forth by the church that people with mental or physical illnesses are blameless, although there is patient responsibility to seek change, accept support, and work at increasing one's skills.

COMMON MORAL AND CLINICAL ISSUES

Although acceptance of ambiguity is both an explicit and implicit part of the Lutheran faith, Lutherans tend to face moral and spiritual turmoil when their process of scriptural study and discourse fails to conclude with an acceptable stance or viewpoint. When individuals face their life decisions at a time when there are no clear church statements but rather many differing opinions, Lutherans experience both internal conflict and external estrangement in the church community. Such moments can involve significant psychological and spiritual distress. One area in which the church is currently trying to resolve difference and establish a comfortable consensus is in the area of sexuality.

Lutheran Views on Sexuality

At the present time, the ELCA is undergoing a major study on human sexuality and homosexuality. Specifically, at the 2001 Churchwide Assembly, voting members representing all ELCA churches across the United States adopted a resolution to: (a) study homosexuality with reference to the blessing of same-sex unions and the ordination of a person who is in a committed same-sex union and (b) develop a social statement on sexuality. This study will follow the procedure outlined earlier whereby various study documents ("Journey Together Faithfully") have been distributed among the various ELCA congregations as a means for individual Lutherans to engage in a dialogue among each other in order to begin forging position statements that will be voted on eventually. Overall, the study is geared to occur over a 6- to 7-year period.

Although the church does not yet have a formal position on same-sex relationships, a large contingency among ELCA members supports the sanctity of such relationships. Those ELCA congregations that wish to "advertise" to the public that they are receptive to gay and lesbian members call themselves "Reconciled in Christ." Homosexuality is openly discussed in mainstream Lutheran publications and is at the heart of the current nationwide study being conducted by the ELCA. Typical of their approach, the ELCA has requested mental health professionals, ethicists, clergy, as well as lay members to provide consultation, advice, and feedback about this issue.

Until the decisions are made resulting from this study in 2007–2008, Lutherans can look to a previously adopted statement issued by the ELCA. In 1996, the ELCA published the message entitled, *Sexuality: Some Common Convictions.* Although not articulating new policy, this statement attempts to express the Lutheran church's perspectives about human sexuality in contemporary society as a means of providing guidance for the members of the church.

In this statement, the ELCA suggests that "sexuality is a mysterious, life-long aspect of human relationships. Through sexuality, human beings can experience profound joy, purpose, and unity, as well as deep pain, frustration, and division." Drawing on the ten commandments, scriptural implications lead to the following notions: (a) sexuality should be placed in perspective, (b) family relationships should be honored and nurtured, (c) destructive abuses of power that harm others are prohibited, (d) marriage is viewed as a sacred union and social institution, (e) "truth-telling" is an essential aspect of all relationships, and (f) any sexual desire that lures one away from a spouse or family is condemned.

In this context, sexual interactions within marriage are considered a joyous gift from God. Lutherans are not told that sexual intercourse is purely for procreation—it can be a celebration of a loving marital relationship. The specific implication from this notion is that contraception is allowable. Further, whereas the Lutheran perspective indicates that sex should occur within a marital relationship, it does acknowledge the concept that many adults are single (through choice, divorce, or death of a spouse) and are sexual beings. Consistent with the paradoxic approach taken by the Lutheran church about many difficult social and moral issues, it does not explicitly allow single adults to engage in sex, nor does it prohibit them in a direct manner. According to the 1996 message, "this church seeks to be a place where, as sexual beings, single adults can find guidance for their particular spiritual, ethical, psychological, and social issues." Moreover, the Lutheran church acknowledges that some marriages may not be "safe spaces," but places where spouses or children may be abused. For those marriages that cannot be reconciled, although considered tragic, the Lutheran church does suggest that divorce may be the best option (remember that Lutherans do not consider marriage to be a sacrament). Remarriage is also permitted, if not affirmed.

With regard to specific prohibitions about human sexuality, the Lutheran church opposes adultery, sexual abuse (both physical and emotional), promiscuity, prostitution, practices that spread sexually transmitted diseases, pornography, and advertising in the media that exploits stereotypes of male and female sexuality (e.g., using sex as an allure to sell a product).

The concluding statement of this message typifies how the Lutheran church attempts to understand the reality and foibles of human nature within the context of a loving relationship with God:

> to a world obsessed with sexual self-fulfillment, divided by differences over sexuality, and weary of how sexuality is abused, the message of the grace of God lightens our burdens, lifts our spirits, renews our commitments, and reminds us of the deepest basis for mutual respect—the love of God we have in Jesus Christ (ELCA, 1996).

CONCLUDING REMARKS

Given that Lutheran church doctrine offers much individual freedom among its followers in interpreting scripture, as well as its support of secular professionals in the mental health fields, it is not unusual for a Lutheran experiencing emotional or behavioral problems to seek counsel from a nonclergy counselor. More importantly, it appears that little in the official church teachings interferes with conventional psychotherapy principles and strategies. However, given that the majority of Lutherans identify themselves as following the basic tenets of the church (e.g., the importance of faith), it may behoove the therapist, if providing services to a Lutheran, to request whether he or she wishes to focus on their beliefs in therapy. The contents of this chapter provide the reader with the notion that the ELCA fosters independent thinking; rather than dictate "proper lifestyle behaviors," it provides a context within which one's life and faith fit together.

REFERENCES

Beck, J. (1995). *Cognitive therapy: Basics and beyond.* New York: Guilford.

Butman, R. E. (1999). Christian growth: Psychospiritual wholeness. In D. G. Benner & P. C. Hill (Eds.), *Baker encyclopedia of psychology.* Portland, OR: Baker Books.

Enright, R. D. (2001). *Forgiveness is a choice: A step-by-step process for resolving anger and restoring hope.* Washington, DC: American Psychological Association.

Evangelical Lutheran Church in America. (1991). *Church in society: A Lutheran perspective.* Retrieved from www.elca.org

Evangelical Lutheran Church in America. (1996). *Sexuality: Some common convictions.* Retrieved from www.elca.org

Evangelical Lutheran Church in America. (2001). *Our ministry of healing: Health and health care today.* Retrieved from www.elca.org

Evangelical Lutheran Church in America. (2003). *Constitutions, bylaws, and continuing resolutions, adopted by the constituting convention of the ELCA.* Retrieved from www.elca.org

Evangelical Lutheran Church of America. (a) *Essential questions: Christianity and Lutheranism* Retrieved from www.elca.org

Evangelical Lutheran Church of America. (b) *Chronic mental illness: A congregational challenge.* Retrieved from www.elca.org

Hayes, S. C., Strosahl, K. D., & Wilson, K. G. (1999). *Acceptance and commitment therapy: An experiential approach to behavior change.* New York: Guilford Press.

Inskeep, K. W. (2001). *Religious commitment in the Evangelical Lutheran Church in America: Findings from the Faith Practices survey, 2001.* Retrieved from www.elca.org

Journal of Lutheran Ethics. (2002). *Faith and science: An interview with James Houck.* Retrieved from www.elca.org

Kabat-Zinn, L. (1994). *Mindfulness meditation for everyday life.* New York: Hyperion.

Lewinsohn, P. M., & Munoz, R. (1992). *Control your depression* (rev. ed). New York: Fireside Publishers.

Linehan, M. (1993). *Cognitive-behavioral treatment of borderline personality disorder.* New York: Guilford.

Nairn, T. A. (2001). The Christian moral life: Roman Catholic and Lutheran perspectives. *Journal of Lutheran Ethics, 1.* Retrieved from www. elca.org

Nezu, A. M. (2004). Problem solving and behavior therapy revisited. *Behavior Therapy, 35,* 1–33.

Nezu, C. M., & Nezu, A. M. (2003). *Awakening self-esteem: Psychological and spiritual techniques for improving your well-being.* Oakland, CA: New Harbinger.

Nielsen, S. L., Johnson, W. B., & Ellis, A. (2001). *Counseling and psychotherapy with religious persons: A rational emotive behavior therapy approach.* Mahwah, NJ: LEA.

Noll, M. (2003). American Lutherans yesterday and today. In R. Cimino (Ed.), *Lutherans today: American Lutheran identity in the 21st century* (pp. 3–25). Grand Rapids, MI: Wm. B. Eerdmans Publishing.

Novaco, R. W. (1975). *Anger control: The development of an experimental treatment.* Lexington, MA: Heath.

Olson, D. V. A., & Perl, P. (2001). Variations in strictness and religious commitment within and among five denominations. *Journal for the Scientific Study of Religion, 40,* 757–764.

Paterson, R. (2000). *The assertiveness workbook.* CA: New Harbinger.

Religioscope. (2004). *Total number of Lutherans worldwide climbs to nearly 66 million.* Retrieved from www.religion.info

Solari-Twadell, A. (1999). Health and wholeness. *Christian Century, 3,* 19.

SECTION II

The Mainliners

CHAPTER SIX

Mainline Protestants: Christian Faith in the Reflective Tradition

Donald L. Bubenzer, Amy B. Quillin, and Paul Ashby

In writing about Mainline Protestants, the authors are taking a view that religion and spirituality are perhaps most helpfully understood from a cultural rather than a psychological perspective. This view is taken for two reasons. First, it seems as though religion is an expression of culture if culture is understood as a "socially transmitted system of ideas—ideas that shape behavior, categorize perceptions and give names to selected aspects of experience" (Locke, 1998, p. 3). Second, world religions long preceded the development of the discipline of psychology; thus, trying to apply psychological lenses and language to religious schema and symbols may not be helpful or appropriate. If therapists attempt to draw forth different realities and experiences by the language chosen to describe them, then it might behoove those in the helping professions to learn the language of those served. Therefore, the reader is invited to enter the culture of Mainline Protestantism and suspend the desire to automatically translate what is written into the language of psychology. Perhaps the thought and language of Mainline Protestantism might inform psychological thinking and practice.

OVERVIEW OF MAINLINE PROTESTANTISM

Mainline Protestants represent the historic churches that were the dominant expression of Protestantism in America from the time of the landing of the Mayflower until the 20th century movements of fundamentalist and Pentecostal churches, which then came to surpass the numbers within Mainline churches. Major denominations among mainline churches include: Episcopal, Presbyterian, Lutheran, United Methodist, American Baptist, United Church of Christ, and Disciples of Christ churches. The roots of these bodies for the most part were formed in protest against the centralized authority and perceived misuse of power of the Roman Catholic Church in Europe during the 16th century.

EPISTEMOLOGICAL APPROACHES INFORMING THE FAITH

Their approach to theology is more defining of "Mainline" than the denominations that compose them. Mainline theology approaches fundamental doctrines and core beliefs with the paradoxical use of reason and logic in formulating theology but rejects any absolute truths other than postulating that all truth is God's truth. The Mainline Epistemological approach has absorbed the Kantian philosophical awareness of the limits of human knowledge. Therefore there is no conflict between scientific discovery and spiritual wisdom, because both belong to God. Yet on that foundation is the understanding that no philosophical insight, Holy Scripture, religious experience, faith group, nation state, or scientific formulation can claim a monopoly on the truth.

The epistemological tools of the Mainline tradition reflect a humble acceptance of the limitations of human knowledge combined with the use of human reason to explore dimensions of faith with historical awareness. It is the poignant humble awareness of the human mind's limitations that undermine any attempts to proclaim any scripture text as an absolute dogma or create creeds that are promoted as timeless truth. Any attempt on humans' part to grasp eternal truth is fragmentary and fractured by the limits of human understanding.

The sources of authority in the Mainline tradition all reflect the use of critical reason and historical awareness. It is in the thoughtful reflection of these sources that life is pursued. Those sources include:

• Scripture as interpreted through historical-critical analysis, meaning the word of God is shaped by "historically conditioned human beings who are capable of error" (Solle, 1990, p. 28).
• Confessions of faith, church constitutions, theological constructs, and denominational resolutions are affirmed as part of the faith while acknowledged as products of a particular time in history and not eternal truth.
• A willingness to accept and adopt new discoveries and teachings of science and the social sciences as complementary to theology rather

than as a source of conflict. For example, although fundamentalists are still at war with the idea of evolution and fossil records, leading Mainline churches and pastors embraced the discoveries of Darwin in the 19th century. In 1897 Congregational minister, Lyman Abbott wrote, *The Theology of an Evolutionist*. A hallmark of Mainline churches since Schleirmacher's, *Speeches on Religion,* has been to both honor and accommodate the highest realizations of culture as compatible with the deepest values of faith.

• Mainline morality is defined by the Christian call to love one's neighbors; embrace the Enlightenment values of justice, equality, liberty, and acceptance of diversity; and foster a spirit of tolerance. The blessing of the Enlightenment is that it freed the Protestant traditions from repressive dogmatism and promoted "the centrality of human welfare and the necessity of free inquiry into truth" (Ward, 1991, p. 200).

• A central source of authority for Mainline churches is symbolized in the compassion of Jesus. The heart of the church's preaching, teaching, and mission is to follow the ways of Jesus and become the "Good Samaritans" who serve the world in mercy and justice. It is the calling of Mainliners to bring healing through taking notice of the needs of others and acting to bind up the wounds of the world. The ethics of Mainline churches was shaped by the dawn of the Social Gospel movement in the early 20th century. A leading proponent of this view was Walter Rauschenbush, whose experience as a pastor in the Hell's Kitchen neighborhood of New York City led him to see the inadequacy of a revivalist theology that "saves souls" and allows people to "rot" in the environments of crime, ignorance, and poverty. His writings helped Christians focus on the ethics and teachings of Jesus and related faith to social transformation. Rauschenbush wrote, "A theological God who has no interest in the conquest of justice and fraternity is not a Christian. It is not enough for theology to eliminate this or that autocratic trait. Its God must join the social movement" (Rauschenbush, 1917, p. 178).

• In Mainline Protestant faith, salvation is realized by life in a community of faith. Baptism is not simply an individual experience but an embrace with love and acceptance into a family of faith. The process of salvation by God's grace through faith is viewed as more than a one-time experience or single religious event in a lifetime. It is a life-long commitment to grow in faith, hope, and love. Mainline churches reflect the theme of Christian nurture first proposed by Congregational pastor Horace Bushnell in 1847 as an alternative to revival practices in the 19th century.

For Mainline Protestants the interpretation and living of the faith is based upon text, context, and the people of God (Solle, 1990). The text of scripture is not an isolated document. Scripture is interpreted through religious traditions that are shaped by history and culture and then lived via the imagination of a community of faith. In the Mainline tradition, it is honestly admitted that the community interprets the text through its own history, culture, theology, and experience of faith. There can be no "pure" or neutral interpretation when each generation has blind spots created by the limitations of their particular time and experience. At the same time church leaders, such as Martin Niemoller and Dietrich Bonhoeffer, who dared to oppose the evils of oppression in Nazi Germany and Archbishop Desmond Tutu, who addressed the tyrannical government and heinous prejudice in South Africa and worked for a just peace, are honored. The Mainline tradition is a faith that acts not with perfect knowledge from texts but with a calling to follow the compassion of Christ. With the preceding sources in mind Mainline Protestants engage in reflective practices that lead to the dialogue of meaning and action that continues their faith story. The call to compassion, then, informs Mainliners' thinking of human development, healthful living, and helpful change.

Mainline Protestants have been steeped in the view that the Bible and other faith documents are a collection of stories and sources holding witness of God as written through the inspired (and perhaps at times not so inspired) hands of humans. Although these stories and their writers were dealing with issues in a historical and cultural context, the meaning of many of these stories remains informative for life today and for the future. These stories and sources were and are to be interpreted in the historical context through a process termed critical analysis. Critical analysis was theology's response to the increasing influence of scientific objectivity and the prevailing epistemology of the Enlightenment. Although important and still quite prevalent, critical analysis does not hold the dominance it enjoyed even 20 years ago. It is important to remember, however, that critical analysis is one other tool by which to interpret the text; it is not the sole lens through which the text is understood. Walter Brueggemann (1993), a noted Old Testament theologian in the Mainline tradition, explained that critical analysis; that is, interpretation informed by historical awareness, was once presumed to be "knowledge." Its place was not questioned in a culture-bound world where the prevailing epistemology posited that within this modern context, the objective method (objectively examining the historical context) automatically led to knowledge.

However, because the dominance of scientific positivism has been questioned, the modes of theological interpretation in the critical analysis tradition also have been questioned, at least by Mainline Protestants. New practices of knowledge and meaning making are beginning to arise within the Mainline tradition. As Brueggemann (1993) noted, the certainty with which various constructs were once viewed has been abandoned.

This loss of certainty has furthered the practice of reflective thought among Mainline Protestants.

Many reasons exist for questioning the modernist view of knowledge and power. Perhaps the most cogent of these was presented by Kenneth Gergen in his book, *The Saturated Self* (1991), in which he argued that the certainty of the world and the self in part began to be seriously questioned with the development of technologies that allowed people with both similar and disparate views of reality to communicate with each other, resulting in ways of knowing and being that both validated those ways of knowing and also raised questions. A case in point is the legitimization of gay and lesbian lifestyles and the related questioning of heterosexual lifestyles as being the only "God-given" way of living. As gay and lesbian folks have communicated with each other through the available technologies, they, as a segment of the human population, have realized they are a significant and legitimate community. Likewise, many Christians who live within the reflective–interpretive tradition as Mainline Protestants have moved away from seeing homosexuality as aberrant and toward seeing it as potentially as redeeming as heterosexual lifestyles. The focus is not on the form but on the qualities of the relationship. The filters for this view include "gospel" concepts such as love, commitment, and acceptance.

PERSONALITY IN THE FAITH: BUILDING ONE'S STORY IN A STORIED TRADITION

For Mainliners, identity is not static but moves as the context and one's historical religious imagination meets the potentiality of the future (Brueggemann, 1993). Further, Brueggemann noted that there is evidence that identity itself is processive, that people are underway rather than having a fixed identity, in a process by which one is continually constituted and reconstituted. Paul Ricoeur (1995) described this storied self as an ongoing project, a task to be performed. Often this task or project is expressed as one's faith journey, one's growth within God's vision.

From the Mainline Protestant perspective the Bible is a collection of stories, some with historical dimensions. However, the purpose of these stories, the reason for which they were written (for the most part), and certainly for which they are used is heuristic, stimulating reflection on what it means to live one's own story in the presence of a revealing God.

Stories are the connection of events and meaning into a coherent perspective across time (Bruner, 1986). Michael White and David Epston (1990) in applying Bruner's ideas, wrote that, in general, people ascribe meaning to their lives by plotting their experience into stories, and that the stories they develop shape their lives and relationships. Stories privilege the particulars of lived experience and it is in those particulars, rather than in the rational argument the scientific method uses, that the story takes on its lifelikeness. It is the lifelike qualities that invite the listener to ponder the meaning and make application to their own lives.

At the close of his novel, *Cities of the Plains,* Cormac McCarthy (1998) wrote about constructed identity as a storied, ongoing project. In a dialogue between two characters he draws together Bruner's idea that stories are made up of landscapes of action and meaning that are strung together over time. One of the characters notes that the events of the world, that which happens in life, often comes uninvited and one is left to weigh and sort those happenings into the story that becomes identity. McCarthy notes (p. 283) the placing of events (actions) on an axis of meaning constitutes the story. Likewise, Mainline Protestants may speak of the weighing and sorting of the events in their life against their reflections and imagined meanings of the faith that constitute their faith journey, or their story of change over time and their growing identity in the faith.

Finally, essayist William Kittredge (1999) in his books, *Taking Care: Thoughts on Storytelling and Belief,* wrote to this evolving, multistoried nature of one's life. Kittredge indicated that each person has many stories available to him or her to live. A person experiences trouble when the story being lived is not his or hers, or does not work anymore, but is being continued. Further, Kittredge spoke to the idea that stories are culturally based and provide instructions from a society to its members, telling them what is valuable and how to conduct themselves if they are to preserve the things they cherish. Kittredge noted that both individuals and society may suffer from what is termed "narrative dysfunction." Such dysfunction comes from inhabiting stories with assumptions and plots that are no longer helpful. Kittredge too, views lives as ongoing projects; evolving stories that allow people to situate themselves within a particular context.

From a Mainline Protestant perspective, these "useful" stories, these ongoing projects have key elements that are timeless (e.g., compassion, justice, and mercy; a view of all people as children of God; a belief that the Holy Spirit is present in all life, the idea that health [salvation] is only possible in community; a view that humans exist through God's grace [undeserved gift] and are called to be a graceful and forgiving people). The Mainline story is about living in the light of union with God; that is, to travel the path and grow in the timeless qualities noted in the preceding. However, the application of these ideas changes as identity develops and the context of the world shifts.

The story that Mainline Protestants live becomes their identity and their task is to live their story faithfully. When one's task is to live faithfully, the concept of normal or abnormal personality is not congruent with the faith. Normalcy is not a relevant question to the faith. Perhaps those who have lived most faithfully might even be considered, in a world of comparative records and competencies, normal curves, and deviance to be most abnormal. For example, Francis of Assisi is reported to have disrobed in a public setting and to have handed his clothes to his father as a way of declaring himself divorced from aristocracy and committed to an ascetic (godly) life (Bodo, 1985). Consequently, the question of normality is not a religious question, although to practice the faith (to practice generosity, love, and respect for all people) is considered to be characteristic of healthy personhood.

Abnormality in its broadest sense is the failure to live one's story faithfully, a place of being stuck in one's story, and unable to move forward. This arrested movement within the journey may be viewed as the abdication of one's will to choose, or the belief that one's story has little impact on others and vice versa, or an inability to see oneself as part of a larger story.

Abnormality also may be the inability or unwillingness to engage within the larger story, to attempt to live in isolation removed from others, to live contrary to the propensity for connectedness that is viewed as inherent in humans.

However, people live in an environment where they are assaulted every day with reminders that the world is not so always hospitable, where they witness and sometimes participate in injustice, vengeance, and arrogance. People experience convergence of what they know to be right ways of living amid the daily deluge of an arrogant, consumerist mentality. In such a world people can feel out of place, alone, and restless, as though in a wilderness, which Walter (1988) terms a place of unsettled experience. This is a place where the story is forgotten or no longer fits.

From a Mainline faith perspective, therapy is one avenue to reclaim one's story, to become unstuck. From this perspective, therapists come alongside their clients and walk with them back into their journey. In this way counselors serve as historical tour guides, helping clients find and reclaim their place, putting themselves back into the historical narrative that holds creations of their past and hopeful imaginations of their future. Identity then can be the opposite of wilderness. Identity is a story of located experience. The task of remembering is one of again finding one's story. Constructing fragmented parts of past experience in a way that gives the past meaning for the present and projected future results in a story, one's identity. Therefore, memory is not just calling something to mind but also taking a stance, valuing, and bringing forward what is good and powerful (Taylor, 1996).

HUMAN DEVELOPMENT AS LITURGY

The writer of Ecclesiastes declared, "There is a time for everything, and a season for every activity under heaven: a time to be born, and a time to die . . . a time to weep and a time to laugh . . . a time for war and a time for peace" (3:1–8, New International Version). That people mark time—days, weeks, seasons, years—indicates that people have histories, are dependent on memory, and are gifted with the opportunity to create and draw forth the history that is lived. Development of all creation, then, for those in the Mainline traditions, may be viewed from the perspective of the cyclical nature of life's seasons and rhythms and the promise that viewing life in this way leads to growth over time in one's faith journey.

This developmental perspective has both cyclical and longitudinal qualities that allow for the vagaries of life's events and subsequent emotions. Within the Mainline tradition, history—one's own or others'—reminds one that the pain and frustration experienced today will likely be moderated by a friend's compassion, a community's embrace, or even the passing of time. That there is a time for everything, and that life's seasons will visit again, invites graciousness with oneself and others. One is reminded and encouraged to embrace the opportunities presented to others and to oneself in those periods and recognize the possibilities that can be created from those opportunities.

Cyclical Development

The cyclical or rhythmic qualities of life are expressed in the church calendar or the seasons of the church and remind us of life's fluidity and circularity. Perhaps the Sabbath itself represents the smallest unit of circularity in the church calendar. Sabbath is seen as a reminder that life is a gift. It sets a boundary in our lives as a place where we recall that we do not own this gift of life (Brueggemann, 1977). Sabbath is a time for a celebrative and reflective renewal of the covenant with God, a time to replenish one's story and realign it with the principles of the faith. The seasons too remind one that this gift of life offers choices in the ways people participate in creation. The rituals of the church also express the cyclical seasonal qualities of life in ways that highlight the faith story, the events and people that have helped establish the faith, exemplars, and mythical communities of support, which provide hopeful promise to the stories that are one's privilege yet to craft.

In the early days of the Protestant church, when many of its members did not have access to formal education and could not read or write, clergy taught the church's ways and beliefs within the church calendar—Advent, Christmas, Lent, Easter, Pentecost, etc. The stories of each season emphasized certain understandings of God's character. Even today, the ritual and ceremony related to each period of the church calendar is an invitation to enhance one's development in the faith through the sights, sounds, words, and smells employed. The engagement of the various senses summons people to enter the story more deeply and personally.

For instance, Advent—the time leading up to the mythical events surrounding the birth of Christ—may be seen as a time when people are reminded of the hope in life, peace, and living in goodwill toward all humankind. The season is one of preparation, offering an opportunity to evaluate one's actions and meanings in the light of Advent's promise. Thus, a therapist who wants to use advent as an anchoring point might ask, "Have there been times in your life when you have felt the particular hopefulness of the season?" and explore that response. This idea might be followed with a discussion of sources of hopefulness in the client's life at the moment. Further it might be asked, "If these threads of hopefulness were to grow in your life, how would that happen?" Threads running through this discussion might include the people and events of the client's faith history that he or she finds as sources of hope. Thus, one can see how the idea of narrative, time, actions, and meanings can be integrated into a therapeutic approach.

Pentecost, an event marking the arrival of the Holy Spirit as a guide for the faithful after the death of Jesus, also might offer therapeutic opportunity in working with Mainline clients. Pentecost can be viewed as a season that encourages people to ponder the spirit(s) within their own lives and address with intentionality those they want to nurture and those they want to release. For instance, do they live within and embody a spirit of compassion, empathy, justice, generosity, and community feeling? Pentecost offers an opportunity to examine and be intentional about the development of those aspects of the larger Holy Spirit, and to celebrate the gifts of those spirits within others. Again, the cultivation of a community of support, the drawing forth of historical faith figures who embodied aspects of the faith, and the awakening of memories of desired spiritual qualities and the projection of the development of those qualities in the future through possible actions may be useful when working with clients from the Mainline tradition.

Longitudinal Development

Over time, the church's sacraments or nodal celebrations may come closest to marking what is commonly thought of as developmental stages, in psychological terminology. The sacraments and rituals noted in the following are not necessarily exhaustive, nor are they necessarily celebrated in all Mainline traditions; rather, they represent Mainliners' views of development. In each instance the event holds implications for a variety of members of the community of faith.

Baptism for most of the Mainline denominations is symbolically an infant's induction into the faith as a receiver of the Holy Spirit. The ceremony is usually a faith community event and involves a commitment on the part of the parents that they will raise the child according to the tenets of the faith, expose the child to Christian teachings, and model for him or her beliefs and behaviors consistent with church teachings. At times, the ceremony also involves godparents, who assume some special responsibility for the Christian upbringing of the child. Likewise, the members of the congregation also take a vow to assist in the rearing of the child in supportive ways expressive of the faith community. Some denominations may have commitment ceremonies for infants and see baptism as an adult activity where the individual commits his or her own life to the faith.

Confirmation marks the occasion when a young adult makes a public confession of his or her faith, confirming what was previously proclaimed by the parents at baptism. The ceremony itself usually follows a period of instruction in the faith and assumes reasoning capabilities of the young adult. After learning about the ways of the faith journey and the commitments of the church the young adult, enters willingly into the community. The ceremony confirms the growing independence and responsibility of the youth and usually marks the time when he or she becomes a voting member of the congregation with all of the rights and privileges of such membership. Again, the ceremony is designed to allow the parents and community to see the adolescent in more of an adult role and for the adolescent to see herself or himself unfolding, being involved in a process of transformation into an adult.

The sacrament of marriage celebrates the love relationship between two people who choose to commit themselves in love and faith, to one another and to a larger responsibility in life. Many Mainliners and some Mainline denominations extend the sacrament of marriage beyond the sole domain of heterosexual marriages and provide equal credence to gay and lesbian commitment ceremonies as viable expressions of committed love. Again, the ceremonies unite two people but also recognize families and the larger church community as an important source of hope and support for the couple. Amid the joy and ebullience celebrated in this sacrament the seriousness of the commitment is recognized in the promise to offer love even during the difficult times of life. Children often are associated with marriages and commitments, and when parents present their children for baptism, life's fluidity and circularity are poignantly revealed.

Although not a formal sacrament, death marks the final earthly passage in the Mainline tradition, the culmination of one's earthly life story. It is hoped that the commitments of the faith have prepared one to face death with dignity, knowing the story has been well crafted. Death usually is celebrated via funerals or memorial services. The services are often a time for remembering the life story of the departed and recalling what that story has to offer to the faith stories of those who are left. These ceremonies can be powerful celebrations of events and meanings that serve as inspirations to others. Such ceremonies can be powerful rituals that allow people to begin to say goodbye and invite the new life, resurrection, which allows aspects of the deceased person's spirit into their lives. As with most theological issues, Mainline members hold varied views about the meaning of eternal life. Some believe that life continues in some other form after earthly death, whereas others view eternal life as consisting of the lasting qualities exhibited in the lives lived by others (i.e., love, compassion). Those in the latter category take a "wait-and-see" attitude about the afterlife.

Because Christianity is a communal activity, there are continual opportunities to engage in the developmental activities offered in the cyclical church year and the special event celebrations of weddings and commitment ceremonies, baptisms, confirmations, and funerals. Each offers a renewal opportunity for all participating members.

PSYCHOLOGICAL HEALTH AND PATHOLOGY: CARE AND NEGLECT OF THE SOUL

Predicated on the affirmation that God accepts and loves all of creation, despite its foibles, psychological health inherent in many Mainline faith traditions proceeds from the love and acceptance of oneself and others (Matthew 7:12, Luke 6:31). Again, although faith does not ask the polarizing questions of "good" health or "bad" adjustment, those are issues for the medical and psychosocial worlds. From the Mainline perspective, the questions are, "How does one live faithfully?" or "What holds authority in one's life?" Yet, one might say that from a faith perspective love and acceptance find their source in a transcendent God whose commitment is to individuals, local and global communities, and the larger created world. That God loves and cares for all of creation, even the most seemingly insignificant life forms—the lilies of the fields (Luke 12:22) and the grass on a hill (Psalm 147:8)—serves as a model to follow. Mainline Protestants see an inclusive love as the authority in the journey or story of their lives.

Although what makes for psychological health is not the driving question, the nature and quality of one's relationship to God, others, ourselves, and the environment and the way in which those relationships intersect might be thought of as indicators of psychological health. The way people love themselves is inextricably bound to how they view and interact with others; the way they love others has implications for how they treat the environment; and their love and gratefulness to God as the source of love is the capstone of life.

Fredrick Buechner (1991) stated that the command to love your neighbors as yourself might also mean that you love yourself as your neighbor; that is, extending to yourself what you might extend to your neighbor—acts of caring, nourishing, understanding, comforting, and strengthening. That people have histories and that their stories connect, intersect, overlap, and run together with others' stories makes relating well with others—with neighbors, who may include the people next door or in another country who speak other languages, and worship other gods—a cornerstone of spiritual and perhaps ultimately psychological health. Buechner (1969) also described the differences and similarities of *eros* and *agape* love. Sometimes thought of as sexual love (eros) and sacred love (agape), he redefined them as seeking love (eros) and giving love (agape). He concluded that the similarities between the two concepts far outweigh the differences, and are, in fact, essentially the same, springing from the same source. To become fully human, he argued, people need to recognize the need to be givers and receivers of love. The seeker's need to receive love's sacrifice is no less a need than that of the giver's to extend the sacrifice. The desire for connectedness to oneself, to one another, and God requires that one nobly offer the gift of love to one's neighbors, and also humbly receive love's gift.

The failure or inability to love one's neighbors as one's self, and in Buechner's terms, one's self as one's neighbors, portends a disconnection from one's story. Ironically, the most helpful response to this state of mind is reengaging with one's community and reestablishing relationships. Taylor (1996) stated that more stories from the perspectives of different storytellers is the best remedy to disconnected, faulty, or stuck narratives. The more stories one hears and willingly becomes a part of, the more complete the story becomes, the more one has to offer to others' stories, and the more receptive one becomes to the ebbs and flows of the larger story of which one is a part.

Those from the Mainline faith traditions also likely believe that people should love the environment as they love themselves and their neighbors: to care for it, nourish it, and try to understand it in ingratiating ways (Buechner, 1991). Creation is alive, and its tendrils are entwined in people's stories—certainly in communal and global stories, but also in individual stories. Land and the environment, in general, are gifts that unite humanity, although history records countless times in which desire for land domination divided peoples. Again, the Mainline response to this gift of creation is to live humbly, extend mercy, and practice justice.

Berry (2002) describes the disconnection of words and actions where faith proclamations run contrary to the ways people respond to the land. It is contradictory, for instance, to proclaim love for one's neighbor but disregard the land, and the fruit of the land, on which that neighbor depends. Dumping toxic waste into the water supply, poisoning the air with noxious gases, or filling wetlands for needless commercial development belie contempt not only for the land but for one's neighbor.

To raise the issue of psychological health against a context in which the concept of psychology had not yet arisen is difficult. It was not until the 17th century that the concept of soul care began to be formulated. Nevertheless, in making the connection to psychological health it seems that psychological health requires keen awareness. It is an embodied awareness that personal stories intersect with the stories of others, the land (environment), and a transcendent God, and that intersection is an invitation to find comfort and strength in others' stories, glean pieces of one's identity from them, and then in humble awareness that these are gifts, offer back to others—the community, the environment, and God—the gift of people's stories and the spirit(s) that inhabit them.

Recalling Buechner's (1969, 1991) views of love, Barry Lopez (1986) pushes the love idea even further. He writes that agape is an expression of spiritual affinity and wonderment at sharing life with other life. Love, indeed is indicative of health. He notes that people trust their future life to their intelligence but then raises the question of whether intelligence is reason or love. To the Mainline Protestant, it is both.

Spiritual pathology in the Mainline tradition, on the other hand, is to live in fear, prejudice, rigid orthodoxy; it is to take a knowing rather than a learning posture, to live a disrespectful life, where that which is sacred and worthy of respect is not seen (Palmer, 1998).

HUMAN CHANGE AS TRANSFORMATION

Personal Change

Mainline denominations see change as a process that in general takes place over long periods of time but that may be punctuated by benchmark events, for example, the transfiguration of Moses (Exodus 34:29–35), the transfiguration of Jesus (Matthew 17: 1–13), or the baptism of Jesus (Matthew 3:13–17, Mark 1:9–11, Luke 3:21–22). These benchmarks are usually highlights in a process of change. Long processes of preparation and change precede them and change occurs after them. Further, change always takes place in a context. There is often an audience to the change and a community of support around the change. Often there is a spiritual presence of the core faith values: social justice, mercy for the poor, widows, orphans, forgiveness, or a movement to greater wholeness (living more fully the faith story). Also, Mainline Protestants often see the benchmarks of change in biblical characters' lives as heuristic in nature rather than historical. It is not as though history is denied but rather written or constructed for a purpose other than to record history. The purpose or meaning has greater value that the factual events.

Walter Brueggemann (1993) indicated that in the Mainline tradition people do not generally change because of moral persuasion or doctrinal arguments. Rather, people change because they are offered or discover new models, images, and pictures of how life might fit together and these have the particularity of narrative to guide them. Transformation is a slow process of entering a counter story about self, neighbors, world, and God and of disengaging from a story that is no longer credible.

Cultural Change

Mainline Protestants also consider people to be participants in the process of change from various vantage points. At times, they are the primary recipients of change, may be distant witnesses to change, or may be participants in a greater movement of change that by its existence transforms culture. Niebuhr (1951) examined differing perspectives of Christ and culture and the various ways Christian traditions understand the intersection of the two. Mainliners likely embrace the view of the Christ of culture and the belief in the transformative power that humans, exemplifying the life (characteristics) of Christ, have as a community within the culture. Contrary to other views that disdain culture and work to separate the so-called Christian life from what they see as godless and sick, the Mainliners take more of a prophetic vision and in fact seek contact with culture. They espouse the belief that the gospel's audience is universal, not the domain of a select few, and that the characteristics of the gospel—love, justice, compassion, mercy, humility—embodied in individuals and within the community offer the possibility of radical change. From this prophetic view, Mainliners enter discussions relative to peace, the economic system, education, and issues that make for a healthy society and world.

Niebuhr (1951) points out the necessity for relatedness. The questions and certainties that arise from faith and stories are not lived in solitude, but in community. From the Mainline perspective, change often is thought of from the perspective of offering a critique of society. The role is not only to care for those who are oppressed, who live outside the power structure but to change the very structures that are responsible for the oppression.

COMMON MORAL ISSUES:
PRACTICES OF INCLUSION

Because of their emphasis on social justice and mercy, the valuing of all people, community, and the intrinsic worth of all creation, Mainline Protestants consider the discussion of moral issues and advocacy for positions, social policy, and actions consistent with the faith to be central to their mission.

For the most part, Mainline Protestant denominations are democratic rather than autocratic institutions. Moral positions are discussed and debated at all levels of the church organization. Votes on moral stances and actions are cast by designated delegates with the results being accepted as the position of the church. Thus, seldom does a central head of a denomination make a pronouncement concerning a moral issue that is not a product of the members through some form of representation.

The extent to which such a moral position is imposed upon a particular church or minister varies by denominational structure. In a congregational structure most authority lies at the level of the local congregation. From this perspective, churches call and employ their own minister and adopt their own faith statements. The minister has to be acceptable to the denomination. In some Mainline denominations, ministers may be assigned by a central authority to a church but even then there is usually a mutual agreement to the assignment. Likewise the degree to which moral positions are imposed on a church also vary, but in general there is tolerance of varying perspectives.

For example, as a denomination within the congregational structure, the United Church of Christ has taken a position of being an "open and affirming" denomination. The phrase means that people of various gender and relationship orientations are not only welcome within the denomination but the lifestyles themselves are viewed as potentially sacred. However, geographical regions of the United Church of Christ may or may not be "open and affirming" depending on their perspective on the issue, and individual churches have the right to decide if they are open and affirming. Ministers within the denomination can live openly gay and lesbian lifestyles and have the choice of performing wedding or commitment ceremonies between gay and lesbian couples.

Mainline churches often adopt positions relative to the moral issues of the day. These might include current issues such as abortion, the women's rights, the appropriateness of military action, the potential oppressiveness of capitalism, and the death penalty. A task of the Mainline church is to transform society in the light of the faith, to be a moral voice, rather than to live apart from society or be a tool of the state (Niebuhr, 1951).

CLINICAL ISSUES:
THE DISENFRANCHISED NARRATIVE

The diversity of thought within Mainline Protestantism makes it difficult to conceive of clinical issues that are specific to these faith traditions. Furthermore, and contrary perhaps to some of the more fundamental faith traditions, Mainliners are likely to view counseling, psychotherapy, and psychiatry as legitimate means of addressing concerns they might encounter. Mainline Protestants would not likely hold the view that "clinical issues" are the result of sin or something inherently evil in human nature.

It may be helpful, however, to think about some of the issues encountered by clients and thus by therapists in a different light rather than from the "diagnostic" clinical perspective. The clinical perspective might connote sterility, isolationism, and individuality apart from one's community. From this different light, however, issues encountered may stem from the paradoxic interplay of connection and disengagement, the way that this paradox plays itself out in the life of one's stories, and the confluence of those stories with those of communities, histories, the dominant culture, and the narratives of the larger world people inhabit.

Disengagement is necessary—although sometimes radical—when, as stated, people become stuck in their stories, or when life seemingly conspires to stifle people's voices and mitigate the power of individual or communal narratives. Breuggemann (1991) warns that those who pursue and work for peace and justice in this world will at times encounter hostile resistance, and he specifies what is necessary to stay the course in the pursuit of peace and justice. The acts of peacemaking, he indicates, necessitate a kind of disengagement from apparent power structures, and these acts require an imagination that embraces another world order, speak from a different voice, lay claim to a different memory, and sets its sight on another humanity.

This imaginative disengagement, and the intensity with which one embraces it, however, require that one be intimately connected in some supportive community that validates him or her and the radical work. To question or actively work against (or be perceived to work against) the agenda of a dominant cultural or national story; for instance, the belief that true patriotism exhibits itself in the full support of a war one believes is unjustified, is to risk the dominant culture's bemused ridicule at best and vengeful wrath at worst. Barring the strength of a community that supports, encourages, and is even like-minded in its efforts to participate in such peacemaking efforts, the divergence of the dominant story with those of the peacemakers can elicit self-doubt and isolating loneliness. The result of this isolation can be evidenced in what is commonly known as clinical symptomology.

Distancing oneself from stories that are not helpful, and, therefore, not healthful, can at times require enormous courage and commitment to purpose. To be challenged to see and live one's story in a different light, particularly when it is juxtaposed against a dominant story that contradicts or invalidates the emerging story one is committed to see and live, can feel overwhelming. It is those times, especially, that people may bring those stories, or hopes of creating new stories to a counselor with the expectation of finding support and encouragement in birthing and strengthening those new narratives.

In light of this distance and engagement, which is sometimes necessary, and the perils that distance can pose, the necessity of connection for creating and sustaining healthful stories is eminently obvious. When rightly connected, that is, connected in ways that foster healthy growth and deepening relationships, to the poser of stories, others, the environment, and God, people create sacred spaces for the birthing, nurturing, and wonderment of all these stories and storytellers.

The level of experienced connectedness with emotions and the way meaning is made of them in the light of stories directly affects the quality of connection with others. Palmer (1998) contends that only as people achieve a level of peace and acceptance within themselves is it possible to truly experience community with others. Outward participation with one's community demonstrates an inward graciousness toward oneself. Participation in the life of community affords opportunities to engage in endeavors, even seemingly mundane ones, with a sense of transcendence, create and appreciate the creative acts of others, give and receive compassion and mercy, challenge and be challenged, experience beauty and passion, and participate in a cohort of truth seekers. Truth, as defined by Palmer is an ongoing and transcendent conversation transacted passionately and respectfully about matters that in some way make a difference. Conversation by definition necessitates "the other"—other stories, other voices, other opinions, and other experiences. This passionate, disciplined, and eternal conversation invites the global voices of those long past and those not yet present. The conversation proceeds whether engaged in or not; it is about "things that matter," and such realization can enliven and enlarge the stories. Additionally, those in the Mainline tradition would likely concur with Berry (2002) in professing that divine love embraces the totality of the entire world and invokes its health and wholeness. This love, incarnate among the world's inhabitants, insists that the health of individuals is inextricably bound to the health of communities. When people fail to recognize the interdependence of the stories and do not work toward healthful communities, the passion and integrity of the conversations and narratives are jeopardized.

Finally, as stated, from a Mainline perspective, connectedness to the created order, the environment, is an indication of the quality of individual and communal well-being. Both Palmer (1998) and Berry (2002) would likely agree that one possible way to understand the sometimes pervasive malaise experienced, particularly in the West, is to examine the disconnectedness of people from the land. When individuals, or local or global communities become isolated—from others, themselves, the land, and the transcendent—events are set in motion that conspire to disfigure and skew the shape of joys and sorrows, divest the stories of vitality and life, and reduce the multifaceted scope of interactions with all creation to a flat, one-dimensional exchange. Connectedness, the link to one's communities, is life. Nothing, not even the seemingly individual and isolated act of breathing, transpires within the universe in isolation (Berry, 2002). Berry contends, for instance, that everyone depends on an ultimate unity that births innumerable phenomena and allows for myriad unseen connections that enable people to draw breath and live their lives.

THE COMPLETED STORY

In summary then, Mainline Protestants are more concerned with faithful living than with prescribed ideas of normal or abnormal development. They hold a deep appreciation for the ability to craft their stories and an abiding respect for the historical and cultural contexts within which these stories are created. Mainliners espouse the characteristics exemplified by Christ—love, justice, mercy, compassion—and recognize that individual and communal health is enhanced by embodying the spirit of those characteristics. Finally, recognizing that all this transpires in the context of community and shared stories, and that well-being is linked to the vibrancy of local and global conversations, those in the Mainline Protestant faith traditions would likely view faith's intersection with emotional and psychological health as seamless, understanding that all truth is God's truth and that all the earth's inhabitants converge, at some point, in their dependence on one another.

REFERENCES

Berry, W. (2002). *The art of the commonplace: Agrarian essays of Wendell Berry.* Washington, DC: Counterpoint.

Bodo, M. (1985). *The way of St. Francis.* New York: Image Books.

Brueggemann, W. (1977). *The land: Place as gift, promise, and challenge in Biblical faith.* Philadelphia: Fortress Press.

Brueggemann, W. (1991). *Interpretation and obedience: From faithful reading to faithful living.* Minneapolis: Augsburg Fortress.

Brueggemann, W. (1993). *Texts under negotiation: The Bible and postmodern imagination.* Minneapolis: Fortress Press.

Bruner, J. (1986). *Actual minds, possible worlds.* Cambridge, MA: Harvard University Press.

Buechner, F. (1969). *The hungering dark.* New York: HarperCollins.

Buechner, F. (1991). *Telling secrets: A memoir.* New York: HarperCollins.

Gergen, K. J. (1991). *The saturated self.* New York: Basic Books.

Kittredge, W. (1999). *Taking care: Thoughts on storytelling and belief.* Minneapolis: Milkweed Editions.

Locke, D. C. (1998). *Increasing multicultural understanding: A comprehensive model.* Thousand Oaks, CA: Sage.

Lopez, B. (1986). *Arctic dreams: Imagination and desire in a northern landscape.* New York: Bantam Books.

McCarthy, C. (1998). *Cities of the plains.* New York: Vintage Books.

Neibuhr, H. R. (1951). *Christ and culture.* New York: Harper & Row.

Palmer, P. J. (1998). *The courage to teach: Exploring the inner landscape of a teacher's life.* San Francisco: Jossey-Bass.

Rauschenbush, W. (1917). *A theology for the social gospel.* New York: Library of Theological Ethics.

Ricoeur, P. (1995). *Figuring the Sacred: Religion, narrative, and imagination.* Minneapolis: Fortress Press.

Solle, D. (1990). *The window of vulnerability: A political spirituality.* Minneapolis: Fortress Press.

Taylor, D. (1996). *The healing power of stories: Creating yourself through the stories of your life.* New York: Doubleday.

Walter, E. V. (1988). *Placeways: A theory of the human environment.* Chapel Hill NC: The University of North Carolina Press.

Ward, K. (1991). *A vision to pursue.* London: SCM Press.

White, M., & Epston, D. (1990). *Narrative means to therapeutic ends.* New York: W.W. Norton & Co.

SECTION III

The Outsiders

CHAPTER SEVEN

Evangelicalism

Mark A. Yarhouse and Stephen R. Russell

Evangelicalism is a word that possesses both historical and theological significance. According to Noll, Bebbington, and Rawlyk (1994), the term describes "a fairly discrete network of Protestant Christian movements arising during the eighteenth century in Great Britain and its colonies" (p. 6). In addition to this historical view, Evangelicalism also may be understood as a category of religious doctrine that transcends denominational and confessional boundaries (Noll et al., 1994; Pierard, 1984). The major components of this theological view include a recognition of the authority of the Bible, an emphasis on individual conversion or "new birth," an encouragement toward personal and community activism, and a faith in the redeeming work of Jesus Christ.

The term Evangelicalism originates from the ancient Greek noun *euangelion*, which means "good or joyful news," as well as the Greek verb *euangelizomai*, to "announce good tidings of or to proclaim as good news" (Pierard, 1984, p. 379). In this way, the term stresses both the historical emphases on spreading the *gospel* or "good news" as well as an ongoing dedication to sharing faith with others. In order to gain a proper understanding of the Evangelical tradition, one must consider both the historical and theological components.

Although Evangelicalism often is regarded as a contemporary phenomenon, most Evangelicals recognize their roots from the beginnings of the Christian church. Pierard (1984) argues that the "Evangelical spirit" has arisen throughout history:

> The commitment, discipline, and missionary zeal that distinguish Evangelicalism were features of the apostolic church, the fathers, early monasticism, the medieval reform movements (Cluniac, Cistercian, Franciscan, and Dominican), preachers like Bernard of Clairvaus and Peter Waldo, the Brethren of the common Life, and the Reformation precursors Wycliffe, Hus, and Savonarola" (p. 380).

According to Pierard (1984), the term Evangelicalism was first given to the Lutherans, whose goal was to rededicate Christianity to a clear teaching of the gospel and the authority of Scripture. The word later came to be applied to both Lutheran and Reformed congregations in Germany.

Although certain aspects of the Enlightenment challenged previously accepted religious ideas, a number of movements focused on the essential nature of supernaturalism and divine revelation as expressed through the Bible. These movements included, but were not limited to, Methodism (John and Charles Wesley); German pietism (Spener, Francke, and Zinzerdorf); and the Great Awakening (Jonathan Edwards). Many historians trace the beginning of the Evangelical movement to the mid 18th century and the revivals associated with Jonathan Edwards and George Whitefield.

By the 19th century Evangelicalism had become a prevalent part of the public domain through the messages of the Charles H. Spurgeon, Charles Finney, and D.L. Moody. Those who identify as Evangelical, according to Mouw (2000, p. 22), rely heavily on what are often called "parachurch" organizations—groups and ministries that carry on their work at one step removed from the "institutional" church. Examples of Evangelical organizations can be traced back to 17th century pietism and the formation of "house churches" and "conventicles," places where Christians met in small groups for prayer, Bible study, and support and encouragement. Recent examples include organizations such as the YMCA, founded by George Williams, and the Salvation Army, founded by Catherine and William Booth. With the onset of the 20th and 21st centuries, Evangelicalism took additional forms, including the development of the National Association of Evangelicals (1942), Fuller Theological Seminary (1947), and *Christianity Today* (1956). Throughout this time, speakers such as Billy Graham have become well-known figures among Evangelicals, as have efforts to establish educational institutions for the training of Evangelicals in various areas of scholarship.

EVANGELICALISM VERSUS FUNDAMENTALISM

As this chapter begins to examine the issue of scholarship and, in particular, the issues of psychology as an area of scholarship, distinction should be made between fundamentalism and Evangelicalism. Harris (1998) notes several key differences between these two groups, including that fundamentalists tend to: (a) be suspicious of scholarship and science in particular, with a tendency to be antiintellectual, (b) have a "mechanical" view of how the Bible was written, (c) make more literal interpretations of the Bible and tend to endorse only one view of the second coming of

Christ, (d) reject involvement with Christians who do not endorse their view, and (e) tend to deny social activism as a practical outworking of their faith.

In contrast to fundamentalists, Evangelicals: (a) encourage scholarship and the engagement with science in order to develop a more accurate understanding of God's creation (and of their faith); (b) approach hermeneutics or the interpretation of Scripture with an appreciation of the cultural context in which it was written; (c) recognize that the Bible is a collection of many different writing forms, including poetry, metaphor, prophecy, and symbolism, and that there are legitimate points of disagreement among scholars as to the second coming of Christ; (d) identify and defend the essentials (i.e., non-negotiable teachings) of Christianity while not letting "secondary" differences keep them from cooperation with others; and (e) see a praxis dimension to integration in that their faith leads them to address social injustices (Harris, 1998).

There are important distinctions between fundamentalists and Evangelicals, some of which contribute to a willingness among some Evangelicals to play an active role in the field of psychology. This chapter now turns to important aspects of Evangelicalism that shape a unique approach to the study of psychology.

IMPORTANT ASPECTS OF EVANGELICALISM

Making a distinction between fundamentalism and Evangelicalism begins to identify important aspects of Evangelicalism. Although Evangelical Christians share a host of common beliefs with other religious groups, Evangelical historians (Marsden, 1984; Noll et al., 1994) posit four main tenets that are common of all Evangelicals. According to Noll (1994):

> In one of the most useful general definitions of the phenomenon, the British historian David Bebbington has identified the key ingredients of Evangelicalism as conversionism (an emphasis on the "new birth" as a life-changing religious experience), biblicism (a reliance on the Bible as ultimate religious authority), activism (a concern for sharing the faith), and crucicentrism (a focus on Christ's redeeming work on the cross)" (p. 8).

Despite denominational or confessional affiliation, each of these beliefs is central to the lives of Evangelical Christians.

Conversionism refers to an understanding that a person experiences a crisis of faith and makes a personal, individual decision about a relationship with Christ. He or she has what is referred to as a "conversion" experience or a "second birth," having been "reborn" spiritually. For

Evangelicals, this personal, spiritual rebirth is a pivotal decision that leads to changes in one's behavior over time. These changes are not so much necessary as they are a natural extension of the changes that are believed to occur within the person who has had a conversion experience. Changes vary significantly from person to person, but generally they are believed to be an important part of sanctification, a Christian concept that reflects a person being "set apart" for God's purposes, being made (from the inside out) more in the image and likeness of Christ.

Biblicism refers to the Evangelical emphasis on seeing Scripture as the ultimate authority. Although Evangelicals look to Scripture, tradition, and reason as authority, they will give greater weight to Scripture in guiding their approach to both reason and tradition. In the area of reason, which includes science, this may mean looking at Scripture not as a handbook for scientific inquiry, as though it was written to explain specifically how to raise emotionally healthy children or how to intervene with someone suffering from an eating disorder, but to look at Scripture for broader principles that inform one's deepest understanding of personhood.

Tradition, too, although important, is viewed by Evangelicals as needing constant reform. The source of information for reformation is going to be Scripture. As with reason, tradition may need to be revisited so that no one tradition becomes privileged over the broader principles understood by the Evangelical as directly relevant to living out one's faith.

Activism refers to a heartfelt desire to share one's faith with others. This is probably most directly tied to the actual name, Evangelical, as this can be traced to the Greek word for "good news," which is what Evangelicals refer to as the gospel; that is, the sharing with others that God has made a way for them to be reconciled to Him through faith in the person and work of Jesus (Pierard, 1984). Activism, then, is seen in spreading the gospel or one's religious faith commitments with others.

By placing emphasis on sharing personal testimonies of how God has changed their lives, Evangelicals also focus on Christ's redemptive work. In fact, for the Evangelical, this is the whole point of sharing the gospel, because the gospel is the story of God redeeming a people through the work of Jesus the Messiah.

These four tenets do capture the essence of Evangelicalism. Some of the unique ways in which Evangelicalism has been shaped by its cultural context in America might be added to this. What appears to be rather unique about American Evangelicalism is that it is characterized by individualism, pragmatism, and empiricism.

There is certainly an emphasis place on *individualism* in American Evangelicalism. The focus is on personal sin and, as Marsden puts it, "the important spiritual unit was the individual." Sinners essentially stand alone before God:

The Christian community provided emotional support, encouragement, and example; but ultimately the decision to accept the message
of salvation was, in the democratic American . . . tradition, essentially
the decision of each individual, as was the decision to conquer sin
(1980, p. 37).

Historically, emphasis on individualism should not be taken to mean
that Evangelicals disregard social justice issues. In fact, this was one of
concerns that distinguished Evangelicals from fundamentalists, the latter
often seeing social justice as a potential distraction from the more pressing issue of saving souls (and that what is truly compassionate is the saving of a soul rather than addressing social inequities) (Marsden, 1980).

Pragmatism is seen in Evangelical social concern. Historically,
Evangelicals supported public and private social programs as "compli-
mentary outgrowths of the regenerating work of Christ which saved souls
for all eternity" (Marsden, 1980, p. 91). If the individual was to first repent for personal sin and have a saving relationship with Jesus, then the
good works that follow would reflect a concern for social action. This follows from philosophical pragmatism, in which, for proponents of the
Social Gospel, "the only test of truth was action" (p. 91). Indeed, there is
a sense in which American Evangelicals, although they often share a common language, cannot speak to the validity of another's faith based on
statements alone, but also on actions, pragmatic expressions of one's
faith. For the Evangelical, both beliefs and actions are important and inseparable (Marsden, 1980).

Empiricism essentially claims that what is known in one's mind is a
product of sensory experience. The modern sciences relied on empiricism,
and American Evangelicalism came into its own in the context of these
historical developments. Evangelicals came to have "faith" in this
method, in part because the method involved observation and analysis of
data derived from immediate observation of God's world. For the
Evangelical, empiricism is important because, as Brantley (1993) observed, people see for themselves and are in the presence of those things
they know.

Not only were Evangelicals interested in empiricism insofar as it
supports the scientific method, but also in approaching Scripture.
Evangelicalism developed an approach to theology that reflected modernist assumptions: If the Bible contained facts that could be known by a
rational individual of some intelligence, then that person could be shown
the truths of Scripture, so that inductive reasoning could be applied to the
Bible as it was being applied to the rest of God's world. Evangelicals,
then, cared deeply about science because they were certain that scientific
reasoning would lead to the discovery of truth—both in the natural world
and in the pages of the Bible.

PSYCHOLOGY IN EVANGELICALISM

Epistemological Tools Acknowledged and Supported by Evangelicals

Some of the epistemological tools acknowledged and supported by evangelicals have been discussed. From an evangelical perspective, how a person comes to know things are true is through observation of the created world (natural revelation), and accurate discernment of truths revealed in Scripture (special or divine revelation).

As Evangelicals reflect on knowledge of the created world, they tend to function as critical realists, and this perspective has often been contrasted with perspectivalism, imperialism, and postmodern relativism (Jones & Yarhouse, 2000). Perspectivalists argue that science and religion are two complementary epistemologies that approach the subject matter (e.g., human behavior) from two distinct perspectives. There is no integration of the two perspectives; they are both deemed appropriate within their distinct explanatory framework. There is no real dialogue between science and religion, and Evangelicals have historically rejected this position.

In contrast, imperialism is the view that science and religion *compete* to describe the same reality. Both science and religion are vying to replace the other. Many argue today that science has all but replaced religion with respect to public explanatory frameworks and access to knowledge. Fundamentalists may experience the relationship between science and religion as an exchange between competing descriptions of reality; Evangelicals, however, reject this view just as they reject perspectivalism.

Another perspective that contrasts with an Evangelical critical realism is postmodern relativism. From this perspective, science cannot promise society access to truth because the postmodernism despairs that truth exists, or, if it does, that it is accessible to people. As Modernism has faltered and scientific rationality called into question, one alternative has been postmodernism, the view that the authority of the narrative replaces the authority of science. Science, like so much of what has historically been seen as authoritative, is deconstructed, it is just another narrative structure along side so many others.

Evangelicals are more closely identified with critical realism. They tend to believe "there is a real world out there where it is possible to know and know truly (hence, 'realism'), but . . . also . . . our theories and hypotheses about that world, and our religious presuppositions and beliefs about reality, color and shape our capacity to know the world (hence, 'critical realism')" (Jones & Yarhouse, 2000, p. 15). From this perspective, religion and science both deal with reality; they deal with different and overlapping aspects of reality. So Evangelicals support a dialogue between science and religion, a dialogue in which science can influence religion and religion influences what is believed about empirical reality. Evangelicalism's interest in the study of psychology makes sense as psychology is a topic in which truth claims from both science and religion intersect.

The Theory of Personality Inherent in Evangelicalism

Evangelicals have generally held that neither Scripture nor theology has historically taught a theory of personality in the way that it is viewed in contemporary psychology (Jones & Butman, 1991). The focus of Scripture and Christian theology is to identify and apply an understanding of what it means to be in fellowship with God. Historical pastoral care has, however, developed approaches to personality that reflected scriptural principles:

> Even in ancient times, pastoral theologians found it necessary to develop models for understanding personality that were built upon, but went beyond, scriptural revelation in order to develop guidelines for pastoral care. In doing this, Christian pastoral thinkers have frequently turned to contemporary nonreligious scholarship about dimensions of personhood to construct more complete models of ministry. . . . While some seem to regard this as heresy . . . , we regard this as a strength as long as the distinctives [sic] of the Christian faith are preserved and given pre-eminence" (p. 40).

So there is a kind of intersection between principles derived from Scripture and contemporary scholarship on the provision of services to others. However, what are the broad scriptural principles that might inform a theory of personality?

Certainly for the Evangelical, some understanding of the human condition or the human predicament is a part of an understanding of human personality. Van Leeuwen (1985) correctly observes that a consideration for a biblically based theory of personality is that the Bible "speaks not only of the inborn personality heritage common to all human beings but also of the possibility of a second birth and a completely 'new creation' in Christ" (p. 224). In terms of a common or shared heritage, humans are in conflict: They are created for relationship with God, and exist in tension that is tied to their rebellion against God. As Van Leeuwen puts it, ". . . the basic human tendency that we all share at birth is in the nature of a conflict between total loyalty to the God who created us and total loyalty to oneself and, by extension, to any of a variety of idols that we try to force into that 'God-shaped void' of which Augustine wrote" (pp. 224–225). This conflict is within the person and between the person and the Creator-God.

From an Evangelical perspective, then, human beings were made to be in relationship with God. To be human is to be relational; humans are made to be in relationship with God and others. The relationships humans pursue are flawed, however, as people express their sinful nature through thoughts and behaviors, and thoughts and behaviors are extensions of their fallen condition. From an Evangelical perspective, "The righteous response to this dilemma is to balance the tension and choose to live in humble submission to the Creator as a dependent being with responsible choice" (Jones & Butman, 1991, p. 51).

Also, from an Evangelical perspective, humans live in the time between the times, meaning a time when Christ is victorious over sin but humans do not yet live in that experience fully. This is a time of redemption—God redeeming a people, setting them apart for God's own purposes. This purpose is to be set apart, to be made holy. The implication for psychology is that symptom relief is not the focus of the Evangelical Christian. Rather, a primary focus is to live life in loving gratitude to God and in obedience to God's revealed will.

The Theory of Human Development

Again, there is no specific evangelical theory of human development. However, an Evangelical explanatory framework makes assumptions about human nature and development. According to Roberts (1997, p. 76), an understanding of human nature has to answer the question, "What are we made for, what would our most fundamental yearnings and interests be if they were fully wise and self-conscious, fully in accord with our essential nature as persons?" From an Evangelical perspective, human beings were made to delight in relationship with God, oneself, one's fellows, and one's physical surroundings (Wolterstorff, 1983). For a human being to flourish, he or she must address these most fundamental yearnings, and these associations are not merely relationships but are tied into essential aspects of what it means to function properly as human beings.

Roberts (1997) suggests several ways in which human beings are structured to actualize their potential. These include human agency and inwardness. Concerning human agency, Roberts notes that humans have a kind of limited freedom and that that freedom allows expression and shapes character over time. God gives people increasing access to the possibility to choose even greater freedom:

> The word of God enables us to see possibilities, without the seeing of which we would lack the real options needed for our freedom. We are liberated from our bondage to sin by a word of grace that declares we have been made righteous in Christ. And thereby actions become open to us that would otherwise have remained in the dark night of pure potentiality (p. 82).

As Roberts (1997) observes, humans are more than the sum of their behaviors. They are shaped too by the inward aspect of what it means to be human, by the ways in which the heart and mind are shaped by what they come to care about, think about, and plan for:

> Proper personhood as actualized in the Christian virtues, by consequence, is not merely a set of dispositions to behave properly, but above all a rightly qualified inwardness—patterns of thought, wish, concern, emotion, and intention shaped by the Christian story and the truths about God, ourselves, and the world, that follow from that story (p. 84).

Human beings have wishes, desires, and longings, and an Evangelical understanding not only brings these to the foreground but notes how thoughts and motivations reveal who they really are, and what they really care about.

The Theory of Psychological Health and Pathology

The authors have suggested that there is no Evangelical theory of personality or human growth and development. The same is true for a theory of psychological health and pathology. There is no distinctively Evangelical theory of health and pathology. However, there is an Evangelical perspective that informs such a theory, and it probably best understood as a background explanatory framework for human incompleteness.

From an Evangelical perspective, human incompleteness is reflected in humans' understanding of sin. Evangelicals have historically been identified with a focus on specific acts that can be identified as sin, and an Evangelical perspective identifies the effects on a client of his or her own sin.

This understanding, however, is only one of several ways Evangelicals incorporate an understanding of sin. Another perspective on sin is to consider sin as a state or condition. In this way, sin is ubiquitous—the human condition is affected by the fall and tainted by sin. As McMinn (2004) observed, it is the "white noise" or background experience in which people live their daily lives.

This fallen condition is a distortion of what life was supposed to be like. It is no surprise, then, that there is something like a manual for making diagnoses of mental illness, as these diagnostic categories reflect specific distortions. The entries are concrete illustrations of the fallen human condition (McMinn, 2004). For example, in the section on clinical depression, an Evangelical would look at low serotonin levels as a reflection of the fallen state insofar as in the prefallen state such neurotransmitters would be properly balanced: "but in a fallen world we live in imperfect bodies, which we take care of imperfectly and end up with all manner of maladies and ailments" (p. 13).

A third perspective on sin is to identify the effects of others' sin on clients (McMinn, 2004). For example, a survivor of date rape who presents with symptoms of acute stress disorder or posttraumatic stress disorder owes her experiences of psychopathology to the direct result of sin done to her in the form of a sexual assault. A more subtle expression of the affects of sin on clients might include adult children of verbally abusive parents, who then struggle themselves with parenting and childrearing. In this case, the effects of others' sin make it increasingly difficult for the adult child of abuse to make choices that reflect the good later in life.

An additional challenge is that Evangelicals believe that humanity suffers from the noetic effects of sin, that is, the idea that "sin blunts our intellect and even our ability to discern sin . . ." (McMinn, 2004, p. 14). That Christians fail to "see" sin is itself a symptom of sin.

Finally, an Evangelical Christian reflection on sin is not limited to reflections on sin in emotional or psychological disturbance, even if the discussion is broadened to sin as a state or condition and the effects of others' sin on clients' lives. There is also a praxis-oriented dimension to an Evangelical explanatory framework that identifies sin within the very structures of society and works to transform those structures to reflect God's original intent. An Evangelical Christian framework reflects on the current situation in society and seeks to be instrumental in its transformation. Applying this to models of health and psychopathology, the Evangelical will want to reflect on the care being provided to those who suffer from symptoms of psychopathology, as well as the ways in which society in general and the mental health community in particular conceptualizes these mental illnesses and provides care for those in need (Yarhouse, Butman, & McRay, 2005). As Wolterstorff (1983, p. 62) puts it, "We owe it to God and to our fellow human being to see to it that our society's array of institutions adequately serves the life of its members—that they serve the cause of justice and shalom."

To push further, the Evangelical Christian asks questions about the mental health care system. In doing so they follow Wolterstorff (1983) in asking whether the system is functioning properly. Does the mental health care system work well? Are the functions being assigned to the mental health care system better addressed by other systems? What role ought the community of Christians play in addressing the concerns of those suffering from psychopathology? What is the place of prevention? How much of what is done in the mental health community is to turn a profit rather than meet needs? Is it worth reflecting upon the familiar model of treatment that is the 50-minute hour? What would it mean to think creatively about alternative approaches, including preventive efforts?

Of course, sin is not the beginning and end of an Evangelical understanding of health and pathology. It is, however, an important foundational consideration. Evangelicals recognize that there are many pathways to the conditions currently described in the *Diagnostic and Statistical Manual* (DSM), and that these pathways represent, to varying degrees, several of the various expressions of sin discussed in the preceding.

There is no established Evangelical view on psychological health. However, many voices have offered what might be taken to be an Evangelical framework for understanding psychological health and well-being. For example, return to Roberts' (1997) discussion of what it means to be a human being. One claim he makes is that people are word-eaters ("verbivore," as Roberts puts it). People eat and digest words, assimilating them into "the construction of the self":

> In being verbivorous, humans are unique among the earth's creatures. We have a different kind of life than nonverbal animals, a kind of life that we can call generically 'spiritual.' Since we become what we are by virtue of the stories, the categories, the metaphors and explanations in terms of which we construe ourselves, we can become spiritual Marxians by thinking of ourselves in Marxian terms, spiritual Jungians if we construe ourselves in Jungian terms, and so forth. It is because we are verbivores that the psychologies have the 'edifying' effect on us . . . : They provide diagnostic schemata, metaphors, ideals for use to feed upon in our hearts, in terms of which our personalities may be shaped into one kind of maturity or another (p. 81).

The Theory of Human Change Inherent in Evangelicalism

Again, there is no one answer to how change takes place that is unique to evangelicalism. However, various approaches to change are typically reviewed, criticized, and aspects of a given theory are integrated into clinical practice if not inconsistent with broader biblical principles or Christian theology (e.g., Jones & Butman, 1991). In other words, if a theory of human change is not incompatible with Christianity, it is viewed as a potential resource to the Evangelical psychologist.

So there are various models of human change. For example, cognitive-behavioral, person-centered, and psychodynamic approaches are three of the most prominent theories of human change. None of these is rejected out of hand. Nor are they embraced uncritically. They are examined and critiqued, as Evangelicals in the field search to mine the resources therein (see Jones & Butman, 1991).

Take, for example, a cognitive-behavioral approach to change. Evangelicals reject an utterly reductionistic approach central to behaviorism, as well as determinism seen in the broader theory. However, evangelicals see themselves as able to use cognitive-behavioral strategies for behavior change while rejecting the broader philosophical commitments inherent in the theory (Jones & Butman, 1991).

POTENTIAL CONFLICTS

Common Moral Issues

Evangelicals recognize that there are points of conflict between a Christian and secular view of psychopathology: "While recognizing that personal discomfort and societal norms both contribute to a consideration of what is normal, the Christian would see both these dimensions as flowing out of God's law as manifested in human consciousness (a revelation sometimes flawed by sin)" (Johnson, 1987, pp. 223–224). At the same time, Christians should expect to experience disagreement between sin and what society determines is normal (Johnson's examples include homosexuality, pride, and materialism), just as one might find society pathologizing behaviors that reflect spiritual insight or maturity, such as sacrificial living.

As Johnson (1987) suggests, the moral conflicts for students studying psychology include providing clinical services to people making weighty moral decisions (e.g., abortion, divorce) or working with clients who are actively engaging in behavior that the church has historically viewed as immoral (e.g., homosexual behavior, premarital or extramarital sex). The Evangelical student studying psychology can approach these dilemmas in several ways. Two approaches are probably most common. The first is to increase one's own sense of self-awareness so that one can acknowledge to oneself specific beliefs and values that touch on moral issues. This can aid in determining whether or not to refer a client to another clinician.

The second approach is to clearly demarcate one's roles and responsibilities. As a licensed clinical psychologist, the clinician has made a contract with society to provide clinical services within an existing framework of scientifically derived diagnosis, case conceptualization, and treatment. Although there may be moral conflicts with specific acts, these conflicts are set aside in light of one's role as a psychologist. The mental health focus of one's role governs one's actions in the context of delivery of mental health services.

Common Clinical Issues

At least two broad considerations can be discussed here. The first is a discussion of common clinical presentations that might come to the attention of an Evangelical. The second is whether Evangelicals ought to share their religious beliefs with others in the form of evangelism.

Evangelicals may be more likely than nonEvangelicals to receive referrals for clinical problems that might not be seen or taken seriously by other mental health professionals, or at least this might be the person's fear. Interestingly, there are some issues, such as birth control, that are probably of greater concern to some Christians (e.g., Catholic Christians) than to Evangelicals, as Evangelical Christians tend to be as a whole more open to various methods of birth control (with the exception of "morning-after" approaches). Other issues are of greater concern to Evangelicals. For example, a woman may come to an Evangelical psychologist for postabortion counseling in part because she may assume that she and her therapist share an understanding for why her decision to have an abortion may continue to be emotionally traumatic. She may also believe that the psychologist is willing to draw on religiously congruent interventions in pursuit of psychological and spiritual healing from an abortion (Reisser & Coe, 1999).

Probably the most politicized and thus hotly contested clinical issue today is that of the person distressed by his or her same-sex feelings. If a conservative Christian experiences same-sex attraction, he or she might report distress and seek professional services based on his or her view of the authority of Scripture and the interpretation that the revealed will of God is that all people limit full genital intimacy to heterosexual marriage. The client who contends with same-sex attraction and experiences conflict with his or her religious beliefs may seek out an Evangelical psychologist to help cope with the dilemma (of experiencing same-sex attraction) or to change same-sex attractions to opposite-sex attractions.

With both postabortion counseling and sexual identity counseling the client might seek out an Evangelical psychologist as much because the professional would at least take an *emic* perspective. That is, the psychologist would see the issue not with reference to universal terms, but through the eyes of those within the specific community of interest; seeing the person's struggles with an abortion or with same-sex behavior through a religious evaluative framework.

Other clinical issues that might lead a conservative Christian to seek out an Evangelical psychologist involve other sexual disorders not otherwise specified in the DSM, including nonparaphilic disorders, such as sexual addictions, internet pornography, and compulsive masturbation. Again, Evangelical Christians might seek out Evangelical psychologists because of the concern that nonreligious professionals might not take these behaviors seriously or might not view them as clinical concerns but as manifestations of "repressed" sexuality inherent in conservative expressions of religion.

A final cluster of clinical concerns include marital and family issues, such as marital therapy, when to pursue separation or divorce, parenting skills and parent–child and parent–adolescent relationships. The concern here might be that a nonEvangelical might not understand the Evangelical client's biblically informed view of marriage and sanctions against divorce, respect for parental authority, and the appropriate use of corporal punishment. Along these lines, Evangelical students studying psychology may express concern about seeing a cohabiting couple. They may prefer to work with marital couples who, by virtue of being married, are often viewed as making choices consistent with a biblically sanctioned structure for intimate relationships.

In addition to these clusters of clinical concern, the second broad clinical issue that often comes up for students in training is whether or not to evangelize or share the "good news" of the gospel with their clients. Some students may go on to identify themselves as Christians through informed consent. By doing so they are communicating with prospective clients that a certain world view shapes their understanding of persons, and they may choose to be rather specific in how their faith shapes their practice. Others, whether they include this as part of their informed consent, still rely on their role as defined by the social contract to function as a psychologist in their professional role with clients. Because evangelizing has not been studied empirically as an intervention per se, they would refrain from sharing their faith. Although they might be open to answering questions, clients may have about their world view, their primary focus for case conceptualization and treatment planning derives from the scientific base that is meant to inform all of clinical practice. From this perspective, they can entrust the ultimate care of the client to God's sovereign will, while being faithful to God by honoring a commitment they made to the society in which they live to provide mental health services within an existing framework that is based on scientific foundations for the provision of clinical services.

CONCLUSION

A distinctively Evangelical perspective on psychology brings with it a biblically based focus on distinct aspects of personhood. This broad consideration informs visions of health and pathology, as well as human growth and development. Although there is no distinctively Evangelical view of mental health and pathology, existing models are held up against the biblical standard for points of agreement. In those areas where there is agreement—and there are many—Evangelical psychologists train and practice based on the best the field of psychology has to offer. In areas of disagreement, the Evangelical makes clear his or her concerns and makes referrals as needed to others who can provide clinical services.

REFERENCES

Brantley, R .E. (1993). *Coordinates of Anglo-American romanticism: Wesley, Edwards, Carlyle & Emerson.* Gainesville, FL: University of Florida Press.

Harris, H. A. (1998). *Fundamentalism and Evangelicals.* New York: Oxford University Press.

Johnson, E. L. (1987). Sin, weakness, and psychopathology. *Journal of Psychology and Theology, 15*(3), 218–226.

Jones, S. L., & Butman, R. E. (1991). *Modern psychotherapies: A comprehensive Christian appraisal.* Downers Grove, IL: InterVarsity Press.

Jones, S. L., & Yarhouse, M. A. (2000). *Homosexuality: The use of scientific research in the church's moral debate.* Downers Grove, IL: InterVarsity Press.

Marsden, G. M. (1980). *Fundamentalism and American culture.* New York: Oxford University Press.

Marsden, G M. (Ed.) (1984). *Evangelicalism and modern America.* Grand Rapids, MI: Eerdmans.

McMinn, M. R. (2004). *Why sin matters: The surprising relationship between our sin and God's grace.* Wheaton, IL: Tyndale.

Mouw, R. J. (2000). *The smell of sawdust: What Evangelicals can learn from their fundamentalist heritage.* Grand Rapids, MI: Zondervan.

Noll, M. A. (1994). *The scandal of the Evangelical mind.* Grand Rapids, MI: Eerdmans.

Noll, M. A., Bebbington, D. W., & Rawlyk, G. A. (1994). *Evangelicalism.* New York: Oxford University Press.

Pierard, R. V. (1984). Evangelicalism. In W. A. Elwell (Ed.), *Evangelical dictionary of theology.* Grand Rapids, MI: Baker Books.

Reisser, T. K., & Coe, J. H. (1999). Postabortion counseling. In D. G. Benner & P. C. Hill (Eds.), *Baker encyclopedia of psychology and counseling* (2nd ed., pp. 886–888). Grand Rapids, MI: Baker.

Rennie, I. S. (1988). Evangelical theology. In S. B. Ferguson & D. F. Wright (Eds.), *New dictionary of theology* (pp. 239–240). Downers Grove, IL: InterVarsity Press.

Roberts, R. C. (1997). Parameters of a Christian psychology. In R. C. Roberts & M. R. Talbot (Eds.), *Limning the psyche: Explorations in Christian psychology* (pp. 74–101). Grand Rapids, MI: Eerdmans.

Van Leuwen, M. S. (1988). *The person in psychology: A contemporary Christian appraisal.* Leicester, England: Inter-Varsity Press and Grand Rapids, MI: Eerdmans.

Wolterstorff, N. (1983). *Until justice and peace embrace.* Grand Rapids, MI: Eerdmans.

Yarhouse, M. A., Butman, R. E., & McRay, B. W. (2005). *Modern psychopathologies: A comprehensive Christian appraisal.* Downers Grove, IL: InterVarsity Press.

CHAPTER EIGHT

Conservative Christianity: A New Emerging Culture

John R. Belcher

IMPORTANT ASPECTS OF CONSERVATIVE CHRISTIANITY

People often lump together Christian fundamentalists and conservative Christians, such as Pentecostals, Charismatics, and Evangelicals. It is true that there are some conservative Christians who also agree with many of the principles of Christian fundamentalists. However, most conservative Christians are neofundamentalist at best. Beginning in the 1950s, neo-fundamentalism, which was less militant and outspoken than Christian fundamentalism, began to emerge (Carpenter, 1997). Whereas Christian fundamentalism was rooted in a bedrock antimodern and antiliberal mentality that also believed in premillennailism and the verbal inerrancy of the Bible (Marsden, 1980; Sandeen, 1978), neofundamentalism borrowed some principles from Christian fundamentalism but was more willing to partially negotiate with modernity and adopt some of its practices.

Marsden (1980) correctly noted that fundamentalism shared its roots with other conservative Christian movements, such as Wesleyans, Pentecostals, Evangelicals, and Charismatics. Note that these various movements do not, with few exceptions, work together; they are not in-terdenominational. There have been some attempts to dialogue (Gros, 2003); however, these discussions usually have not reached significant agreement. The Holiness churches, for example, have been involved in conversations with other Christians since 1957. Usually, however, these discussions are not particularly fruitful because the various factions and movements often divide over some point of theological or practice difference.

Although much as been written about Christian fundamentalists (Carpenter, 1997; Gasper, 1963; Marsden, 1980), less is written about conservative Christians. During the 1880s and into the early 1900s, Christian fundamentalists established a wide network of Bible colleges, missionary training schools, and religious magazines (Wacker, 1985). There was no such similar undertaking among other Christian conservative groups. Instead, conservative Christianity, with little fanfare, grew steadily and increased its visibility after the 1900s. As Brinkley (1998, p. 276) notes, many secular and mainline Protestant Americans were bewildered by the fact that "active faith" had not vanished and not been "consigned to the provincial backwaters of society." Many Americans assumed that as Christian fundamentalism faded during the early 1900s, all vestiges of active Christian faith also would disappear.

A major shift in both American politics and religion took place with the election of Ronald Reagan in 1980. The country shifted to the right; people began to turn away from established institutions, such as mainstream Protestantism, and join conservative Christian churches. The fact that the political shift and the faith shift occurred simultaneously should not be overlooked. People who joined conservative Christian churches criticized mainline churches for being overly concerned with social issues and not focused enough on spiritual ones. "Soul winning" became the goal of these churches, which was a major shift from the Social Gospel movement (Gill, 1976; Saucy, 1997; Stanley, 1990). Saucy (1997, p. 298) sums up best the central aim of much of the conservative Christian movement, "Christians should withdraw from the world ruled by Satan in the church and radically practice the ethics of the Kingdom among themselves."

The notion that the world was sinful and controlled by Satan was a major platform of the movement. Much of the rhetoric of the movement encouraged people to separate or at least be suspicious of "worldly" institutions, such as higher education. Preachers encouraged their congregations to only "trust" their fellow congregants. Mainline Protestantism and the Catholic Church were considered apostate. The fact that many conservative Christians were distrustful of nonconservative Christians meant that the doctrine of ecumenicalism was "dead;" conservative Christians founded their own Bible colleges, seminaries, and ordination practices. Mainline Protestants and the Catholic Church had sought cooperation among denominations; they had worshiped together and cooperated on social ministries. However, conservative Christians sought separation. The phrase, "Are you a Christian?" became a code word that signaled that you were of the right faith; you could be trusted.

The separateness of the conservative Christian movement led to a significant gulf in Christianity. The greatest challenge to the movement is that people purposely can become "cut off" from the world. This can create potential psychological problems as people become increasingly isolated from the mainstream. As long as their communities are healthy and supply all of a person's needs, the challenge is not great; however, when these communities began to grow "petty" and judge people, then the community can further isolate individuals. The greatest challenge is when someone attempts to leave these communities; he or she may be labeled as "traitor."

As people become more entrenched in these communities; the growing pressure is directed, both covertly and overtly, to encourage the person to separate from the mainstream. For example, Boy Scouts of America has historically provided an opportunity for boys to develop a set of skills. Most mainline Protestant churches and the Catholic Church support the movement. However, the conservative Christian community has developed their own program for boys; Royal Rangers. Both movements are very similar; encouraging rank achievement and outdoor activities. However, Royal Rangers is an attempt to show boys that they are different from the world; their friends who may be in Boy Scouts are not altogether "worthy." More importantly, Royal Rangers begins a tradition in which children began the cultural shift of isolation.

Conservative Christianity is hard to define because it is made up of many faith movements as well as denominations. Unlike their mainline Protestant counterparts, conservative Christian churches are not members of a body, such as the World Council of Churches; they do not seek unity. Instead, members of conservative Christian bodies worship independently; what they have in common, such as a belief in God, is obscured by many disagreements over what to outsiders may seem as minor issues, such as speaking in tongues, the manifestation of the Holy Spirit, and the cessation of the Charismata (Ruthven, 1997). Movements and denominations that span the conservative Christian movement (CCM) include, but are not limited to:

The Church of God (Cleveland, TN)
The Church of God (Anderson, IN)
The Vineyard
The Assemblies of God
Wesleyan churches
Holiness churches
Nazarene churches
The Presbyterian Church of America (PCA)
Independent churches that are variations of the above

People who belong to these churches purchase Christian music and books by authors such as T.D. Jakes, Joyce Meyers, Chuck Swindoll, Bob Carlye, Gary Smalley; they listen to radio shows broadcast from Focus on the Family (Bob Dobson); belong to Christian counseling associations, such as the American Association of Christian Counselors; and attend nonmainline seminaries, such as Regent, Fuller, Bethel, and Liberty University. Their leaders vary in educational level; some are not educated beyond high school, some have attended nonaccredited Bible colleges, and others are graduates of conservative Christian seminaries, such as Fuller Theological Seminary. They work and live among non-Christians, mainline Protestants, Catholics, and Jews, yet, to varying degrees, they maintain an antimodern and antiworldly stance both in daily living and worship. Those conservative Christians who aspire to read more scholarly materials also have their own set of journals, such as *Wesleyan Theological Journal, The Pneuma Review, Journal of Pentecostal Theology, Journal of Psychology and Theology,* and the *Journal of Psychology and Christianity.*

To someone raised as a mainstream Protestant or Catholic, the life of a conservative Christian is both strange and bewildering. For example, to varying degrees women are thought to be subordinate to men. Admittedly, there are women within these movements who argue that women are gaining more acceptance and are entering ministry (Leclerc, 2003); nevertheless, each of these movements places limits on women both in the family and the church to some degree (Saiving, 1979). Some churches, such as the Vineyard, are subtle in their approach toward women, allowing them to be preachers, but encouraging them to subordinate themselves to their husbands on spiritual matters. Other churches, such as the Church of God, are more blatant; informing women through doctrine that there are limits to how far a woman can rise within the movement and what is to be her proper place in the home.

Not surprisingly, many women within these movements only pay "lip service" to the teachings of their church, while pursuing private independence. Moreover, they may remain silent in church, attend women's groups, and assume the "proper" role, but hold a job, earn a living, and "run" the house. There are also women within these movements who willingly and by all appearances gladly practice submission to their husbands. Interestingly, many of these women are well educated and accomplished; they are not uneducated and ignorant about what their submission means and requires.

Another hallmark of the movement is an antimodernism stance; not in the sense of antitechnological, for most of these churches are fairly technologically sophisticated. Instead, antimodernism refers to that which is not of God. A popular conservative Christian periodical uses the phrase "Christian Worldview," which on further study does not include mainline Protestants and Catholics; for they are not viewed as "Christian" (McMinn, 2001).

The notion that mainline Protestants and Catholics are not Christian may come as a surprise to many Catholics, Jews, and mainline Protestants; however, much of the rhetoric from the conservative Christian community argues this very point. Not only is conservative Christianity concerned about the nonchurched, but it is also concerned about the "lost souls" attending Christian churches but not what some within the movement would describe as Bible-believing churches. American society has been slow to catch on to this subtle although important nuance; the Christian community is now composed of conservative Christians (who are "true" Christians) and other Christians who are not "true" Christians.

A big difference between the two groups, conservative and nonconservative Christians, is that the former reject "bureaucratic structure," which predominates in the latter (Miller, 1999). The Vineyard movement for example, encourages its adherents to dress casually, the pastor generally dresses casually, people come and go during the praise and worship, and there are no defined elders, deacons, pastoral board, etc. The Church of God (Cleveland, TN) is more formal; their pastors ware business suits, but use no vestments and allow local churches to be somewhat autonomous. Much of the appeal of these churches is their stark differences between themselves and mainline churches.

This brief review of the history and development of the conservative Christian movement points to the fact that the movement is rapidly growing, while the mainstream Protestant community is losing membership. One of the important hallmarks of the movement is the fact that it encourages its followers to separate themselves from the world and mainstream Christianity to varying degrees. It is important for people to realize that the movement considers the world to be controlled by Satan and things of the world are then viewed as tainted by sin. For example, science is suspect, as are medicine and education.

THE EPISTEMOLOGICAL TOOLS ACKNOWLEDGED AND SUPPORTED BY CONSERVATIVE CHRISTIANITY

Theology is good place to begin to distinguish between the conservative Christianity and mainstream Protestantism. The theology of mainline Protestantism is basically postmillennial or a-millennial; Jesus has been resurrected and people are living in the age of the church. From this perspective, there will be no return of Christ, for he has already come.

Mainline Protestantism also generally believes that Christ or God are active to varying degrees in the lives of people. Conservative Christianity believes in a more active God, who intervenes in the daily lives of people. People can develop their relationship with God through scripture, which the movement believes is without error.

Some people and movements within the conservative Christian movement, such as Charismatics and Pentecostals, believe that gifts of the Holy Spirit, such as prophecy, direct divine revelation, healings, miracles, and other similar gifts are active—meaning they did not cease with the apostles. The view in which they are seen as having ceased is referred to as cessationism, which is generally practiced among mainline Protestants and Catholics.

Conservative Christians generally believe that the world cannot improve; it is destined to end, because that is biblically ordained. Some Evangelicals are more hopeful; however, there continues to be the belief that the world is headed toward disaster. Prophecies and the like, such as exorcisms, signal that the world is experiencing the final days. Mainline Protestants and Catholics hold to a different view. The world is not destined to end and, because they are generally cessationist, it is up to men and women in cooperation with God to create a world that embraces social justice.

Theologians such as Walter Rauschenbush (1907, 1917), and Max Stack-house (1968) argued that the church had a responsibility toward the poor and disenfranchised that relied on men and women as opposed to divine intervention. Men and women would do the right thing because they were Christian. It was the belonging to Christianity, responding to the Christian ethic, rather than God's active intervention, that commanded people do something for the poor; to seek social justice. Conservative Christians view men and women as inherently corrupt and although they can and should repent, it is not suggested that they are able to make changes in the world. Only God in His divine wisdom is able to create a better world; the Scriptures clearly indicate that such an intervention is not His ultimate plan.

For conservative Christians, the Social Gospel of Rauschenbush missed the point of the Gospels; where was an active God? The postmillennial-cessationist equation did not include an exalted Christ. Conservative Christians talked about the coming parousia (Dunn, 1998a), which is also consistent with many early Jewish writings (Davis, 1994). To many conservative theologians, the Bible clearly and specifically described Jesus' return. The fact that mainline Protestant churches either chose to overlook it or miss it was testimony that they (conservative Christians) had been chosen by God to lead a lost people. Conservative Christian theologians chose to develop their own theological paths that radically deviated from mainline Protestantism (Blumhofer, 1993; Dunn, 1975, 1998b; Fee, 1996; Turner, 1998).

Charismatics and Pentecostals generally believe that a person is anointed to "preach the word;" their educational credentials, which the two movements have often viewed as worldly, are not so important. The process of ministerial credentialing for a Charismatic or Pentecostal is one where a person could be "walking outside the Lord" (is not a believer); usually has sinned (e.g., drinking, indulging in unapproved sexual activity, using drugs); and has been saved (attends a church service or services where he or she becomes "convicted" or convinced or sinfulness). Many of these people are so "thankful" for their "deliverance" from sin that they decided to preach; they are anointed. They feel "led" to preach (the belief is that the Lord called them to preach). The fact that they might have only finished high school and have had no formal training in theology, preaching, or psychology is often viewed as irrelevant. In fact many people within Charismatic and Pentecostal circles often view the lack of formal post-high school education as a plus. Many Charismatic or Pentecostal pastors lack the skills to prepare and deliver a sermon; therefore, many of their sermons are repetitive and tend to focus narrowly on one scripture without appreciation of its wider implications.

In Charismatic and Pentecostal circles, people say, "we are going to have church today." The phrase "church today" means a particular kind of emotional experience in which the preacher attempts to "work-up" the congregation so that they "feel the presence of the Holy Spirit." A worship service without emotion is not generally viewed as acceptable. Therefore, a minister who delivers a well-researched "cognitive" sermon is most likely to face challenges from the congregation. Comments such as, he is "full of himself," is preaching "over our heads," and "he thinks he is better than us" are common. Most sermons are marked by the pastor condemning something or someone, such as homosexuals. Not surprisingly, many people drawn to Charismatic and Pentecostal churches look for emotion over substance in their worship experiences.

Evangelical churches, such as the PCA, represent a stark contrast to Charismatic and Pentecostal communities. PCA pastors generally hold advanced degrees. Most of these pastors hold a master's of divinity degree. Higher education is not looked at negatively in PCA churches, although the right kind of education is encouraged, such as attendance at a church-based university. Sermons are more intellectual and not as focused on emotion. These churches are part of the conservative Christian movement; they believe in the infallibility of the Scriptures and believe that women should be subservient to men. The demographics in PCA churches are different from their Charismatic and Pentecostal counterparts. PCA churches tend to attract a more educated middle-class group of people as opposed to the less educated and lower-middle-class people who attend Charismatic and Pentecostal churches. The PCA and the Charismatic and Pentecostal churches do not cooperate; it should be noted that a hallmark of the movement is to not to seek cooperation or ecumenicalism.

The Charismatic and Pentecostal churches tend to view the scientific method with great skepticism; generally they do not believe in any of its theories or outcomes. Divine inspiration is paramount, along with a rock solid belief in the authority of Scripture. The PCA churches are more open to the scientific method; however, this group remains highly skeptical of theories that find, for example, that sin (e.g., homosexuality) is normal. Similar to Charismatics and Pentecostals, the PCA believes strongly in divine inspiration and the authority of Scripture.

The obvious reason that the scientific method is held in such little regard and is generally viewed with suspicion is that it often conflicts with Scripture. In the final analysis, scriptural authority provides the answer to all human problems.

THEORY OF PERSONALITY

Conservative Christians do not generally hold to sophisticated theories of personality. Instead, most conservative Christians assume that problems in living are the result of a struggle between good and evil. The term spiritual warfare is frequently used to describe this struggle. Whereas modern psychology and psychiatry postulate a personality that is shaped and developed over time, conservative Christians assume that anyone, no matter what kind of life they have lived, can be changed by the "healing power Jesus." Jesus is the ultimate mental health professional; the notion that someone might develop a personality core that is unchangeable, such as antisocial, is unthinkable to the conservative Christian. The process by which someone recovers from problems, which traditional theorists might label a personality disorder, is to seek Jesus and pray for healing. The church then is like a mini-mental health center, providing support, encouragement, and structure for the person with problems.

Whereas most theories of normal personality posit that individuals possess much individual freedom and a healthy identity is developed by learning, the conservative Christian movement encourages individuals to seek a group identity; the role of an individual identity in which someone expresses individual freedom is discouraged. Learning that seeks to encourage individual expression or thought also is discouraged. Group values and group allegiance are encouraged. For example, Bible study is important in the conservative Christian movement; however, people are encouraged to express themselves only if they quote accepted doctrines.

Over time, people who belong to the movement come to realize that individual expression is discouraged.

A person with an abnormal personality is thus viewed as someone who seeks individual expression at the expense of the group. This is not to suggest that conservative Christians are not healthy. On the contrary, most are healthy. The challenge comes about if a "free thinker" or someone who is an individual thinker attempts to attend a conservative Church. They may find themselves being "put down" or challenged in their apparent reluctance to identify with the group. Many mental health professionals may at first be confused or overwhelmed by the seeming unwillingness of conservative Christian clients to place their own values or preferences above the group.

Living involves a lifelong struggle between good and evil and the only way to control this process is through Jesus Christ. Rather than relying on mental health professionals and theories of personality to treat and understand mental illness, people are asked about their prayer lives, their relationship to Christ, and their relationship to the church. Psychotropic medication is rarely recommended. In fact some conservative Christian pastors refer to psychotropic medications as from the "world" and not of God.

The challenge for many conservative Christian pastors is that the mental health community generally encourages individual growth and as the person grows he or she may begin to challenge values or positions held by the movement. Moreover, the "world," in the opinion of many conservative Christian pastors, is overly concerned about individual rights. For many people with mental health problems, the conservative Christian movement provides a refuge from harsh realities of a "world" that they find threatening. Belonging to a movement that offers to provide support, encouragement, and belonging to someone who may never have experienced such resources is enticing. Because higher education is often discouraged, and because it is "worldly," conservative Christians are encouraged to seek treatment for their problems from conservative Christian practitioners.

HUMAN DEVELOPMENT

Conservative Christians do not think about human development as traditional psychologists do. People are born, and they remain lost until they "give" (are converted) their lives to Jesus Christ. Conservative Christians describe this process as being "born again." Baptism becomes the focus of life. When people are baptized and reborn, their old life ceases and a new one begins. Ideally, the "new life" is without sin. Walking with God means that the person does not want to engage in behaviors that led to their problems. On Sundays and through midweek services, the conservative Christian is admonished to live a Godly life.

Most textbooks on human development divide life into stages, with pathologically free people successfully moving through developmental milestones. For conservative Christians, the only developmental milestone is to be "born again" or baptized. At that point a new life begins. The notions of genetic predisposition or family or environmental influences are considered to be "worldly." A person is thought to be able to overcome anything through Jesus Christ. In many respects, the conservative Christian view of human behavior is very optimistic, unlike the deterministic models that mental health professionals often posit.

The challenge for many conservative Christians comes about when people develop a problem, such as major depression. Despite a belief in Jesus Christ, they may still become depressed. Many conservative Christians are perplexed by this apparent contradiction. Jesus Christ is supposed to be ultimate healer, yet the person is afflicted with depression. Because the conservative Christian movement tends to dismiss such factors as genetic predisposition, a person suffering from depression is often left in limbo; he or she is often told by the pastor not to seek the use of psychotropic medication, yet the patient suffers.

The conservative Christian movement's view of self-actualization also differs from the position held by many human behavior theorists. Self-actualization is found through one's relationship with Jesus Christ and the church. Apart from that relationship, there is no possibility for self-actualization. Religious development seeks to convince people that relationship with Jesus Christ is only correct goal for Christians. Theories of science or value systems that do not support the view that Jesus Christ is the ultimate truth are judged as suspect. For example, Muslims or Jews are not capable of self-actualization because they do not know Jesus (i.e., believe that he is the Son of God).

Many conservative Christians can recite the day, time, and year of their conversion. "Before I was a Christian—I did bad things—but now I am living a good life." There is a notion of "backsliding," in which conservative Christians believe that they "slip" into old ways. Conservative Christians talk about rededicating their lives to Christ. Most Sunday services are dedicated in part to an altar call, where the unsaved and the saved commit and recommit their lives to Christ.

The notion of committing one's life to Christ means that the person rejects all other "worldly" truths and decides to live the remainder of life as a dedicated follower of Jesus Christ. The goal is convert others to this same mind set and normal human development begins at this point. One's life before the day of commitment is viewed as superfluous. The "Christian" adopts "a change of mind, a new understanding and a new set of desires" (Rankin, 2003). Admittedly, the theological significance and understanding of the "change" differs from movement to movement and denomination. For example, PCA believes that the believer must be born again, but does not believe that the Holy Spirit is part of that process, and also does not believe that the believer is "sanctified" after that transforming event (Morgan & Yarhouse, 2001). Over time the born again believer will put the newfound faith into practice.

Charismatics and Pentecostals tend to take a different approach to conversion by emphasizing the work of the Holy Spirit in the life of the believer (McMahan, 2002). Converts to these two movements speak about being filled with the Spirit and often report being "flooded" by the experience. More traditional Pentecostals speak in tongues as the initial evidence of the Holy Spirit (Synan, 1975).

The conservative Christian movement does not view religious development in the same way as do mainline Christians. For many mainline Christians and the Catholic Church a person moves through a set of classes, which culminate in "confirmation" in which the person joins the church. Conservative Christians generally find fault with this process. Individuals seeking a relationship with Christ must, in the eyes of the movement, come to a decision. The decision leads them to being "born again" or experiencing a "rebirth" in which they reject their old life. It is that rejection that is important to the movement.

A confirmation class does not ask people to reject their pasts and become "reborn." Therefore, conservative Christians argue they have merely gone through an educational exercise in which they have learned about Christ and the church. They have not had an experience of the heart in which Christ has entered their life. Once they have chosen Christ (i.e., made the decision), they reject human freedom because it is generally viewed as synonymous with sin. The movement generally believes that when people seek freedom they are seeking separation from Christ.

In the mainline Protestant and Catholic Churches, a child is baptized at birth. The conservative Christian movement does not believe in infant baptism. A person must be of the age where a decision can be made to embrace Christ. Children in the conservative Christian movement are encouraged to make a correct decision; in fact, most youth programs are structured around some kind of altar call.

PSYCHOLOGICAL HEALTH AND PSYCHOPATHOLOGY

Conservative Christians generally do not understand health and illness in the same ways as do other Christians. Illness, whether physical or mental, is the result of sin. This does not necessarily mean individual sin, although that plays an important role, because people are born into a world of sin. The way sin is kept in check is through prayer and living a Christian life. The notion of psychological ill health and psychopathology are foreign terms for many conservative Christians; the *DSM-IV* generally is not used or appreciated by the conservative Christian movement. Depression is often seen as alienation from God and the way to treat it is through prayer, not medication and cognitive behavioral therapy. Anxiety generally is viewed as sinful because people are too concerned with their own needs and desires and are not focused enough on God.

Some conservative Christians believe in waiting on God, a behavior often referred to as "tarrying." Some evangelists have been known to encourage believers to throw away their medications and depend on God. The fact that people in conservative Christian churches may experience problems in living is frequently blamed on society. They believe that if people were living a more Christian life; refraining from TV, radio, newspapers; and attended church many problems would disappear. Many people with mental health problems, such as people with attention deficit/hyperactivity disorder, may be described as being bad or needing exorcism.

Some of the more educated elements of conservative Christianity are beginning to turn to traditional mental health providers, but there is a general distrust of mental health professionals. Conservative Christians often "check out" therapists with questions such as, "are you a Christian?" When they mean Christian, they do not mean a mainline Protestant or Catholic, but, for example a Charismatic. It should be pointed out that conservative Christians prefer their children to be home schooled, educated in Christian schools, and attend Christian colleges. There is the fear that if they become too "tainted" by the world, they will become corrupted. Some denominations, such as PCA, are more sophisticated in their outlook but retain some views that are fearful of traditional mental health.

People who "turn" their lives over to God generally are believed to be able to overcome mental health problems. In fact, many conservative Christians exhibit a great deal of motivation to maintain a positive outlook on life and remain upbeat in the face of biological or psychological problems. The danger for people in the movement is when they are unable to maintain their upbeat attitude. They may experience isolation or ridicule because they have "failed." Many pastors are uncertain as to how to explain this phenomenon.

THEORY OF HUMAN CHANGE

There is only one theory of human change; people change as a result of Jesus Christ. Anything else is superfluous. Conservative Christians generally do not believe in traditional mental health theories or theorists. Interestingly, many conservative Christians continue to manifest problems after conversion; however, the movement generally holds that the ultimate problem is that the convert has not fully turned his or her life over to Christ. People with problems or in need of change are encouraged to "seek Christ" and then they will change. Recently, the conservative Christian movement has become concerned about marriage and has conducted regional seminars designed to encourage men to be "good husbands" and wives to be "good wives." "Good" generally means that the wife is to be submissive to the husband and the husband is to live a godly life.

This may appear overly simplistic, but the simplicity of it is also the reason why conservative Christianity is very attractive to many people. Rather than relying on psychological theories of change, people with problems are encouraged to go to the altar and give their lives to Christ. Then they are told to become active in church and model their lives after people in the church. Obviously, this formula for success is not always successful. Conservative Christians would argue that there is nothing wrong with the formula, only that the person is not committed enough to the process.

It is almost as if conservative Christians live in their own world devoid of scholarly and worldly influence. Much like the Amish, who actively avoid the world, conservative Christians are also encouraged to avoid the world and its "evil" ways.

The formula for change is simple and easily available. Individual redemption (repentance), conversion, and rebirth are the core elements of the formula. After rebirth, a person is supposed to grow closer to Christ. When people do not change, the movement argues it is because people are not correctly following the formula. The formula stresses sin, guilt, and repentance.

COMMON MORAL ISSUES

Conservative Christians are consumed by the phrase, "the avoidance of evil." More importantly, they believe that one of the main reasons people experience problems is because they choose to involve themselves in "worldly pleasures." There is often a laundry list of moral offenses to which pastors and evangelists frequently refer. Conservative Christians assume that the Bible should be taken literally and their lenses through which to interpret the Bible are very narrow. The list of moral offenses includes:

Alcohol use

Drug use

Profanity

Many TV shows that show too much skin, use profanity, and/or promote worldly values

Thinking about things in a non-godly manner

Sexual immorality (this includes homosexuality)

Conservative Christians attempt to live their lives in a "godly" way,
free of worldly temptations. Generally, on Sunday mornings, pastors in
the more conservative Christian churches, such as the Church of God,
seek to remind their congregations of the temptations of the world and
how they can avoid them. Much Bible study and Christian education is
also designed to accomplish this goal.

The conservative Christian movement has much to say about appropriate sexual behavior. Only sex within the bonds of heterosexual
marriage is viewed as appropriate. Premarital sex is wrong, as are homosexual relationships. In addition to these prohibitions, the church also encourages women in particular to dress in such a way that they do not
encourage men to look at them inappropriately. For example, in the PCA
church, women generally are not allowed to teach men because it might
lead a man to become distracted.

COMMON CLINICAL ISSUES

People drawn to conservative Christian churches often have mental health
problems, such as depression, isolation, anxiety, or substance abuse issues.
They use the church as a kind of mini-mental health center, so church becomes a therapeutic process. Many conservative Christian churches provide
for a time of "healing" during the service in which the elders of the church
"lay their hands upon" or "anoint with oil" a person seeking "healing."
Because problems in living (which generally means mental health problems)
generally are viewed as the result of a struggle between good and evil as well
as personal failure (a person has given over to sin), the church through its
various functions provides what the mental health community refers to as
treatment. A pastor might pray for someone, or a person might seek the
counsel of an elder or pastor or participate in a "healing" service. In addition to these interventions, men's and women's groups in the church provide support, encouragement, and structure to those who need assistance.
Few of the clergy in these churches understand mental illness or substance
abuse; as mentioned before, they do not generally use the *DSM-IV*. Instead,
their pastors believe that God can and will take away people's problems.

Members of conservative Christian churches manifest marital problems; however, the analysis of these problems generally differs from the analysis of many mental health professionals. The conservative Christian community generally urges women to view their husbands as being in charge of the family. Men are encouraged to accept this responsibility, obey God's laws, and care for their wives. Marital conflicts are assumed to take place because wives are not being submissive or husbands are not obeying God's laws and caring for their wives. As has been mentioned, the conservative Christian movement believes that problems in living arise because people are not following God's laws. The formula for improvement involves "drawing closer" to God.

There are conservative Christian mental health therapists who hold advanced degrees. They represent a mixed group of professionals. Some of these professionals pray with their clients, encourage their clients to seek healing, but also provide a diagnosis and offer standard treatments, such as recommending medication and cognitive behavioral therapy. Other professionals within the movement, even though professionally trained, have distanced themselves from the mental health community and do not offer their clients diagnosis or standard treatments. These professionals, for example, may encourage married women to accept the belief that men are in charge and encourage them to seek forgiveness for their "waywardness" (i.e., not believing their husbands are in charge).

As an example, a 28-year-old man visited a Church of God with apparent substance abuse problems. He was a heavy drinker, abused his wife, and had problems keeping employment. He met with the pastor, and they prayed for healing. The man received healing and he ceased drinking and abusing his wife, and began to take employment more seriously. He became a faithful follower of the church and believed that his recovery was because of God. This example demonstrates the unique "draw" of the conservative Christian movement. The process of change is straightforward; repent of your sins and follow God's laws and your problems will cease. In the example, the man was "convicted" (a quasi-supernatural experience in which a person accepts or is convinced by God that he or she is in the wrong) of alcohol and spousal abuse (i.e., accepted the fact that these things were wrong), and began to attend church. The church became a mini-mental health center for his spouse and him because it provided a structured environment that both encouraged him and continually reminded him of his past.

Many people are "drawn" to the movement because of its simplicity. Rather than undergoing weeks of therapy in which the outcome is somewhat uncertain, the movement offers some "plain truth;" believe and you will experience relief from your problems. This kind of approach appears to be particularly appealing to people with substance abuse as well as personality problems.

For example, a man suffering from what would best be described as borderline characteristics, such as engaging in self-defeating behaviors that resulted in him experiencing significant relationship and substance abuse problems, visited a conservative Christian church. He had visited multiple therapists, taken different kinds of medication (e.g., Prozac, Paxil), and had been told that his life was a "mess." The pastor and congregation reached out to the person, offering "healing" and counsel. The person experienced "healing," obeyed God, attended church several times a week, and joined a men's group. The relief he experienced was new and refreshing; he had not experienced this relief from traditional mental health professionals. The difference appeared to be the structure provided by the church. He was given a plan, a direction, and told how to behave. Mental health professionals were not as direct with him and they were not able to provide a comprehensive structured environment. In essence, the conservative Christian church provided a kind of therapeutic community for the client.

REFERENCES

Blumhofer, E. L. (1993). *Restoring the faith: The Assemblies of God, Pentecostalism, and American culture.* Chicago: University of Illinois Press.

Brinkley, A. (1998). *Liberalism and its discontents.* Cambridge: Harvard University Press.

Carpenter, J. A. (1997). *Revive us again: The reawakening of American fundamentalism.* New York: Oxford University Press.

Davis, P. G. (1994). Divine agents, mediators and New Testament Christology. *Journal of Theological Studies, 45,* 479–503.

Dunn, J. D. G. (1975). *Jesus and the Sprit: A study of religious and charismatic experience of Jesus and the First Christians as reflected in the New Testament.* London: SCM Press.

Dunn, J. G. D. (1998a). *The theology of Paul the Apostle.* Grand Rapids, MI: William B. Erdmans Publishing Company.

Dunn, J. G. D. (1998b). *The Christ and the Spirit. Volume I Christology. Volume 2 Pneumatology.* Grand Rapids, MI: William B. Erdmans Publishing Company.

Fee, G. (1976). Hermeneutics and historical precedent: A major problem in Pentecostal hermeneutics. In R. Spitler (Ed.), *Perspectives on new Pentecostalism* (pp. 118–132). Grand Rapids, MI: Baker Book House.

Fee, G. D. (1996). *Paul, the spirit, and the people of God.* Peabody, MA: Hendrickson Publishers.

Gasper, L. (1963). *The fundamentalist movement.* The Hague: Mouton.

Gill, A. (1976). Christian social responsibility.) in R. Padilla (Ed.), *The new face of evangelicalism: An international symposium at the Lausanne covenant* (pp. 82–95). Downers Grove, IL: InterVarsity Press.

Gros, J. (2003). *The church in ecumenical dialogue: Cultural choices, Essential contributions.* Paper presented at the Second Joint meeting of the Society for Pentecostal Studies and the Wesleyan Theological Society. March 20–23, Asbury Theological Seminary, Wilmore, KY.

Leclerc, D. (2003). *Gendered sin? Gendered holiness? Historical considerations and homiletical implications.* Paper presented at the Second Joint Meeting of the Society for Pentecostal Studies and the Wesleyan Theological Society. March 20–22, 2003. Asbury Theological Seminary, Wilmore, KY.

McMahan, O. (2002). A living stream: Spiritual direction within the Pentecostal/Charismatic tradition. *Journal of Psychology and Theology, 30,* 336–345.

Marsden, G. (1980). *Fundamentalism and American culture: The shaping of twentieth-century Evangelism 1870–1925.* New York: Oxford University Press.

McMinn, M. R. (2001). A psychology of sin & a sin of psychology. *Christian Counseling Today, 9,* 12–14.

Miller, D. E. (1999). *Reinventing American Protestantism: Christianity in the new millennium.* Los Angeles: University of California Press.

Morgan, D., & Yarhouse, M. (2001). Resources from Reformed spirituality for Christian spiritual formation in clinical practice. *Journal of Psychology and Theology, 29,* 62–71.

Rankin, S. W. (2003). A perfect church: Toward Wesleyan Missional Ecclesiology. *Wesleyan Theological Journal, 38,* 83–124.

Rauschenbush, W. (1907). *Christianity and the social crisis.* New York: Macmillan.

Rauschenbusch, W. (1917). *A theology for the social gospel.* New York: Macmillan.

Ruthven, J. (1997). *On the cessation of the Charismata: The Protestant polemic on postbiblical miracles.* Sheffield, England: Sheffield Academic Press.

Saiving, V. (1979). The human situation: A feminine view. In C. Christ & J. Plaskow (Eds.), *Women spirit rising.* New York: Harper & Row.

Sandeen, E. R. (1978). *The roots of fundamentalism: British and American Millenarianism, 1800–1930.* Grand Rapids, MI: Baker.

Saucy, M. (1997). *The Kingdom of God in the teachings of Jesus.* Dallas: Word Publishing.

Smith, J. W. V. (1980). *The quest for holiness and unity: A centennial history of the Church of God.* Anderson, IN: Warner Press.

Smith, T. L. (1967). *Revivalism and social reform in mid-nineteenth-century America.* Nashville, TN: Abington Press.

Stackhouse, M. L. (1968). *The righteousness of the kingdom.* New York: Abingdon Press.

Stanley, B. (1990). Evangelical social and political ethics: An historical perspective. *Evangelical Quarterly, 6,* 19–36.

Synan, V. (1975). *Aspects of Pentecostal-Charismatic origins.* Plainfield, NJ: Logos International.

Turner, M. (1998). *The Holy Spirit and spiritual gifts.* Peabody, MA: Hendrickson Publishers.

Wacker, G. (1985). The Holy Spirit and the spirit in the age of American Protestantism, 1880–1910. *Journal of American History, 72,* 45–62.

Wacker, G. (2000). *The Christian right. The beginning: 1800 to 1980.* The National Humanities Center. Retrieved from www.nhc.rtp.nc.us.8080

CHAPTER NINE

Fundamentalism

Sara Savage

OVERVIEW AND HISTORY OF THE FUNDAMENTALIST ORIENTATION

Christian fundamentalists are committed to the faith expressed in the Christian creeds; they are intrinsically oriented believers. The intrinsic individual embraces a creed, internalizes it, and attempts to follow it fully. Such a believer *lives* his religion.

In the context of Christian history, fundamentalism is a relatively recent development. Protestant fundamentalism first emerged in America in the 19th century at a time of major paradigm shift in religious thought. The Bible was being subjected to critical analysis as if it were just any historical, secular text. Higher biblical criticism examines the human and cultural origins of Scripture, using archaeological and linguistic methods. The fundamentalist response to this involved vigorous campaigns against higher criticism, Darwinism, and other liberalizing influences. The faith was felt to be under threat. The movement peaked between 1910 and 1915 with the publication and distribution of 3 million copies of *The Fundamentals,* a series of 12 booklets that defended "fundamental" beliefs, written by Presbyterian scholars at Princeton. Henceforth, Protestant fundamentalists were the first to earn their name as those who would battle for the fundamentals of the faith.

The key tenets formulated within the booklets encapsulate the primary beliefs of present-day fundamentalists as well. These are: (a) the authority and inerrancy of the Bible (Scripture); (b) the verbal inspiration of Scripture (the words, not just the ideas, are inspired); (c) the substitutionary atonement of the death of Christ (Christ died to atone for

humanity's sins, and to assuage God's righteous anger against humanity);
(d) the bodily resurrection of Christ; and (e) millennialism (the second
coming of Christ at the end of the age) (Marty & Appleby, 1992). The
belief that the Bible is inerrant; therefore, it is safe from the scourge of
higher criticism, is central to Christian fundamentalism.

Fundamentalist revivals were followed by public humiliation in
1925 as a result of the famous Scopes antievolution trials. After this de-
feat, fundamentalists quietly retreated from the public scene for approximately 50 years, bowing to science. Perhaps coincidentally, from 1979
onward (the year of the Iranian Revolution and the oil crisis in the United
States), a new era of Protestant fundamentalism began, along with
Muslim, Hindu, and other fundamentalisms worldwide, as a force to
which to be reckoned. This second appearance of Christian fundamentalism is more of a middle-class phenomenon, in contrast to the older,
more rural U.S. form. The reason for this apparently sudden emergence
is a subject of much debate. A common thread is that the current rise of
fundamentalisms reveals a distinctively modern reaction against the
'mixed offerings' of modernity (Percy, 1996). Although fundamentalists
may appear antimodern and backward looking, this explanation under-
estimates Christian fundamentalists' central unwavering purpose: the defense of the faith.

As "true believers," Christian fundamentalists have a strong sense of
separate social identity. They are in this world, yet not of it: belonging to
the right church, reading the right Christian books, and listening to approved preachers provide clear social and cognitive boundaries. In things
pertaining to the faith, they inhabit a relatively closed world; however,
Fundamentalists are not "Luddites." Fundamentalists oppose secular rel-
ativist, liberal values, yet they are adept at using the technological and
communication tools of modernity with which to do so.

Fundamentalism is not just about the private practice of religion. It
is about getting things done. Although Christian fundamentalists obey
the authorities in the land ("All authority comes form God," Romans
13:1), biblical authority is their highest authority, and society should be
shaped, wherever possible, in that direction. The U.S. presidential cam-
paign for Pat Robertson was a serious attempt at gaining political power.
Other forms of wielding influence have come and gone, ranging from the
stars of televangelism, the Moral Majority, the *700 Club,* and the rise of
the Christian Right in the 1980s.

There is exponential growth of fundamentalist churches in Latin
America, Africa, and Asia, and the continuance of fundamentalism in the
United States appears to defy theories of secularization. In the United
States alone, there are an estimated 15 million self-identifying Protestant
fundamentalists, despite the pejorative nature of the term.

DEFINITIONS

Who is a Christian fundamentalist? The label is problematic. It is useful to think in terms of narrow and broad definitions. The narrow definition applies to "card-carrying" self-identifying fundamentalists, and many conservative Evangelicals. Denomination alone does not signify Fundamentalist status. Terms such as "Bible believing" may or may not denote Fundamentalism; it must be remembered that Fundamentalists believe the tenets of creedal Christianity, as do all conservative Christians, so a more subtle distinction is necessary.

A helpful way forward is provided by Rokeach (1960) who distinguishes the *way* a person holds beliefs from the belief content per se. In Rokeach's model, it is accepted that all people rely extensively on various authorities for information about the world (e.g., history books, the media, "expert" opinion). In an open system, authority-derived beliefs are held in an open manner, awaiting confirmation from experience or other sources of information (Kirkpatrick, Hood, & Hartz, 1991). In a closed system, the authority belief (here, the inerrancy of Scripture) is accorded absolute status, and thus beliefs derived from the authority are beyond question ("the Bible tells me so"). Thus, a closed system is governed by a meta-belief: a belief that the beliefs are inerrant.

In a closed system, peripheral beliefs (e.g., that women should keep silent in church) are held independently of other peripheral beliefs (Jesus sent Many Magdalene to announce his resurrection to his disciples). Thus any disconfirming effect of one peripheral belief on another is avoided. In a closed system, disconfirming evidence is screened out through avoidance, institutional narrowing, or the confines of a particular discourse. If an authority belief is threatened, it is feared that a whole "domino effect" on the belief system would ensue. As this would be unsettling in the extreme, thinking and interacting tend to proceed on the basis of avoiding threats to the authority belief. Using Rokeach's ideas, Fundamentalists can be defined as those whose belief system is organized as a closed system.

A *broader* definition of Christian fundamentalism encompasses the arguments of scholars such as James Barr (1981). He contends that evangelicals as a whole are also inherently Fundamentalist in that their defense of scriptural inerrancy governs their interpretation of the Bible. Percy (1996) argues that Pentecostalists and Charismatics are also Fundamentalists as they too refer to Biblical inerrancy as a legitimating authority belief. Although this is so, it must be also recognized that for the latter particularly, another form of authority is also at work: subjective experience (or experience of the Holy Spirit). At times, this consolidates inerrancy, and at other times it modifies it. (Hence, readers are advised to cover the Pentecostalism, Evangelicalism, and Fundamentalism chapters en masse because these orientations can overlap in different combinations).

Therefore, it is helpful for clinicians and psychotherapists to think in terms of *fundamentalist tendencies*. It must not be assumed that there is one discrete fundamentalist population out there. Rather there is a broad spectrum of conservative creedal Christianity worldwide, whose members adhere to the inerrancy of Scripture to greater or lesser saturation. For some, this authority belief is undiluted, for others this combines (with various outcomes) with other religious and social influences. Any ideology can be organized as a closed system. Neither "liberal authoritarians" nor fundamentalist Marxists brook dissent; however, such an elastic definition of fundamentalism can simply be a way of labeling "people we don't like."

Because of the complex issues involved in defining Fundamentalists, it is most fruitful to concentrate on the cognitive aspects of Fundamentalism, which flow from the way beliefs are held, rather than focusing on the content of the beliefs per se, or social influences. The latter indeed can vary. For simplicity's sake, this chapter uses the term "Fundamentalist," yet what is meant by that term are those Christians who have fundamentalist tendencies.

Some researchers emphasize the apocalyptic nature of Fundamentalism ("the end of the world is nigh"), and this dimension certainly does amplify the effects of belonging to a subgroup (the rest of the population is under God's judgment!). As some argue, this can contribute to paranoid tendencies in some people. However, it is my opinion that apocalyptic thinking is additional, rather than primary, to the fundamentalist rationale. An activist faith requires things to be happening; and if the domain of this world is thwarting fundamentalist advance, then the heavenly realm can provide a substitute domain for religious (even militarist) ultimate victory. Excessively apocalyptic readings of the daily news and the Bible can undoubtedly produce some strange obsessions and flight from reality, but this often signifies that a local movement is "running out of steam," and is seeking a less resistant (and non-falsifiable) horizon of activity. Overemphasis on apocalypse can indeed be dangerous if combined with authoritarian leadership ruling a closed subworld. Waco is a tragic example of the mishandling of an apocalyptic cult. Among Christian fundamentalists, the underlying motive for apocalyptic focus is to "hurry" God's purposes (and ultimate victory). Apocalyptic focus is likely to fade when individuals can find more reality oriented horizons for their spiritual growth.

The global rise in Fundamentalism has launched over a thousand studies. Christian fundamentalists have been investigated by psychologists for a range of pathologies. Many researchers, flabbergasted by the continuing rise of Fundamentalism, begin with the assumption that there must be something wrong with Fundamentalists; they must be mad, bad, or stupid. It is common for researchers to expect that Fundamentalists are deficient cognitively, morally, politically, psychologically. As research has progressed, many of these assumptions have been qualified.

A stereotyped image of a Fundamentalist does share some surface qualities with the authoritarian personality defined as having very high regard for and tendency to acquiesce to authority, a rigidity in thinking, and a preference for clear structure and for conventional values. Yet, when Batson and Ventis (1982) reexamined the authoritarian literature, they found that when the I-E (intrinsic–extrinsic) dimension was accounted for, the correlations between intrinsically religious individuals and authoritarianism become negligible. In other words, Fundamentalists who are *intrinsically* religious (where religious faith is an end in itself, rather than a *means* to an end) are not prone toward authoritarianism. Fundamentalism was negatively correlated with racism, but positively correlated with prejudice against women, homosexuals, and communists. The idea that prejudice is personality-based among Fundamentalists has been refined to a correlation between aspects of the belief system and specific intolerances.

EPISTEMOLOGICAL TOOLS ACKNOWLEDGED AND SUPPORTED BY THE FAITH

Far from being irrational in their approach to religion, Fundamentalists display a preference for hard facts and proper techniques. Even though many U.S. Fundamentalists espouse creationism (which may, or may not, involve a worked out opposition to evolution), fundamentalists are not anti-science. Barr (1981) notes how Christian fundamentalism stresses the material–physical accuracy of the Bible and how it takes its method from a Newtonian model of natural science. In the United Kingdom, physics, chemistry, and engineering university departments are awash with Christians (including some with Fundamentalist tendencies). Somewhat fewer are found among departments of the biological sciences, and fewer still in the social sciences.

Philosophically, fundamentalism challenges the notion of truth as the outcome of social and cultural conditions. Fundamentalism regards truth as unchanging. There is a strong conviction that "the Truth is out there," and it must be defended. Truth can be known as an object in the material world, and for the Fundamentalist, religious truth needs to be "as good as" (thus similar to) scientific truth. Having this kind of truth produces a sense of confidence from which Fundamentalists are loathe to be parted.

A certain perceptual style is in evidence. In the author's research on the moral reasoning of Fundamentalists and non-Fundamentalists (Savage 1998, 2002), it was found that Fundamentalists tended to represent the moral problem focusing on the person, action, or issue, in and of themselves, apart from the social context, similar to the way the "figure" of a picture is focused on, ignoring the background. This figure perspective includes the tendency to form attributions to the person rather than to the situation (Ross, 1977). The figure perspective also includes seeing actions and issues in and of themselves, apart from the social context. The contrasting ground perspective preferred by non-Fundamentalists emphasizes the person, action, or issue in relationship with others or embedded within a wider social context, similar to the way one looks at the background of a picture.

Thus Fundamentalists have a tendency to think that people have a great deal of agency. The social constraints on persons, actions, and issues tend to be overlooked. Although a fair amount of research indicates that Fundamentalism tends to be punitive, the punitive solutions to moral dilemmas chosen by Fundamentalists result more from this figure perceptual style, seeing persons, actions, and issues as things in and of themselves, apart from the social context, rather than from a desire to punish others. Underlying this figure perceptual style is an empiricist philosophic stance: Things are as they appear because one's senses provide a direct, veridical grasp on reality. Harris (1998) argues that this epistemology informs Christian fundamentalism in a diffuse, background way. It is not focal knowledge with most Fundamentalists, but rather represents the substratum upon which a theory of literal scriptural inerrancy could most easily be built. Thus, Fundamentalism can be considered "a-psychological" in that the mediating processes of selection, interpretation, or emotional bias are ignored.

For the strict Fundamentalist, objective truth is preferred, and this is what the Bible is considered to be: Scripture is considered to be divinely inspired (the words, not just the meanings, are inspired). The Bible is understood to contain everything people need to know for salvation, and for living the Christian life; it is an infallible guide to moral choices. Although Christians believe that prayer involves a two-way communication between God and humans, for the Fundamentalist, Scripture is the most trustworthy channel for God's *personal* word to individuals. Charismatics and Pentecostalists are open to God's communication through vision, dreams, prophesy, and intuitions. Many Fundamentalists feel this is too subjective.

To summarize this section, Fundamentalists' relationship with science is somewhat paradoxic. A Newtonian model of science has shaped the Fundamentalist view of truth more than perhaps many realize. A publicly antiscience stance is becoming rare, but biblical authority always supersedes scientific authority, and if that entails denying evolution, so be it.

THE THEORY OF NORMAL PERSONALITY INHERENT IN THE FAITH

To be normal is to be moral; to be moral means to make the correct choice, to choose righteousness rather than sin, to choose Christ rather than darkness. All of human history and each individual's life leads up to one key event: conversion.

St. Paul's Damascus road experience serves as a prototype for conversion. Every fundamentalist ideally has his or her own "Damascus road" experience in which conversion occurs suddenly, is an emotional experience, and is felt to be caused by external forces acting on a passive recipient, and is understood to be a once-off life changing event (Richardson, 1985).

Traditional evangelistic campaigns seek to elicit this kind of experience. "Before and after" contrasts are expected in testimonies of Fundamentalists' conversion. It is important to have a born again experience that can be tied down to a specific point in time. For many, this provides a helpful way to jump start a new beginning. Whatever acts one has committed before conversion are forgiven. The past is washed clean. The newly converted Christian is now a new creation in Christ.

The experience of new life often is profound. Conversion is often accompanied by a leap in self-esteem; central to Christian teaching is that the believer is esteemed by God as a son or daughter, and accepted into the body of fellow believers. It is believed (and often experienced) that the power of sin is broken. The Christian is free, from henceforth, to choose acts of righteousness, obedience, love, mercy, and kindness. In Latin America, there is sociologic evidence of Fundamentalists' "betterment" in every sphere of life (reduction in domestic violence, alcoholism, marriage breakdown, along with improvements in education and standard of living).

Faithful fundamentalist Christians are expected to live sober lives, and to donate money (e.g., a "tithe," 10% of the income) to church and charitable causes. Fundamentalists aspire to having a happy marriage and family, and to live as responsible citizens. However, moral debate tends to be focused on the individual, rather than social issues; there is little emphasis on wider issues such as poverty or social inequality. This emphasis on rational individualism has great resonance with U.S. culture. Indeed, some elements in fundamentalist Christianity (biblicism, patriotism, respect for law, order and free markets) are culturally normative in the United States, despite its otherwise countercultural appearances.

To fall short of the new life in Christ is to sin; but all is not lost. Sin is to be confessed (to God in prayer, more often than to a human intermediary), and Scripture promises that God's forgiveness, through Christ, flows freely. A new beginning is again possible. There is a strong emphasis on grace (God's freely bestowed favor and forgiveness). At the same time, believers are exhorted to live in a manner worthy of their calling, entailing an exercise of choice. Any substance or method that may alter consciousness is to be shunned. Although not necessarily teetotal, most Fundamentalists do not indulge in drink or drugs.

Dancing, and other activities that stir up the lusts of the flesh are avoided. Even so, Fundamentalists are not overly hung up on the body; bodies are simply ignored. Fundamentalists are committed to a strict sexual morality (sex is to be celebrated only in the context of heterosexual Christian marriage), but they are not sex-haters. Most would agree that the spiritual sins, such as pride, rebellion, witchcraft, or doubt, are more serious in God's eyes than the sins of the flesh. The ultimate sin is to deconvert, to lose one's faith. There can be great anxiety about the "unforgivable sin," made worse by the fact that many people are not too sure what that might mean! (Biblical commentators suggest that the gospel references to the "unforgivable sin" pertain to a persistence in calling the activity of the Holy Spirit as "devilish." To persist in this is to so confuse light with darkness as to close the door on the possibility of repentance. Clinicians can assure anxious clients that this "unforgiven" condition is not accompanied by worry over one's spiritual state.)

Thus, to be "normal" is to be on a journey from darkness toward light, from sin to righteousness, from self-centeredness toward God. The rigid contours of the fundamentalist orientation can provide people with the firm leverage they need to change their lives. For many, the payoff can be well worth the price of having to conform to an inflexible, demanding religion.

THEORY OF CHANGE INHERENT IN THE FAITH

Jesus preached "Repent, for the kingdom of heaven is at hand," and repentance, a change of heart and mind, a turning toward God, is understood to be the main vehicle for human change. It is understood that the Holy Spirit instigates and undergirds this process, but that humans must consciously cooperate. In practice, Fundamentalists understand repentance as a turning away from specific actions (acts that contravene the Ten Commandments or actions that are incompatible with the Christian faith: indulging the flesh, anger, revenge, swearing, lust, jealousy, and dishonesty). This working definition of sin as actions, rather than sin as an orientation or condition of separation from God, others and ourselves (which is actually closer to the New Testament understanding of sin), produces an emphasis on doing rather than being. Failures to do the right thing produce a cycle of trying, failing, feeling guilty, repenting, *ad infinitum*. The effort to be righteous can produce a judgmental attitude toward others; more often it produces a harsh attitude toward the self. Research indicates that the sense of well-being, increased self-esteem, and freedom from depression and anxiety that conversion often brings about can take a downturn as the Christian life becomes harder to live out over time (Loewenthal, 1996).

An aspect of repentance is the renewing of the mind with Christian truth, and the reading of Scripture is the main resource for this practice. A daily quiet time that includes the reading of Scripture is considered vital. There is a useful concordance between the Christian concept of the renewing of the mind and cognitive therapy. Clinicians can harness this concordance and use higher-order principles, such as compassion and truth, to encourage fundamentalist clients to bring into conscious awareness their own cognitive style, as this will act as a filter to their perception of God. As distorted cognitions are uncovered, the client has begun to move beyond the a-psychological, empiricist implications of Fundamentalism. From this place, it then might be easier for Fundamentalists to begin to uncover memories and associated emotions.

Another vehicle for change is seen in the practice of being filled with the Holy Spirit. The author has argued elsewhere (Mayo, Savage, & Collins, 2005) that many Christians, including Fundamentalists, rely on an implicit "container" model of the person. The Christian person is an earthly container that houses the Spirit of God. Container-like metaphors describing the relationship between God and humans abound in Scripture ("We have this treasure in earthen vessels . . . ," 2 Corinthians 4:7). Historically, this metaphor underwent a later twist when early Christian thinking incorporated the dualism of neo-Platonism. Neo-platonic philosophies presented the material stuff of the universe as not only different from the spiritual stuff, but inferior, and in some quarters, inherently evil. For the Fundamentalist, thinking about the human person as an earthly, material container filled with God's Spirit in practice means that the inferior "container" is to be ignored, as all hope for betterment is pinned on the "filler." Thus, the metaphor implies that the container is, and should be, inert. Passivity in the face of life's problems can result.

The container model also implies hierarchy, and this is further echoed in cartesian body/mind dualism. The mind, and, thus, all those who have access to the things of the mind, are accorded greater value. Fundamentalism clearly elevates rational belief over emotions and subjective experience. The elevated status of White, rational, cerebral men within fundamentalism (as well as the wider church) is an unquestioned social norm. Features of the earthly container such as emotions or bodily needs should be ignored; they are "subjective."

The person as container encourages focus on what "substances" fill the containers. There is great concern among Fundamentalists over what kinds of ideas, images, or conversation fill the containers. The container model of person also tends to engender an expectation for instant, almost magical, solutions to life's problems. Saying the right prayer or believing the right thing is crucial in the hope that the desired result will "happen by faith," delivered directly to the container, without the need for mediating processes.

THEORY OF DEVELOPMENT INHERENT IN THE FAITH

Although the conversion experience, with its before and after contrasts, dominates the idea of human development, there is an understanding that children develop physically, mentally, and spiritually. Adults too should develop, particularly in relation to the faith: "When I was a child, I talked like a child, I reasoned like a child. When I became a man, I put childish ways behind me" (1 Corinthians 13:11).

Genetic influences are rarely incorporated, if ever, into fundamentalist teaching on human development, beyond the obvious processes of child development. Early experience in shaping development often is not considered; being born again is believed to supersede previous experience. As argued, the container model of person focuses on the "substances" that go into the container (right thoughts, right groups of people, right teaching) as crucial for development. There is widespread anxiety about cultural influences taking people away from the faith, often resulting in a fortress mentality.

For Fundamentalists, the concept of self-actualization requires some redefining. Fundamentalists are suspicious about anything to do with the self. Self is often equated with sin (as in selfishness or self-centeredness). Fundamentalist advice about the self is to ignore it ("JOY: Jesus first, Others second, Yourself last"). Obedience to God's will and His commands are the priority. Nevertheless, a number of heroes of the faith have observed, almost with surprise, that in following Christ they have been led on a path that entails becoming all that they are; service becomes the path of freedom. An understanding of self-actualization as entailing development of a person's "signature strengths" can resonate with Fundamentalists' belief in the virtue of developing one's unique God-given talents and attributes *in order to serve the Kingdom*. Self-actualization in the jungian sense may be difficult for Fundamentalists (at least in the early stages of therapy), but self-actualization recast in terms of Seligman's (2002) "authentic happiness" has a greater concordance. Fundamentalists would be motivated to identify the very best in themselves, as gifts from God, so that they can work for the Kingdom, improve the world, and attain authentic happiness.

THEORY OF PSYCHOLOGICAL HEALTH AND PATHOLOGY INHERENT IN THE FAITH

There are resources within this orientation that contribute to health. The born again fundamentalist Christian is brought into relationship with God through Christ, and is accepted, forgiven, and loved. The believer is brought into fellowship with like-minded others. There are clear ethical norms and rules for behavior. Each believer is encouraged to discover his or her own unique calling ("God loves you and has a plan for your life"). Existential anxieties are placed within a superordinate, eternal framework.

The converse of the preceding entails an understanding of pathology. To be lost, in darkness, in sin, "away from fellowship," confused, or doubting describes the understanding of pathology. Even common psychological problems such as depression are understood as involving spiritual darkness. The inference is that a spiritual solution (e.g., more prayer or more faith) is both necessary and sufficient.

Some circles consider demon possession to result from extreme exposure to darkness and sin. Dabbling in the occult is considered by some to risk demon possession (as would addictions and persistent "perverse" behavior). The limitations of the container model of person come to the fore here; the only answer to the extremes of mental distress is to get the bad, evil substances out of the container through exorcism or deliverance. The potential to misinterpret symptoms of mental illness as demon possession, and the dire consequences of this mistake, have been catalogued elsewhere (Howard, 1997). In Fundamentalism, there is little worked out understanding of mental illness beyond spiritual darkness as the logical extension of the container model of person.

Although Fundamentalists may appear extremely naive in terms of their understanding of mental illness, they are not naive in terms of recognizing evil as a reality that extends beyond the individual and that can take on a life of its own. In Charismatic and Pentecostal circles, there is a budding psychological understanding termed "intergeneration sin." Here, the religious beliefs considered wrong (e.g., witchcraft, Freemasonry) and the unrighteous actions of parents and other relatives are understood to have a direct negative impact on the believer. Hints of psychodynamic theory can be detected here, and these could be drawn out fruitfully in the context of therapy. However, the concept of intergenerational sin tends to be cast in the container model whereby the evil influences of the previous generation need to be cast out by prayer alone. The concept of intergenerational sin could be harnessed by mental health practitioners by stressing that prayer is like a workshop in which the client wrestles with reactions, perceptions, and desires, in order to bring them into God's perspective of love and truth. This more dynamic understanding of prayer as a workshop (rather than as an incantation) could help to ameliorate Fundamentalists' expectation of instant solutions to deeply ingrained problems.

The Fundamentalist orientation can provide for some the basis of a healthy, productive life; for others, the expectation of new life in Christ provides an unattainable standard that becomes a harsh taskmaster. The failure to experience the promised land can produce great pain. Because the orientation purports to provide all the needed resources, there is a sense of shame or failure in having to get outside help from professionals when it does not all work according to plan. It can feel like backsliding to turn to psychologists. A few may even fear that psychology itself is of the devil because it appears to not be in the Bible.

COMMON MORAL ISSUES

Sensitive therapeutic support needs to take into account Fundamentalists' moral givens, especially if these are at odds with clinician's own moral stance. For Fundamentalists, sex before marriage is not condoned, and marital faithfulness is paramount. Marriage is highly esteemed; it is expected that every reasonable effort should be made to save a troubled marriage. However, the tacit assumption that wives should silently endure abuse is no longer the norm. Abortion is condemned; the sacred quality of a human life is at stake, and Fundamentalists are loathe to play God; however, other means of birth control are accepted.

Homosexuality is not considered acceptable, yet there is little in the orientation apart from repentance and prayer to help those struggling with issues of sexuality. A terrible burden of guilt can be incurred when sexual orientation does not respond to will power. Although it is not helpful to challenge a client's *moral* stance on homosexuality, Fundamentalists are not antiscience, and a discussion of the genetic markers for homosexuality, and research showing the extremely modest success of efforts toward changing sexual orientation is useful. A libertine solution is not helpful; rather, it is more beneficial for Fundamentalists to find a way to live responsibly with their homosexuality. Some fundamentalist clients may wish to try to change their sexual orientation, and they will need support while they explore this.

Although the required submission of women may mean that issues of dependence, codependence, anger, and inferiority are simmering for women, feminist discourse is likely to be dismissed. Therapists and clinicians might encourage women to study the gospels and examine how Jesus treated women in the context of the patriarchal culture of his day. What seeds of emancipation and empowerment are evident in the gospels? Again, a libertine solution is not acceptable; rather, it is more helpful to encourage female fundamentalist clients to find ways of achieving emancipation responsibly (within the existing marriage, if at all possible).

The commandment to "honor your mother and father," which Fundamentalists take literally, may be misconstrued to enforce the denial of childhood abuse. Subjective guilt is likely to be incurred when childhood experiences show a client's parents in an extremely negative light. Clinicians can reassure clients that the journey toward forgiving abusers begins (not ends) with bringing the experience of abuse to light.

In this context, it is important to disentangle notions of Christian forgiveness from condoning, minimizing, or tolerating abuse. Appealing to Fundamentalists' sense of justice helps motivate the exposure of wrongs suffered. It is helpful to draw upon research concerning the psychological stages of forgiveness. Forgiveness needs to be understood as a potentially lengthy process involving various phases such as the following:

1. The uncovering phase, in which the reality of the offense and its perhaps permanent consequences are faced; the denial, hurt, shame, and anger uncovered
2. The decision phase, in which forgiveness as a *possibility* is explored, even if for simply pragmatic reasons—the old strategies are no longer working—culminating in a decision to forgive
3. The work phase, in which strategies such as reframing the offender, developing empathy, or role-taking as a future "forgiver" are employed to facilitate forgiveness
4. The deepening phase, in which deeper meaning, support from others, and some emotional release occurs through the process of working through the suffering (Enright & North, 1998)

Understanding the work involved in the journey of forgiveness helps steer the fundamentalist client away from a desire for instant solutions; at the same time forgiveness as a therapeutic goal harnesses the cooperation of the fundamentalist client, and perhaps overcomes resistance to unveil past emotions and experiences.

Wherever issues of grave sin are involved (whether it is sin committed against the client, or real or imagined sins committed by the client), divine forgiveness is a key resource. The client can be encouraged to take a two-pronged approach: (a) prayer (perhaps with the client's minister) to deal with the need for God's forgiveness for self or other and (b) therapy to help the client's journey toward forgiving self and others.

COMMON CLINICAL ISSUES

Fundamentalists' suspicion of any authority outside of the fundamentalist interpretation of the Bible is a serious issue in clinical practice. Any direct attack on Fundamentalists' meta-belief (inerrancy of Scripture) will be met with a vigorous closed response (Savage, 1998). Clinicians and therapists are advised *not* to adopt such a strategy; it simply entrenches defensive tendencies, and usually results in the fundamentalist client terminating the relationship. A more indirect approach to fostering greater elasticity in the organization of the belief system is possible. The process of therapy or counseling itself erodes the a-psychological assumptions implicit in Fundamentalism.

Help from mental health professionals is likely to be considered only after every other source of help within the Fundamentalist orientation has been exhausted. A person who seeks help for himself or herself probably has sifted through this, but a referred person may be more resistant. A fundamentalist client nearly always prefers the mental health professional to profess the Christian faith (and believe the Bible). If this is not the case, the mental health professional needs to assure their fundamentalist clients that their religious faith is respected, and that the goal of the therapy accords with a truth-seeking life.

As discussed, fundamentalism provides an entree, more easily, to behavior-focused interventions. On the surface, choosing moral behavior resonates more easily with behaviorist approaches (or cognitive behavioral therapy), rather than with psychotherapeutic approaches. There may be initial resistance to psychotherapy because it is understood that past experiences have been "covered" or "washed away" through Christ's atonement. Approaching past traumatic events with the goal of forgiveness may provide some clients with a more acceptable motivation to unveil the past.

Hypnosis or Eastern meditation practices (e.g., yoga) are eschewed. Some fundamentalist clients feel uneasy taking medication for depression. Science is an ally here; the clinician can help the client by providing a clear explanation concerning how the medication interacts with brain chemistry. "Objective" facts (science and medicine) can help to assuage the fear of altered mental states.

Another clinical issue concerns the highly negative press that Fundamentalists regularly attract. Mental health professionals need to examine their own attitudes toward fundamentalist clients, make an effort to sift through what is adaptive from what is maladaptive, and distinguish between the normal and the abnormal within Fundamentalism. For example, Fundamentalists routinely talk about God guiding and speaking to them. This is accepted parlance for a sense of personal relevance that can come from Scripture or a sermon; it does not necessary indicate a psychotic episode.

Although there is a widespread assumption that Fundamentalism corresponds with psychopathology, meta-studies based on previous research indicates that this is not the case as long as social class is held constant, and the items are religiously neutral (Wulff, 1997). Batson, Schoenrade, and Ventis (1993) reviewed the mental health and religion literature accounting for the different religious orientations (intrinsic, extrinsic, and Quest). Their review reported that intrinsically religious people (among whom Fundamentalists number) showed high levels of purpose of life, and low levels of depression and various anxieties. In other studies, Fundamentalists of different religions are found to share greater optimism (Sethi & Seligman, 1993, 1994) and greater marital happiness (Hansen, 1992), although their families may not share such adaptive functioning in other areas (e.g., emotional openness) (Denton & Denton, 1992). Fundamentalists do not suffer from the negative self-esteem that may be associated with an emphasis on sin, guilt, and judgment (Hood, 1992). However, prevalence does not necessarily match what is encountered by clinicians among fundamentalist clients; Fundamentalism, although adaptive for some, can intertwine unhelpfully with any disorder.

A "religious mental health examination" may help to provide insight concerning the function the fundamentalist orientation is performing in the client's life. Draper, Meyer, Perzen, and Samuelson (1965) provide guidelines. Sample questions follow:

1. What is the client's earliest memories of religious experiences?
2. What are the client's favorite Bible verses or characters, and why are they important to him or her?
3. What is the worst sin the client could commit?

4. What does prayer mean to the client?
5. What does the client pray about?
6. What would one ask for if God would grant any three wishes?

These questions are all good projective techniques. Oates (1978) says that the responses to these questions could be categorized into the following:

1. Conventional responses: Responses that are expected within the orientation
2. Personal responses: Responses indicating where the client is appropriating the meaning of a religious idea for himself or herself
3. Bizarre responses: For example, a minister who had raped his wife while dating her denied it was a sin or that she might resent him because he had later married her. (recounted in Powell, Gladstone, & Meyer, 1991).

The religious mental health status examination is one way of seeking to understand when the fundamentalist belief system is functioning as an escape from reality, or as a basis for taking responsibility and acting in love.

It is important also for clinicians to distinguish between those for whom Fundamentalism is currently providing a sacred canopy that is adaptive (or partially adaptive) from those for whom Fundamentalism has become maladaptive. When a Fundamentalist feels he or she has outgrown Fundamentalism, the process of *leaving* Fundamentalism is often destabilizing. Yao (1985) has dealt with dozens of people exiting Fundamentalism who have experienced extreme guilt, confusion, and loss of a valued social group. Leavers may feel they are backsliders, or even apostates (people who have renounced the faith). When relationships with the Fundamentalist church breaks down, a person's entire world view can be dismantled. This can contribute to depression, anxiety, and other clinical disorders.

Clinical work with people exiting Christian fundamentalist communities indicates excessive rumination and dwelling on past experience of Fundamentalism. However, there were fewer psychotic indicators among the fundamentalist group in comparison with those exiting religious communities involving consciousness-altering methods (e.g., drug taking or chanting). Yet a person who exits Fundamentalism does so devoid of the anchoring belief system that once made sense of life. Total loss of Christian faith may ensue in some cases, but for others, exiting Fundamentalism can be part of ongoing religious development.

Whether a person leaves or remains within Fundamentalism, religious development is normal and desirable. However, James Fowler's seminal model of religious development needs careful handling to be helpful to Fundamentalists. The teleological nature of Fowler's stage wise framework suggests that Stage 3 synthetic–conventional faith, in which a fundamentalist orientation is thought to reside, is best outgrown, and that believers should move on to more critical, liberal orientations of Stages 4, 5, or 6. It may be more helpful for the fundamentalist client to think of religious development as an *enlargement* of faith, rather than a dismissive moving on. What has been beneficial can be retained and augmented. To acknowledge that one's current organization of faith is inadequate for the present challenges does not need to entail a devaluing of the former. Nevertheless, the transitional phase is unsettling. Religious development inescapably involves disengagement (moving away from what held life together), dis-identifying with the social group, disenchantment, and disorientation. Therapy on its own may not be sufficiently religiously informed to enable a client to enlarge or reformulate his or her religious beliefs; therefore, clients should be encouraged to seek support from ministers experienced in spiritual direction or religious development. The therapist, too, may benefit from a relationship with a local minister experienced in issues of religious development.

Clinicians can encourage the fundamentalist client to draw on the strength imparted by the fundamentalist orientation to risk the onward journey of religious development. The Christian faith is itself a paradox and a journey; Christ is both fully human and fully divine; Christians live in the Now and the Not Yet. The fundamentalist client does have access to key resources that can fuel the onward journey: forgiveness, compassion, and a love of truth.

REFERENCES

Barr, J. (1981). *Fundamentalism* (2nd ed.). London: SCM Press.

Batson, C. D., & Ventis, W. L. (1982). *The religious experience.* Oxford, UK: Oxford University Press.

Batson, C. D., Schoenrade, P., & Ventis, W. (1993). *Religion and the individual: A social psychological perspective.* New York: Oxford University Press.

Denton R. T., & Denton, M. J. (1992). Therapist's ratings of fundamentalist and non-fundamentalist families in therapy: An empirical comparison. *Family Process, 31,* 175–185.

Draper, E., Meyer, G., Perzen, Z., & Samuelson, G. (1965). On the diagnostic value of religious ideation. *Archives of General Psychiatry, 13,* 202–207.

Enright, R., & North, J. (Eds). (1998). *Exploring forgiveness.* Madison, WI: University of Wisconsin Press.

Fowler, J. W. (1981). *Stages of faith: The psychology of human development and the quest for meaning.* San Francisco: Harper & Row.

Hanson, R. A. (1991). The development of moral reasoning: Some observations about Christian fundamentalism. *Journal of Psychology and Theology, 19(3),* 249–256.

Harris, H. (1998). *Fundamentalism and evangelicals.* Oxford, UK: Clarendon Press.

Hood, R. W. (1992). Sin and guilt in faith traditions: Issues for self-esteem. In J. F. Schumaker (Ed.). *Religion and mental health* (pp. 110–121). London: Oxford University Press.

Howard, R. (1997). *Charismania: When Christian fundamentalism goes wrong.* London: Mowbray.

Kirkpatrick, L. A., Hood, R. W., & Hartz, G. (1991). Fundamentalist religion in terms of Rokeach's theory of the open and closed mind: New perspective on some old ideas. *Research in the Scientific Study of Religion, 3,* 157–179.

Loewenthal, K. M. (1996). *Mental health and religion.* London: Chapman & Hall.

Marty, M. E. P., & Appleby, R. S. (1992). *The glory and the power.* Boston: Beacon Press.

Mayo, B., Savage, S., & Collins, S. (2005). *Ambiguous Evangelism.* London: SPCK.

Oates, W. E. (1978). *The religious care of the psychotic patient.* Philadelphia: Westminster.

Percy, M. (1996). *Words, wonders and powers: Understanding contemporary Christian fundamentalism and revivalism.* London: SPCK.

Powell, J., Gladstone, J., & Meyer, R. (1991). Psychotherapy with the fundamentalist client. *Journal of Psychology and Theology, 19(4),* 344–353.

Richardson, J. (1985). The active vs. passive convert: Paradigm conflict in conversion/recruitment research. *Journal for the Scientific Study of Religion, 24,* 163–179.

Rokeach, M. (1960). *The open and closed mind.* New York: Basic Books.

Ross, L. (1977). The intuitive psychologist and his shortcomings: Distortions in the attribution process. In L. Berkowitz (Ed.). *Advances in experimental social psychology* (vol. 10, pp. 173–220). New York: Academic Press.

Savage, S. (1998). Fundamentalism and moral reasoning, Doctoral dissertation, University of Cambridge, 47-10521.

Savage, S. (2002). A psychology of fundamentalism: The search for inner failings. In M. Percy & I. Jones (Eds.). *Fundamentalism, church and society.* London: SPCK.

Seligman, M. E. P. (2002). *Authentic happiness: Using the new positive psychology to realize your potential for lasting fulfilment.* New York: Free Press.

Sethi, S., & Seligman, M. E. P. (1993). Optimism and Fundamentalism. *Psychological Science, 4,* 256–259.

Sethi, S., & Seligman, M.E.P. (1994). The hope of fundamentalists. *Psychological Science, 5,* 58.

Wulff, D. (1997). *Psychology of religion* (2nd ed.). New York: John Wiley & Sons.

Yao, R. (1985). *Fundamentalists anonymous: There is a way out.* New York: Luce Publications.

SECTION IV

The Church of Jesus Christ of Latter-Day Saints

Psychological Models Inherent in Doctrine and Practices of The Church of Jesus Christ of Latter-Day Saints

Dianne L. Nielsen, Daniel K. Judd, and Stevan Lars Nielsen

MEMBERSHIP AND ORGANIZATION

At the end of 2004, membership of the Church of Jesus Christ of Latter-day Saints[1] stood at 12,350,000 in 160 countries of North and South America, Asia, Europe, Africa, and the Pacific Rim (Watson, 2005). If the growth of the Church from births and conversions continues at current, exponential rates, membership will exceed 50,000,000 by 2050 (Stark, 1996). With headquarters in Salt Lake City, UT, the Church is led by

[1]The complete name of this religious institution, by official policy, is "The Church of Jesus Christ of Latter-Day Saints," called "the Church" (for convenience and brevity), in subsequent references within the same work. Members are often called "Mormons" or "Latter-day Saints;" labels readily understood and not offensive. However, the institutional policy regarding the title of the Church discourages the unofficial and incorrect titles, "The Mormon Church" or "The LDS Church."

This chapter is intended to be an accurate description of The Church of Jesus Christ of Latter-day Saints and its doctrines. However, it is neither an official statement of the Church nor of Brigham Young University, which is operated by the Church. Extensive official information about the Church is available at www.lds.org, where Gospel Principles, a detailed description of Church doctrine, is available for review and my be downloaded at no charge at: http://www.lds.org/gospellibrary/materials/gospel/Start%20Here_01.pdf

President Gordon B. Hinckley and two counselors, called the First Presidency, and by a Quorum of Twelve Apostles. Mormons believe the First Presidency fill the roles of Peter, James, and John, as presiding apostles, with the Quorum of Twelve serving as did Andrew, Philip, Thomas, Paul, and the other apostles called anciently by Jesus Christ.

Under the direction of this general leadership, local congregations, known as branches, wards, districts, and stakes, are directed by lay priests, called Bishops or Presidents, who are ordained, but not remunerated for their services. Leaders of local congregations serve temporarily, usually for a space of several years. Participating Latter-day Saints generally serve in a variety of voluntary congregational positions throughout their lives, teaching or organizing ministering activities for children, youth, and adults.

The Latter-day Saints have a strong proselyting tradition, with 51,000 full-time missionaries serving worldwide (Watson, 2005), most at their own expense. Most missionaries serve primarily to teach interested persons about church principles. Others serve primarily in humanitarian assignments, working to ameliorate conditions of poverty, disease, malnutrition, lack of educational opportunity, and other social ills. All missionaries are encouraged to give service to individuals and communities where they live.

BASIC BELIEFS AND PRACTICES

In common with many other religions, Mormons believe in God, in each individual's duty to serve God and others, in revelation and scripture inspired by God, and in the spiritual foundation and meaning of human existence. In common with other Christians, Mormons believe Christ is the Son of God and the Redeemer of humanity. The Church teaches that individuals have a duty to learn and obey God's commandments, serve others, and participate in prescribed ordinances. Latter-Day Saints believe that Christ's gracious atonement is necessary for salvation, because mortals are unable to save themselves from the effects of sin.

Deity

Mormons believe in a godhead that includes God the Eternal Father, Jesus Christ, His son, and the Holy Ghost. Unlike many Christians, Mormons believe that although members of the godhead are united in purpose, they are separate beings, and that the Father and Son have glorified corporeal bodies, whereas the Holy Ghost is a personage of spirit.

Premortality

Mormons believe that humans lived with God as spirit beings before their mortal birth and even before the creation of the earth. Mormons believe in a literal adversary and tempter, Satan, who with his followers, attempts to lead humans away from God's plan and enslave them. According to the Latter-day Saint perspective, Satan and his followers were similar to other prehuman spirit beings in the premortal existence, but fell because they rebelled against God's plan.

Restoration

In common with Protestants, Latter-day Saints believe that authority from Christ's original church was lost. Unlike most Protestants, however, Mormons trace the authority of their religion to a restoration rather than a reformation. Latter-day Saints believe this restoration occurred in the early 19th century through divine revelation to Joseph Smith, Jr. (1805–1844), accepted by believers as a prophet. Joseph Smith, Mormons believe, received priesthood authority through divinely appointed ordination by Peter, James, and John, acting under the direction of Jesus Christ.

Scripture

In common with many other religions, Mormons accept and study the Old and New Testaments as revealed Scripture. Unlike other religions, the Church accepts three additional scriptural canons: the Book of Mormon,[2] the Doctrine and Covenants of the Church of Jesus Christ of Latter-day Saints,[3] and the Pearl of Great Price.[4] The Book of Mormon is believed to be an account of God's dealings with people who lived anciently in the Americas, and who were visited by Christ after his resurrection. The Doctrine and Covenants (D&C) is a compilation of instructions and doctrines from the early days of the Church (1823–1847) recorded by Joseph Smith. A few sections are more recent (1890, 1918, and 1978) and were recorded by later presidents of the church, who are also considered prophets by Mormon adherents. The Pearl of Great Price is a selection of materials touching significant aspects of the faith and doctrines of the Church, first published in 1851. Because these works are canonized sources, accepted by believers as doctrinally pure, the authors of this chapter have sometimes cited passages from them to illustrate the Latter-day Saint belief system.

[2]The Book of Mormon is available in its entirety at: http://scriptures.lds.org/bm/contents
[3]The Doctrine and Covenants is also available at http://scriptures.lds.org/dc/contents
[4]The Pearl of Great Price is also available at: http://scriptures.lds.org/pgp/contents

Ongoing Revelation

Joseph Smith wrote, "We believe all that God has revealed, all that He does now reveal, and we believe that He will yet reveal many great and important things pertaining to the Kingdom of God" (Ninth Article of Faith from the Pearl of Great Price), describing the Mormon belief in continuing revelation. Several examples of major changes, accepted by believing Mormons as revelations, have occurred in the 175 years since the church's organization. In the 19th century, Mormons practiced polygamy, which was ended by official declaration, viewed as revelation, in 1890 (D&C: Official Declaration 1). In the 20th century, a practice of racial distinction for priesthood ordination was ended (D&C: Official Declaration 2). During the 21st century, a major change in temple construction practice has occurred. These alterations in organization or practice are seen by Latter-day Saints as examples of God's continuing instruction to the Church, adapting doctrine or practice to present conditions.

Family

Latter-day Saint followers accept as doctrine a 1995 publication entitled, "The Family: A Proclamation to the World" by the Church's First Presidency and Quorum of Twelve Apostles. The Proclamation (included as an Appendix) summarizes principles and admonitions about families. This document states that: Individuals are commanded by God to marry, have children, provide for them, and teach them in loving, stable families; happiness in family life is most likely when founded on principles taught by Christ; the family is the most basic unit of society, which individuals and governments should protect and promote; and finally, disintegration of the family unit imperils society.

The Proclamation states that the ideal human family is modeled after God's relationship with humankind. According to Mormon doctrine, human beings are the offspring of heavenly parents. Mothers and fathers, like heavenly parents, are inherently equal partners. Gender is an eternal characteristic, present in the premortal existence and continuing after death. The Proclamation on the Family states that family relationships may be continued after death through sealing ordinances performed by priests with the proper authority.

History

Like many devout believers throughout history, early Mormons were persecuted for their beliefs, moving repeatedly through regions of New York, Pennsylvania, Ohio, Missouri, and Illinois seeking greater tolerance. The state of Missouri issued an official order of proscription against members of the Church, forcing exodus to Illinois. Persecutions continued in Illinois, culminating in the murder of Joseph Smith in June 1844. Joseph Smith was killed by a mob in Carthage Jail, IL, after surrendering himself to official custody. When persecution of the Church continued, the main body of Latter-day Saints left the United States in 1846. Groups of Mormons traveled by foot and ox-drawn wagons to frontier regions that now comprise Utah, parts of Idaho, Arizona, Nevada, and Mexico. As many as 5,000 of the Church's 70,000 members died during this migration across wilderness territory, a 7% mortality rate two to three times greater than expected mortality for the time (Black, 1998). Institutional memory continues for hardships endured during this time. Even outside of the United States, many congregations commemorate the arrival of the first Mormon settlers in the Salt Lake Valley on July 24, 1947. July 24th is a state holiday in Utah, where 70% of the population are Mormons.

Although the majority of Church members emigrated, a smaller group of Latter-day Saints remained in Illinois, forming the Reorganized Church of Jesus Christ of Latter-Day Saints, which has recently taken the name Community of Christ. These two faiths share a common early history, but are separate religions with many diverging doctrines. This chapter does not present doctrines of the Community of Christ.

PSYCHOLOGY IN MORMONISM

Epistemological Tools

Sources of Knowledge

Latter-day Saints view learning and knowledge as highly desirable, and members are encouraged to seek truth energetically. Joseph Smith recorded that truth is "knowledge of things as they are, and as they were, and as they are to come" (D&C 93:24), further explaining that "the glory of God is intelligence, or in other words, light and truth" (D&C 93:36). Believers are encouraged to seek "out of the best books, words of wisdom; seek learning, even by study and also by faith" (D&C 88:118). Knowledge is not delineated into distinct realms of natural versus supernatural or temporal versus eternal. A member of the Quorum of the Twelve wrote:

> The Church of Jesus Christ of Latter-day Saints accepts newly revealed truth, whether it comes through direct revelation or from study and research. We deny the common conception of reality that distinguishes radically between the natural and the supernatural, between the temporal and the eternal, between the sacred and the secular. For us, there

is no order of reality that is utterly different in character from the world of which we are a part, that is separated from us by an impassable gulf. We do not separate our daily mundane tasks and interests from the meaning and substance of religion. We recognize the spiritual in all phases and aspects of living and realize that this life is an important part of eternal life. We aspire to the best of which we are intrinsically capable and will think our thoughts, fashion our ideals, and pursue every task firm in the faith that in a very real sense we are living in the presence of God here and now (Brown, 1965, p. 18).

Latter-day Saints believe that truth may come by revelation, and also through academic study and scientific research. Mormons believe that God has revealed truth throughout history through both secular and religious sources. In 1978, the First Presidency wrote:

The great religious leaders of the world such as Mohammed, Confucius, and the Reformers, as well as philosophers including Socrates, Plato, and others, received a portion of God's light. Moral truths were given to them by God to enlighten whole nations and to bring a higher level of understanding to individuals. The Hebrew prophets prepared the way for the coming of Jesus Christ, the promised Messiah, who should provide salvation for all mankind who believed in the gospel. Consistent with these truths, we believe that God has given and will give to all peoples sufficient knowledge to help them on their way to eternal salvation, either in this life or in the life to come (Kimball, Tanner, & Romney, 1978).

In the 19th century, Brigham Young, second President of the Church, wrote:

Whether a truth be found with . . . the Universalists, or the Church of Rome, or the Methodists, the Church of England, the Presbyterians, the Baptists, the Quakers, the Shakers, or any other of the various and numerous different sects and parties, all of whom have more or less truth, it is the business of the Elders of this Church (Jesus, their elder brother, being at their head), to gather up all the truths in the world pertaining to life and salvation, to the Gospel we preach, to mechanisms of every kind, to the sciences, and to philosophy, wherever it may be found in every nation, kindred, tongue and people, and bring it to Zion (quoted in Widtsoe, 1941, p. 248).

Church theology holds, thus, an *inclusive* view of truth but an *exclusive* view of priesthood authority.

Personal Revelation

Church theology emphasizes that a personal, spiritual witness of truth is essential to salvation. The first worship service of each month is a "fast and testimony meeting" during which, following a day of fasting and prayer, members are invited to give their testimony; that is, to declare their personal, spiritual witness of truth as they understand it. Spiritual experimentation is viewed as necessary for obtaining a spiritual witness.

Latter-day Saints believe that patterns of spiritual experimentation are evident in the Old and New Testaments, for example, when God challenged Israel to pay tithing, saying, ". . . prove me now herewith, saith the Lord of hosts, if I will not open you the windows of heaven, and pour you out a blessing. . . ." (Malachi 3:10). Another challenge to experimentation appears in Christ's statement, "My doctrine is not mine, but his that sent me. If any man will do his will, he shall know of the doctrine, whether it be of God or whether I speak of myself" (John 7:17).

Spiritual experimentation is also described in the Book of Mormon, which ends with this explicit spiritual challenge:

> And when ye shall receive these things [the Book of Mormon], I would exhort you that ye would ask God, the Eternal Father, in the name of Christ, if these things are not true; and if ye shall ask with a sincere heart, with real intent, having faith in Christ, he will manifest the truth of it unto you, by the power of the Holy Ghost. And by the power of the Holy Ghost ye may know the truth of all things (Moroni 10:4, 5).

Latter-day Saints are encouraged to use a spiritual–experimental approach in seeking verification from God about other spiritual truths.

Theory of Personality

Considering implications of Mormon doctrine for a comprehensive theory of personality, Mormon psychologists Scott Richards and Allen Bergin wrote:

> There is a spiritual core to human personality. Personality is influenced by a variety of systems and processes, but the eternal spirit is the core essence of identity. Healthy human development occurs as people hearken to the enticing of the Spirit of Truth. The Spirit of Truth helps people understand, value, and regulate their lives in harmony with universal principles that promote human growth and healthy functioning. Personality development and functioning are optimized when people are able to affirm their eternal spiritual identity; follow the influence of the Spirit of Truth; and regulate their behavior, feelings, and thoughts in harmony with universal principles and values (1997, p. 100).

Considering religious assumptions and also personality theorists, such as Erikson (1963), Gilligan (1982) and Randour (1987), Richards and Bergin proposed six psychospiritual constructs pertinent to the development of human personality:

1. Eternal identity versus mortal overlay
2. Free agency versus inefficacy
3. Inspired integrity versus deception
4. Faithful intimacy versus infidelity
5. Benevolent power versus authoritarianism
6. Health and human welfare values versus relativism and uncertainty

Eternal Identity versus the Mortal Overlay

In the Mormon view, each individual, as a spirit son or daughter of heavenly parents, has an eternal, spiritual identity and divine potential. Identity begins before birth and persists across time, including after death. Experiences of mortality, including problems such as birth defects, biological deficiencies, imperfect parenting, or social chaos, may serve developmental functions as individuals learn through these experiences. Latter-day Saint doctrine proposes that even as Jesus Christ learned through experiences of mortality (Hebrews 5:8), so human potential is also refined through experience. A passage in the Doctrine and Covenants, believed by Latter-day Saints to be a divine admonition to Joseph Smith during a time of persecution, states: "If thou art called to pass through tribulation; . . . know thou, my son, that all these things shall give thee experience, and shall be for thy good. The Son of Man hath descended below them all" (D&C 122: 5, 7, 8). The mortal overlay, including urges of the flesh and temptations from Satan, experiences of problems and affliction, were expected and accepted by humans during a spiritual existence before birth as part of God's plan for individual development.

Free Agency versus Inefficacy

Latter-day Saints believe that individuals are divinely endowed with moral agency and with associated responsibility for choices. Moral agency may be limited through individual choices, as in addictions, by the actions of others, as in abuse or deception, or by biological factors, such as brain disorders or genetic deficiencies. Individuals, by acting in accordance with spiritual understanding, and by exercising faith, may develop greater spiritual capacities, and increase self-regulative ability.

Inspired Integrity versus Deception

Rogers (1961) emphasized the importance of emotional congruence. Acceptance of reality (Hayes, Strosahl, & Wilson, 1999), mindful awareness (Linehan, 1993), and toleration of the truth, frustrations notwithstanding (Ellis, 1994), are broadly recognized as hallmarks of psychological health. In the words of Richards and Bergin:

> Integrity . . . is a sensitive attunement to the Spirit of Truth. It includes a resilient willingness to face the facts, to 'be true,' to be nonoffensive, to avoid blaming others, and to accept responsibility for one's defects and bad conduct even when it hurts to do so. Integrity is 'egoless' in the sense that the prideful protection or advancement of the ego is given up and that one elects to absorb the painful truths that defenses and deceptions have hidden from oneself and others (1997, p. 105).

Faithful Intimacy versus Infidelity

The Proclamation (Appendix) states that sexual expression is God-given, and is appropriate only in marriage. The Mormon ideal for marriage includes respect, love, and compassion and necessarily includes negotiation and support, mutual protection, and honest communication—aspects of emotional intimacy and maturity. Expressing physical intimacy outside of a committed relationship is likely to neglect or impede interpersonal growth. Children can be expected to model the faithful, mature relationships they see in their parents and express similar relationships with parents, siblings, and friends. The Proclamation proposes that family life is of central importance, and should be founded on relationships of love and mutual caring, fidelity and commitment. Parents are encouraged to treasure children as "an heritage of the Lord" and to create a protective atmosphere in the home where love, productive work, discipline, and wholesome recreation are planned and conducted.

Benevolent Power versus Authoritarianism

Personalities exist in the social context of relationships with other personalities. From the sexual intimacy of marriage to accomplishment of household chores, from administration of classrooms to business interactions, relationships include real and imagined individual differences in ability, status, and power. Maintaining relationships in families, organizations, and communities depends on groups of people appropriately balancing assertion, deferment, and disagreement (Richards & Bergin, 1997).

Several interesting passages present the Mormon view that humankind tends toward overcontrol of others. Joseph Smith wrote, "We have learned by sad experience that it is the nature and disposition of almost all men, as soon as they get a little authority, as they suppose, they will immediately begin to exercise unrighteous dominion" (D&C 121:39). That is, social differential almost invariably leads to authoritarianism.

A more benevolent model of influence is proposed in a later passage of the same scripture, suggesting that influence should be maintained, instead, by:

> persuasion, by long suffering, by gentleness and meekness, and by love unfeigned; By kindness, and pure knowledge, which shall greatly enlarge the soul without hypocrisy, and without guile—Reproving betimes with sharpness when moved upon by the Holy Ghost; and then showing forth afterwards an increase of love (D&C 121:41).

In other words, relationships will work best when social power is exerted through social buffering based on mutuality, persuasion, knowledge, honesty, and affection rather than through coercion or position.

Health and Human Welfare Values versus Relativism and Uncertainty

Mormon doctrine holds that humans were not created *ex nihilo* for an arbitrary purpose, but from preexisting, premortal spirit beings for a benevolent purpose, which God identified as His fundamental goal. A passage from The Pearl of Great Price is believed by Mormons to be a statement of deity: "For behold, this is my work and my glory, to bring to pass the immortality and eternal life of man" (Moses 1:39). This sets humans as beings of great worth, encouraging something akin to Rogers' unconditional positive regard (1961) and Ellis' unconditional acceptance (1994). A Book of Mormon passage reads, "Adam fell that men might be, and men are that they might have joy" (2 Nephi 2:25), a statement that may give believing Mormons confidence about the goal of their existence.

Implications

Mormon doctrine imbues human beings with great potential, as eternal beings passing through a developmental stage of mortality including trials and temptations (the mortal overlay). According to this religious perspective, individual agency may be enhanced or limited according to choices and experiences of earth life. Relationships with others, including intimacy and exercise of power, further impact individual development. Finally, choices of working for human well-being (seen as cooperation with God, in this religious context), influence an individual toward growth rather than stagnation, and happiness rather than despair.

These beliefs about human nature comprehend features of many psychological theories. Based on doctrinal belief in the inherent tension between the temporary, mortal overlay and the eternal, human spirit, between temptations and spiritual prompts, Mormons will recognize and resonate with features of psychodynamic models. Given Latter-day Saint belief in premortal life, Mormons agree with many psychological observations about constitutional differences in temperament. Based on admonitions for parents to teach their children, many Latter-day Saints readily accept psychological aspects of learning models.

Theory of Development

The Proclamation on the Family (Appendix) includes the Mormon developmental model, which is of cosmological proportion. As children are born to parents whom they may grow to emulate, so all humans are children of God—children of heavenly parents—whom they may grow to emulate. In the Latter-day Saint view, human development across the life span can be seen as a simulacrum of eternal development across infinity. The term "developmental milestone" is not specifically used in Mormon doctrinal explanations, but the concept of a developmental milestone is a well-suited analogy for the Plan of Salvation, and is adopted here:

Premortal Milestones

Mormons believe all humans had an existence before birth, with at least two critical developmental milestones. First, premortal spirit beings learned the Plan of Salvation proposed by God, our Heavenly Father (see Job 38:7), and were presented with the choice of accepting or rejecting this plan. Mormons believe that one third of premortal spirit beings, led by Satan, rejected this plan. They missed birth, the second critical developmental milestone.

Mortality

Latter-day Saints believe mortal birth affords human beings opportunities for specific experiences, tasks, and tests that may be seen as developmental milestones. Individuals must be born, take possession of a body, and work to develop intellect, self-control, and mastery of urges or temptations. Individuals must learn and follow both human laws and God's laws. Individuals must learn to heed the prompting of personal conscience, consisting of a God-given sense of moral rectitude. Individuals must hear the Plan of Salvation and accept or reject it. Mormons believe that God requires several formal ceremonies or ordinances as signs of acceptance, including, for example, baptism by immersion in water.

Maturity

Latter-day Saints are expected to accomplish some tasks at specific ages: Children are generally expected to be intellectually and morally ready—accountable—to choose baptism and church membership at age eight. Parents are commanded to teach children so they will be ready to decide for or against baptism and other milestone decisions. Boys may be ordained to the Church's lay priesthood at age 12, and, if worthy, may take on new ordinations at 14 and 16. Boys may receive a higher priesthood at 18 and volunteer for missionary service at age 19. Girls and women may fill positions of responsibility in the Church, and may serve as missionaries, but they are not ordained to the priesthood.

Exceptions to general age-related tasks arise, of course. Physical limitations and developmental deficits may preclude accountability. Latter-day Saints believe that God, who is infinitely fair, determines when each person has had sufficient maturity, instruction, and ability to complete milestones. Mormons believe that everyone will eventually have a fair opportunity, either in mortality or in the spirit existence that immediately follows mortality and precedes resurrection. According to Latter-day Saint doctrine, children who die before accountability are believed saved by the grace of Jesus Christ. With greater opportunity and capacity come higher standards during God's judgment.

Spirit Paradise and Prison

Immediately after death, those who have been obedient to the commandments will find themselves in a paradise of rest from the pains, anxieties, and sorrows of life. Those who ignored or wilfully disobeyed available truth will find themselves imprisoned in vivid, painful awareness of their disobedience and its consequences; self-deceptions will be stripped away, and all will be remembered. This spirit prison is a kind of hell. Spirits in both spirit worlds will interact, congregate, and attempt to influence and teach one another.

Physical ordinances such as baptism, ordination, and marriage will be impossible without physical bodies. Latter-day Saints believe that performing such ordinances vicariously for the dead will give many of the dead a postmortal opportunity to accept saving ordinances. Paul mentions one of these vicarious ordinances, baptism for the dead, in 1 Cor. 15:29. Mormons believe Jesus Christ restored more detailed instructions for vicarious work for the dead.

Resurrection and Judgment

When all human beings have had fair opportunity to hear and decide, all will appear before God to be judged. Mormons believe this judgment occurs at the time of physical resurrection. This has occurred for some, Peter, James, and John, for example, but not for most. At the resurrection, spirits will receive an immortal body and the existence they prepared to receive. According to Latter-day Saint doctrine, this resurrection and final judgment will include three different degrees of blessing (1 Cor. 15:40-42):

> There are also celestial bodies, and bodies terrestrial: but the glory of the celestial is one, and the glory of the terrestrial is another. There is one glory of the sun, and another glory of the moon, and another glory of the stars: for one star differeth from another star in glory. So also is the resurrection of the dead. It is sown in corruption; it is raised in incorruption.

Mormons believe these states of glory will continue on eternally. The highest, or celestial glory, where God dwells, will include continuation of family relationships established during mortality.

Hell

Even most humans who have seriously flouted God's laws during mortality will, at the resurrection, escape the sufferings of the spirit prison and move on to a glorious existence. The glory of this existence, however, is as much less than the glory of the Celestial reward as the stars are less bright in their appearance than the brilliance of the sun. Some few souls will, however, be consigned to what Mormons believe is an eternal hell, an outer darkness where they are left to suffer in their own implacable hatred and rejection of the blessings God has offered His children. These utterly damned souls are those who, for example, had full spiritual knowledge of the truth, including a compelling spiritual witness of Jesus, and chose to work vigorously against the truth. Although Latter-day Saint writings about this state are sparse, it seems likely that most, if not all of the suffering is self-inflicted arrogance and hatred.

Implications

Mormons are likely to view life as the current chapter in a multivolume series of developmental stages, begun before birth and continuing after death. Parents are commanded to teach their children so that they will be prepared for baptism and learn to choose in accordance with prompting of conscience or spirit. In the Church's view, failure to teach commandments places responsibility for children's sins on parents, so Latter-day Saint parents often take their parental responsibilities very seriously. The physical body and temptations create tensions as described in the preceding and bodies and abilities differ for constitutional reasons.

This heavy emphasis on teaching, training, developing, and achieving has led some members of other Christian faiths to criticize Mormonism as not really believing in Jesus Christ, or at least not believing in his grace.

The Latter-day Saint view, however, considers that after all that people can do—and they should strive to do much—salvation comes only by the gracious atonement of Jesus Christ (2 Nephi 25:23).

Theory of Psychological Health and Pathology

Joy

The Plan of Salvation is also called the Plan of Happiness in the Book of Mormon. Mormons believe that God desires His children's long-term happiness. Joseph Smith taught, "Happiness is the object and design of our existence; and will be the end thereof, if we pursue the path that leads to it; and this path is virtue, uprightness, faithfulness, holiness, and keeping all the commandments of God" (Smith, 1976, pp. 255–256). Latter-day Saints believe that joy may come as a spiritual gift, as recorded in this passage, recorded as a promise of Christ: "I will impart unto you of my Spirit, which shall enlighten your mind, which shall fill your soul with joy" (D&C 11:13). Another source of joy, in the Mormon view, is the earth, which was designed for the blessing of humankind. A passage from the D&C states, "all things which come of the earth, in the season thereof, are made for the benefit and the use of man, both to please the eye and to gladden the heart" (D&C 59:18).

Joy in Missionary Service

The greatest joy is found in service to others, particularly helping to bring others to knowledge of truth, and to repentance. Luke, chapter 15, which includes the parables of the lost sheep, the lost coin, and the prodigal son, describes this joy. In the parables of the lost coin and the prodigal son, return of sinners to the fold is celebrated with partying. On a similar theme, Joseph Smith wrote that Jesus told him:

> Remember the worth of souls is great in the sight of God; For behold, the Lord your Redeemer suffered death in the flesh; wherefore he suffered the pain of all men, that all men might repent and some unto him. And he hath risen again from the dead, that he might bring all men unto him, on conditions of repentance. And how great is his joy in the soul that repenteth! Wherefore, you are called to cry repentance unto this people. And if it so be that you should labor all your days in crying repentance unto this people, and bring save it be one soul unto me, how great shall be your joy with him in the kingdom of my Father! And now, if your joy will be great with one soul that you have brought unto me into the kingdom of my Father, how great will be your joy if you should bring many souls unto me! (D&C 18:10–16).

Joy in Religious Service

Mormons believe that service emulates God's benevolence to humankind, giving a taste of the love God has for His children. A typical congregation in the United States includes as many 100 service positions. Adult women are members of the Relief Society, the oldest women's organization in the United States. The Relief Society motto is, "Charity Never Faileth." The responsibility of the Priesthood organizations, to which boys and men belong, is providing temporal and spiritual service to Church members. Every able Priesthood and Relief Society member in a congregation is charged to attend to the welfare of one or more families in the congregation.

Joy in Service for the Dead

Many Church members perform ordinances on behalf of individuals who have died. In the Mormon view, these ordinances may have vicarious benefit. Preparation for this work consists of genealogical documentation of the lives of the dead by researching and validating names, dates of birth, christening, marriage, and death. After proper documentation, vicarious ordinance work for the dead soul may take place in temples devoted to this work. Church members believe it is especially important to complete such work for ancestors. In support of this effort, the Church of Jesus Christ of Latter-day Saints has developed a major network of genealogical resources and temples.

Patriarchal Blessings

Healthy living includes individual initiative and effort. Latter-day Saint practice offers a spiritual guide to individuals who seek it, a blessing that gives counsel and direction about an individual's life and efforts. These blessings, given by priests called as Patriarchs, are modeled after the blessings Jacob gave his 12 sons. Members believe it is important to prepare carefully for the blessing, then treat it as a sacred document, which they ponder and contemplate as a revelatory guide.

Sin as Pathology

Harm is obvious with some sins, such as theft, robbery, assault, or rape. Even when victims or harm are not obvious, however, Mormons believe sin causes a harmful separation from God, seen as a kind of spiritual death. Separation from God harms the soul, reduces resistance to temptation, distorts one's perceptions (e.g., sin may cease to seem wrong), darkens one's outlook, misdirects one through false belief, discourages through separation from the peace, enlightenment, and joy that come from the Spirit, and harms others when spiritual prompting is lost and duties are misunderstood, neglected, or misdirected.

Emotional Distress and Mental Illness

Although sin may cause emotional problems, Mormon belief does not hold that emotional problems are inevitable evidence the sufferer has sinned. The Book of Mormon contains these comments:

> For it must needs be, that there is an opposition in all things. If not so . . . righteousness could not be brought to pass, neither wickedness, neither holiness nor misery, neither good nor bad. Wherefore, all things must needs be a compound in one; wherefore, if it should be one body it must needs remain as dead, having no life neither death, nor corruption nor incorruption, happiness nor misery, neither sense nor insensibility (2 Nephi 2:11).

This passage presents the view that suffering often arises because of the nature of reality. The context for this passage, in the Book of Mormon account, was egregious abuse within a family, including contention and assault. This excerpt is well known and frequently memorized by Mormon seminary students, and presents a dialectical view of opposing forces inherent in mortal life. From this dialectical perspective, psychological problems can be viewed as inevitable features of the "mortal overlay," which contribute to human understanding and experience.

Psychological pathology can arise from a range of such opposing forces, including the sins or carelessness of others, natural accidents, misunderstandings, ignorance, genetic predispositions, developmental problems, and other factors. Latter-day Saint perspectives of these conditions and of their treatment fit mainstream conceptions of mental illness.

Implications

The Church acknowledges the need for professional mental health treatment as an adjunctive and parallel process to pastoral care. The Church maintains a professional mental health network called LDS Family Services, available in many areas worldwide. The Church's university system, Brigham Young University, with campuses in Utah, Idaho, and Hawaii, has counseling centers staffed by mental health professionals, including psychologists, social workers, consulting psychiatrists, and nurse practitioners.

Common Moral Issues

Several lifestyle patterns set Mormons apart from most mainstream cultures. Practicing Mormons do not smoke, and they do not drink alcohol, coffee, or tea. Also, Mormon beliefs include Sabbath observance, modest dress, and sexual abstinence outside of marriage. These practices are counterculture in many settings and may pose moral dilemmas for individuals born to Church membership but undecided about their level of commitment. Latter-day Saint adolescents, in particular, may face questions of moral commitment and religious identity.

Mormonism is viewed as a cult by some. Although this seems like a misperception to these authors, it is nonetheless a social reality. Because of this negative perception, or because of strong familial ties to other religious traditions, those who convert to the LDS faith often face opposition from family and friends. Considerations about degree of commitment and willingness to sacrifice social ties may be common for such individuals as they weigh their decision in light of competing values.

Another area in which Latter-day Saints may face moral concerns involves the doctrinal acceptance of ongoing revelation. Consistent with belief in a living prophet, the Mormon view includes the possibility for unforeseen changes in Church organization or policy, as the prophet receives revelation pertinent to current conditions. Such changes could pose a moral dilemma.

Common Clinical Issues

Express Scripts, one of the largest pharmacy benefit management companies in the United States, posted reports of state-by-state prescription use based on convenience sampling of prescription purchases during the year 2000 (Motherall, 2001; Motherall, Cox, Mager, Henderson, & Martinez, 2002). The reports showed that in a large sample of Express Scripts members, Utah had, on average, the highest antidepressant use rate in the United States. Antidepressant purchases in Utah (where 70% of residents are Mormons) were nearly three times the average use of the lowest state. *Los Angeles Times* reporter Julie Cart (2002) speculated that this pattern may arise because Mormons, especially Mormon women, are more likely to experience depression because their religion creates perfectionism in them.

In 1978, Burgoyne and Burgoyne noted a higher incidence of depression among Mormon women in Utah. Spendlove, West, and Stanish (1984), surveying women in the Salt Lake metropolitan area, did not find significant differences in levels of depression among demographically similar Mormon and non-Mormon women. The study found that previously identified risk factors for depression, including lack of education, low income, children in the home, and perceived lack of support from a spouse, contributed to depression in both groups, but no significant differences between LDS and non-LDS women were found. A later study by Williams (1999) specifically examined perfectionism and other factors in Mormon women compared to Protestant women, finding no significant difference in depressive symptoms. Perfectionism correlated significantly with depression for both groups.

A range of studies find that involvement or commitment to the Church, generally defined by temple attendance (as described in the preceding) has either overall positive effects on mental health or ameliorative effects relative to general societal problems, including delinquency (Jensen, Jensen, & Wiederhold, 1999; Top, Chadwick, & Garrett, 1999), drug abuse (Hawks & Bahr, 1999), stress in larger families (Wilkinson & Tanner, 1999), and suicide (Hilton, Fellingham, & Lyon, 2002; Merrill & Salazar, 2002; Zhang & Thomas, 1999). These studies leave unanswered questions about negative consequences for formerly committed, now disaffected church members. Do the disaffected, for example, face greater risks for mental illness than those who never believed?

Implications

Current research suggests that Mormons suffer from approximately the same mental health problems at levels similar to non-Mormons. Growing evidence suggests that the rate and severity of such problems may be lower and less severe among more committed Latter-day Saints, but causal relationships in either direction have not been demonstrated; that is, it is not clear that practice leads to subsequent improvement in mental health or that reducing commitment leads to subsequent mental illness.

CONCLUDING REMARKS

It seems likely that Latter-day Saints will not reject psychology or conventional psychotherapeutic models. Indeed, some features of psychology and personality theory may resonate with basic Church doctrine. However, a history fraught with persecution may lead the average Latter-day Saint to be more sensitive than the average conservatively religious individual to attitudes critical or skeptical of religion in general and of the Church in particular. Therapists interested in establishing a good working relationship with a Mormon are advised to begin by demonstrating a neutral or sympathetic stance toward all religion.

Mormons, and certainly practicing Mormons, can be expected to bring the Church with them to psychotherapy. For example, practicing Latter-day Saints will feel an urge to share the Church, so a therapist should not be surprised if the Latter-day Saint client attempts to refer the therapist to the Mormon missionaries, particularly after a working therapeutic relationship has been established.

REFERENCES

Black, S. E. (1998, July). Do we know how many Latter-day Saints died between 1847 and 1869 in the migration to the Salt Lake Valley? *Ensign, 28(7),* 40.

Brown, H. B. (1965). *The abundent life.* Salt Lake City, UT: Bookcraft.

Burgoyne, R. H., & Burgoyne, R. W. (1978). Belief systems and unhappiness: The Mormon woman example. *Dialogue: A Journal of Mormon Thought, 11(3),* 48–53.

Cart, J. (February 20, 2002). The Nation: Study finds Utah lead nation in anti-depressant use. *Los Angeles Times,* p. A.6.

Ellis, A. (1994). *Reason and emotion in psychotherapy: A comprehensive method of treating human disturbances* (Revised and updated) New York: Birch Lane Press.

Erikson, E. H. (1963). *Childhood and society* (2nd ed). New York: Norton.

Gilligan, C. (1982). *In a different voice: Psychological theory and women's development.* Cambridge, MA: Harvard University Press.

Hawks, R. D., & Bahr, S. H. (1999). Religion and drug use. In D. K. Judd (Ed.), *Religion, mental health and the Latter-day Saints* (pp. 169–178). Provo, UT: Religious Studies Center, Brigham Young University.

Hayes, S. C., Strosahl, K, & Wilson, K. G. (1999). *Acceptance and commitment therapy: An experiential approach to behavior change.* New York: Guilford.

Hilton, S. C., Fellingham, G. W., & Lyon, J. L. (2002). Suicide rates and religious commitment in young adult males in Utah. *American Journal of Epidemiology, 155,* 413–419.

Jensen, L. C., Jensen, J., & Wiederhold, T. (1999). Religiosity, denomination and mental health among young men and women. In D. K. Judd (Ed.), *Religion, mental health and the Latter-day Saints* (pp. 67–70). Provo, UT: Religious Studies Center, Brigham Young University.

Kimball, S. W., Tanner, N. E., & Romney, M. G. (1978). Statement of the First Presidency regarding God's love for all mankind. As cited in J. E. Faust (1980, May). Communion with the Holy Spirit, *Ensign,* 12.

Linehan, M. (1993). *Cognitive-behavioral treatment of borderline personality disorder.* New York: Guilford.

Merrill, R. M., & Salazar, R. D. (2002). Relationship between church attendance and mental health among Mormons and non-Mormons in Utah. *Mental Health, Religion & Culture, 5,* 17–33.

Motherall, B. (2001). Fact sheet: Regional variation in prescription drug use. Unpublished report. Retrieved June 25, 2005 from http://www.ex-press-scripts.com/ourcompany/news/ outcomesconference/2001/factsheets/regionalVariation.pdf

Motherall, B., Cox, E. R., Mager, D., Henderson, R., & Martinez, R. (2002). *Executive summary: Express Scripts prescription drug atlas.* Unpublished report. Retrieved June 25, 2005, from http://www.express-scripts.com/ourcompany/news/outcomesresearch/ prescriptiondrugatlas/entireStudy.pdf

Randour, M. L. (1987). *Women's psyche, women's spirit: The reality of relationships.* New York: Columbia University Press.

Richards, P. S. & Bergin, A. E. (1997). *A spiritual strategy for counseling and psychotherapy.* Washington, DC: American Psychological Association.

Rogers, C. R. (1961). *On becoming a person: A therapist's view of psychotherapy.* Boston, MA: Houghton-Mifflin.

Smith, J. (1976). *Teachings of the prophet Joseph Smith: Selected and arranged by Joseph Fielding Smith.* Salt Lake City, UT: Deseret Book.

Spendlove, D., West, D., & Stanish, W. M. (1984). Risk factors and the prevalence of depression in Mormon women. *Social Science and Medicine, 18,* 491–495.

Stark, R. (1996). So far, so good: A brief assessment of Mormon membership projections. *Review of Religious Research, 38,* 175–178.

Top, B. L., Chadwick, B. A., & Garrett, J. (1999). Family, religion, and delinquency among LDS youth. In D. K. Judd (Ed.), *Religion, mental health and the Latter-day Saints* (pp. 129–168). Provo, UT: Religious Studies Center, Brigham Young University.

Watson, M. F. (2005). Statistical Report, 2004. Retrieved June 7, 2005, from http://www.lds.org/conference/talk/display/0,5232,23-1-520-9,00.html

Widtsoe, J. A. (Ed.). (1925). *Discourses of Brigham Young.* Salt Lake City, UT: Deseret Book.

Wilkinson, M. L. & Tanner, W. C. (1999). The influence of family size, interaction, and religiosity on family affection in a Mormon sample. In D. K. Judd (Ed.), *Religion, mental health and the Latter-day Saints* (pp. 93–106). Provo, UT: Religious Studies Center, Brigham Young University.

Williams, M. K. (1999). Family attitudes and perfectionism as related to depression in Latter-day Saint and Protestant women. In D. K. Judd (Ed.), *Religion, mental health and the Latter-day Saints* (pp. 47–66). Provo, UT: Religious Studies Center, Brigham Young University.

Zhang, J. & Thomas, D. L. (1999). Familial and religious influences on suicidal ideaiton. In D. K. Judd (Ed.), *Religion, mental health and the Latter-day Saints* (pp. 215–236). Provo, UT: Religious Studies Center, Brigham Young University.

The Family: A Proclamation to the World

We, the First Presidency and the Council of the Twelve Apostles of The Church of Jesus Christ of Latter-day Saints, solemnly proclaim that marriage between a man and a woman is ordained of God and that the family is central to the Creator's plan for the eternal destiny of His children.

All human beings—male and female—are created in the image of God. Each is a beloved spirit son or daughter of heavenly parents, and, as such, each has a divine nature and destiny. Gender is an essential characteristic of individual premortal, mortal, and eternal identity and purpose.

In the premortal realm, spirit sons and daughters knew and worshiped God as their Eternal Father and accepted His plan by which His children could obtain a physical body and gain earthly experience to progress toward perfection and ultimately realize his or her divine destiny as an heir of eternal life. The divine plan of happiness enables family relationships to be perpetuated beyond the grave. Sacred ordinances and covenants available in holy temples make it possible for individuals to return to the presence of God and for families to be united eternally.

The first commandment that God gave to Adam and Eve pertained to their potential for parenthood as husband and wife. We declare that God's commandment for His children to multiply and replenish the earth remains in force. We further declare that God has commanded that the sacred powers of procreation are to be employed only between man and woman, lawfully wedded as husband and wife.

We declare the means by which mortal life is created to be divinely appointed. We affirm the sanctity of life and of its importance in God's eternal plan.

Husband and wife have a solemn responsibility to love and care for each other and for their children. "Children are an heritage of the Lord" (Psalms 127:3). Parents have a sacred duty to rear their children in love and righteousness, to provide for their physical and spiritual needs, to teach them to love and serve one another, to observe the commandments of God and to be law-abiding citizens wherever they live. Husbands and wives—mothers and fathers—will be held accountable before God for the discharge of these obligations.

The family is ordained of God. Marriage between man and woman is essential to His eternal plan. Children are entitled to birth within the bonds of matrimony, and to be reared by a father and a mother who honor marital vows with complete fidelity. Happiness in family life is most likely to be achieved when founded upon the teachings of the Lord Jesus Christ. Successful marriages and families are established and maintained on principles of faith, prayer, repentance, forgiveness, respect, love, compassion, work, and wholesome recreational activities. By divine design, fathers are to preside over their families in love and righteousness and are responsible to provide the necessities of life and protection for their families. Mothers are primarily responsible for the nurture of their children. In these sacred responsibilities, fathers and mothers are obligated to help one another as equal partners. Disability, death, or other circumstances may necessitate individual adaptation. Extended families should lend support when needed.

We warn that individuals who violate covenants of chastity, who abuse spouse or offspring, or who fail to fulfill family responsibilities will one day stand accountable before God. Further, we warn that the disintegration of the family will bring upon individuals, communities, and nations the calamities foretold by ancient and modern prophets.

We call upon responsible citizens and officers of government everywhere to promote those measures designed to maintain and strengthen the family as the fundamental unit of society (available at http://www.lds.org/library/display/0,4945,161-1-11-1,00.html).

SECTION V

The Judaic Traditions

CHAPTER ELEVEN

Liberal Judaism

Ira S. Halper and Amy Ruth Bolton

OVERVIEW AND HISTORY OF THE FAITH

The Jewish community in the United States is diverse in a religious sense. Liberal or non-Orthodox Jews comprise the majority of this community and include members of the Conservative, Reform, Reconstructionist, Humanist, and Renewal movements as well as a significant number of unaffiliated and secular Jews. The majority of the Jews who responded to the 2000–2001 National Jewish Population Survey (United States) by saying they belonged to a synagogue, gave a Liberal affiliation.

The Liberal denominations of Judaism have their roots in the European Enlightenment of the 18th century. The Enlightenment was "a process of 'letting in the light' into the presumed darkness of the age that preceded it. The 'light' that was . . . to be let in was the light of reason. Reason, not received tradition or external authority, was to be the ultimate source of truth in all areas of human understanding" (Gillman, 1993, p. 7). The ideologies of present-day Liberal Jews can be traced back to Jewish religious reformers in 19th century Germany. The two major movements are Conservative Judaism and Reform Judaism. The Conservative and Reform movements share several basic principles but differ on others. Both believe that to deal effectively with modernity, Judaism must be studied in a scientific way. This means using the methodology of modern criticism in the study of the Hebrew Bible and the later rabbinic literature, comparing Jewish practices with those of other religions, and accepting as fact that throughout its development, Judaism was influenced by the conditions that existed outside of the Jewish community. Thus, neither the Torah (the first five books of the Hebrew Bible) nor the rabbinic literature are studied as the explicit words of God, and the laws of the early rabbis are no longer considered eternally binding.

In Conservative Judaism, decisions about which ideas and practices are to be preserved and which changed are made by the leadership of the movement. The rabbis and scholars of every historical period significantly influence the lives of Jews, but they in turn are influenced by the needs of the community. Thus, there is a sharing of authority, which is different than the more authoritarian structure of traditional Judaism. There is also a contrast with one of the basic principles of Classical Reform Judaism, its emphasis on personal autonomy in determining what a Jew is to believe and practice. Conservative Judaism takes the position that the process of revelation did not end with the giving of the Torah at Mount Sinai. It continued in the teaching of the early rabbis and continues in the decision of modern rabbinic authorities in response to the changing needs of their community.

In a series of Statements of Principles, the first in 1885 and the most recent in 1999, the Reform movement has articulated the central tenets of Reform Judaism. The aggressively worded Pittsburgh Platform of 1885 defined classical Reform Judaism as, a "progressive religion, ever striving to be in accord with the postulates of reason" (Meyer, 1988, p. 388). Although recognizing the importance of the God-idea in the Bible, the Pittsburgh Platform explicitly rejects those ceremonies and rabbinical laws that are "not adapted to the views and habits of modern civilization" (Meyer, 1998, p. 388). It is of interest that the 1999 Statement includes a paragraph on commandments:

> We are committed to the ongoing study of the whole array of *mitzvot* (commandments) and to the fulfillment of those that address us as individuals and as a community. Some of these . . . sacred obligations . . . demand renewed attention as a result of the unique context of our own times (Stevens, 2003, p. 110).

At the same time, the 1999 Statement of Principles acknowledges the diversity of Reform Jewish beliefs and practices.

The smaller Reconstructionist movement was founded by Mordecai Kaplan, a rabbi and faculty member of the Conservative seminary in New York. Kaplan conceptualized Judaism as the evolving religious civilization of the Jewish people. He also developed a theology in which God is neither identified with things in the world (natural), nor is God beyond the world (supernatural). Reconstructionist Judaism calls this theology "transnatural." Thus, God works through us rather than upon us. There are also Reconstructionist Jews who have difficulty relating to the identification of God as Process. They experience God as a being with whom they can converse and from whom they derive strength. Reconstructionist

Judaism rejects the belief that the words of the Torah are the divine revelation at Mount Sinai and that traditional commandments of Judaism come from God. The authority of Jewish tradition is dealt with by taking the position that the past has a vote, not a veto. Reconstructionist synagogues have a strong and explicit commitment to lay participation. "The nature of liturgical and ritual observance is normally determined by group consensus after collective study" (Alpert & Staub, 2000, p. 153).

Although they themselves may not be adherents to traditional Jewish law, Conservative congregants tend to desire and expect from their clergy a higher level of ritual observance than do Reform congregants. In addition, individuals who worship at Conservative congregations are often seeking a service that includes more Hebrew and that is based upon the structure of the traditional prayer service. In contrast, Reform worshipers look for a more creative service that includes more English. The design of a Reconstructionist service typically includes quotation, affirmation, and conversation. Quotation is traditional prayer in Hebrew. Affirmation is contemporary English prose and poetry that relate to the traditional liturgy. Conversation is discussion and dialogue rather than a sermon (R. Hirsh, personal communication, August 26, 2004).

Humanistic Judaism is a relatively new and small movement that combines Jewish culture and identity with humanistic values. Jewish Renewal, also relatively new and representing a small minority of Liberal Jews, describes itself as a non- or post-denominational movement whose focus is on spiritual experience and the mystical teachings of Judaism.

The Jewish mystical tradition can be traced back several thousand years and includes *Kabbalah,* a movement that flourished from the 12th to the 16th century. "Mystics seek intimate knowledge of the divine which goes beyond intellectualization and rational thinking. . . . Mystics are not necessarily anti or nonintellectual . . . but they *are* interested in the *experience* of the sacred in a way that is *intuitive, direct,* and *intense*" (Holtz, 1984, p. 306). Mysticism has influenced liturgy, Bible commentary, and practice of Jews throughout the ages. The Jewish meditation that some Liberal Jews use today to enhance their spirituality is rooted in this tradition. To the dismay of some members of the Jewish community, contemporary pop religionists have tried to revive *Kabbalah* as a movement in a superficial way that is very different than the serious spiritual and intellectual tradition of Jewish mysticism.

The most current and authoritative study of the American Jewish population is the National Jewish Population Survey (2000–2001). The survey findings lead to the following portrait of American Jews: most American Jewish adults observe the High Holy Days, Passover, and Chanukah in some way. Majorities read Jewish publications or books with Jewish content and regard being Jewish as very important. They report that half or more of their close friends are Jewish. Smaller numbers report involvement in other religious and communal activities, such as lighting *Shabbat* (Sabbath) candles, keeping kosher (observing traditional dietary laws) at home, and attending religious services once a month or more.

Forty-six percent of American Jews affiliate with a synagogue either personally or as a member of a household. Those who affiliate divide as follows: Reform 38%, Conservative 33%, Orthodox 22%, Reconstructionist 2%, other 5% (United Jewish Communities, 2004, p. 7).

Jews of all denominations believe in one God. There is no concept of the Trinity or of Jesus as the Messiah. Some Liberal Jews view God as having great power and intervention to aid them in their daily lives; others believe that God is not there to help them in their everyday lives but is there to offer strength and solace. Some view God not as an external being but as a divine force within each individual. Many Liberal Jews are unaccustomed to speaking directly about God. It is easier for them to talk about Jewish communal life or religious practices. For many Liberal Jews, however, God does play a role in their lives, and efforts to help the individual clarify or express religious beliefs may help in the healing process of psychotherapy. There is little focus in Liberal Judaism on the afterlife and no strongly defined picture of a heaven or hell. Liberal Jews can be serious about their religion, and Judaism can be important to them. It is of interest, however, that theological issues and issues related to scriptural authority tend to be absent in the treatment of Liberal Jewish patients.

Individual autonomy tends to be valued by Liberal Jews, and individual choice and faith in human abilities tend to be valued over divine omnipotence, even for those with a strong sense of God in their lives. An important implication for psychotherapy is that reliance on the individual rather than outside authority means that one has the power as well as the responsibility to improve one's psychological state and one's life. There is no religiously based stigma attached to psychiatric illness in the Liberal Jewish communities, and Liberal Jews tend to have an accepting attitude toward psychological and psychiatric treatment.

Judaism is a religion that focuses on action. Liberal Jews focus on living this life rather than hoping to achieve a new and better afterlife. There tends not to be a lot of religious guilt among Liberal Jews about what they are thinking or feeling but rather about how they are acting or not acting. Some Liberal Jews feel inadequate in terms of their religious practices, particularly in the Conservative movement, where there is some emphasis on the importance of following Jewish laws.

Traditional Jewish law covers virtually every area of human life. It addresses worship and holidays, personal and business relationships, sexuality, and diet. Liberal Jews vary widely in their level of ritual observance and practice. A significant percentage attends public synagogue worship services during the High Holy Day season but does not attend services any other day of the year. A small number of affiliated Liberal Jews attend weekly *Shabbat* services on a regular basis, as well as worship services on other major Jewish holidays. With respect to home observance, many liberal Jews celebrate the holidays of Passover and Chanukah. Most Liberal Jews do not observe the Jewish dietary laws or adhere to the traditional laws of *Shabbat*. Some Conservative Jews, however, keep a strictly kosher home. A smaller minority also keeps the laws of *Shabbat*, refraining from such activities as cooking and working. Study, community service, social action, and philanthropy are other vehicles through which many Liberal Jews express their religious observance.

EPISTEMOLOGICAL TOOLS ACKNOWLEDGED AND SUPPORTED BY THE FAITH

As children of the Enlightenment, Liberal Jews are comfortable with the scientific method. Jews have been called the People of the Book, and the emphasis on learning has been passed down to modern Liberal Jews, extending well beyond religious subjects. The basic tenets of psychoanalysis, such as the unconscious and psychic determinism, are congenial to Liberal Jews, and it is no accident that Sigmund Freud and a disproportionate number of the early psychoanalysts were Jewish. The collaborative empiricism of cognitive therapy is equally congenial to Liberal Jews.

Classic texts continue to be important to Jews. The Torah is the first five books of the Jewish Bible, according to tradition given by God to the Children of Israel at Mount Sinai. The Talmud, or Oral Law, was the originally orally transmitted legal commentary on the Torah (Telushkin, 1991). The Talmud was codified and committed to writing by the early rabbis beginning about 200 CE (Common Era, corresponding to AD). Its many volumes include ethical discussions and folklore as well as legal debates. Midrash is another body of early rabbinic literature that flowered between the years 400 and 1200 CE. The medieval period produced Bible commentaries and works of Jewish philosophy. In recent years there has been a renewed interest in *Kabbalah* and the texts of Jewish mysticism, the most well-known of which is the *Zohar,* a book that emerged in the 13th century. The *Hasidic* movement began in Eastern Europe in the 18th century. Its charismatic leaders told "of a God who was present and directly accessible throughout His universe, . . . and of an essential role that each Jew had to play in the joyous transformation of matter into spirit, of mundane into holy" (Holtz, 1984, p. 362). The teachings of the Hasidic masters form part of the classic Jewish literature. There is also a wealth of more contemporary literature that builds on traditional texts.

Some Liberal Jews are attracted to the intellectual facet of Judaism. There are many opportunities for Jews of all movements to pursue Jewish studies, ranging from informal classes at synagogues and Internet learning to doctoral programs in Jewish Studies at major universities.

Although curiosity and intellectual aggressiveness can be assets in psychotherapy, the emphasis on academic achievement can be a burden to Jews who are unable to compete successfully at a high level in this arena.

THE THEORY OF NORMAL PERSONALITY
INHERENT IN THE FAITH

There is no specific theory of normal personality inherent in the faith of Liberal Jews. Because Liberal Jews tend to view the world in a natural rather than a supernatural way, they seek rational explanations for unusual sensations and perceptions. In Judaism there is a belief that each individual is inherently good but has the freedom to choose both good and evil actions. Individual freedom and choice are core values of Liberal Judaism, and there is a recognition that one chooses and is responsible for one's own actions and life choices.

Jewish tradition discourages denial of the reality of death, and the rituals connected with the loss of loved ones can be supportive and therapeutic (Telushkin, 1991). The casket is closed at the funeral, and the finality of the loss is reinforced by the expectation that the immediate family will pour the first shovelfuls of earth over the casket. After the funeral, the mourners return home or to the home of the deceased, where they sit *shiva* for 7 days. *Shiva* is the Hebrew word for seven. Jewish law requires Jews to observe the rules of *shiva* for the death of a parent, sibling, child, or spouse. Friends and family visit the bereaved, and there are daily prayers. The mourners do not return to work until after the *shiva* week unless economic necessity dictates otherwise. *Shiva* is followed by less intense periods of mourning, a full year when a parent dies, and 30 days for other close relatives.

Traditionally, the mourner's *Kaddish* is recited three times a day during the mourning periods. This prayer extols the greatness of God. It is significant that a prayer with a positive theme was selected to memorialize the dead. Four times a year, on Yom Kippur and three other major holidays, *Sukkot, Pesach* (Passover), and *Shavuot,* a memorial prayer called *yizkor* (remember) is recited in the synagogue for deceased relatives. The dead also are memorialized annually in the *yahrzeit* rituals on the anniversary of the death. A 24-hour-candle is lit, and the Mourner's *Kaddish* is recited in the synagogue. Although Liberal Jews tend to be selective about their observance of the rituals connected with the death of loved ones, they still may derive comfort from these traditions.

Collective memory as well as individual memory is important to Jews. The Patriarchs and the Matriarchs of ancient Israel appear prominently in Jewish liturgy and literature. The Torah and excerpts from the writings of the Prophets are read each *Shabbat* in Liberal as well as Orthodox synagogues.

Although memories of the *Shoah,* the Holocaust, are fading, this collective tragedy is still present in the memory of 21st century Jews. A sense of vulnerability, potential if not actual today, is reinforced by identification with the embattled State of Israel and by the virulent anti-Semitism of the Islamic world. This sense of vulnerability is reinforced by the attitude of Europe, where criticism of Israeli policies toward Palestinians merges into anti-Semitism.

Consistent with its emphasis on behavior, the concept of original sin is absent in Judaism. The soul that comes from God is pure, and atonement for sin is possible by prayer to God and a change in behavior toward humans. Although observant Jews can feel guilty about not observing *mitzvot,* this is not an issue for the average Liberal Jew. Liberal Jews want to lead a moral life, as defined by the standards of secular society as well as the Jewish community and Jewish tradition. Sin, however, plays only a small role in the theology of most Liberal Jews except on the High Holy Days.

THE THEORY OF NORMAL HUMAN DEVELOPMENT INHERENT IN THE FAITH

There is no specific theory of human development inherent in the faith of Liberal Jews; however, children are extremely important in both Orthodox and non-Orthodox families. Many Liberal families maintain the ancient custom of *brit milah,* the ritual circumcision of Jewish boys symbolizing the covenant between God and the Jewish people, and the birth of girls is celebrated with a ceremony in which the baby is given a Hebrew name. Although Jewish day schools are more popular in the Orthodox community, it is not uncommon for more observant Liberal Jews to send their children to Jewish day schools, sometimes with considerable financial sacrifice, even when good public schools are available.

The *bar mitzvah,* the ceremonial event at age 13 which in the Jewish tradition marked the beginning of manhood for the Jewish boy, remains an important life cycle event for many Liberal Jewish families. *Bar mitzvah* means literally, son of commandment. Traditionally, this is the time when a Jewish boy becomes obligated to observe the ritual commandments such as daily prayer and the moral commandments such as charity. A similar ceremony, the *bat mitzvah,* literally meaning daughter of commandment, has been added by Liberal families for girls. The *bar or bat mitzvah* leads the service and reads from the Torah. This life cycle event can be a source of stress for the boy or girl and the family. This time of heightened emotion can be particularly difficult in the case of divorce or blended families.

Interfaith dating and marriage has become a source of great concern for the Jewish community and for some Jewish parents. Before the 1960s anti-Semitism limited the interaction between Jews and non-Jews socially and in the workplace, and intermarriage was much less of a problem. In the years since that time, Jews have been treated extraordinarily well in the United States compared to other periods in history and compared to the anti-Semitic attitudes and behavior that has resurfaced in Europe. In a society where Jews can live wherever they want to live, work wherever they want to work, and marry whomever they want to marry, intermarriage has become a major challenge to the continuity of the Jewish people. There is concern that once intermarriage occurs, a family is lost to Judaism.

The issue of intermarriage brings up the question, "What is Judaism?" In *Judaism as a Civilization,* Mordecai Kaplan contended that Judaism is not simply a religion, not simply a way of behaving or believing, and not simply a matter of peoplehood. It was all of this and more. A civilization, Kaplan contended, is a dynamic complex of language, history, institutions, beliefs, practices, arts and ties to a land. One "belongs" to or participates in a civilization by identifying with any or all of these dimensions (Gillman, 1993, p. 78). Thus, Judaism is an ethnic group as well as a religion.

The ethnic facet of Judaism makes intermarriage more problematic for many Jewish parents, and such marriages are potentially the cause of considerable confusion and conflict. The conversion of the non-Jewish partner is a solution that satisfies many Liberal parents; such converts can become more serious about their religion than their born-Jewish spouses. Jewish grandparents can experience much pain as they see grandchildren growing up without a Jewish education and with minimal identification with a community that has been important to them and to their families.

Judaism as a civilization is a concept that has importance beyond the Reconstructionist movement. There are many Liberal Jews who spend little or no time thinking about their relationship with God and who do not attend religious services on a regular basis but nevertheless may have a strong identification with Judaism. They send their children to secular schools but also send them to Supplementary Religious Schools. They enjoy holidays and family events at their synagogues and encourage their children to become a *bar* or *bat mitzvah.* An interesting (and for those involved, unhappy) phenomenon is the young adult who comes from a family that has a casual attitude toward Judaism and who becomes interested in more traditional beliefs and practices. The young person studies classic texts, becomes involved with Jews who are Orthodox, and becomes an Orthodox Jew, to the consternation of parents who consider Orthodoxy foreign and antithetical to the way they raised their child.

Jews tend to place a high value on family relationships, and many are very involved in an appropriate way in caring for elderly relatives. The Jewish community helps by devoting a significant amount of resources to services for the elderly. Jews have a tradition of taking care of their own. Many Liberal Jews give money to Jewish charities, and a number of them do volunteer work for Jewish charitable organizations. Many Liberal Jews have a passionate interest in, and identification with, the State of Israel. Synagogues sponsor organized trips to Israel for youth groups and adult members of their congregations. A number of Liberal Jews visit Israel on their own.

THE THEORY OF PSYCHOLOGICAL HEALTH AND PATHOLOGY INHERENT IN THE FAITH

There is no coherent theory of psychological health and pathology inherent in the faith of Liberal Jews; however, references to psychopathology appear as early as the Bible. King Saul suffered from depression and suspiciousness with fits of anger, and David played the harp to soothe him. There are statements about mental illness and the legal status of the mentally ill in later Jewish texts as well.

The intense relationships in Jewish families can give rise to psychological conflicts and inhibitions. Not living up to family expectations can cause emotional distress, and the guilt-provoking Jewish mother is the subject of Jewish humor. On the other hand, the closeness of Jewish families can provide emotional support for individuals suffering from depression and other psychiatric disorders. Jews tend to be involved in the affairs of family members to an extent that may be interpreted as pathological by outsiders. This involvement may serve an adaptive function in a Jewish family.

For complex historical reasons, Jews have a record of achievement in industrial and postindustrial societies. The pressure to succeed can be problematic for Liberal Jews who feel they are not achieving enough vocationally and economically and can be magnified by the belief they are not measuring up to family standards.

THE THEORY OF HUMAN CHANGE INHERENT IN THE FAITH

For all denominations, Judaism is a behaviorally oriented religion; faith alone is insufficient to be a good Jew. Because Liberal Jews tend to place a high value on individual autonomy and freedom, the work of personal change, whether psychological, behavioral, or religious, is the responsibility of the individual. Jewish tradition recognizes and encourages this potential for individual growth through the concept of *teshuvah*, literally, return, and often translated as repentance. This concept is emphasized most dramatically during the High Holy Day season in the fall, on the holidays of Rosh Hashanah and Yom Kippur. On these days, communal and individual prayers in the synagogue focus on atonement for transgressions in the hope for a renewed commitment to improvement in the new year. God is depicted as a powerful King sitting upon the throne of Judgment. Redemption is possible, but it is significant that prayer on Yom Kippur, the Day of Atonement, is insufficient. Addressing sins between person and person and changing behavior for the better are also necessary.

The High Holy Days are the times of highest synagogue attendance among Liberal Jews, including a significant percentage who do not attend worship services at any other time during the year. Many Liberal Jews may be consciously attuned to repentance and return to God only at this time of year, although the idea of *teshuvah* is found in liturgy throughout the year.

Although the emphasis is on individual redemption, communal worship is important as well. Liberal Jews who are serious about their religion are expected to pray as part of a religious community on a regular basis. Traditionally, parts of the liturgy must be omitted if there is not a *minyan* or quorum present. Liberal Judaism tends to favor the concept of a loving God and a supportive Jewish community that wants to help people grow and succeed rather than a punitive God and a community that chastises.

COMMON MORAL ISSUES

The average Liberal Jew does not think much about the Biblical or rabbinic basis for positions on moral issues. Nevertheless, many do approach contemporary moral questions with views that are influenced by the Jewish values with which they were raised and that are prevalent in the Liberal Jewish community. Some Conservative rabbis and their congregants attempt to use a traditional Jewish legal process to address contemporary ethical concerns and decisions (Dorff, 1998).

Liberal Jews tend to have a sense of responsibility to the community at large as well as to the Jewish community. The ideals of *tzedakah* (translated as charity but derived from the Hebrew word for justice) and *tikkun olam* (repairing and improving the world) are highly valued in the Liberal Jewish world. Jewish philanthropists make significant monetary contributions to both Jewish and non-Jewish causes. Synagogues sponsor social action projects such as cooking in a soup kitchen, working in a nursing home, and providing aid to battered women.

Many Liberal Jews have an interest in social justice, a tradition that can be traced back to the ancient Prophets. Jews were active in the civil rights movement of the 1960s. The Religious Action Center of the Reform movement lobbies actively in Washington for liberal causes. Jews are joiners, and there are a large number of Jewish organizations. Some raise money for Israel and for needy Jews in the United States. The American Israel Public Affairs Committee is an organization based in Washington, DC that lobbies on behalf of Israel. The American Jewish Committee and the Anti-Defamation League were formed to fight anti-Semitism. Hillel is devoted to meeting the needs of Jewish students on college campuses. There is even a Conference of Presidents of Major American Jewish Organizations.

With the exception of a small percentage of Conservative synagogues, the Liberal movements are egalitarian with respect to gender. Female as well as male rabbis, cantors, and congregants lead services and read from the Torah. Prayer books in the Reform and Reconstructionist movements are gender neutral. The situation in the Conservative movement is more complex and is evolving. The decision to ordain women as rabbis in 1983 caused a rift in the Conservative movement, leading to the formation of the nonegalitarian Union for Traditional Judaism. Nevertheless, the majority of Conservative synagogues and Conservative Jews take the equality of women in religious as well as secular life for granted. There are women serving as rabbis, cantors, and synagogue presidents in Conservative congregations throughout the United States.

The Jewish tradition recognizes that sex not only involves physical pleasure; it is a form of communication in which marriage partners convey their love for one another. The tradition recognizes that both men and women have sexual needs, and the Torah and the rabbis who interpreted the Torah took the position that both spouses have a right to regular sex within marriage. Marriage and sex are also important because of the potential for bringing children into the world. In addition to the richness that children bring to marriage and life, procreation is necessary for the survival of Judaism. The emphasis on children in Judaism magnifies the negative feelings that infertile Jewish couples may experience.

Human life is sacred in the Jewish tradition. Abortion is permitted in some circumstances, but it is not viewed as a morally neutral matter of individual choice. Traditional Jewish law forbids abortion in most situations. Some authorities have ruled, however, that abortion is permitted and even required in certain circumstances. According to this interpretation, abortion is permitted when risk to the woman's life or health, physical or mental, is greater than that of a normal pregnancy but not so great as to be a clear and present danger to her. Abortion is required when the life or health of the mother, physical or mental, is threatened by the pregnancy. The threat to mental health has been interpreted both stringently and leniently. Abortion cannot be justified by traditional Jewish sources for reasons having to do with the health of the fetus; although some authorities justify the abortion in the case of a fetus with a major defect on the basis of preserving the mother's mental health. Although the preceding considerations may be important to Liberal Jews who have a serious concern about Jewish law, the majority have a pro-choice attitude toward abortion.

Homosexuality presents a challenge to Liberal Jews, who look to the Torah and rabbinic sources for guidance in moral matters. The book of Leviticus in the Bible is clear about its position on male homosexual behavior; it is abhorrent and warrants the death penalty. Later rabbinic authorities understood lesbian sex to be prohibited as well. Elliot Dorff (1998), one of the foremost contemporary Conservative rabbinic authorities on Jewish ethics, notes that the tradition assumes gay behavior is a matter of choice. Although one may lack understanding of the biological factors that underlie homosexuality, experience with gay and lesbian individuals contradicts the idea that homosexual behavior reflects a lifestyle choice. Gay and lesbian individuals appear to be as compelled to be attracted to the same sex as heterosexual individuals are compelled to be attracted to the opposite sex. The position that God created a minority of humans who have sexual drives that cannot be legally expressed is theologically problematic.

One can argue that Judaism sanctifies marriage and monogamous, loving sex between heterosexuals and should sanctify similar relationships between homosexuals. Some Liberal rabbis have performed commitment ceremonies for gays and lesbians. The Reform and Reconstructionist Rabbinical Seminaries ordain openly homosexual or bisexual rabbinic candidates. The issue continues to be debated in the Conservative movement, and for now, no openly gay, lesbian, or bisexual student can be admitted to either of the Conservative movement's seminaries.

The process of dying presents another challenge to non-Orthodox Jews, who look to Jewish law for guidance in decision making. Traditionally, the body is God's possession; the use of the body is granted by God during an individual's lifetime. Jews are prohibited from injuring themselves or killing themselves.

> Either of these actions is viewed as harming or destroying what belongs to God. . . . The only three occasions on which a Jew is supposed to prefer death at the hands of others or even suicide . . . [is] where the alternative is being forced to commit murder, idolatry, or adultery/incest, . . . all choices for the sake of God, not for oneself (Dorff, 1998, p. 181).

Advances in medical science have blurred the line between active and passive euthanasia and have made decision making more complex from a moral standpoint. Liberal as well as Orthodox Jews and their families may be challenged by difficult decisions at the end of life. Should a large dose of medication be used to relieve pain, even if that dose might hasten the patient's death? Should pneumonia be treated in the terminally ill patient? Should machines be turned off? Should artificial nutrition and hydration be withheld? Family members often want to know if their decisions about care are appropriate according to Jewish standards. At the end of life, even individuals who have been nonobservant may turn to their religion for guidance and support.

There is a famous story about the death of Rabbi Chananyah, who was burned at the stake by the Romans for teaching the Torah. He refused to inhale the flames to hasten his death. The Romans had attached tufts of water-soaked wool to his chest to make his death slower and more painful, and Rabbi Chananyah allowed his students to bribe the executioner to remove them. From this and other sources later Jewish authorities arrived at the position that it is acceptable to remove impediments to the natural course of dying but not to actively cause one's own death or someone else's. It should be noted that Judaism's opposition to euthanasia is not based on the idea that suffering is redemptive.

COMMON CLINICAL ISSUES

Depression can interfere in a major way with interpersonal relations. Thus it is not surprising that depression can interfere with a person's ability to relate to God. Just as depressed individuals often cut themselves off from family and friends, they may also cut themselves off from religious supports, ceasing to attend religious services, decreasing participation in community activities, and becoming unable to connect with prayer.

Survivors of the Nazi Holocaust are uniquely scarred by the atrocities they witnessed and endured. Multiple generations of families were wiped out, and loss is a prevailing theme in the psychology of Holocaust survivors and their families. Depression and chronic anxiety is common in Holocaust survivors. Guilt troubles some survivors; they ask themselves how they survived when so many others perished. The horrors of the Holocaust may be as salient to the memories of the survivors as if they just happened. Memories can be triggered easily by current events. Some survivors still suffer recurrent nightmares or flashbacks.

Children of survivors also can be affected. Survivor families tend to be particularly close-knit, and many survivor parents are overly protective of their children. Children of survivors may exhibit a role reversal in which they parent their parents (C. Silow, personal communication, March 2, 2004).

Prayer, both scripted and personal, is a means for Jews to deal with unhappiness. God is viewed as a source of strength, a healer of both body and soul. Traditional prayers and Psalms from the Bible address issues ranging from joy and celebration to anger and despair. The mystical Jewish literature includes themes of self-examination, overcoming negative emotion, and achieving spiritual and emotional peace. Liberal Jews have built on this tradition and developed healing services that include new as well as traditional prayers and time for personal sharing of physical and emotional concerns. Pastoral counseling with rabbis is an important resource for some Liberal Jews struggling with psychological issues; rabbis also can be helpful by connecting congregants to support services in the Jewish community. Liberal rabbis are generally very willing to refer to and collaborate with mental health professionals.

Liberal Jews seek help for clinical problems found in other religious and ethnic groups. Although there are no uniquely Liberal Jewish issues or disorders, it is common for the intense relationship of the Jewish family to become a topic of discussion in psychotherapy.

REFERENCES

Alpert, R. T., & Staub, J..J. (2000). *Exploring Judaism: A Reconstructionist approach*. Elkins Park, PA: The Reconstructionist Press.

Dorff, E. N. (1998). *Matters of life and death: A Jewish approach to modern medical ethics*. Philadelphia: The Jewish Publication Society.

Gillman, N. (1993). *Conservative Judaism: The new century*. West Orange, NJ: Behrman House.

Holtz, B. W. (1984). *Back to the sources: Reading the classic Jewish texts*. New York: Summit Books.

Kaplan, M. (1994). *Judaism as a civilization: Toward a reconstruction of American Jewish life*. Philadelphia: Jewish Publication Society of America.

Meyer, M. A. (1988). *Response to modernity: A history of the Reform movement in Judaism*. New York: Oxford University Press.

Stevens, E. L. (Ed.). (2003). Central Conference of American Rabbis Yearbook 1999, 2000, 2001, 2002. New York: Central Conference of American Rabbis.

Telushkin, J. (1991). *Jewish literacy*. New York: William Morrow.

United Jewish Communities. (2004). The National Jewish Population Survey 2000–2001. Retrieved September 15, 2004, from http://www.ujc.org

CHAPTER TWELVE

Orthodox Judaism: Features and Issues for Psychotherapy

Kate Miriam Loewenthal

IMPORTANT ASPECTS OF ORTHODOX JUDAISM

What are the most fundamental aspects of Orthodox Jewish beliefs and lifestyle? Which are most salient for psychology and psychotherapy?

Since the destruction of the second Temple nearly 2,000 years ago, many Jews were dispersed from the land of Israel, but the longing for a restoration of the Temple, and of a complete return of the Jewish people to the land of Israel, has remained a key feature of Jewish prayers and identity in the centuries that followed.

There are about 14 million Jews in the world today. About 3 to 4 million live in Israel, with a similar number in the United States and the former Soviet Union, and the remainder scattered in communities in every continent. Orthodox Jews can be broadly divided into two categories:

1. The strictly or ultra-Orthodox. In Israel, Jews in this group are called the *charedim*. The men wear conservative dark clothes, black skullcaps *(yarmulkes),* and black hats, and are often bearded. The women wear modest dress (skirts and sleeves below the knees and elbows, high necklines, and the hair covered, sometimes with a wig). There are many groups within *charedi* circles, of which the most noticeable are the pietistic *Chasidim,* numerous groups, each clustered around a charismatic

leader, a *Rebbe*. They are particularly likely to encourage religious enthusiasm and mystical experience.

2. The Traditionally and Modern Orthodox. In Israel, Jews in this group may be called *daatim* (although his term sometimes covers the ultra-Orthodox as well). Men dress more casually than in ultra-Orthodox circles, but may wear skullcaps (often crocheted and not black), and the dress of women, although modest, may not completely follow the strict dress code of the ultra-Orthodox.

The dress of the two groups has been described because dress sends important signals about religious identity and group membership. The strictly Orthodox may comprise about 10% of world Jewry, although estimates are hard to obtain. Estimates of the numbers of traditionally and modern Orthodox are even harder to make, but perhaps about one-third to one-half might identify themselves as traditionally or modern Orthodox.

Judaism is the oldest monotheistic religion, and belief in the unity of G-d, the origin and continuous source of creation, is by definition central. Orthodox Jews believe that G-d revealed teachings to humanity, via Moses, and passed down and elaborated by generations of pious scholars. (In Jewish law it is said that the name of G-d should not be spelled out in full since the paper may finish up in an unsuitable place.) There are laws applying only to particular categories of people—Jewish kings, for example, women who have recently given birth to a child, priests, and non-Jews. However, there is a large body of law and custom widely accepted and practiced by all Orthodox Jews. There are minor variations in detail between different subgroups of Orthodox Jews. The common features of all varieties of Orthodox Judaism include observance of the dietary laws, Sabbaths, and festivals; the sanctity of marriage (strict monogamy); encouragement of regular prayer and religious study; and a high value placed upon the Jewish home and family as the center of religious life. The education of children is an esteemed activity. Especially among the more strictly Orthodox, children are regarded as blessings of which one cannot have too many—therefore, family size is normally very large: Averages have been estimated at about six children per family. The core ethical teaching is widely quoted as, "Love your neighbor as yourself" (Lev 19:18), and Jewish communities are characterized by high levels of communal good works, with a wide range of charitable and support institutions (Holman & Holman, 2002). Mystical experience and religious enthusiasm are valued particularly among the more strictly Orthodox, famously in Hasidic groups.

Orthodox Jews, then, have monotheistic religious belief, a love of Israel, and follow strict laws about diet, Sabbath observance, sexual behavior, and other aspects of daily life. Family life, education, and practical kindness are all highly valued.

THE EPISTEMOLOGICAL TOOLS ACKNOWLEDGED AND SUPPORTED BY ORTHODOX JUDAISM

What are legitimate sources and kinds of knowledge for Orthodox Jews? Among the very strict, secular study is not highly regarded. Some areas of study may promote values that are seen as antithetical to Jewish values; for example, with respect to sexual behavior. For strictly Orthodox men, particularly in Hasidic circles, a lifetime career in religious study (often teaching) is the most esteemed career track. The intellectual demands are high, but the focus of study is Jewish law and lore, with no significant attention given to wider cultural, literary, artistic, or scientific topics. Women in such circles may have a wider education than men; however, women prioritize marriage and family commitments. These are likely to be heavy given the value place on having as many children as possible. Women commonly contribute to the family livelihood, sometimes being principal breadwinners in order to free their husbands for religious study. Time usually is made for communal charitable activities by both men and women. University education is rare, but technical training may be undertaken; the computer industry is very popular. Small business management and administration is another popular livelihood and, in some strictly Orthodox circles, medical and paramedical training and careers are religiously acceptable and commonly undertaken, including counseling and psychotherapy.

The traditionally and modern Orthodox do not eschew secular study and, as is well known, Jews have made significant contributions to science, medicine, and the arts. Medicine, law, and business are popular careers. As among the strictly Orthodox, women are free to devote themselves fully to family care if they wish, but it is common for women to be economically active.

Literal interpretation of Scripture—in its normally understood sense of the term—is not valued by Orthodox Jews. Scriptural study is said to involve several levels—the *P'shat,* the plain meaning—proceeding to more profound levels of mystical and kabbalistic interpretation and understanding. Every level of understanding (including the plain meaning) is open to different interpretations. Scriptural study normatively involves a small piece of text in center of the page, surrounded by hundreds or even thousands of words of commentary, offering diverse interpretation. "These and these are the words of the living G-d" and "There are seventy faces to the Torah" are commonly quoted in the face of apparently irreconcilable views, expressing Judaism's valuing of diversity of interpretation. Nevertheless, scriptural interpretation is not a free-for-all, and only interpretations offered by competent Orthodox religious authorities are accepted.

Although academic education is regarded with some suspicion, "pure" science, medicine, and mathematics are regarded as legitimate areas of activity by most Orthodox religious authorities. The Code of Jewish Law (*Shulchan Aruch,* which is adhered to by the strictly orthodox; see Ganzfried, 1850) states that when choosing a teacher, one should be careful that she or he be a G-d fearing individual. However when choosing a medical practitioner, one is obliged to seek the most professionally competent, regardless of her or his religiosity.

The guidance of the Code of Jewish Law is unclear about psychotherapy and counseling—is one getting "teaching" or medical help? In practice, the more strictly Orthodox and their rabbis have been negative about using mainstream psychotherapy and counseling services for reasons that become apparent later in this chapter. Spitzer (2003) regards it as essential that Orthodox and Hasidic patients with psychiatric and psychological disturbances are seen only by professionals from a similar cultural background. Spitzer and others argue that the behavior and feelings of Orthodox patients cannot be understood by others, and appropriate help and treatment can only be developed by those with a full immersion in the cultural and religious values and practices of the community.

THEORY OF PERSONALITY

The psychic structure inherent in Judaism involves a divine soul *(Nefesh Elokis)* and an animal soul *(Nefesh HaBehamis)*. One aspect of the animal soul is the intelligent soul *(Nefesh HaSichlis)* (e.g., the Hasidic work, *Tanya* by Shneur Zalman of Liadi). This is not unlike Freud's later structural theory, which suggested three psychic functions: id, ego, and superego, which correspond roughly to the animal, intelligent, and divine soul. Indeed, the similarities between Freud's thinking and that of Jewish tradition have been noted by several commentators (Bakan, 1958). The divine soul apprehends spiritual reality, and strives to cleave to G-dliness. The animal soul seeks material and self-centered pleasures, and the intelligent soul may be employed by either. The animal soul and the divine soul often have conflicting interests, and different Jewish mystical and ethical systems propose various methods of dealing with this conflict of interests, notably whether to suppress the animal soul and its demands by abstinence and fasting, or train the animal soul by teaching it to enjoy things done for the service of G-d. The latter path probably has been more popular. Judaism does not regard the animal soul as the work of the devil, but as a source of challenges to be dealt with in the right way. The source of animal soul is divine, although this is not obvious and apparent; hence, the apparent "reality" of evil.

Among Western Jews, the study of Jewish mysticism was largely confined to Hasidic circles, although it was more widespread among Asian Jews. More recently, Jewish mysticism has become a more popular topic for Orthodox study generally. Study includes the mystical systems of the *Zohar, Lurianic kabbalah,* and systems for contemplation and meditation.

The idea of a lifelong moral struggle that humans are inherently equipped to win, but in which they have complete free choice, is the simple but pervasive theme underlying Jewish ethical teaching and accounts of personal development. It is closely tied to the Jewish view of human development.

HUMAN DEVELOPMENT

Jews view human development as a lifelong process. In Judaism, no one has ever "made it," in the sense that some religious traditions offer the hope of enlightenment or salvation, after which there is a personal transformation and struggles for salvation ended. Even the totally righteous individual is engaged in a constant developmental struggle. Awareness of G-dliness is seen as an inherent human potential, but achieving this awareness is an ongoing process, and a necessary precondition to the spiritual–moral struggles that are the main purpose of existence.

Education, too, is a lifelong process. Training in religious awareness and spiritual work begin before birth, and all Jews are seen as having an obligation both to learn and grow, and facilitate the learning and growth of others. The study of religious texts and adherence to the myriad details of Jewish law are the key vehicles of this process. The following are some examples.

- Pregnant women and young children should avoid contact with non-kosher animals; for example, they should not be given toy bears to play with, as they may cause spiritual harm by their predatory nature.
- Very young children should be taught to say blessings before and after eating and drinking, to remind them that the food is not there solely to be enjoyed, but is from G-d, and the strength derived from eating is to be used for good activities.
- Teachers and parents should encourage children and adolescents to study and lead a religious life, but this should be in a way of pleasantness and firmness, without shouting, shaming, or using physical force: These latter methods produce short-term compliance but have no beneficial long-term effects.

- One very popular area of personal development in Orthodox circles is the study and practice of the laws relating to guarding the tongue *(Shmiras HaLoshon)*. Bad-mouthing, slander, and even gossip and chat, all may cause tremendous harm to the tellers, listeners, and object of discussion (Pliskin, 1977). Careful attention, detailed knowledge, and continual awareness are needed to maintain and develop standards in everyday social talk (Glinert, Loewenthal, & Goldblatt, 2004).
- Giving charity is seen as an obligation for all; even the poorest person should give a proportion of what she or he receives. This should be done several times daily, and implies the acknowledgment that G-d is the source of all material goods.

These are just a few examples of Judaism's approach to ongoing personal development and its relation to involvement in family and society. The age of transition to full adult moral and spiritual responsibility is clearly given as 12 (for women) and 13 (for men).

PSYCHOLOGICAL HEALTH AND PSYCHOPATHOLOGY

Traditional Jewish sources are said to describe a range of psychopathology that corresponds to what people are familiar with today (Loewenthal, 1995). Accounts of well-being and psychopathology also can be found in traditional sources, and there are many references in the book of Psalms and elsewhere to the importance of religious faith and trust: Positive well-being is suggested to result from trust in G-d, not consorting with bad people, not relying on the powerful and mighty, and serving G-d with joy. The other important therapeutic tool frequently advocated in traditional Jewish sources is the importance of offering assistance, comfort, and all forms of practical support to those in need: giving charity regularly to the chronically poor, consoling the bereaved, visiting and assisting the sick, lending money to those who have suffered financial setbacks to enable self-support. These are religious obligations and commandments *(mitzvot)*, and it is known that these forms of social support have powerful protective effects in preventing the onset of psychopathology among those who have suffered severe stress.

Interviews with lay people and religious leaders in the Orthodox Jewish community indicate that normatively, the causes of mental illness are seen as both social (particularly all forms of stress) and biological (perhaps particularly for psychosis) (Cinnirella & Loewenthal, 1999; Greenberg & Witztum, 2001; Loewenthal & Cinnirella, 1999).

The idea that psychological disorder is *solely* spiritual in origin (e.g., the results of the machinations of the evil inclination, *Yetzer Hora*), appears not to be widespread. However, all agree that succumbing to evil inclinations is spiritually unhealthy and psychologically damaging, although there are other causal factors in mental illness as well.

THEORY OF HUMAN CHANGE

Although there are frequent references to the importance of religious trust for well-being, this is not usually seen as a panacea, particularly not for serious psychopathology, either in religious traditions or among contemporary religious leaders or among the lay Orthodox Jewish public.

Jewish tradition has always endorsed the obligation to seek medical treatment, and the doctor is empowered by G-d to heal.

Medical treatment for psychosis, particularly medication, is seen as appropriate. There are no problems in Jewish law in seeking and obtaining this help.

However, there are reservations among Orthodox Jewish authorities on seeking counseling and psychotherapy for "minor" disorders (depression, anxiety) and social problems. Religious law appears to have no problem with taking medication. Many lay people, however, doubt whether medication does more than "relieve symptoms" without touching the underlying causes (Loewenthal & Cinnirella, 1999). Own-group counselors and psychotherapists who have had religiously approved training and are known to be G-d-fearing individuals may be consulted. However, some lay people have reservations about own-group counselors, particularly with respect to confidentiality and the level of professionalism (Loewenthal & Brooke-Rogers, 2004): "I wouldn't consider going to someone like Mrs X. I might be sitting next to her at a *simcha* (festive meal) the next evening, and I wouldn't like the idea that she might say something I don't want everyone to hear."

Some religious leaders suggest that religious faith, prayer, and other activities may be sufficient:

> We treat such problems in the community. We give the person with difficulties a boost, talking about belief, and trust in G-d, saying we must not despair . . . everything is from Heaven. We encourage him to listen to *nigunim* (Hasidic song), to read stories of miracles from the great rabbis (ultra-Orthodox rabbi, quoted by Greenberg & Witztum, 2001).

Thus, although faith, prayer, and other religious activities are widely seen as helpful, particularly in promoting positive well-being, a small minority endorses religious beliefs and activities as the sole panacea for psychological disorders.

COMMON MORAL ISSUES

There are several areas in which the values of Orthodox Judaism may conflict, or appear to conflict, with the needs of psychotherapeutic work. These conflicts and apparent conflicts are primary reasons for the reluctance of many Orthodox rabbis to unconditionally endorse the use of counseling and psychotherapy, although Orthodox counselors and therapists have received training and guidance in dealing with these issues and liaise closely with the rabbinate in their day-to-day work, so their work is usually endorsed by the rabbinate.

First, Jewish law does not condone homosexuality, masturbation, or extramarital or premarital sexual relations. Thus, any indication that these practices can be condoned or supported is not appropriate for Orthodox Jews, even though of course all of these practices can and do happen. Therapists who do not share Orthodox Jewish values and beliefs may think or suggest that an Orthodox Jewish client is being made guilty or anxious as a result of religious prohibitions about sexual behavior. Appropriate therapeutic support can be given only by a therapist who understands that the religious prohibitions are givens, and the feelings and conflicts of the client must be dealt with in the context of the client's probable acceptance that the laws about sexual behavior are right, even if she or he does not find them easy or convenient.

On a more minor level, touching and other contact with people of the opposite sex is not approved and therapists need to be aware not to offer to shake hands or touch strictly Orthodox clients of the opposite sex, although necessary contact for medical, life-saving purposes is permitted.

Second, more strictly Orthodox clients may be troubled by the laws regarding respect for parents and teachers and those prohibiting speaking badly of another person, which can make it difficult for clients to talk about abuse. There is complete rabbinic support for disclosing abuse, taking the appropriate steps to prevent its repetition, and dealing with the traumatized individual. However, clients need to be aware that there is such rabbinic support, and of course, as one Orthodox therapist has said, "I can't give guidance on Jewish law, that's not my remit, and clients couldn't and shouldn't accept what I say—it has to come from a *Rov* (rabbi) that the client trusts." It is important for therapists to be familiar with religious law, have appropriate rabbinic contacts, and be able to make suggestions about seeking appropriate rabbinic advice if clients seem likely to have reservations about making disclosures. It is also important for therapists to liaise with rabbinic authorities about child protection issues. Rabbinic authorities have developed policies and practices in this area consistent with the law, and closely liaise with the statutory authorities. It is important to know what these are and act accordingly, because therapists and clients who report child protection issues to the police or social services without appropriate liaison with rabbinic authorities may find themselves ostracized by lay people in the strictly Orthodox community who find it hard to accept that a respected member of the community has behaved abusively. The accused may be hotly defended as an innocent upright person who is being maliciously slandered by a disturbed individual. If lay members of the community can be made aware that there is rabbinic support for the steps being taken, this will defuse any counterproductive attempts to protect the abuser and delay protective measures.

Third, somewhat similar issues can beset attempts to deal with violent or abusive marriage relationships. Marriage is regarded as a holy and desirable state, and every attempt to preserve a marriage is regarded as praiseworthy and religiously meritorious. Nevertheless, there is no rabbinic support for domestic violence or other forms of abuse. Again it is important for therapists to be aware of the complex issues in religious law, and have appropriate rabbinic contacts.

Among the many other issues that may be important is the issue of child-bearing. Jewish law is clearly negative about the use of contraception, unless life is endangered, in which some but not all forms of contraception are permitted. Moreover, among the strictly Orthodox children are regarded as a blessing. Family sizes may be very large, and women (and men) may find themselves with inadequate resources to cope with parenting the very large numbers of children with which they have been blessed. It is important for the therapist not only to liaise with rabbinic authorities acceptable to the client, but also to have a good knowledge of the many support organizations within the community that specialize in this central dimension of Orthodox Jewish life.

These are the salient moral dilemmas involved in psychotherapy and counseling with Orthodox Jewish clients. There are clear conflicts with values that are normative in wider society, and there are complex issues in Jewish law that might best be dealt with by a therapist who is familiar with the strictly Orthodox community, its personnel and mores. However, many clients prefer to seek help and support from professionals from outside the community. This is often the case when the client seeks anonymity, and does not want to risk disclosing unpleasant and shameful secrets to someone who is part of the same community. It can be helpful for therapists and counselors to be aware of the issues and conflicts that may be troubling their clients, and reflect on and assess their own views on these moral dilemmas and how these views might affect their therapeutic practice.

COMMON CLINICAL ISSUES

Prevalence studies have suggested that patterns of psychiatric disorder differ in the Jewish community compared with other groups. Bipolar disorder is said to be more prevalent, as are mood disorders in general. Mood disorders are now established to result from the higher prevalence of major depressive disorders in Jewish men, and are possibly connected to the lower prevalence of alcohol abuse among Jewish men (Levav, Kohn, Dohrenwend, et al., 1993; Levav, Kohn, Golding, et al., 1997; Loewenthal, Goldblatt, Gorton, et al., 1995; Loewenthal, MacLeod, Goldblatt, et al., 2003).

There are assertions that obsessive-compulsive disorder (OCD) is more common among Orthodox Jews than other groups, but there are no reliable prevalence data. Lewis (1998) has concluded that although obsessionality as a personality trait is more likely among the religious (probably as a result of the religious valuing scrupulosity), OCD as a psychiatric disorder is not more likely in any of the religious groups studied compared with the general population. Greenberg and Witztum (1994) concluded that religion can provide the framework for the expression of OCD symptoms, but is unlikely to be a direct cause.

Nevertheless, prevalence is not necessarily reflected in the referral situation. The clinical problems and dilemmas in the consulting room are not a clear reflection of the distinctive patterns of prevalence of disorder in the Jewish community.

Important clinical dilemmas in the diagnosis and treatment have been reported in dealing with Orthodox Jewish clients.

First, there are difficult diagnostic issues that arise with religious behavior and ideas. Clients may fear misjudgment, which may be well founded. They may be reluctant to seek professional help for psychological distress for fear of being misunderstood. There is ample evidence to show that clinicians may indeed misjudge religious behavior as evidence of psychopathology, and may see religious clients as more likely to be disturbed (Gartner, Hermatz, Hohmann, et al., 1990; Littlewood & Lipsedge, 1997; Loewenthal, 1999; Yossifova & Loewenthal, 1999). For example, an Orthodox Jewish man who declined to shake hands with a woman psychiatrist (on religious grounds) was diagnosed as withdrawn and catatonic. Only advisors from the patient's own religious group are able to clarify whether the behavior is pathological or normative. Spitzer

(2003) asserts that Orthodox Jewish professionals are better qualified to detect whether a particular religious practice is pathological or normative. Greenberg and Witztum (2001) offer some helpful guidelines in making this decision about Orthodox Jewish clients. Again, rabbinic advice may be necessary, especially if it is appropriate to tell the client that a particular piece of behavior is not religiously advisable; for example, spending several hours repeating a particular phrase from the prayers to make sure it has been said correctly.

The other major group of clinical issues focuses on treatment. Which treatments are acceptable? Which treatments are seen as likely to be helpful?

Psychotherapy may not be acceptable: Therapists may be seen as unsympathetic, lacking in knowledge of the values and mores of the Orthodox Jewish community, and likely to misjudge religious behavior and ideas. Own-group therapists may not be trusted: The concerns here have to do with confidentiality and professionalism. Prayer, religious trust, and direct consultation with rabbis and other religious leaders are inexpensive, confidential, and relatively accessible. Therefore, religious support may be sought as a first resort, and there is considerable evidence that at least some significant forms of psychopathology may be helped by prayer, religious faith, and other religious means (e.g., Koenig, McCullough & Larson, 2000; Loewenthal et al., 2000). A common issue today is the extent to which therapists may recommend or even employ religious techniques. MacLachlan (1997) has recommended treatment plans that incorporate clients' beliefs about the causes of their distress and symptoms, and that cover all feasible methods of alleviation. Greenberg and Witztum (2001) offer fascinating accounts of interventions such as combinations of medication, and a range of psychotherapeutic techniques such as visualization, cognitive and psychoanalytic therapy, and religious techniques (including forms of exorcism). An important feature of Greenberg and Witztum's work is close liaison with the religious authority most acceptable to the client. They have emphasized the importance of working within the client's frame of interpretation. Symptoms may be seen as *idioms of distress*. The therapists' acceptance of the cultural–religious framework improves client trust, and work within the framework can produce beneficial results. The following example is a case in point.

Ezra was a 24-year-old married man who had been a Jewish penitent for 2 years. He was brought by his brother to the clinic because of "bizarre behavior." During the previous 6 months, while Ezra had been immersed in studying the *Zohar* (the key Jewish mystical text), he had heard voices and experienced dreams in which his late father appeared as a threatening black apparition. Ezra engaged in ascetic practices: He fasted frequently, wore tattered clothes, and visited the graves of *Zaddikim* (Jewish saints). He lit ritual candles on these graves and at home. After the birth of his first child, a girl, these practices became more intense, and 4 months later he was brought by his brother to the clinic and admitted. Ezra appeared unkempt, and was not completely oriented to place and time. His cooperation was minimal. He was depressed in mood, but his formal thinking was normal. He reported visions of a personal angel, and also nightmares in which his father appeared, dressed in black and with a sad, suffering face. These visions and nightmares had started after the birth of his daughter.

Ezra was the younger of two sons of North African descent. His father had been a quiet, sad man, who had begun drinking in mid-life, and had become a chronic alcoholic. At home, he would drink himself to oblivion, and fall asleep in his own vomit. One night, when Ezra was 15, his father called Ezra to bring him a glass of water. Ezra brought the water, but when his father asked him to stay with him, Ezra refused. In the morning, his father was found dead.

Ezra became depressed and guilt-ridden. He blamed himself for his father's death. He began taking hard drugs. His brother persuaded him to quit drugs, and join the army, which he did. After 2 years' military service, Ezra left the army, became religiously observant, and married. He prayed for a boy to name after his father.

He was shocked when his daughter was born. He began to hear a voice, which he identified as belonging to his personal angel. The angel said that instead of protecting him, he was punishing him for the neglect that led to his father's death. The angel told him to fast, wear tattered clothes, visit the graves of saints, abstain from sexual relations, and generally afflict himself so that he might be forgiven.

The therapists suggested to Ezra that in Jewish law it is forbidden to mourn a dead relative for more than 1 year. They appreciated that he was seeking an ecstatic religious experience that would signify that he had been forgiven, and attempted to encourage this; for example, by asking him to bring his father's photograph to sessions. Ezra wrote a letter to his father asking for forgiveness, and also looked intently at his father's picture and wept in a therapeutic session. The therapists also asked Ezra to investigate the angel: What were its intentions? What was its name? Was it really an evil spirit in disguise? In the 13th session, the therapists, together with Ezra's brother (who was a religious authority), attempted to exorcise the angel. Leading the ritual, the brother asked one of the therapists to read a formula from mystical–magical work *The Book of the Angel Raziel,* which Ezra used to summon the angel. During the reading, Ezra began to sway, moving his body and head in an increasingly rhythmic and vigorous manner. He added his own ecstatic singsong two-syllable phrase, and seemed to enter a trance. Suddenly, he became quiet and informed the others that the angel was present. Ezra's brother told the angel that on behalf of the religious court, he was ordering the angel to leave and return no more, neither for good nor bad, and not even to reveal mystical secrets. Ezra seemed stunned and confused, because of his long, intense, ambivalent relationship with the angel. One of the therapists explained that from then on the angel had no right to disturb him because the angel belonged to another realm. The brother, tense and emotional, told Ezra to complete the exorcism by blowing out the candles. Ezra did this, and he was declared a free man, under his own control.

The therapists had intended to convert the angel from a punitive enemy to an ego-supportive ally. Ezra's brother had thwarted this intention by stating that the angel must not return again, for good or bad. However, ultimately the angel behaved according to the therapists' expectations by returning occasionally, and always in the role of an ally (Witztum, Buchbinder, & Van Der Hart, 1990).

Although prevalence studies have suggested particular patterns of disorder in the Jewish community, in the consulting room the most common clinical issues focus on diagnosis and treatment: When is religious behavior pathological? Which treatments are religiously acceptable? Which religious treatments can be recommended or even used?

ADDITIONAL RESOURCES

The following is a brief list of some useful sources of further information, and research and clinical support for some of the suggestions made.

- Useful journals include *The Journal of Psychology and Judaism, Mental Health, Religion and Culture, The International Journal for the Psychology of Religion,* and *Social Science and Medicine.*
- Important books include Greenberg and Witztum's fascinating accounts of their mental health work among ultra-Orthodox Jews in Jerusalem, and Littlewood & Lipsedge's (1997) mesmerizing accounts of their mental health work among Hasidic Jews in North London. Bulka (1987), Spero (1985), and Spitzer (2003) all offer helpful suggestions about working with Orthodox Jewish patients.
- Useful articles on psychotherapy with Orthodox Jewish patients include Rabinowitz (2002), and Margolese (1998).
- More general works on religion and mental health, which can help to put the understanding of psychological issues among Orthodox Jews into the broader context of work on religion and mental health, include Koenig et al. (2001), Loewenthal (1995), and Pargament (1997).

REFERENCES

Bakan, D. (1958, reprinted 1990). *Sigmund Freud and the Jewish mystical tradition*. London: Free Association Books.

Bulka, R. P. (1987). *The Jewish pleasure principle*. New York: Human Sciences Press.

Cinnirella, M., & Loewenthal, K. M. (1999) Religious and ethnic group influences on beliefs about mental illness: A qualitative interview study. *British Journal of Medical Psychology, 72*, 505–524.

Ganzfried, S. (1850). *Code of Jewish Law (Kitzur Shulchan Aruch)* (translated in 1927 by H. Goldin as *A Jew and his duties*). New York: Hebrew Publishing Company.

Gartner, J., Hermatz, M., Hohmann, A., & Larson, D. (1990). The effect of patient and clinician ideology on clinical judgment: a study of ideological countertransference. Special issue: Psychotherapy and religion. *Psychotherapy, 27,* 98–106.

Glinert, L., Loewenthal, K. M., & Goldblatt, V. (2004). Guarding the tongue: An analysis of gossip control among orthodox Jewish women. *Journal of Multilingual & Multicultural Development*.

Greenberg, D., & Witztum, E. (1994) The influence of cultural factors on obsessive compulsive disorders: Religious symptoms in a religious society. *Israel Journal of Psychiatry and Related Sciences, 31*, 211–220.

Greenberg, D., & Witztum, E. (2001). *Sanity and sanctity*. New Haven, CT: Yale University Press.

Holman, C., & Holman, N. (2002). *Torah, worship and acts of loving kindness: Baseline indicators for the Charedi community in Stamford Hill*. Leicester: De Montfort University.

Koenig, H. G., McCullough, M. E., & Larson, D. B. (2000). *Handbook of religion and health*. Oxford, UK: Oxford University Press.

Levav, I., Kohn, R., Golding, J. M., & Weismann, M. M. (1997). Vulnerability of Jews to affective disorders. *American Journal of Psychiatry, 154*, 941–947.

Levav, I., Kohn, R., Dohrenwend, B. P., Shrout, P. E., Skodol, A. E., Schwartz, S., et al. (1993). An epidemiological study of mental disorders in a 10-year cohort of young adults in Israel. *Psychological Medicine, 23*, 691–707.

Lewis, C. A. (1998). Cleanliness is next to G-dliness: Religiosity and obsessiveness. *Journal of Religion and Health, 37*, 49–61.

Littlewood, R., & Lipsedge, M. (1997). *Aliens and alienists* (3rd ed.). London: Unwin Hyman.

Loewenthal, K. M. (1995). *Mental health and religion*. London: Chapman & Hall.

Loewenthal, K. M. (1999). Religious issues and their psychological aspects. In K. Bhui & D. Olajide (Eds.), *Cross cultural mental health services: Contemporary issues in service provision*. London: W.B. Saunders.

Loewenthal, K. M., & Brooke-Rogers, M. (2004). Culture sensitive support groups: How are the perceived and how do they work? *International Journal of Social Psychiatry, 50*(3), 227–240.

Loewenthal, K. M., & Cinnirella, M. (1999). Beliefs about the efficacy of religious, medical and psychotherapeutic interventions for depression and
schizophrenia among different cultural-religious groups in Great Britain.
Transcultural Psychiatry, 36, 491–504.

Loewenthal, K. M., Goldblatt, V., Gorton, T., Lubitsh, G., Bicknell, H., Fellowes,
D., et al. (1995). Gender and depression in Anglo-Jewry. *Psychological
Medicine, 25,* 1051–1063.

Loewenthal, K. M., MacLeod, A. K., Goldblatt, V., Lubitsh, G., & Valentine, J.
(2000). Comfort and joy: Religion, cognition and mood in individuals under stress. *Cognition and Emotion, 14,* 355–374.

Loewenthal, K. M., MacLeod, A. K., Cook, S., Lee, M. J., & Goldblatt, V. (2003).
Beliefs about alcohol among UK Jews and Protestants: Do they fit the alco-
hol-depression hypothesis? *Social Psychiatry and Psychiatric Epidemiology,
38,* 122–127.

MacLachlan, M. (1997). *Culture and health.* Chichester, UK: John Wiley & Sons.

Margolese, H. C. (1998). Engaging in psychotherapy with the orthodox Jew: A
critical review. *American Journal of Psychotherapy, 37,* xx.

Pargament, K. (1997). *The psychology of religion and coping.* New York:
Guilford Press.

Pliskin, Z. (1977). *Guard your tongue: A practical guide to the laws of Loshon
Hora.* Brooklyn: S. Weissman.

Rabinowitz, A. (2002). Psychotherapy with Orthodox Jews. In P. S. Richards &
A. E. Bergin (Eds.), *Handbook of psychotherapy and religious diversity.*
Washington, DC: American Psychological Association.

Shneur Zalman of Liadi. (1796). *Likkutei Amarim—Tanya* (bilingual edition
translated in 1973 by N. Mindel, N. Mandel, Z. Posner, & J. I. Shochet).
London: Kehot.

Spero, M. H. (1985). *Psychotherapy of the religious patient.* Springfield, IL:
Charles C Thomas.

Spitzer, J. (2003). *Caring for Jewish patients.* Abingdon, UK: Radcliffe Medical
Press.

Witztum, E., Buchbinder, J. T., & Van Der Hart, O. (1990). Summoning a punishing angel: Treating a depressed patient with dissociative features. *Bulletin
of the Menninger Clinic, 54,* 524–537.

Yossifova, M., & Loewenthal, K. M. (1999). Religion and the judgment of obsessionality. *Mental Health, Religion and Culture, 2,* 145–152.

SECTION VI

The Islamic Traditions

CHAPTER THIRTEEN

Psychology and Sunni Muslims

Saba Rasheed Ali

In order to understand the tacit psychological assumptions and world view of Sunni Muslims or Islam from a Sunni perspective, one has to have a basic understanding of the religion of Islam and its unique history. Muslims were not always divided into the two main sects of Sunni and Shiite; this division occurred in the mid-7th century after the death of Prophet Muhammad (the last and most well known prophet of Islam). This chapter attempts to provide the reader with an overview of Islam, including the major tenets, as well as the similarities among Islam, Christianity, and Judaism, and focus on the events that preceded Muslims before the emergence of the Sunni and Shiite sects. Much of the information contained in these sections is religious principle and historical information common to both Shiite and Sunni Muslims.

Next, this chapter provides a brief introduction to the historical divisions and ideological differences between Sunni and Shiite Muslims. The preceding sections allow the reader to better comprehend the psychology of Sunni Muslims, including information on epistemological tools used to determine Sunni ways of knowing, views of personality and normal or abnormal development, psychological health, and human change processes. The last two sections discuss how common moral and clinical issues are viewed and approached by Sunni Muslims.

OVERVIEW OF ISLAM

In order to provide a better understanding of Islam and Muslims, one must first understand the terminology used in Islam. For example, the word Islam itself comes from the Arabic root word *salaam* (peace), and literally translates from Arabic to English as "surrender." Islam is the word for the religion, whereas the word Muslim literally translates as "one who submits to the will of Allah" and characterizes a follower of Islam. A commonly mistaken term used synonymously with Muslim is Muhammadan. This term has been mostly used by non-Muslims to describe the "followers of Muhammad." However, Muslims believe that Muhammad was the last messenger of God; they do not worship Muhammad. In fact, it is against religious doctrine in Islam to ascribe godlike powers to Muhammad, and Muslims find it offensive when the term "Muhammadan" is used to describe a follower of Islam (Ali, Liu, & Humedian, 2004).

For Muslims, Allah is the word for the God of all humanity. Allah is not a separate deity confined only to Muslims. In fact, many Arab Christians also use Allah when referring to God. The *Qur'an* (or Koran) is the holy book for Muslims and also has a literal translation into English as recitation. The majority of the religious terminology in Islam is Arabic, the original language of the *Qur'an*. More definitions of important terms are provided in the following sections in discussion of important Islamic tenets.

HISTORY OF ISLAM

Muslims believe that the religion of Islam officially began in 7th century Arabia, when the first words of the holy *Qur'an* were revealed to Muhammad ibn Abduallah. At this time (610 CE), Muhammad was an Arab businessman in the city of Mecca and every year at the same time would meditate in a cave in the Mountain of Hira. During this annual meditation, Muhammad would keep a fast, pray, and give charity to economically disadvantaged members of society. According to most Islamic historians (Armstrong, 2000; Esposito, 1988; Haykal, 1976), Muhammad used this time for contemplation and was deeply concerned with the state of religious affairs in Arab society, particularly in the city of Mecca. His main concern was the treatment of the elderly, poor, and women in Arab society. These groups were essentially disenfranchised members of this society. One of his main concerns was that Arabia had deviated from its tribal responsibilities, which included caring for all members of its society, especially those who were disenfranchised. Most Islamic historians believe that in a quest for wealth and power, the Quraysh tribe (Muhammad's tribe and the most powerful in Mecca) had abandoned these values (Armstrong, 2000; Haykal, 1976). Muhammad's retreats to the Cave of Hira were to seek answers to the plaguing issues of Arabian society and find ways to assist the society to return to the roots of religious identification, which prescribed social justice and equity (Armstrong, 2000; Lippman, 1995).

Muslims believe that the first words of the *Qur'an*, the call to Islam, were predicated on this need for social justice and equity in Arabian society. On the 17th of Ramadan (the Muslim holy month) 610 AD, while Muhammad was meditating in the cave of Hira, the angel Gabriel brought the first of 6,340 verses of the *Qur'an*. Over the course of the next 22 years, the Angel Gabriel continued to bring the message of God to Muhammad, who in turn spread the religion to the people of Arabia until he died in 632 AD (Ali, Liu, & Humedian, 2004).

The Holy *Qur'an*

The scripture of Muslims is contained in the *Qur'an*. The original language of the *Qur'an* is Arabic, but it has been translated into almost every major language in the world. The *Qur'an* is divided into 114 *surahs*, or chapters. These *surahs* are organized from the longest to shortest. Muslims believe that some of the verses of the *Qur'an* were revealed to Muhammad from the Angel Gabriel in answer to a specific community question or crisis (Armstrong, 2000). Therefore, it is customary practice among many Muslims to learn the historical issues of 7th-century Arabia, in conjunction with the Prophet's sayings *(hadith)* and teachings *(sunnah)*, in order to understand *Qur'anic* prescriptions and instructions in context. Although some of the verses provide immediate guidance for the specific context, Muslims believe that these verses also contain broader universal guidance for future generations of Muslims. Included in this broader guidance are the basic principles of the Islamic religion known as the five pillars of Islam (Lippmann, 1995).

BASIC TENETS OF THE ISLAMIC FAITH

Although there is great variation in cultural practices and adherences to many of the principles of Islam, five basic principles are commonly accepted by all Muslims as the pillars or foundational principles on which the religion is based (Esposito, 1998). The first pillar of Islam is the belief *(iman)* that there is one God and that the Prophet Muhammad was his last and final prophet. *La liha illallah Muhammedoor Rasoola* (there is only one God and Muhammad is his messenger) is known as the *shahaada*. This is the only phrase that one needs to recite in order to convert to Islam and is considered the basis of the religion. Lang (1996) characterizes this phrase as not only a declaration of faith, but also as a sociopolitical statement that implies recognition that there is only one God for all humanity. This recognition elucidates the issues of social equity, in which God will only judge human beings according to their actions and deeds toward others and not according to their religion, race, ethnic background, wealth, or power. The *Qur'an* states, "We have created for you from a single soul, male and female, and made you nations and tribes, so that you may come to know one another. Lo! The noblest among you in the sight of God is he who is best in conduct" (*Qur'an*, 49:13).

The second major tenet of Islam is prayer (*salat*). Prayer is prescribed for five times during each day. Prayers involve a series of Arabic recitations and prostrations toward the Kaaba (the Muslim Holy Shrine in Mecca) and are uniform across all Muslims. The timing of these prayers is as follows: before sunrise (*fajir* prayer), early afternoon (*zuhur* prayer), midafternoon (*aser* prayer), just after sunset (*maghrib* prayer), and before retiring for bed (*isha* prayer). All of these prayers can be individually or congregationally performed. A special prayer, the *juma* prayer, is allocated for Friday (*juma*) of every week. This prayer is performed in a congregation (*jumat*) and is obligatory for males, but optional for females. Congregational prayers also are performed on the holidays of *Eid ul Fitr* (ending of Ramadan) and *Eid ul Adha* (ending of Hajj or pilgrimage).

Zakat, the third major tenet of the Islamic faith, is a form of charity that is compulsory upon all Muslims. It has been characterized as one of the most important of the Islamic duties. *Zakat* originally meant self-purification and was not just a charitable act, but also considered a "loan to God" (Schimmel, 1992, p. 35). Haykal notes: "Concerning zakat and charity, the *Qur'an* talks at length, clearly and emphatically. It has classified charity among the highest deserving virtues of the greatest reward; indeed, it has placed charity alongside the conviction of God, thus leading us to believe that the two are equal" (1976, p. 535). The most common estimate of *Zakat* practiced among Muslims in the United States is that 2.5% of all savings and earnings are donated annually. This percentage is to be given to the "less fortunate" and is commonly paid at the end of *Ramadan* during *Eid ul Fitr* (Lippman, 1995).

Islam also prescribes fasting (*sawm*) for its followers; this is the fourth pillar of Islam. This prescription is completed in the month of Ramadan and requires Muslims to refrain from liquids, food, and sexual activity for the entire period from sunrise to sunset. During this month, Muslims are required to continue their daily activities (e.g., work, family obligations), but to also use this as a time for self-reflection and spiritual discipline designed to increase empathy for the poor and needy (Esposito, 1998). Ramadan is the 9th month of the lunar calendar and typically lasts 30 days. Because Muslims follow the lunar calendar, the timing of the month of Ramadan falls at different points of the Roman calendar from year to year.

The final tenet of the Islamic faith is the pilgrimage to Mecca *(Hajj)* that is to be performed once in a lifetime. Lippman describes *Hajj* as: ". . . the unifying force in Islam. It brings together in the experience of faith the polyglot peoples of a multiracial, international religion; it is the event in which all sects within Islam participate side by side" (Lippman, 1995, p. 22). Once the pilgrims have arrived in Mecca they are required to perform a complex series of rituals to commemorate the lessons of the Prophet Abraham (the same Abraham that both Christians and Jews endorse as the founder of their religions). The *Kaaba* is the central shrine in this commemoration and is located in the Great Mosque in Mecca. This pilgrimage, which begins once a year on the 10th day of *Zul-Hajjah,* the 10th month of the lunar calendar, is only obligatory for those who can afford to perform it.

OTHER RELIGIOUS PRACTICES

Restrictions

Islam prohibits gambling and consumption of pork and alcohol. In addition, eating meat from an animal that has not been slaughtered is prohibited in the *Qur'an.* Muslims are required to only eat meat that has been slaughtered in the name of God *(halal)* and has not had any polytheistic gods names invoked at the time of slaughter *(haram).* Meat that has been slaughtered by people of the book *(ahl al khitab)* is permissible. Muslims consider both Jews and Christians as people of the book. There are different explanations for the prohibition against alcohol and pork, but most of these are speculations by Muslims and Muslim scholars; the *Qur'an* does not give specific reasons for these restrictions.

Gender Roles, Customary Dress, and Family Values

Cultural practice heavily influences the treatment and expectations of Muslim women, and there are many complex and comprehensive texts that specifically address these issues. The author refers the reader to these texts for further information on these issues (see Haddad & Esposito, 1998; Haddad & Lumis, 1987; Wadud, 1999). However, it is important to understand that Islam does prescribe modest dress for both men and women. The *Qur'an* states in Surah al Nur:

> Say to believing men that they should lower their gaze and guard their private parts: that is more pure for them. Surely God is well-acquainted with whatever you do. And say to believing women that they should lower their gaze and guard their private parts, and that they should not display of their adornment except what [ordinarily] appears thereof, and that they should draw their head coverings over their breasts and not display their adornment (24:30–31).

This verse *(ayat)* has been interpreted in many different ways, so that some Islamic cultures and governments regulate women's dress and require women to cover themselves completely *(burqa)*, whereas others believe that the meaning of modesty is open to interpretation and tend to take these verses more liberally (Haddad & Lumis, 1987).

Similarities with Judaism and Christianity

Muslims view Islam to be a continuation of Judaism and Christianity (Armstrong, 2000; Lang, 1996; Lippman, 1995) and trace the religion's roots to the time of Adam. The Prophet Muhammad is believed to be one in a succession of prophets who brought God's message to people in various parts of the world, with the first of the Prophets being Adam. In addition, Muslims believe that Jesus and Moses were both Prophets of God sent to the Jewish people, whereas Muhammad was sent to bring the same message to the people of Arabia. Many of the stories of the Old Testament are retold in the *Qur'an*, including the stories of Moses, Noah, and Adam and Eve. In addition, there is one *surah* or chapter of the *Qur'an (Surah Maryam)* dedicated to Mary, mother of Jesus. In this *surah* the story of the virgin birth is retold. The religion deviates from Christianity after the death of Jesus. Muslims do not accept Jesus as the Son of God or the Savior, but as a prophet who was sent to bring his message to the people of Israel. Therefore, portions of the New Testament such as the letters of St. Paul, are not incorporated into the *Qur'an*. However, Muslims do believe portions of the Christian version of Jesus and his crucifixion. The Muslim version is that Jesus was nailed to the cross, but did not actually die on the cross. It is believed that Jesus was taken directly to heaven and replaced by another body.

History of the Division Between Sunnis and Shiites

Although this chapter is intended to focus on the psychology of Sunni Muslims, it is almost impossible to describe Sunni Muslims without first contrasting Sunni with Shiite Muslims. Political divisions first brought about this division around 657 AD. After the death of the Prophet Muhammad in 632 AD the Muslim community was left to establish leadership. Because the *Qur'an* had clearly indicated that Muhammad was the last prophet, the Muslims in Arabia were forced to find a successor who could provide governance to the community, but this leader would not fulfill the role of spiritual and religious leader vacated by the Prophet. Abu Bakr, who was a very close companion of the Prophet, emerged as the first community leader or *Calipha*. Abu Bakr was selected to this post by a small group of Muslims (Lippman, 1995). Hence, not all Muslims in the Muslim community believed that Abu Bakr was the rightful leader or successor to Muhammad. Another small group of Muslims believed that an actual blood relative of the Prophet had a legal and moral right to the caliphate and thus, believed that Ali (the cousin and son-in-law of Muhammad) was the rightful successor. The decision to appoint Abu Bakr as leader instead of Ali began the schism between Sunni and Shiite Muslims. Ali did eventually ascend to the Caliphate, but only after two successors to Abu Bakr (Umar and Uthman). When he finally ascended to the post of *Calipha*, political strife emerged that resulted in Ali's murder and subsequently the murder of his two sons (Hassan and Husain). These events helped to solidify the schism between the Sunni and Shiite (Shiat Ali or "party of Ali") Muslims.

These historical events and other ideological differences are the basis for the separate sects of Islam. Approximately 15% of Muslims are Shiite. More detail about Shiite Muslim beliefs is provided in the chapter on Shiite Muslims. Approximately 85% of Muslims in the world are Sunni Muslims (Lippman, 1995):

> Sunnites are usually defined as followers of the *sunna*, the path or way of the Prophet. In practice, they are those who historically accepted the authority of the Caliphate, whoever held it and however he attained it, as opposed to those who believe that the office should be hereditary to the Hasemite [Muhammad's clan] line (p. 137).

PSYCHOLOGY AND SUNNI MUSLIMS

Sunni Muslims and Epistemological Tools

Sunni Muslims generally believe in an individual's direct relationship to God. It is through this relationship that knowledge is sought and gained. Divine inspiration comes through reading the *Qu'ran, Sunnah*, and *Hadith*. The *Qu'ran* is considered to be the supreme miracle of Islam because it conveys God's words directly to the followers. There is no clergy among Sunni Muslims; thus, there is no belief that religious knowledge and interpretation are relegated to certain individuals or that an intermediary relationship is necessary in order to obtain knowledge about right and wrong. The Muslim belief is that the *Qu'ran, Sunnah*, and *Hadith* provide the knowledge about right and wrong, but do not necessarily always provide knowledge about every aspect of life or moral dilemma that a person may face. Therefore, Islam supports a person's application of his or her own intellect and reason to determine the right course of action when confronted with a moral dilemma that is not clearly defined by the *Qu'ran, Hadith*, and *Sunnah*. This concept is known as *itjithad*.

Islam in theory is also a religion that has been traditionally rooted in knowledge, science, and education (Boisard, 1979; Eaton, 1985), promoting acquisition of knowledge through science and religious teaching. Sardar notes:

> Islam not only places a high premium on science, but positively encourages its pursuit. Indeed, Islam considers it essential for human survival. The Koran devotes almost one-third of its contents to singing the praises of scientific knowledge, objective inquiry and serious study of the world. The first Koranic word revealed to the Prophet Muhammad is: "Read." It refers to reading the "signs of God" or systematic study of nature. It is a basic tenet of Muslim belief that the material world is full of signs of God; and these signs can be deciphered only through rationale and objective inquiry (2004, p. 28).

In contrast to the contentious relationship between science and religion in Christianity, an Islamic view tends to hold religion and science as "part of the same continuum complementing each other" (Anees, 2002, p. 99). There are a great number of references in the *Qu'ran* to the acquisition of knowledge through the understanding and interaction with the earth and universe and to gain knowledge through education and science is considered an act of worship. The importance placed on science in Islam resulted in the propagation of scientific discovery and invention during the early years of Islamic civilization known as the classical period (8th to 15th century). However, this period of enlightened scientific inquiry did not continue in many modern Muslim countries, where scientific inquiry may not be a high priority (Sardar, 2004).

Theory of Personality

There are a few concepts that are extremely important to understanding Sunni views of personality development. First, the exercising of one's individual freedom and responsibility while submitting to *Allah's* will is central to the faith of Islam. Boisard (1979) writes, "Individual behavior is not imposed by the outside, but is 'internalized' by faith. The believer's commitment arises from the choice he makes to obey" (p. 47). Ideally, this statement means that a Muslim has to choose every day to submit to the will of God, and therefore has choices in the determination of his or her future. Therefore, part of implementing this choice requires one to use the virtues and senses that God has given to each human being. Lang (1996) writes:

> Virtues are abstract concepts and difficult to define, but I believe that we can agree that to grow in virtue at least three things are needed: *Free will,* or the ability to choose; *intellect,* so that one is able to weigh the consequences of his or her choices and learn from them; and third, and

equally important *suffering and hardship*. As we see the *Qu'ran* emphasizes strongly all three of these while discussing man's spiritual evolution. To grow in compassion, for example, is inconceivable without suffering. It also requires the choice, the ability to choose to reach out to someone in need or to ignore him. Intellect is necessary so that one telling the truth may lead to personal loss and suffering, which can be predicted through the use of one's reason (p. 51).

The *Qu'ran* constantly emphasizes certain virtues as part of optimal development of a Muslim and Muhammad is conceptualized to be the ultimate example of these virtues. For Muslims, God cannot be emulated and it is beyond human understanding to know God in His entirety. Christians may refer to God as our Father, but Muslims do not believe that God has those types of relationships with human beings and therefore, would not refer to God in this manner. Muslims refer to God as in many different ways. The 99 Arabic names of God represent qualities attributed to God such as "The Creator" or "The Beneficent." Emulation of Muhammad's personality is considered to be the healthiest and morally correct view of personality. Within the religion there is a strong emphasis on the specific human characteristics that Muhammad embodied such as humility, truthfulness, modesty, kindness, and self-discipline. Self-discipline in the worship of God, while also participating in life fully is expected and considered harder to achieve than simply worshiping God at the expense of life's daily tasks. A Muslim is expected to have an occupation, family, and acquire wealth (but not hoard it) while also remembering to worship God through *salat* and *zakat*. The main focus of one's life is to serve God through daily acts of worship and this focus is manifested in one's personality.

In Islam spiritual, moral, physical, cognitive, and mental development are all considered to be components that form a whole person (Ansari, 2002) and cannot be separated from one another. Central to this notion is the unity of the outward and inward being. Eaton writes:

If we envisage the outward personality as the changing expression or projection of an unchanging nucleus or centre, then we may begin to glimpse an answer to the perennial question: 'Who I am I?' But we cannot stop here; there is one more step to be taken before the question is finally resolved. This centre, called by Muslims (though not by Muslims alone) the 'heart' is indeed the central point to which outward personality corresponds as periphery, but although it is 'within' us, it is not ours. It belongs to God, and is eternally present with Him; and yet, since it is also 'within' us, it is the place where He is present, immanent. In other words, if we penetrate sufficiently deeply into ourselves— through all the layers of dreams and darkness—we come into the open and find everything there; hence the saying of the Prophet: . . . 'he who knows himself knows his Lord' (1985, p. 188).

From a biological perspective it is believed that all of these virtues are contained in the "heart" and have been provided for a person from birth and it is up to the person to access and use the virtues appropriately. However, it is understood that a person who is devoid of certain mental capacities is not necessarily responsible for their actions (e.g., those who have mental retardation or schizophrenia). In these cases, it is expected that the community will assist these individuals.

Optimal Human Development

In Islam, as in Christianity and Judaism, the goal of life on earth is to live consistent with God's commandments and it is believed that one will be rewarded for this in eternal paradise (heaven or *junta*) after death. Therefore, development of a person is looked at as optimal if one is continuously striving to achieve the highest moral character. Self-actualization is obtained through self-knowledge and self-discipline, which are both central to the Islamic tenets. It takes a great deal of self-discipline to maintain a daily schedule of five prayers at the appropriate times and also to keep a fast from sunrise to sunset during the month of Ramadan. These acts of worship are designed to increase one's ability to achieve self-knowledge and actualization through the understanding of suffering and remembrance of God.

Optimal human development is also discussed in the *Qu'ran* in terms of the importance of community and therefore there is a social focus in human development. The *Qu'ran, Sunnah,* and *Hadith* provide multiple references to and examples of optimal social development such as development of character, treatment of others (e.g., family, community members, fellow Muslims) and an emphasis on forming family ties through marriage and procreation.

Islam places a high emphasis on heterosexual marriage (Haneef, 1996). In general, unmarried men and women are warned about forming close ties prior to marriage, but are highly encouraged to seek companionship through marriage. Marriage is mentioned several times in the *hadith* as the second half or completion of one's faith. Differences in gender roles and differences between men and women are readily acknowledged within Islam and the *Qu'ran* at times refers to these differences almost as if they were biological in nature. For example, the personality or "nature" of men and women is often discussed in terms of women's delicate, sensitive, or emotional nature. And yet, there are also numerous examples in Islamic history of women displaying intellectual, courageous, and heroic characteristics.

Regarding development of these inherent personality differences between men and women, Haneef writes: "Because the nature of the male and female are not the same, each has been entrusted with a particular role and function in society: these roles are complementary and each is equally basic and essential to the functioning of the society" (1996, p. 156). Therefore, as part of optimal human development, men and women are expected to fulfill certain roles. For example, men are expected to provide for their families, whereas women are expected to be mothers who care for the children. Motherhood is highly stressed and valued for women in Islam. Most Muslims societies consider it unnatural or deviant for a woman to choose not to be a mother and wife. Equally deviant is a man who chooses not to be a father or husband.

Psychological Health

Much like Mormonism (Koltko, 1990), Sunni Muslims generally believe that their religion is very potent and that if they live their lives consistent with Islamic values they should not need psychotherapy (Hedayat-Deba, 2000). Unfortunately, this can lead to Muslims feeling ashamed when they do seek treatment for legitimate personal crises or mental health issues.

One concept (and certainly not the only view) of mental illness among Muslims is that it can be the result of the disharmony or constriction of consciousness that comes from lack of faith. Lack of faith may occur because a person has concentrated his or her attention on material possessions and egoism, while neglecting spiritual matters. Consistent with this view is the concept that evil and sin are manifested as mentally unhealthy and self-destructive. Lang writes:

> The statements in the *Qu'ran* and in the traditions of the Prophet that state that an evildoer's heart (his spiritual and moral sense) becomes dark, veiled, rusted, hard and hence impenetrable, and that the hearts of the virtuous become soft, sensitive, and receptive to God's guiding light, immediately come to mind. The verses in the *Qu'ran* that convey this idea most powerfully are those that assert that the sinners destroy themselves by their wrongdoing—that they commit *zulm* (sin, wrong, harm, injustice, oppression) against themselves (1996, p. 60).

However, the *Qu'ran,* although strongly emphasizing the individual's responsibility to repent for their sins, also discusses at length repentance and forgiveness, reinforcing the concept that God is forgiving and merciful. The concept of forgiveness in Islam extends beyond God simply forgiving sins, the *Qu'ran* also states that God will help those who seek forgiveness to repair any damage that the individual has inflicted upon others (Lang, 1996). One of the most famous sayings of Muhammad was that "when we go toward God walking, He comes toward us running."

Human Change Processes

The Islamic perspective of health emphasizes that it is a gift from God. This belief is based on the Qu'ranic verse: "If God should touch thee with misfortune, then none could remove it but He; and if He would touch thee with good fortune—it is He who has the power to will anything" (*Qu'ran* 6:17). Therefore, Muslims believe that all healing is directly the result of God's will and any knowledge that a therapist has and uses to assist a client is a divinely revealed science (Ansari, 2003). Hence, psychotherapeutic tenets of human change and Islamic values are not inherently in conflict with one another, because seeking help from God and others to improve one's life is consistent with religious doctrine. However, as mentioned, some Muslims believe that it is shameful to seek therapeutic treatment from others outside of their religious community or family. Therapists who understand these issues may be able to assist their Muslim clients to overcome or deal with this shame by incorporating Islamic teachings into therapy to help Muslim clients cope with their psychological issues.

Common Moral Issues

As with many other religious groups, Muslims are faced with many important moral dilemmas that can cause psychological conflict. Some of these dilemmas are shared with believers of other religions (e.g., sexuality), whereas are other moral dilemmas are unique to Islam. A few of these dilemmas are discussed in this section.

Interest, Usury, and Loans

Moral issues concerned with the accumulation of wealth are unique to Islam. For example, one major moral dilemma facing devout Muslims in the United State is the paying and receiving of interest. Islamic law technically forbids a Muslim to earn interest on loans because it is considered usury (Haddad & Lumis, 1987). This concept is incompatible with the American banking system, where it is virtually impossible to acquire a loan without paying interest. In an extensive qualitative study of American Muslims, Haddad and Lumis (1987) found that some American Muslims have found a way to rationalize the use of American systems of savings and loans. These authors note:

> Some feel that the Islamic injunction against usury means only that one should not pay or collect unreasonable interest, that is, that one should not engage in loan-sharking but that [a] fair interest rate is acceptable. Others believe that although *Qu'ranic* injunction does in fact apply to

all forms of taking and receiving interest on loans, this was meant for Islamic countries and was not intended to make life impossible for a good Muslim in a country where they are a small minority and the economic and commercial institutions do not operate in accordance with Islamic law (Haddad & Lumis, 1987, p. 99).

Sexuality

As with many religious groups, the expression of sexuality can become a moral dilemma for Muslims. Islam forbids sexual intercourse before marriage and in general men and women are discouraged from forming close ties prior to marriage. Within Islam there is an emphasis on both men and women "preserving their chastity" until they are married. However, once a person is married they are highly encouraged to express their sexuality with one another. Marriage is considered a commitment for life. Divorce is not forbidden in Islam, but it is highly discouraged; thus, most Muslim societies tend to have low divorce rates. Additionally, adultery is considered a grave sin.

Homosexuality is also considered a sin in Islam, which poses a difficult moral dilemma for those Muslims who identify themselves as lesbian or gay. A majority of Muslims do not reveal to other Muslims or their families that they are struggling with their sexual orientation for fear of judgment. Most Muslim societies can be extremely hostile toward gay and lesbian persons. Counseling or psychotherapy may be the only safe opportunity for Muslims struggling with sexual orientation to deal with these issues. In these cases a psychotherapist may be able to provide support and a nonjudgmental space for these clients to discuss their issues. It would be very important for psychotherapists to balance a perspective of helping these clients to deal with issues related to sexual orientation and also deal with the hostile reality that exists for gay and lesbian persons within Muslim society.

Common Clinical Issues

Ali et al. (2004) and Hedayat-Diba (2000) outline some common clinical issues that Muslim clients might face. A brief version of these issues is outlined in this section, but the author refers the reader to the references for more in-depth detail about these issues.

Alcoholism

Alcoholism is an important clinical issue and moral dilemma for Muslim societies. There is very little information about the prevalence rates of alcoholism for Muslims because alcohol consumption is strictly forbidden in Islam. Although the consumption of alcohol is forbidden, it cannot be assumed that Muslims adhere to this principle. For example, recent refugees from political strife may turn to alcohol to cope with posttraumatic stress disorder and related issues (Nasser-MacMillian & Hakim-Larson, 2003). This may cause a Muslim to experience his or her alcoholism as a moral conflict; therefore, admitting and dealing with the problem may have different implications than for a person whose religion does not forbid consumption of alcohol. Ali et al. (2004) note that Muslim clients who seek treatment for alcohol-related problems also may feel more comfortable discussing their issues with a non-Muslim therapist, because they may be able to discuss alcohol-related problems without feeling guilty or judged.

Depression and Suicide

There is limited information about depression and suicide rates in Muslim societies. Lowenthal, Cinnirella, Evdoka and Murphy (2001) found that consistent with the prevailing attitude among Muslims that they should be able to cope with psychological difficulties through their faith, Muslims were more likely than members of other religious groups to believe in the ability of Islam and Islamic social support rather than mental health treatment to cope with depression. Therefore therapists might suggest that Muslim clients use Islamic tenets to deal with depression, such as using the five daily prayers for meditative purposes or turning to *Qu'ranic* passages for spiritual lessons (Nielson, 2004). However, caution should be used with these suggestions, especially when the feelings of depression seem to be linked to the client's struggle with their religious identity.

Assessing suicidal ideation might be difficult with Muslim clients, especially with those who are less acculturated to Western culture (Hedayat-Diba, 2000). Islam strictly forbids suicide, and suicide is a criminal act to many Muslims. Therefore, it may be necessary to assess for suicidal ideation by asking about its passive expression; by asking, for example, "Do you wish that God would let you die?" rather than asking if the person has thoughts of suicide (Hedayat-Diba, 2000).

CONCLUSION

The psychology of Sunni Muslims can be highly influenced by their religious beliefs. This chapter outlines the major tenets and beliefs of the faith while also providing some insight into the developmental, personality, cognitive, and moral aspects of these beliefs. Although this chapter does not discuss all the aspects of Islam that might affect a Sunni Muslim's psychological beliefs, it does highlight some of the most important tenets and psychological assumptions that are inherent within the religion. The information outlined in this chapter can assist therapists who work with Muslim clients to incorporate religious beliefs into therapy while also providing a context for understanding their Muslim clients.

REFERENCES

Ali, S. R., Liu, W. M., & Humedian, M. (2004). Islam 101: Understanding the religion and therapy implications. *Professional Psychology: Research and Practice, 35,* 635–642.

Almeida, R. (1996). Hindu, Christian, and Muslim families. In M. McGoldrick, J. Giordano, & J.K. Pearce (Eds.), *Ethnicity and family therapy* (2nd ed.) (pp. 395–426). New York: Guilford Press.

Anees, M. A. (2002). Islam and scientific fundamentalism. *New Perspectives Quarterly, 19,* 96–101.

Ansari, Z. (2002). Islamic psychology. In O. R. Paul (Ed.), *Religious theories of personality and psychotherapy: East meets west* (pp. 325–357). New York: Haworth Press.

Armstrong, K. (2000). *Islam: A short history.* New York: Random House.

Boisard, M. A. (1979). *Humanism in Islam.* Indianapolis: American Trust Publications.

Eaton, C. L. (1985). *Islam and the destiny of man.* New York: State University of New York Press.

Erikson, C. D., & Al-Timimi, N. R. (2001). Providing mental health services to Arab Americans: Recommendations and considerations. *Cultural Diversity and Ethnic Minority Psychology, 4,* 308–327.

Esposito, J. L. (1998). *Islam: The straight path.* New York: Oxford University Press.

Haddad Y. Y., & Esposito, J.L. (1998). *Islam, gender, and social change.* New York: Oxford University Press.

Haddad Y. Y., & Lumis, A. T. (1987). *Islamic values in the United States.* New York: Oxford University Press.

Haneef, S. (1996). *What everyone should know about Islam and Muslims.* Chicago: Kazi Publications.

Haykal, M. H. (1976). *The life of Muhammed.* Delhi, India: Crescent Publishing

Hedayat-Diba, Z. (2000). Psychotherapy with Muslims. In P. S. Richards & A. E. Bergin (Eds.), *Handbook of psychotherapy and religious diversity* (pp. 289–314). Washington, DC: American Psychological Association.

Koltko, M. E. (1990). How religious beliefs affect psychotherapy: The example of Mormonism. *Psychotherapy, 27,* 132–141.

Lang, J. (1996). *Even angels ask: A journey to Islam in America.* Beltsville, MD: Amana Publications.

Lippman, T. W. (1995). *Understanding Islam: An introduction to the Muslim world.* Middlesex, England: Penguin Books.

Lowenthal, K. M., Cinnirella, G. E., & Murphy, P. (2001). Faith conquers all? Beliefs about the Role of religious factors in coping with depression among different cultural-religious groups in the UK. *British Journal of Medical Psychology, 74*, 293–303.

Nasser-MacMillian, S. C., & Hakim-Larson, J. (2003). Counseling considerations among Arab Americans. *Journal of Counseling and Development, 81*, 150–159.

Nielsen, S. L. (2004). A Mormon rational emotive behavior therapist attempts Qur'anic rational emotive behavior therapy. In P. S. Richards & A. E. Bergin (Eds.), *Casebook for a spiritual strategy in counseling and psychotherapy.* Washington, DC: American Psychological Association.

Sardar, Z. (2004). How to take Islam back to reason. *New Statesman, 133*, 28–30.

Schimmel, A. (1992). *Islam: An introduction.* New York: State University of New York Press.

Wadud, A. (1999). *Qur'an and woman.* New York: Oxford University Press.

CHAPTER FOURTEEN

Psychology and Shia Muslims

Amina Mahmood

The previous chapter provided the reader with an introduction to Islam, its history, the commonalities among Islam, Judaism, and Christianity, and the beliefs and practices of Muslims. It also presented a brief overview of the split within the Muslim community into two major groups (Sunni and Shia). The Sunnis constitute the majority of the Muslim population, whereas the Shia comprise approximately 15% to 18% of the world's Muslim population (currently estimated to be 1.2 billion). Although the Sunni and Shia factions of Islam share many commonalities, significant ideological differences distinguish these two groups from one another. To gain a clearer understanding of the psychological assumptions and world view of Shia Muslims, it is important to have a basic understanding of Islam, as well as an awareness of the history of the schism that led to the development of Shiism.

This chapter provides the reader with a detailed account of the factors leading to the emergence of Shiism as a separate sect within Islam. To avoid repetition, only those beliefs and practices that are unique to Shia Muslims or differ significantly from the practice of Sunni Muslims are discussed. The reader is encouraged to gain familiarity with the basics of Islam that are common to both Shia and Sunni Muslims by referring to the previous chapter. It is hoped that the historical account of the development of Shiism will assist the reader in reaching a better understanding of the psychology of Shia Muslims, including epistemological tools, views of personality, optimal development, psychological health, and human change processes. Finally, this chapter assesses some of the common moral and clinical issues that are viewed from the Shia Muslim perspective.

OVERVIEW OF SHIA ISLAM

History of the Sunni–Shia Divide

As mentioned in the previous chapter, the death of the Prophet Muhammad (peace be upon him [pbuh]) in 632 AD created a political division in the Muslim community. The Prophet Muhammad (pbuh) died without appointing a successor. However, the Shia't Ali[1] (those who supported Ali)[2] maintained that the Prophet Muhammad (pbuh) had designated Ali to be his successor (Armstrong, 2000; Lippmann, 1995; Momen, 1985; Pinault, 1992), and point to various *Hadith* (sayings of the Prophet) and verses of the *Qur'an* as evidence (Momen, 1985; Pinault, 1992). Initially the Shia't Ali consisted of a small proportion of individuals in the Muslim community who believed that Abu Bakr (a trusted companion of the Prophet who reigned 632–634) was wrongfully appointed as the *Caliph* (leader), a position they believed should have been filled by Ali. Various sources indicate that the supporters of Ali encouraged him to become their leader. However, Ali refused to do so in order to maintain unity in the Muslim community (Momen, 1985).

After Abu Bakr, another trusted companion of the Prophet Muhammad (pbuh), Umar (632–644), was appointed the *Caliph* of the Muslim community. This caused further resentment among the Shia't Ali, because they believed that the Prophet's wishes to have Ali appointed as his successor were being ignored. After Umar's reign as the *Caliph*, Ali was offered to become the *Caliph* by consensus among the companions of the Prophet and respected leaders of the community on two conditions. First, Ali should rule according to the *Qur'anic* guidelines and principles, and the example of Prophet Muhammad (pbuh). Second, he should maintain the precedents set up by the previous two *Caliphs* (Momen, 1985). Ali refused the latter condition; therefore, the Caliphate was passed onto

[1]The word *al-Shia* means "the party of." So, for instance, followers of Prophet Abraham can be referred to as Shia't Abraham. To put it in today's context, members of the Democratic Party in the United States can be called the Shia of the Democratic Party. Therefore, the word Shia indicates that one is a member of a certain group, be it the democrats, republicans, or followers of a religious or political leader.

[2]Ali was the Prophet's cousin and son-in-law, and it has been narrated that the Prophet had chosen him to lead the Muslim community after his death. While on his deathbed the Prophet had requested one of his companions to bring paper and ink to him so that the Prophet could get his decision to appoint Ali as his successor in writing. This request was not fulfilled in time and the Prophet passed away before his decision could be recorded.

Uthman (644–656), another trusted companion of the Prophet. Uthman's Caliphate created many problems for the Muslim state. Under his leadership nepotism flourished, which is evident in the appointments of his family members (who would later establish the Ummayad dynasty) to positions of power in the administration (Esposito, 1998; Momen, 1985). Many communities within the Muslim empire were discontent under Uthman's rule and they sent delegations to Medina (the seat of government of the Muslim state, in present-day Saudi Arabia) voicing protest against his Caliphate (Momen, 1985). These rebellions by dissatisfied communities eventually led to the murder of Uthman by members of the rebellious factions.

Ali became the fourth *Caliph* of Islam in 656. The Caliphate of Ali was accepted and approved by the vast majorities of Muslims, not only those in Medina but also by those inhabiting the various provinces of the Muslim empire. Momen (1985) states that Ali was the first *Caliph* truly "chosen by a consensus of all the Muslims (p. 24)." Ali's Caliphate dealt with the many internal problems in government remaining from Uthman's administration. During Ali's Caliphate the seat of government was moved to Kufa (in present-day Iraq). Additionally, the first civil war within Islam was fought during this period, resulting from Mu'awiya's refusal to pay allegiance to Ali's Caliphate. Mu'awiya, an infamous figure abhorred both by Sunnis and Shiites, was a relative of Uthman. During Uthman's reign he had been appointed as the Governor of Syria. Mu'awiya faced Ali in the Battle of Siffin in 657 (Momen, 1985).

A segment of Ali's army seceded after Ali agreed to engage in arbitration during this confrontation, which led to the victory of Mu'awiya's army. Those who seceded, known as the Kharjiites, began to pose a serious threat to Ali's government. It was a member of the Kharjiites who assassinated Ali in 661 AD. The period 632–661 AD is known as the period of the "Rightly Guided Caliphs" both by the Sunnis and the Shiites (Armstrong, 2000; Esposito, 1998; Momen, 1985; Pinault, 1992). Ali's son Hasan succeeded his father and became the next *Caliph* of the Muslims. However, Mu'awiya coerced Hasan into yielding the Caliphate (Momen, 1985; Pinault, 1992) which he did not as an "act of feeble cowardice but a realistic and compassionate act" (Momen, 1985, p. 27). Hasan was aware that the people of Kufa were not united, and that Mu'awiya was in control of the empire. Therefore, even though the Shia't Ali sent delegations asking Hasan to start an uprising, Hasan chose to stay away from politics. Hasan died in 669; historians indicate that he was poisoned on Mu'awiya's orders. Mu'awiya was aware that despite Hasan's seclusion from politics there was still the possibility that Hasan may be chosen as the next *Caliph*. Additionally, Mu'awaiya had signed a peace treaty with Hasan that indicated that the Caliphate would be passed to Hasan after Mu'awaiya's death. Therefore, Mu'awiya resorted to eliminating Hasan and thereby securing the succession of his son Yazid to the Caliphate, thus creating the first Muslim dynasty, known as the Umayyad dynasty.

During this stage of development the Shia't Ali were primarily political in nature (Momen, 1985). They believed that leadership of the Muslim community should be limited to members of the immediate family of the Prophet Muhammad (pbuh) and his descendants (i.e., the Ahl al-Bayt;[3] Pinault, 1992), which led to their focus on political activities. It is not until the events of Karbala, which are detailed next, that the emergence of Shiism is seen as a distinct school of thought within Islam.

The Events of Karbala

The battle of Karbala in 680 AD contributed to the consolidation of religious Shiism. Leading up to this battle was the death of Mu'awiya in 680. His successor was his son Yazid. The Shia't Ali in Kufa sent a message to Husayn (Ali's son, Hasan's brother) to lead a revolt against Yazid. The people of Kufa indicated that they would provide military support and fight with Husayn to overthrow Yazid, the corrupt Umayyad ruler. Husayn gathered an army of 72 men, and along with women and children headed toward Kufa. This small army was intercepted and surrounded by Yazid's troops at Karbala. From the 2nd to the 10th of Muharram (the first month in the Muslim calendar) Husayn's army remained at Karbala surrounded by the Ummayad army, while negotiations were underway to resolve the situation. The encampment was in need of the basic necessities of food and water, which were denied them by the Ummayad army. Husayn spoke to his troops on the 9th of Muharram, asking them to leave him to face the enemy alone (Momen, 1985). However, this small band of followers refused to desert their leader and the fighting began on the 10th of Muharram. Members of Husayn's army were already weakened by hunger and thirst and the steady artillery from the enemy took a toll on them. Soon only Husayn and his half-brother Abbas were left. Abbas was killed while trying to get water for the women and children at the camp. A passage from Momen illustrates the helplessness of Husayn and the heartlessness of the Ummayad army:

> Carrying his infant son in his arms, Husayn pleaded for water for the baby but an arrow lodged in the baby's throat killing him. As the troops closed around him, Husayn fought valiantly until at last he was

[3]Certain *Qur'anic* verses (Chapter 22, verse 33, and Chapter 3, verse 61), in conjunction with various *Hadith* are cited as evidence for the leadership of the Muslim community by the *Ahl al-Bayt*, as well as the infallibility of the members of the *Ahl al-Bayt*.

struck a severe blow that caused him to fall face down on the ground. Even then the soldiers hesitated to deal the final blow to the grandson of the Prophet until Shimr ordered them on, and, according to some accounts himself came forward and struck the blow that ended Husayn's life (1985, p. 30).

After Husayn's death his entire household was taken captive and his head was delivered to Yazid in Damascus. It is in Yazid's palace, that Zaynab (Husayn's sister) is said to have held the first *majlis* (lamentation assembly, see Other Religious Practices) to mourn for her brother (Pinault, 1992). Husayn's struggle at Karbala plays a central role in Shiism. It symbolizes for the Muslims as a whole and especially for the Shiites "an expression of the Muslims' longing for freedom, for liberation from unjust rulers, and, in later times (especially in British India), from foreign powers that oppress believers" (Schimmel, 1992, p. 21). The value of social justice, which the religion of Islam emphasizes, became even more important for the Shiites after the events of Karbala. The martyrdom of Husayn is observed in the Shiite world today during the month of Muharram, with specific observances and rituals held during the first 10 days of Muharram.

Consolidation of Shiism

Shiism consolidated itself as a distinct ideology about 200 years after the Prophet's death. The martyrdom of Husayn created a division among the Muslim community that was deeper than political allegiances. Over time the Sunni–Shia split created distinctions in doctrine. It is important to note that the fundamentals of faith (see previous chapter) are common to both the Shiites and Sunnis. There are some differences in practices and additional tenets of faith that are unique to Shiites (discussed in further detail in the following). It is also important to note that disagreements over doctrine within the Shiite camp have led to further splits within the Shiites. For example, Zaydis and Ismailis are two offshoots from the Shiite Muslims. This chapter deals primarily with orthodox or Twelver Shiism,[4] which is most prevalent.

The Basic Doctrines of Faith

There are five basic elements in the Shia doctrines of faith. The first three are common to the Muslim community as a whole (i.e., Shia and Sunni

---

[4]The Twelver Shiites believe that the 12th *Imam* (leader) of the Muslim community went into occultation and will return at the end of time. The offshoot groups of Shiism believe that an Imam prior to the 12th one (e.g., Ismaili's believe it is the 7th Imam) went into occultation. Further explanations about the *Imams* is provided in the section *The Basic Doctrines of Faith*.

Muslims). The two additional elements are unique to Shiism. The first element of Shiism is the belief in the unity of Allah (the Arabic or Muslim word for God). This is also known as *Tawhid*. *Tawhid* involves the recognition that there is no god save Allah and that the Prophet Muhammad (pbuh) is the "Seal of the Prophets." In the declaration of faith that attests to the concept of *tawhid* (i.e., the *shahada* [see previous chapter]), Shiites add another phrase *Ali ul Wali-Allah* (and Ali is God's friend [and vice-regent on earth]). The second doctrine of faith is the belief in the line of prophethood beginning with Adam and ending with the Prophet Muhammad (pbuh). The third doctrine of faith of the Shiites (also in agreement with other Muslims) is the belief in the finality of this life and in the Day of Judgment, when one's life will be accounted for and who will go to heaven and who to hell will be decided.

The fourth doctrine of faith is specific to Shiites. It is the belief in the Imamate. For Muslims as a whole an *Imam* in general refers to someone who leads the prayer. However, it holds a different meaning for Shia Muslims. For Shiites *Imams* are "those members of the *Ahl-e Bayt* who are true spiritual leaders of the Muslim community regardless of any political recognition or lack thereof extended by the Muslim world at large" (Pinault, 1992, p. 5). The *Imam* is the rightful leader of the Muslim community, according to the Shiites, and the only individual qualified to hold political and religious office. The first *Imam* was Ali, and the second and third *Imams* were Hasan and Husayn, respectively. The Shiites believe that the *Imams* are those members of the Prophet's family who have been passed on the esoteric knowledge (hidden knowledge, which cannot be accessed by the lay person) about Islam by the previous *Imam,* beginning with Ali, who was given the knowledge by Prophet Muhammad (pbuh) himself. There are 12 *Imams;* the twelfth *Imam* is known as the "Hidden Imam" or the "Mahdi." It is believed that the twelfth *Imam* was divinely concealed by God in the 10th century and will return as the "Mahdi" or "the one guided by God" to usher in the Day of Judgment. All Shiite *Imams* have been persecuted by the reigning authority of their times, with the exception of the twelfth *Imam*. The Shiites believe that the 12 *Imams* in addition to the Prophet Muhammad (pbuh) and his daughter Fatima, are infallible; that is, they are incapable of making any mistakes or committing any sins.

The 14 infallible *Imams* (the Prophet Muhammad [pbuh], his daughter Fatima, and the 12 *Imams*) are believed to provide means of intercession to God for the Shiite individual. This belief in the infallibility of the *Imams* is one of the main doctrinal issues that distinguishes Shia from Sunni Islam. For the Shiites the *Imam* is "not only a worldly ruler but the highest spiritual authority" (Pinault, 1992, p. 9). The absence of the twelfth *Imam* means the absence of a legitimate ruler because the *Imam* is the only legitimate leader of the community. To resolve this, Shiites choose Ulama (religious scholars) to be their leaders until the *Imam* returns. The member of the Ulama elected to be the leader is highly educated in matters of religion and jurisprudence, and is a *Mujtahid* (one who is qualified to apply the concept of *Ijtihad,* investigative reasoning to resolve situations). There are various ranks within the members of the Ulama. This hierarchy of the Ulama is not present in Sunni Islam. Another distinction between Sunni and Shia Ulama is that Sunni Ulama historically worked with the government of the times; therefore, being on government payroll, were typically subordinated by the government (Pinault, 1992).

The fifth doctrine of faith in Shiism is the concept of God's Justice or *Adl.* Although both Sunnis and Shiites agree on this concept, Shiites have incorporated it into their basic doctrines of faith. This concept emerged via a group of early religious intellectual thinkers known as the *Mutazilities* and was later adopted into Shia doctrine. The *Mutazilites,* an 8th-century philosophically oriented group, the relied on rational thought. One of their main debates was questioning whether God is just, kind, wise, and powerful. Their conclusion was that by attributing the human qualities of being just, kind, wise, and powerful, one is defining a being that is beyond definition. Thus, they concluded that God rather than being just, is justice itself.

Basic Religious Practices

The religious practices of prayer *(salat),* fasting *(sawm),* paying charity tax *(zakat),* pilgrimage *(hajj),* and struggle *(jihad)* are primarily the same in Shiism as in Sunnism, with only minor differences. Shiites sometimes combine the afternoon and late afternoon prayers, and the evening and night prayers, thereby praying three times a day. There is also less emphasis on the Friday congregational prayers in Shiism than in Sunnism. Shiites tend to break their fast when the sun has completely set under the horizon; therefore their fasts last a few minutes longer than those of their Sunni brethren.

Jihad has two meanings. One is known as the lesser struggle, which is the physical defense of the religion against those who want to dismantle it. The other is known as the greater *jihad,* which is one's struggle with one's own ego in order to become a better Muslim. This *jihad* is ongoing throughout a Muslim's life, whether Sunni or Shia.

Basic religious practices unique to Shiism consist of *khums,* or profit sharing. In addition to the charity tax *(zakat)* the Shiites pay one-fifth of their profits to their religious leader. The *khums* tax is levied after one has accounted for all of her or his expenses. This money is used to maintain the religious leader and also is passed out to the poor and needy in the community by the leader. *Khums* originated in the days of early Islam when the Muslim empire was expanding beyond Arabia, when soldiers gave one-fifth of the spoils of war to the government.

The last two basic religious practices consist of Enjoining the Good, and Forbidding Sinful Acts. The Shiites as a minority have faced extensive persecution; these two basics of religious practice illustrate the serious regard Shiites give to social responsibility, social justice, and advocacy. The Sunnis and Shiites share these principles, but the Shiites have included it as one of their basic religious practices.

Other Religious Practices

In addition to the practices mentioned in the previous chapter there are some practices that are unique to Shiism. These include visiting the Shrines of the *Imams*, as well as visiting shrines of Shia saints. Another practice, referred to as "a guiding principle for any Shiite" (Pinault, 1992, p. 9) is that of *taqiyya*, religious dissimulation. This means that Shiites, who are under considerable persecution, may hide their true faith under perceived threat.

There are, of course, religious practices that specifically commemorate the events of Karbala (see section Events of Karbala). The Shiites observe a 40-day period of mourning beginning in the month of Muharram and continuing on into the second month of the Muslim calendar, to commemorate the events of Karbala. *Majalis,* or mourning, assemblies are held in various households or Shia community centers. The story of Karbala is retold at these gatherings. Additionally, elaborate passion plays are conducted that tell the story of Karbala. This practice appears to have been adopted from the Christians, and appeared in Shiism around the 17th century.

The Shiites also engage in *Matam* as an act of mourning. *Matam* involves chest beating with one's hand or self-flagellation where one beats upon oneself with chains or blades. *Matam* is not mandatory but is considered commendable. *Matam* is a symbolic act that allows the Shiites to "be imaginatively present at Karbala" (Pinault, 1992, p. 106). The Majalis also play a similar role by using words (stories and poetry) to help the Shiite Muslim vividly remember the tragedy that occurred at Karbala. The Shiites also believe that their remembrance and mourning of the tragedy of Karbala will earn them intercession on the Day of Judgment from Fatima (Pinault, 1992).

In Iran the government has banned acts of *Matam* that result in blood-letting. Many other Shiite communities across the world prohibit or discourage the Shiite mourner to engage in self-harm during *Matam*.

Although there are Shiite communities (especially in South Asia) where Matam practices do result in self-harm, these practices are colored by the culture in which they are practiced. Regardless of culture, it is considered unacceptable to engage in a mourning practice that can lead to a loss of limb or death. It is left up to the individual to determine whether he is engaging in a practice that will lead to such harm. It should be noted that the intention is more important than the act. Great emphasis is placed on the purity of one's intention in Shiism, as is true of Sunnism.

Another somewhat controversial practice of Shiism is that of *Muta'a,* or temporary marriage. This is a legal marriage agreement that can last from a few minutes to several years. The time limit, along with other concerns, is contractually agreed upon by both parties. The logic behind temporary marriage is to curb immoral ways of engaging in sexual activity prior to marriage. *Muta'a* is a last resort, which should be adopted after other options have failed; that is, one is not able to marry on a permanent basis and is also unable to follow abstinence. A detailed discussion about the logic and practice of *Muta'a* can be found in Rizvi's, *Marriage and Morals in Islam.* There is evidence of the practice of temporary marriage in the early days of Islam, which is why it is still accommodated in Shia jurisprudence. However, it should be noted that temporary marriage, like the practice of polygyny, is rarely practiced.

EPISTEMOLOGICAL TOOLS

A great deal of overlap exists between Sunnism and Shiism in terms of epistemological tools; therefore, only those tools additionally employed by Shiites are discussed herein. The reader should keep in mind that the discussion in the previous chapter is relevant to Shiism unless otherwise stated in the present chapter. Unlike the Sunnis, the Shiites believe that the *Imams* possess esoteric knowledge about the *Qur'an* and the religion that only they can transmit to the population at large. Although Shiism does not negate an individual's direct relationship with God and ability to acquire religious knowledge and interpret it, Shiites rely on their *Imams* to convey the esoteric knowledge that lies within the *Qur'an.* The Shiites (and the Sunnis) believe there are many layers to the *Qur'an.* There is the outermost layer, which is literal and can be comprehended by anyone, but there is also an inner (hidden or esoteric) layer, the meaning of which in Shiism can only be understood and transmitted by the *Imams.* Sunnis believe that anyone can access the *Qur'an* at the inner and outer layers.

In the absence of the *Imam,* the Shiite community relies on the *Ulama* and *Mujtahid* to teach the general populace about the religion. In Sunni Islam the concept of *ijma* (consensus of the majority) is followed in matters where one is unsure of how to resolve the problem at hand. Shiism has rejected this approach and relies primarily on the *Mujtahid*'s (one who practices *ijtihad*) decision. This should not be surprising, as the Shiites are a minority that has been oppressed by the majority Sunnis. The rejection of *ijma* by the Shiites can be traced back to the election of the *Caliphs*. Shiites believed that Ali was the rightful successor of the Caliphate; however, through majority consensus other *Caliphs* were chosen. One should also remember that according to the Shiites, the majority Sunnis have made wrong decisions about Muslim leadership. Because the majority Sunnis have repressed the Shiites, it is understandable that Shiites disdain *ijma* (which requires majority consensus) and prefer *ijtihad*.

With regard to following the *hadith,* the Shiites differ from the Sunnis in that in addition to the Prophet's *hadith,* they give importance to the sayings of Fatima and the 12 *Imams.* The sayings of all the 14 infallible ones provide guidance to the Shiites.

Another point that should be made regards the acquisition of knowledge. All Muslims emphasize the importance of acquiring knowledge. The first words of the *Qur'an* urge people to read and acquire knowledge. As an oppressed minority, Shiites have always maintained a tradition of intellectualism, even during times when censorship of knowledge was introduced into the Muslim empire. In fact some of the greatest Muslim scholars are Shiites. During the decline of the Muslim empire (which was marked by the pervasive censorship of knowledge), Shiite centers of learning flourished throughout the Muslim world. The Shiites' intellectual prowess resulted from their unwavering acceptance of *ijtihad* (investigative reasoning). Conversely, the Muslim world at large (i.e., the Sunnis) had closed the doors to *ijtihad*. Additionally, censorship had crept into society, adversely affecting the proliferation of arts and sciences in the Muslim world.

THEORY OF PERSONALITY

Although the theory of personality development presented in the previous chapter applies to Shiism, it should be noted that the Shiite model of development includes the 12 *Imams* as role models for optimal human development.

The events of Karbala, which are central to Shiism, are a factor in understanding the Shiite views of personality. *Imam* Jafar al-Sadiq (after whom the Shiite school of law [Jafari] is named) said, "Every day is Ashura [the 10th day of *Muharram,* when Husayn was martyred] and every land is Karbala." This signifies the important role of *jihad* in Shiite personality development. The implication of the quote is that Shiites should strive to remove injustices daily. Martyrdom while fighting for justice is honorable. Martyrdom does not solely imply death. The definition of martyrdom is dying while fighting for a justifiable cause. Examples that illustrate martyrdom frequently involve people who die while engaged in war. At another level martyrdom can be interpreted, for instance, as the failure of erasing racial discrimination from society even when all options were used to do so. Therefore, *Imam* Jafar's quote serves as a mechanism to mobilize Shiites into taking action against the undesirable and unjust systems present in society.

Contradictory to the message of *Imam* Jafar is the concept of *taqiyya,* in which the Shiite is allowed to hide her or his identity for fear of persecution or imminent danger to one's faith. Therefore, many Shiite Muslims learn to balance the concept of *taqiyya* with the decree to work toward a just and fair society.

OPTIMAL HUMAN DEVELOPMENT

As mentioned in the previous chapter, living consistently with God's commandments is the goal of the Muslim. Amini (1997), a Shiite scholar, talks about the two dimensions of human existence to explain optimal human development in Islam. The human being possesses a lower or animal dimension, and a higher or spiritual dimension. It is the struggle *(jihad)* between these two dimensions that eventually leads to self-actualization when the higher or spiritual dimension gains control of and subdues the lower or animal dimension. The process of self-actualization occurs as one adheres to the teachings of the religion. This includes following the basic practices of the religion, and more importantly establishing one's intention. The intention *(niyyat)* with which one approaches an act of worship, education, or charity is considered extremely important. There is no distinction between the secular and religious life in Islam; therefore, every act of a Muslim is considered a religious act. The intention is important because God does not look merely at the performance of the act itself; rather, the intention of the person performing the act weighs heavily on whether the person gets rewarded for it.

Social justice and social responsibility play important roles in Islam and are greatly emphasized in Shiism because of their history as an oppressed minority. Remembrance of one's history plays a central role in Shiite Islam, and this is evident in the religious practices during *Muharram,* which remind the Shiites about the events of Karbala. This reminder gives immediacy to the past and mobilizes the Shia Muslim to advocate for social justice. Therefore, the Shia Muslim is highly attuned to instances of oppression and is encouraged to take steps toward eradicating it and advocating for a just society.

PSYCHOLOGICAL HEALTH

As mentioned in the previous chapter, the "heart" is considered to be the "celestial jewel" that "controls the degree of human-ness within a human being" (Amini, 1997). If one has a healthy heart; that is, if one is a true believer and adheres to one's religion, one will be psychologically at peace (Amini, 1997). Psychological health for the practicing Muslim is established by following the faith, remembering God, and engaging in moral activities (Amini, 1997). Therefore, one view defines mental illness as that of straying from the righteous path of religion. Refer to the previous chapter for a further discussion of psychological health and Islam.

HUMAN CHANGE PROCESSES

Islam takes a scientific approach toward disease and illness. Nevertheless, psychological illness is still stigmatized in Muslim cultures. As described in the previous chapter, the health of the heart symbolizes psychological health and well-being. Therefore, a sickness of the heart symbolizes distress and possible mental illness. Amini (1997) says that it is "important for us to be knowledgeable about the health and sickness of the heart, must identify symptoms of disease; and should understand the causes and factors in order to implement all the health care hygienic measures to prevent its spread." As far as treatment is concerned, it is the Prophets who "are the real physicians and specialists of the soul" and they "are in a position to help lead human beings in following the straight path and can prevent their deviations" (Amini, 1997). Individuals are encouraged to take steps to treat themselves by identifying "these diseases within our souls through *Qur'anic* verses and guidelines issued by the Holy Prophet (S) and infallible *Imams* (A) and must seriously strive for their treatment" (Amini, 1997). It is believed that healing may occur by reciting, understanding, and applying of the *Qur'anic* injunctions, as well as following the guidelines set by the 14 infallible ones.

In addition to taking steps toward self-treatment, the individual is encouraged to consult "spiritual physicians" if self-treatment does not work. If self-treatment fails, the individual should consult a "wise friend" who may be knowledgeable about such issues, and will maintain confidentiality (Amini, 1997). A shroud of secrecy surrounds the sickness of the heart, and one is not encouraged to reveal too much about it to others except those sought for treatment purposes.

This caution against revealing the "sickness of the heart" translates into the hesitancy of Muslims to seek about psychotherapeutic treatment.

Islam encourages Muslims to seek treatment and recognizes the existence of psychological illnesses. Nonetheless, Islamic culture at large is one in which seeking psychotherapy is looked down upon, because psychological matters should be treated by the religious or spiritual leaders in the community, or by consultation with family members and close friends. It is important for the psychotherapist who is working with a Muslim client to be aware of the basics of the religion of Islam. Having an understanding of the Muslim culture and the stigma associated with seeking help from someone who is not part of the community can benefit the therapeutic relationship. The client can be informed of the psychotherapist's knowledge about the cultural and religious background of the individual, which can be helpful in relationship building with the client. Additionally, an awareness of the Muslim faith will hopefully help the psychotherapist in making clinical judgments, as well as choosing treatment options. With the exclusion of the belief in the healing powers of the *Imams,* the information in this section is applicable to both Sunni and Shiite Muslims.

COMMON MORAL ISSUES

In addition to the issues mentioned under this heading in the previous chapter, Shiites are greatly concerned with social justice and social advocacy. Shiites become mobilized when faced with an unjust or oppressive system, and consider it a religious duty to attempt to overthrow the system so that society can move toward freedom and justice. Psychological distress may occur for Shiites when they are unable to act upon their religious duties of enjoining the good and forbidding the evil. Examples may include the inability to mobilize an urban community into caring for the homeless or being unable to stop incidents of discrimination or hate crimes that occur within their community. Islam as a whole advocates social justice and social responsibility; however, the unique history of Shiism leads the Shiites to place greater emphasis on these principles than do other Muslims.

COMMON CLINICAL ISSUES

A fairly detailed discussion of clinical issues among Muslims is explicated in the previous chapter. Additional clinical issues that may arise are outlined in Ali, Liu, and Humeidan (2004), one of which (post-9/11 anxiety) deserves specific mention here along with two others not mentioned previously.

Post-9/11 Anxiety

Muslims are commonly viewed as the enemy through the western lens, and are often considered to be terrorists. This perception has gained immense favor since the 9/11 tragedy in 2001. To protect themselves, Muslims living in western societies may practice *taqqiya;* that is, they may hide their true religious identity. Although this is acceptable to Shiites because of their need to engage in the practice during periods of oppressive regimes, it can nevertheless cause psychological dissonance, leading to anxiety, depression, and fear. Additionally, those Shiite Muslims who immigrated to these western countries in order to escape persecution and oppression, and have subsequently found themselves back in the precarious position they recently fled, may suffer distress unique to their situation. Given the negative views held by many Westerners, Shiite (and Sunni) Muslims may be hesitant to seek therapy from a non-Muslim therapist for symptoms arising as a result of the 9/11 attack (Inayat, 2002).

Mourning Rituals During *Muharram*

The Shiite Muslim's practice of mourning rituals (*matam* and *majalis*), which include chest beating and self-flagellation in their severe forms, may be misconstrued as signs of abuse by someone not familiar to the rituals of Shiite Islam. Although it is unclear whether Shiite Muslims in America still engage in the more severe forms of self-flagellation during the month of *Muharram* (police oversee the processions that are held during *Muharram* in cities such as New York), there is a likelihood that recent immigrants, refugees, or Shiite Muslim Americans who engage in the practice may have scars or bruises from this practice that could be misinterpreted by the uninformed. In countries where self-flagellation and chest beating are practiced openly during *Muharram* processions, it is usually members of lower social classes with less education who engage in the more severe forms of self-flagellation, whereas better-educated individuals from upper classes practice chest-beating. However, it is important for the non-Muslim to be aware of the important role of mourning the tragedy of Karbala during the month of *Muharram* in Shia Islam and its symbolic meaning.

The Generation Gap

With a new generation of Muslims born and raised in America, one can also expect to see intergenerational conflict and the emergence of conflict in the newer generation of Shiite Muslims (as well as non-Shiite Muslims) with regard to religious beliefs and practices. Language serves as a barrier between immigrants to the United States and their American-born children. Although many children of immigrants understand and may speak the language of their parents' homeland, many do not. These first- and second-generation children have mastered the English language by using it as their predominant language in school and with their siblings, as well as with their parents. Conflict arises when the language of the home country is used during prayer services and other religious events *(majalis, matam)*. Thus, this disables the new generation from adequately comprehending their religious and cultural heritage. Sending this new generation of Muslims to weekend school at the Mosque does not seem to be sufficient for them to completely embrace their faith. The American-born generation of Muslims are growing up in an environment unfamiliar to their immigrant parents, which is a cause for concern for the parents as well as a source of intergenerational conflict as the child adapts to a culture that has not necessarily gained the parents' approval.

CONCLUSION

Religion plays a pivotal role in defining the Muslim's world view. This chapter gives a brief overview of the history and development of Shiite Islam, as well as the major tenets and practices of faith that differentiate Sunni and Shiite Muslims. It is hoped that this chapter as well as the chapter on Sunni Muslims have helped the reader gain some basic knowledge about the religion of Islam, the differences inherent in Sunni and Shia Islam, and an understanding of the central role religion plays in the psychological beliefs of the Muslim. Because no distinction is made between secular and religious life in Islam, it is imperative for those treating Muslim clients to gain a basic understanding of the religion as well as the difference between the different factions and sects. Understanding the subtle and obvious differences between Shiite and Sunni Muslims will increase the multicultural competence of the therapist, which will inevitably lead to a strong working alliance with the client.

REFERENCES

Ali, S. R., Liu, W. M., & Humeidan, M. (2004). Islam 101: Understanding the religion and therapy implications. *Professional Psychology: Research and Practice, 35,* 635–642.

Amini A. I. (1997). *Self-building: a guide for spiritual migration towards God.* Qum, Iran: Ansariyan Publishers. Retrieved January 16, 2005, from http://al-islam.org/selfbuilding

Armstrong, K. (2000). *Islam: A short history.* New York: Random House.

Esposito, J. L. (1998). *Islam: The straight path.* New York: Oxford University Press.

Inayat, Q. (2002). The meaning of being Muslim: An aftermath of the twin towers episode. *Counselling Psychology Quarterly, 15,* 351–358.

Lippmann, T. W. (1995). *Understanding Islam: An introduction to the Muslim world.* New York: Penguin.

Momen, M. (1985). *An introduction to Shi'i Islam: The history and doctrines of twelver Shi'ism.* New Haven, CT: Yale University Press.

Pinault, D. (1992). *The Shiites: Ritual and popular piety in a Muslim community.* New York: St. Martin's Press.

Schimmel, A. M. (1992). *Islam: An introduction.* Albany, NY: State University of New York Press.

SECTION VII

The Spiritual Traditions

CHAPTER FIFTEEN

The Spiritualistic Tradition

Rebecca Murray and Michael E. Nielsen

Spirituality is a broad term that frequently conveys different meanings to different people. The word itself has Latin origins, with *spiritus* meaning breath, evoking images of starting and sustaining life. Indeed, most writings about spirituality link the term to the concept of soul and one's very essence. Definitions of spirituality abound, and many can be found in the psychological literature beginning with James and Jung, moving through the work of the humanists and transpersonalists, and culminating in the contemporary writing of psychologists who are interested in the connection between mental health and spirituality (Elkins, 1998). In practice, a spiritualistic orientation to religious matters suggests an amalgam of beliefs that draw from Hinduism, Buddhism, Taoism, and other religions originating in eastern Asia. These beliefs may or may not include elements of Christianity or Judaism, as well as paganism.[1]

IMPORTANT ASPECTS OF THE SPIRITUALISTIC TRADITION

The current interest shown by psychologists in spirituality is exemplified in the lead article of a recent *Monitor on Psychology* (APA, 2003) that discussed the importance of mental health professionals addressing spirituality with clients. Like many writers, the authors of that work frequently interchanged the terms spirituality and religion—not recognizing

[1]*Spirituality* and *spiritualistic tradition* refer to an interest in matters of the spirit, drawing primarily from Eastern religious traditions. It does not necessarily include what is commonly referred to as *spiritualism*, a practice aligned with occult practices such as speaking with the dead.

important distinctions made between spiritual and religious concerns. This distinction is critical, as a substantial number of people consider themselves *spiritual* but not *religious;* they are moving away from the doctrines of organized religion, yet feel a pressing need to find health and happiness through a deep connection to self, others, and something divine (Forman, 2004). The authors share the assertion that a failure to distinguish sufficiently among spirituality, religiosity, and faith has hindered both research and clinical practice (Larimore, Parker, & Crowther, 2002). Therefore, this chapter examines key components of spirituality that arise from a review of the spirituality literature, and emphasizes the importance of subjective experience, the natural experience of transcendence, and the human need for connectedness.

Subjective Experience

Contemporary definitions of spirituality emphasize its unique, personal nature drawn from individual subjective experience. Some aspects of spirituality may be found in organized religion, such as a feeling of peace and wholeness, clarity of purpose and worth, and a sense of contact with the divine. An essential distinction between organized religion and spirituality is that practitioners of spirituality place great credence in their individual subjective experience. At its heart, the spiritualistic tradition places high value on the belief that there are many different paths to enlightenment or to the divine, and one path is not inherently more valid or justified than another. Of course, this stands in sharp contrast with the position taken by many traditional organized religions.

One can see in this attitude important connections with psychological theories about religion. William James (1902/1982), in his famous Gilford Lectures on Natural Religion, called attention to personal forms of religion and emphasized them over institutional forms. Institutional religion consists of the more ecclesiastical or organizational elements of religion. James focused instead on ". . . personal religion, pure and simple" (p. 29), which he defined as, ". . . the feelings, acts, and experiences of individual men [sic] in their solitude, so far as they apprehend themselves to stand in relation to whatever they may consider divine" (p. 31). This definition is quite consistent with the spiritualistic tradition, which largely rejects church doctrine in favor of a larger, more inclusive, relationship with God as that entity or force is personally defined. Although a direct and personal connection with God is emphasized by sects within traditional religions (e.g., monasticism in Catholicism and Orthodox Christianity), those who gravitate toward a spiritualistic tradition are especially likely to seek a personal spiritual experience, as opposed to the *interpretation* of spiritual experience that is so often part of religious practice.

The desire for spiritual experiences unfiltered through the lens of church-based doctrine is consistent with assumptions behind the intellectual movement of postmodernism. Postmodernists claim that social and psychological knowledge are limited by the context in which they are acquired, and that a natural result of knowledge being passed from person to person, institution to person, and so on, is that it becomes tainted by politics and subjective values. Understanding the effect of context and subject values on knowledge leads to emphasizing and valuing personal emotional experience over the chimera of absolute truth that is offered by science, the church, and other institutions (Jankowski, 2002; Lines, 2002).

The person who follows the spiritualistic approach to life sees important potential benefits for doing so. These are expressed well by Firestone, Firestone, and Catlett (2003):

> In our search for meaning, we believe it is important to reach our own conclusions—that is, to develop our own beliefs and speculations about the vital questions in life based on our own personal experiences rather than ideas and beliefs mediated through diverse religious or secular systems. When values and ethics are developed from within rather than outer-directed, a person can charter the course of his or her life in a manner that is harmonious and well-integrated. He or she will exhibit a clear and distinct point of view, manifest internal consistency, avoid self-deception, dishonesty, and compartmentalization, and maintain a powerful sense of self (p. 377).

Natural Experience of Transcendence

For the purpose of this chapter, transcendence is discussed in the tradition of Maslow, and transcendence is defined as the natural human capacity to experience a mystic state in which one is transported from current time and space, and gain an understanding of self and the divine. Maslow (1976) noted that religion in all its forms has at its foundation the mystical experience of a seer or prophet, who attempts to interpret his or her transcendent states to the masses. Such enlightening peak experiences can become normal occurrences for all people, according to Maslow.

Pratt (1920), a student and successor of James, agreed with Maslow that mystical experiences were commonplace. He distinguished between more extreme mystical experiences, which typically are ascribed to spiritual gurus, and milder forms of mysticism that tend to gain far less attention. Pratt proposed that all mystical events involve both cognitive and affective components, regardless of intensity. According to Pratt, a mystical experience is one in which a truth about the divine is understood, and one is left with a feeling of joy.

Pratt's description of mystical experience is similar to Maslow's account of peak experiences as well as similar to Existential and Transpersonal descriptions of transcendence; all can be spiritual in nature (Frankl, 1969; Grof, 1985). In fact, in their analysis Greenwald and Harder (2003) note that "blissful transcendence" characterizes spiritual experience as described in a variety of writings. As a group, these theoretical perspectives and research indicate that profound, otherworldly, joyful experiences may indeed be quite common. Of course, such experiences are not the exclusive province of spiritualistic pathways, but they can serve to draw individuals to a personally defined spirituality.

Connectedness

The intense emotional connectedness that comes from spiritual experience can motivate one to behave in socially responsible ways. This fact, combined with the observation that the experiences of human spirituality are universal, lead Greenwald and Harder (2003) to conclude that spirituality has an evolutionary role in that it promotes behavior consistent with humanity's survival. In contrast, Jankowski (2002) expresses concern that postmodern spiritual practices overemphasize an individualistic connection with God and in so doing limit connections with other people. To Jankowski, too much emphasis on "vertical spirituality" (connection with God) reduces one's ability to achieve an effective "horizontal spirituality" (connection with others).

Jankowski's critique is thought provoking, and a number of scenarios can be imagined that may lead individuals who embrace the spiritualistic tradition to become egocentric or at least spiritually or emotionally isolated from other people. For example, without sufficient ability to evoke the ideas and metaphors of a given doctrine, it may be difficult to talk to others about one's spirituality. This is complicated by the fact that a transcendent experience, by most definitions, is ineffable and cannot be completely or even adequately conveyed to someone else. Because those who follow the spiritualistic tradition are unlikely to be part of a formal worship community, they do not benefit from the sense of community that can come from belonging to a religious group. Indeed, those who do not associate with a religious group may feel out of sync with the majority in this culture who do identify themselves as belonging to a particular religious group. Despite this, following a personal spiritualistic path may actually enhance one's connections with others.

The spiritualistic premise is that an authentic and congruent experience with the divine, especially in the context of transcendence, leads to an increased experience of unity with all things. The sense of wholeness that comes from genuine spiritual experience actually *demands* connection with others. From time to time one may need to withdraw and seek solitude in order to affirm his or her spirituality, but the natural consequence of spiritual practice is a renewed desire to nurture one's connections to nature and other people.

Although a sense of unity may be gained from experiences in more highly structured religions, particularly a sense of unity with people who share doctrinal beliefs, a spiritualistic orientation to religious matters typically assumes that organized religion may actually reduce authentic connections to God and others. This is because organized religious rituals lend themselves to being performed perfunctorily and also because natural human dynamics generate in-group–out-group biases that promote feelings of unity with some individuals at the expense of others. In contrast, personally defined spirituality generates feelings of wholeness and interconnectedness that do not succumb to in-group–out-group dynamics and tensions.

THE EPISTEMOLOGICAL TOOLS
OF THE SPIRITUALISTIC TRADITION

The spiritualistic tradition takes its epistemological cue, in many ways, from a very broad form of empiricism that places a premium on individual subjective experience. This is important to note, because changes in psychology and other sciences have deemphasized the subjective in favor of matters that are objectively, operationally definable. As a result of this narrow empirical view, many psychologists and other scientists shy away from spirituality, as Grof notes when he states, "Western psychology and psychiatry thus tend to discard globally any form of spirituality, no matter how sophisticated and well-founded, as unscientific" (1985, p. 333). In a similar vein is Bugental's (1987, p. 4) assertion, "We have come to react with repugnance or shame to that which is labeled, 'subjective' and to confuse the term with sentimentality, undisciplined permissiveness, and moral 'softness.'"

Rather than consider this to be a lack of discipline, a spiritualistic approach argues that paradigmatic constraints in psychology actually limit the ability to investigate the essence of humanness. Jung said, "If I recognize only naturalistic values, and explain everything in physical terms, I shall depreciate, hinder or even destroy the spiritual development of my patients" (1933, p. 188). Malone and Malone (1992) echo this sentiment, and state emphatically that regardless of the intellectual embarrassment one may feel, issues of the spirit and soul must be addressed if the significance of life, connections to each other, and experience in the world are to be fully grasped.

Psychologists and scientists in other fields that study the human condition must recognize that we are approaching a shift in paradigm to a model that "will change our concepts of reality and of human nature, bridge the gap between ancient wisdom and modern science, and reconcile the difference between Eastern spirituality and Western pragmatism" (Grof, 1985, p. 16). One form that this paradigm shift is taking is in the greater acceptance of qualitative research methods (Bevan & Kessel, 1994), which offer psychologists an opportunity to examine spiritual and other matters in a nonreductionistic framework. Qualitative methodology is quite consistent with the spiritualistic tradition, given that the key questions to examine concern issues of internal processes and how people create meaning from their experiences.

Qualitative research exploring spirituality may give those who espouse the spiritualistic tradition a language for describing their experience, validation for their spiritual path, and a means of connecting with others who follow this tradition. For example, Forman's (2004) qualitative studies at the Forge Institute suggested that the experience of spirituality is, ". . . accessed through not strictly rational means" (p. 66). To capture the essence of this, Forman wrote:

> But here we are, at the pinnacle of perhaps the most rational and technologically developed civilization in history, and our Grassroots Spirituality movement resists the whole rationalistic bugbear altogether. 'Live from the right side of the brain' . . . 'transcend thought . . . 'synchronicity' . . . 'turn off your computer, Luke, and trust the Force'—these are our new watchwords (p. 67).

Rational thought, narrowly defined empiricism, and technology are less useful than more qualitative methods for understanding the spiritualistic experience in its complexity, subtlety, and power.

THE SPIRITUALISTIC TRADITION AND THEORIES OF PERSONALITY

One view of personality particularly influential in the spiritualistic tradition is that of Carl Jung. His influence is not, of course, limited to the spiritualistic tradition, as followers of a wide variety of religions including Christianity, Judaism, Hinduism, and Buddhism have looked to Jung for insight into personality (Fadiman & Frager, 2002). Whatever influence he may have had in other religious traditions, it is clear that Jungian theory can serve as a source of enlightenment to the spiritualistic approach to religious matters, as a brief examination of Jung's life and theory will show.

Born the son of a Protestant minister, Jung did not adopt the rites or teachings of organized Christianity. Instead, he focused on developing a personal spirituality by drawing on several influences. As described in his autobiography, Jung began at an early age to seek some sort of reconciliation between his personal view of God and more traditional Christian teachings. Eventually, he concluded that Christian dogma obscured the truth (Jung, 1961). "I was disillusioned and even indignant, and once more seized with pity for my father, who had fallen victim to this mumbo-jumbo" writes Jung (1961, p. 59).

Jung advocated the idea that religion, in the forms commonly practiced, encourages a simplified and incomplete understanding of spiritual matters because it promotes an overreliance on rules and serves to shelter people from life's grand questions concerning suffering, death, and other problems people face. In a foreshadowing of postmodernism, Jung recognized that religious practices and teachings are highly interwoven with the social and political contexts surrounding them, and are ultimately affected by those contexts.

Although Jung expressed reservations about religious practices, he did not completely abandon religion. In fact, much of his life was spent exploring world religions in order to find what gems of wisdom he could from them; he sought to incorporate these into his psychological theory and practice. Through these studies he concluded that religions can facilitate psychological health to the extent that they help one gain a profound and personal connection to God. In contrast, religious moralizing, dogma, and paternalism thwart one's efforts to achieve such connection.

Jung preceded several other psychological theorists who saw in spirituality a critical focus of human growth and development. An important reason for humanistic psychology's development was the desire to incorporate spirituality in psychology and clinical practice. Transpersonal psychology grew from humanistic psychology's roots in order to address issues of transcendence, consciousness and cosmic awareness. Transpersonal psychologists such as Ken Wilbur (1998) have published widely about spiritual matters where it is evident that spirituality forms a central concern. Other theorists also illustrate the important role of spirituality in healthy growth and development. Among them are Malone and Malone, who suggest that:

> Being our real selves brings us to our soul, our spirit, the breathing in and out of which exuberant life is made. When being our selves, we learn to be whole. Such experiences then provide the ongoing nourishment necessary for the healthy existence of both the I and the me. They allow us to be truly spiritual, to live in a way that involves our breath of life, our soul (1992, p. 27).

Sentiments such as these illustrate the crucial role that many psychologists, particularly those from the humanistic and transpersonal schools, see for spirituality. Their theories offer a foundation for understanding the prime concerns of the spiritualistic tradition and the focus on personality growth to be found in spiritualistic theories of personality.

THE SPIRITUALISTIC TRADITION
AND HUMAN DEVELOPMENT

Just as there is no doctrine associated with the spiritualistic tradition, the tradition does not propose a formalized stance on human development. However, several psychological theories of human development are quite consistent with the thrust of the spiritualistic tradition. Because of their pivotal roles in this area, the authors draw from Jung, followed by consideration of Maslow's humanistic and transpersonal views.

Jung proposed that the culmination of psychological growth is "individualation," which reflects an innate desire to become one's own self. People have a fundamental drive to achieve a feeling of wholeness through individuation. Although this can be blocked during development, individuation propels people to seek a state of selfhood.

Individuation requires an awareness of the ego as well as a sense of moving beyond the ego in order to develop self. According to Jung people tend, before middle age, to emphasize the ego and its goals. Gaining knowledge of the world and seeking external achievements and accolades from others are the focus of the person at this point. Once a person has met ego-related goals, she or he begins to critically examine the assumptions and ideals that have shaped her or his life. When this occurs, the person is on the cusp of experiencing a change that can lead to a profound sense of wholeness. In large part this comes from having integrated spirituality into one's life. Ultimately, Jung asserted that psychological healing is not accomplished unless the person experiences God.

Maslow's concept of self-actualization is quite similar to Jung's idea of individuation. As is true with individuation, the impetus for self-actualization is considered to be innate and represents the pinnacle of human growth and development. In its simplest form, self-actualization can be defined as the process of becoming fully one's self, enabling one to achieve one's potential. Developmentally, self-actualization results from long-term growth and the realization of one's capacity. Like individuation, self-actualization is accomplished upon the realization of one's true self, beyond ego. Maslow agrees with Jung about the integral role spirituality plays in this process of self-actualization or individuation, suggesting that a spiritual center is necessary if one is to experience one's highest self. Maslow also agreed with Jung about the fact that this process occurs in the latter half of life.

THE SPIRITUALISTIC TRADITION AND PSYCHOLOGICAL HEALTH AND PSYCHOPATHOLOGY

Although the spiritualistic tradition relies heavily on analytic, humanistic, and transpersonal psychology, the spiritualistic assertion that spiritual health is an important aspect of psychological health extends beyond these psychological categories. For example, Bourne's (2000) cognitively oriented self-help book for anxiety disorders features a multidimensional approach that includes the "existential and spiritual level."

The Alcoholics Anonymous (AA) movement is also noteworthy. Bill Wilson, cofounder of AA, was greatly influenced by Jung. In a letter to Wilson, Jung interprets the alcoholism of one of his own patients as a "spiritual thirst" (as cited in Fadiman & Frager, 2002). Indeed, the second of the famous twelve steps asserts that a power greater than oneself is the force that will "restore sanity." For many in the AA program (and related programs such as Narcotics Anonymous and Overeaters Anonymous) the power is God in the traditional Judeo-Christian sense. However, the literature of the program clearly states that members are to define that power however they wish, and to relate to that power in whatever form works for them. Emphasis is placed on respect for diverse spiritual paths without promoting one over the other, as the belief is that spiritual growth can come in many forms.

A word about diagnosis may be helpful here, because there are conflicting views to be considered about spirituality and psychosis. Sperry (2003) cautioned, "There can be some unusual and troubling spiritual experiences associated with the spiritual journey, and clinicians are faced with the prospects of differentiating such spiritual experiences for major pathology" (p. 7). In order to facilitate efforts to distinguish spiritual experiences from psychosis, for example, Jackson and Fulford (1997) proposed diagnostic criteria for identifying benign spiritual experience (i.e., spiritual experiences dramatically increase the client's readiness to action, whereas the client with psychosis is likely to have a failure of action). However, others argue that spiritual experiences do not necessarily follow the description outlined by Jackson and Fulford (e.g., Marzanski & Bratton, 2002). Spiritually sensitive clinicians must be mindful of the potential of clients to report psychotic-like experiences when undertaking a spiritual journey. This may be true in many religious traditions, but the distinction between psychosis and spiritual experience can be made more difficult by the fact that people who take a spiritualistic path may be without the formal social support systems that might be available in more traditional religious groups.

THE SPIRITUALISTIC TRADITION
AND HUMAN CHANGE

Psychological theories and research addressing the process by which change occurs are abundant, but they tend to focus on affective, behavioral, and cognitive changes and not on spiritual changes. However, there are some models that address more fundamental, spiritual changes that go beyond those defined by the ways that people feel, behave, and think. This level of change may be characterized as the process by which one uncovers and develops a relationship with the innate, centered, authentic core of oneself. Studies of such change often reveal that this level of change has a spiritual component (Murray, 2002).

Consistent with the implications of analytic, humanistic, and transpersonal theories, the authors suggest that change can be generated at a deep and profoundly spiritual level. The question that remains is *how* such change is achieved. In one phenomenological study the therapeutic values of Instruction is Self-Reflection; Corrective Emotional Experience; and Uncovering the Self facilitated deep changes in clients (Murray, 2002). Elkins (1998) agrees that the psychotherapy relationship can be deeply, spiritually healing, but Elkins asserts that ultimately the client must learn to care for her own soul. His program for personal spiritual growth includes components that are arguably analogous to the self-reflection and development in Murray's findings.

Forman (2004) reports on a series of interviews with followers of the spiritualistic tradition, and confirms that their spiritual growth and change came through self-transformation, using methods like those cited by Elkins (1998) and Murray (2002). However, Forman also found that people found spiritual significance in their sense of community and connection with others on their spiritual journey. As Forman explained, "We are both sounding our own inner depths, and also intimately supporting and guiding each other, relying on both our own and on each other's wisdom" (2004, p. 65).

In the spiritualistic tradition, change is grounded in connection. Most importantly, a deep connection to self is the key to effective change, and can be facilitated by psychotherapy, spiritual practice, and other endeavors. Connection to others, a proposed as a major tenet of the tradition, also seems to have a central role in the process of change. As stated, connection to self and the divine facilitates an increasing experience of unity, such that deeper connections with others are sought. Change appears to be born from deep self-exploration in which people connect to the divine, and follow a natural desire to offer our authentic selves for intimate connection to other people. This dynamic cycle is the hallmark of life-affirming change that can come from the practice of the spiritualistic tradition.

COMMON MORAL ISSUES

The moral issues encountered by people following a spiritualistic are in many ways no different than those experienced by other people: Treating others well and honestly; respect for life; supporting others' decisions even when one disagrees with them all are characteristic moral issues. If anything is particularly unique to the spiritualistic tradition in this area, it is that its lack of organization as a coherent religious body means that people following a spiritualistic path engage moral issues without the support or guidance of a hierarchical religious authority figure instructing what the "right" action may be in a given situation. Of course, spiritualistic people, who tend to see moral dilemmas as personal decision points and opportunities for growth, view this positively. Nevertheless, it may leave one feeling at a loss for dealing with the complexities of modern life.

COMMON CLINICAL ISSUES

Forman (2004) and others have suggested that many people are following the spiritualistic tradition. As Elkins (1998) notes, a ". . . spiritual revolution is quietly taking place in our society" (p. 9). Members of this "revolution" represent a very diverse group, and therefore are not likely to have common clinical issues, but the quiet and somewhat solitary aspects of a personally defined spirituality may cause distress for some adherents of the spiritualistic tradition. Therefore, it is wished that clinicians' sensitivity to the dilemmas that some clients of the spiritualistic tradition may experience be heightened.

Human beings are deeply religious by tradition, and religious institutions can be important markers of one's position in society. Churches, synagogues, and mosques are dominant features of towns, cities, and neighborhoods. It is not uncommon, especially in some regions of this country, to be asked, "What church do you go to?" with the expectation that you practice some organized form of religion. If your response is that you do not attend formal religious services, you may be met with any number of responses, including curiosity, confusion, disdain, and judgment. Although people who are not of the dominant faith in their community may experience similar reactions, and indeed prejudice and persecution if they are "different," those who follow the spiritualistic tradition face the added difficulty of not being able to ascribe a label to their spiritual practice that summarizes their stance. Problems associated with this include experiencing guilt about leaving the fold of a traditional religion, or interpersonal misunderstandings about the spiritualistic tradition. Ultimately, these can result in clinical issues for some who follow the spiritualistic tradition.

Clinicians working with spiritualistic clients can improve their efforts by striving to recognize the spiritual path as valid, and by providing experiences in session that empower the client to practice their spirituality in a way that is congruent with their desires, even if that path is not sanctioned or understood by the family of origin or the dominant culture. One important step to such empowerment is clinician sensitivity and self-awareness. As Corey, Corey, and Callahan have said, therapists have an ethical mandate about spirituality:

> There are many paths toward fulfilling spiritual needs, and it is not your role as a helper to prescribe any particular pathway. Instead, your job is to assist your client in exploring their values to determine the degree to which they are living within the framework of this value system. We suggest you monitor yourself for subtle ways that you might be inclined to push certain values in your counseling practice (2003, p. 86).

In some cases clients who espouse the spiritualistic tradition may struggle to adequately describe their experience of spirituality. To help address this, therapists may wish to use a formal Spiritual Assessment to gain an understanding of the client's spiritual experiences and beliefs. Several such measures exist, especially from a Christian orientation, which may or may not be useful for a particular client. Taking a more inclusive perspective, Hall and Edwards (2002) developed the Spiritual Assessment Inventory (SAI), and this is an example of a measure that asks questions about one's relationship with God (a term for the divine that some who follow the spiritualistic tradition may not share) but is otherwise generic in content and therefore may lend itself well to virtually any client. Additionally, the SAI has been developed psychometrically, with intentions for use in research as well as clinical practice.

Formal assessment measures may provide insight into the individual's spiritual state, but the importance of informal assessment must not be forgotten. Including spiritual questions in Intake Interviews at the onset of therapy is a critical step in understanding not only the nature of a client's concerns, but also the psychological resources from which the client can draw. Of course, spirituality can be addressed in the therapy process through spiritual questioning and exploration. Spiritually sensitive therapy demands that therapists seek out and examine the spiritual in their clients (Lines, 2002). This is not to suggest that clinicians promote a spiritual agenda, which would be both unethical and clinically unwise. Rather, it is recommended that clinicians improve their sensitivity to clients' spiritual selves, and be aware of opportunities to assess and explore the spiritual dimensions of the client, if the client so chooses.

REFERENCES

American Psychological Association. (2003). Spirituality and mental health: In practice, on campus and in research. *Monitor on Psychology, 34(11)*, 40–53.

Bevan, W., & Kessel, F. (1994). Plain truths and home cooking: Thoughts on the making and remaking of psychology. *American Psychologist, 49(6)*, 505–509.

Bourne, E. J. (2000). *The anxiety & phobia workbook* (3rd ed.). Oakland, CA: New Harbinger Publications.

Bugental, J. F. T. (1987). *The art of the psychotherapist: How to develop the skills that take psychotherapy beyond science.* New York: Norton.

Corey, G., Corey, M. S., & Callahan, P. (2003). *Issues & ethics in the helping professions* (6th ed.). Pacific Grove, CA: Brooks/Cole.

Elkins, D. (1998). *Beyond religion: A personal program for building a spiritual life outside the walls of traditional religion.* Wheaton, IL: Quest Books.

Fadiman, J., & Frager, R. (2002). *Personality and personal growth* (5th ed.). Upper Saddle River, NJ: Prentice-Hall.

Firestone, R. W., & Firestone, L. A. (2003). Spirituality, mystery, and the search for meaning. In R. W. Firestone, L. A. Firestone, & J. Catlett (Eds.), *Creating a life of meaning and compassion: The wisdom of psychotherapy* (pp. 377–385). Washington, DC: American Psychological Association.

Forman, R. (2004). *Grassroots spirituality: What it is, why it is here, where it is going.* Charlottesville, VA: Imprint Academic.

Frankl, V. (1969). *The will to meaning: Foundations and applications of logotherapy.* New York: New American Library.

Greenwald, D. F., & Harder, D. W. (2003). The dimensions of spirituality. *Psychological Reports, 92(3),* 975–980.

Grof, S. (1985). *Beyond the brain: Birth, death and transcendence in psychotherapy.* Albany, NY: State University of New York Press.

Hall, T., & Edwards, K. J. (2002). The Spiritual Assessment Inventory: A theistic model and measure for assessing spiritual development. *Journal for the Scientific Study of Religion, 41(2),* 341–358.

Jackson, M. C., & Fulford, K. W. M. (1997). Spiritual experience and psychopathology. *Philosophy, Psychiatry, & Psychology, 4(1),* 41–66.

James, W. (1902/1982). *The varieties of religious experience.* New York: Penguin.

Jankowski, P .J. (2002). Postmodern spirituality: Implications for promoting change. *Counseling & Values, 74(1),* 69–79.

Jung, C. G. (1933). *Modern man in search of a soul.* New York: Harcourt Brace.

Jung, C. G. (1961). *Memories, dreams, reflections* (A. Jaffe, Ed.). New York: Pantheon Books (Random House).

Larimore, W. L., Parker, M., & Crowther, M. (2002). Should clinicians incorporate positive spirituality into their practices? What does the evidence say? *Annals of Behavioral Medicine, 24(1),* 69–73.

Lines, D. (2002). Counseling within a new spiritual paradigm. *Journal of Humanistic Psychology, 42(3),* 102–123.

Malone, P. T., & Malone, T. P. (1992). *The windows of experience: Moving beyond recovery to wholeness.* New York: Simon & Schuster.

Marzanski, M., & Bratton, M. (2002). Psychopathological symptoms and religious experience: A critique of Jackson and Fulford. *Philosophy, Psychiatry, & Psychology, 9(4),* 359–371.

Maslow, A. (1976). *Religions, values, and peak-experiences.* New York: Penguin Books Ltd.

Murray, R. (2002). The phenomenon of psychotherapeutic change: Second-order change in one's experience of self. *Journal of Contemporary Psychotherapy, 32(2/3),* 167–178.

Pratt, J. B. (1920). *The religious consciousness: A psychological study.* New York: Macmillan.

Sperry, L. (2003). Integrating spiritual direction functions in the practice of psychotherapy. *Journal of Psychology and Theology, 31(1)*, 3–31.

Wilbur, K. (1998). *The essential: An introductory reader.* Boston: Shambhala Publications.

CHAPTER SIXTEEN

The Varieties of Buddhism

Neharika Chawla and G. Alan Marlatt

HISTORY AND FUNDAMENTAL ASPECTS OF BUDDHISM

I teach one thing and one only: that is, suffering and the end of suffering. (The Buddha)

Buddhism began not with God, but with a man, a historical figure by the name of Siddhartha Gautama, who later became known as the Buddha. The word Buddha simply means "one who is awake," and this experience of "waking up" lies at the heart of the Buddhist faith. In order to develop an understanding of Buddhism as a faith, it is essential to understand the life, quest, and awakening of the Buddha.

Siddhartha was born approximately 2,600 years ago near what is now the border of Nepal and India. His father was a king, and legend has it that at his birth Siddhartha was prophesied to become either a great monarch or a holy man. Because his father was determined for his son to become a powerful ruler, he ensured that Siddhartha was surrounded by every pleasure that the world had to offer, while being completely shielded from suffering. When the young prince was in his twenties, however, he became increasingly curious about the world that lay beyond the palace walls. One day he enlisted the help of a friend and decided to step outside the world that his father had created for him. Once outside, Siddhartha encountered four images, each of which had a profound impact on him. First, he saw a feeble old man, then a corpse, and then a man who was afflicted with disease. Shocked and deeply affected by the suffering he observed all around him, and while struggling with what he had just witnessed, Siddhartha encountered the fourth image: that of a wandering forest hermit. It was this last image that altered his destiny. That night Siddhartha decided to leave the palace with all its pleasures and pursue his spiritual search by joining the hermits.

For 6 years Siddhartha practiced a form of asceticism that involved extreme self-mortification and starvation. One day, as he was about to collapse from hunger, he realized that he was no closer to liberation than he had been when he left his father's palace. As he had earlier rejected a life of pleasure, he now rejected the ascetic life. He understood that what he was looking for was "a middle way"; something in between the two dichotomous extremes of asceticism and indulgence. This realization is one of the cornerstones of Buddhist philosophy and an important aspect of the Buddhist identity. With this thought in mind, Siddhartha sat down under the Bodhi tree and vowed to remain there until he had found an answer to the human situation of suffering. After a prolonged period of meditation, during which he experienced intense mind-states of temptation and fear, Siddhartha emerged "awakened" to the causes and solution of suffering. After this, he became a teacher and began sharing his insight with others.

His first discourse was on the topic of the Four Noble Truths, a teaching that encapsulates the essence of the Buddhist system. The four principles delineate the symptom, diagnosis, prognosis, and treatment plan for addressing suffering (Finn & Rubin, 2000). The first noble truth states that "all life is *dukkha.*" Although *dukkha* is typically translated as suffering, it is better described as a universal sense of dissatisfaction. More specifically, it characterizes a world that consists of dissatisfaction in the guise of pain, loneliness, anxiety, hunger, and loss, to name but a few. It includes large-scale events such as wars and natural disasters, but also includes daily disappointments and frustrations (Levine, 2000). The Buddha also identified specific moments of distress that all human beings experience, such as the trauma of birth and the fear of decrepitude and death. This is parallel to the psychoanalytic view of birth as a major source of anxiety and the existentialist emphasis on a fear of death.

Although the first noble truth identifies the unsatisfactory nature of life, the second noble truth addresses the cause of this dissatisfaction. It states that that all people create their own suffering by becoming attached to the notion of an independent self, which results in craving or aversion toward a world that is fleeting. In short, people have difficulty acknowledging a fundamental aspect of life, that everything is impermanent and transitory. Suffering arises when people resist the flow of life and cling to things, events, ideas, and people as if they were permanent (Finn & Rubin, 2000).

The third noble truth states that there is a potential end to this suffering and that the solution lies in understanding and rooting out greed and attachment. The state that personifies complete liberation from suffering is called *nirvana*. The word *nirvana* literally means to extinguish and what is extinguished is greed and grasping.

Although the third noble truth raises the possibility of liberation, it is the fourth truth that actually prescribes the steps involved in this process. According to the Buddha, this requires "the alignment of eight specific factors: understanding, thought, speech, action, livelihood, effort, mindfulness and concentration" (Epstein, 1995, p. 92). These factors comprise the eightfold path to enlightenment and are discussed in greater detail in subsequent sections.

In his first discourse, the Buddha also described another fundamental Buddhist doctrine: the law of *karma*. The word *karma* literally translates as action. It refers to the law of cause and effect and the idea that every volitional act brings about a certain result (Goldstein & Kornfield, 1987). Although cause-and-effect relationships often manifest over a period of time, they are also evident in how the quality of each moment influences the next moment. "Karma means that nothing arises by itself, that every experience is conditioned by that which precedes it, and that our life is a series of interrelated parts" (Kornfield, 1993, p. 273). Related to this is the doctrine of rebirth. Although the Buddha did not talk specifically of an unchanging physical entity such as a "soul" that passes from birth to birth, he did support the idea of a chain of existence and a dynamic mental continuum. This understanding of the interrelatedness of all phenomena is a fundamental aspect of the Buddhist identity.

That being said however, it is somewhat misleading to speak inclusively about the Buddhist identity without accounting for the differences among the various branches of Buddhism. Since the death of the Buddha an assortment of theories and practices have emerged from his teachings (Ho, 1995), often depending on the characteristics of the cultures in which they have taken root (Smith, 1991). Differences in theory and practice also have led to differences in the identities and beliefs of practitioners.

The oldest branch of Buddhism, Hinayana or Theravada Buddhism, is based on the original teachings of the Buddha and continues to be practiced in Cambodia, Thailand, Burma, and Sri Lanka. Traditionally, Theravada Buddhists were those who viewed the attainment of nirvana as their central purpose and renounced the world to become monks. They saw their progress as being largely dependent on personal effort and commitment and regarded "insight" as being the prime attribute of enlightenment (Smith, 1991).

The second major type of Buddhism, Mahayana Buddhism, is what is practiced in Korea, Japan, Nepal, and Tibet. This variant is somewhat less demanding and thus more relevant for the lay person. Mahayana Buddhists believe that the Buddha did not remain in *nirvana* after his enlightenment but returned to devote himself to the welfare of others.

Therefore the fate of the individual is seen as being connected to that of all life, and compassion is given greater importance than wisdom or personal enlightenment (Smith, 1991). Although the ideal personality for a Theravadin is the *Arhat*, "a perfected disciple who strikes out alone for nirvana and proceeds unswervingly towards the goal," the Mahayana ideal is the *boddhisatva*, "a being who having reached the brink of nirvana, voluntarily returns to the world to be of benefit to others" (Smith, 1991, p. 124).

Mahayana Buddhism has been further divided into a number of schools, including Zen, a form of Buddhism that was strongly influenced by Taoism, and Vajrayana Buddhism, which evolved primarily in Tibet. The word *Zen* derives from the Chinese word *Ch'an,* which in turn derives from the Sanskrit word *dhyana,* which means meditation. One of the distinctive features of Zen Buddhism is the importance it gives to meditation. It undermines the value of words and concepts and highlights the importance of direct experience. A tool that is often used by Zen teachers is a *koan;* a brief question or vignette that serves as a catalyst for deep insight into one's being. In contrast to the simplicity of Zen, the most prominent feature of Vajrayana Buddhism is that it employs a number of meditative and contemplative techniques that engage not just the mind, but also the body. Vajrayana practitioners may use a number of rituals such as chanting, hand gestures, and visualizations as part of their meditation. The ultimate goal of these practices is to merge with the deities that one visualizes and attain nirvana in a single lifetime (Smith, 1991).

Lastly, it is necessary to mention another variation of Buddhism that has emerged in the last three decades, and has had a considerable impact on western life, and especially the field of psychology. This group of Buddhists is comprised of a growing number of Westerners who follow either Theravada or Mahayana teachings and are particularly drawn to mindfulness and the meditative aspects of Buddhism (Finn & Rubin, 2000). Although these Buddhists remain true to the well-worn teachings of the Buddha, they are hammering out a unique philosophy that places a far greater emphasis on being a householder in a larger community, rather than being a monk in a monastery (Fields, 1981). In addition to this group, there are also a number of Buddhist immigrants in the West who engage in practices that are more traditional and specific to their culture of origin (Finn & Rubin, 2000). When considering all of these schools together, there are approximately 350 million Buddhists across the world. Together they comprise 6% of the world's population, making Buddhism the world's fourth largest religion. Given the number of its adherents, it is vital for clinicians to become more familiar with the beliefs and practices of the Buddhist faith so as to better understand and serve the needs of their clients.

THE EPISTEMOLOGICAL TOOLS ACKNOWLEDGED AND SUPPORTED BY BUDDHISM

Do not believe in anything simply because you have heard it. Do not believe in traditions because they have been handed down for many generations. Do not believe in anything simply because it is written in religious books. Do not believe in anything merely on the authority of your teachers and elders. But after careful consideration and analysis, when you find something that agrees with reason and is conducive to the good and benefit of one and all, then accept and abide by it. (The Buddha)

Perhaps the most distinguishing feature of the Buddha's story is that his realizations did not come from a divine source. Rather, they were the result of a strong commitment, intense personal effort, and direct experience. During his lifetime, the Buddha discouraged his disciples from blindly following scripture or tradition. He denied all claims to godliness and insisted that he was a mere human being who had his own weaknesses and flaws. "He preached a religion that was devoid of the supernatural," and stated that all forms of divination were merely simple solutions that distracted one from the practical task of self-advancement (Smith, 1991, p. 97). Even so, not long after his death, many of the ritualistic aspects of worship began to seep into Buddhism, and statues of the Buddha began to adorn temples and monasteries across the world. Despite this, Buddhists have continued to place a great emphasis on self-effort and experience. Even today, the teachings are much less about doctrine than about firm mental discipline (Dockett, Dudley-Grant, & Bankart, 2003). The teachings are not only scientific in their attention to cause-and-effect relationships, but also empirical in their appeal to direct validation (Smith, 1991).

Although Buddhism emphasizes the experiential dimension, it also outlines the steps that are involved in acquiring literal knowledge. These are study, reflection, and cultivation. Study consists of reading the scriptures and learning what the various sages have had to say; reflection involves making an honest personal inquiry into fundamental questions; and cultivation implies making the determination to change one's thinking by acquiring attitudes that lead to fulfillment (Dockett, Dudley-Grant, & Bankart, 2003). Study generally goes hand in hand with practice, which is made up of three components: *sila* or ethical code, *samadhi* or concentration, and *prajna* or insight. *Sila* implies a strong moral basis that prevents one from committing unwholesome deeds and aids in creating a mind that is calm and free from agitation. This then sets the stage for *Samadhi* and *prajna,* which are achieved largely through the practice of meditation. The practice of meditation lies at the heart of

Buddhism (Finn & Rubin, 2000). For Buddhists, this is the key method of testing ones experience and attaining wisdom and insight into the true nature of reality.

In traditional Theravada practice, there are two basic types of meditation: (a) *Samatha* or the development of concentration, and (b) *Vipassana* or seeing things as they really are, more commonly known as insight meditation. The goal of concentration meditation is to bring one's attention to a single object, thus limiting the range of ones mental experience. This has the effect of gradually unifying the stream of consciousness. Vipassana, or insight meditation, uses the power of this unified mind and directs it toward one's current experience as it is unfolding.

Another term that is commonly used in the Buddhist literature and particularly in the western psychological context is mindfulness. Mindfulness has been described as "bringing one's complete attention to the present experience on a moment-to-moment basis" (Marlatt & Kristellar, 1999, p. 68). This effort to become aware of one's immediate experience through calm and focused awareness results in the realization of what in Buddhism are called the three basic characteristics of all created phenomena: suffering, impermanence, and selflessness. Suffering is revealed in the layers of past wounds, pain, sadness, fear, and anger that may arise when one observes the mind in the present. Additionally, one may observe that life often feels unstable and uncertain and that even simple acts of liking and disliking create tension. The characteristic of impermanence is realized by observing the continually changing processes of mind and body, and understanding that the whole complex world is composed of changing sights, sounds, tastes, smells, touch, thoughts, and feelings (Kornfield, 1993). The characteristic of selflessness involves the understanding that there is no separate entity, "I" or "self" aside from this constant flux of experience. It is the clear understanding of these three characteristics that eventually leads one to wisdom.

THEORY OF PERSONALITY

Egolessness does not mean the absence of a functional self or ego— that's a psychotic, not a sage—it means that one is no longer exclusively identified with the self. (Ken Wilber, 1998)

Western conceptions of "self" generally can be traced back to either Plato or Aristotle, and tend to affirm the existence of a separate, individual self (Ramaswami & Sheikh, 1989). Psychology as a discipline is no exception to this. In the western psychological context, having a fully developed sense of self is seen as a source of strength and well-being. This is in radical contrast to Buddhist theory, which completely denies the existence of a separate, autonomous or permanent entity. According to the Buddha, a perceived sense of self is "a mere play of patterns and any identity we can grasp at is transient" (Kornfield, 1993, p. 200). What people experience as "I" is a result of certain physical and mental factors that the Buddha called *skandhas* or aggregates. These comprise of form, feelings, perceptions, consciousness, and mental formations. "Form" refers to the material body and its sense organs. "Consciousness" refers to the six senses: the five traditional ones plus the mind, which in Buddhism is often seen as a sixth sense that receives thoughts, ideas, and concepts, rather than actively creating them (Epstein, 1995). "Formations" refers to volitional attitudes and includes habits and dispositions (Ramaswami & Sheikh, 1989). In Buddhist psychology, an interaction of these factors is what gives rise to all phenomena, including a psychological sense of self.

This raises an important question with regard to how one might explain the development of individual personalities. The response lies partly in the way that Buddhism defines personality. In the Buddhist view, personality is seen as a continually changing flow of complex processes, rather than as a static entity. Nevertheless, certain cause-and-effect relationships and karmic propensities that are repeated over and over again, become the conditions that give rise to one's habits and mental tendencies. These "deeply ingrained patterns of thoughts, words and deeds are what constitute our unique styles of relating in the world" (Dockett, Dudley-Grant, & Bankart, 2003, p. 22). Therefore, even though the Buddha stated that there is no enduring and unchanging self, he did not deny that each person is a distinct and recognizable pattern of elements (Goldstein & Kornfield, 1987). Rather, he suggested that people loosen their identification with these karmic patterns, so that they may experience a greater sense of awareness and liberation.

A simple classification system that is contained in the Buddhist literature describes three basic personality types based on one's karmic conditioning. The first, the desire type, is one whose most frequent states of mind are associated with grasping, wanting, and not having enough. The second, the aversion type, is one who habitually pushes the world away through judgment, dislike, and hatred. The third, the confused type, is characterized by states such as lethargy, delusion, and disconnection (Kornfield, 1993). Although each of these types characterizes a style of relating to the world that is rooted in delusion and suffering, they are not considered to be indicative of "abnormality." They are merely seen as patterns that emerge from ignorance—mistaken beliefs that can be altered through awareness and insight into the true nature of one's being.

HUMAN DEVELOPMENT

Nirvana is not the blowing out of the candle. It is the extinguishing of the flame because of the arrival of day. (Rabindranath Tagore)

In the Buddhist system, the ultimate level of human development is characterized by the experience of *nirvana,* a state of total awakening in which delusion and grasping have been completely extinguished. *Nirvana,* like Western conceptualizations of self-actualization, involves the developing of one's personal potential. However, it goes a step beyond these conceptualizations by suggesting a state that involves complete freedom from all forms of suffering. Thus, mental health, as defined by western psychology, whether in terms of self-actualization or psychoanalysis' fully analyzed patient, is still incomplete according to Buddhism (Finn & Rubin, 2000).

However, a question that plagues a number of Buddhists is related to the attainability of *nirvana.* Is enlightenment something that lies far away in the distance or a reality that lurks just around the corner (Batchelor, 1997)? Various schools of Buddhism have found different ways to answer this question. Some see it as a gradual process that involves small incremental steps, whereas others see it as a sudden experience of awakening. Theravada Buddhism generally tends to take the more gradual approach, whereas Vajrayana practices are specifically geared toward transforming strong emotions so as to harness their energy for the process of awakening. In contrast to the other schools, Zen is unique in its view of enlightenment as occurring in immediate flashes rather than in deliberate sequential steps.

An important developmental aspect of the Buddhist path, particularly the Theravada path, involves the stagelike framework of the eightfold training. Although the stages are seen as interrelated and interdependent, rather than as sequential and invariant, they were originally designed as steps that would lead one to awakening. The first step on the path is "right view," which involves seeing things as they really are and truly understanding the truths of karma, impermanence, and suffering. The understanding implied here is one that is intuitive rather than intellectual. Right view goes along with "right intention," which refers to the volitional energy behind one's actions. "Right speech," "right action," and "right livelihood" comprise the ethical aspects of the path, and involve not causing harm thorough words, deeds, and occupation. "Right effort" involves the purity of one's thoughts and motivations and serves as a prerequisite for the other steps on the path. "Right mindfulness" refers to the clear perception of people's bodies, feelings, and mental states, and is aided by "right concentration," which refers to the unification of one's mental faculties by the development of one-pointed concentration.

PSYCHOLOGICAL HEALTH AND
PSYCHOPATHOLOGY

You are responsible for your own confusion and your own liberation.
(Lama Yeshe)

Although psychotherapy in the West is concerned with classifying suffering into specific categories such as depression, anxiety, and the like, Buddhism begins with the more general framework of suffering (Levine, 2000). The root cause of this suffering lies in an individuals' belief in the existence of a solid and unchanging self. Even though it is extremely useful for a human being to create a center and to act as a structured, unified whole, this tendency soon exceeds its legitimate functions and gives rise to a separate and permanent ego (Ramaswami & Sheikh, 1989). This results in clinging and attachment, which manifest as either craving or aversion. Both of these mental states exaggerate the desirable or undesirable qualities of an object and are responsible for a range of psychological problems. Craving is characteristic of problems such as addiction, whereas states such as anxiety and depression often contain strong elements of aversion.

Another aspect of mental health, as defined by Buddhism, is related to the wholesomeness of one's thoughts. Wholesome thoughts are those that engage in the cycle of cause and effect in such a way so as to result in wisdom and illumination. Unwholesome thoughts, on the other hand, are those that result in suffering if pursued. They are rooted in greed, hatred, or delusion, and lead to the blocking of wisdom or injury to self and others (Thera, 1977). For example, angry thoughts often lead to feelings of tension and anxiety. When taken to an extreme, these thoughts can turn into extreme rage and verbal and physical assaults upon oneself or another. An interesting visual representation of this is the Tibetan Buddhist image of the *mandala* or "wheel of life." The wheel portrays six realms of existence, including various types of hells and heavens that keep people locked into the cycle of birth and death. When interpreted metaphorically, these represent unhealthy psychological states such as envy, greed, anger, hatred, and delusion.

According to Buddhism, classifying one's thoughts based on their wholesomeness is not meant to encourage feelings of guilt or ideas about "good" and "evil." The trouble is not so much that people have these thoughts, but that they overidentify with them, and create a narrative "story line" that reifies the illusion of a separate, autonomous self-identity. Whatever is thought about, believed, welcomed, and paid attention to, is what the tendency of the mind becomes. Therefore, "every mental disorder results from particular combinations of unhealthy or unwholesome factors that have perceptual and affective elements" (Ramaswami

& Sheikh, 1989). The Buddha also described certain hindrances or emotional states such as desire, ill-will, sloth, restlessness, and doubt, which interfere with one's mental development and make one's thoughts unwholesome. They serve as obstacles on the path to both healing and spiritual progress (Thera, 1993). The Buddhist approach to the transformation of unwholesome thoughts and the prevention of mental disorder involves the practice of meditation. Insight and mindfulness are considered to be both necessary and sufficient for the elimination of unhealthy factors and the creation of healthy factors (Ramaswami & Sheikh, 1989).

THEORY OF HUMAN CHANGE

The goal of meditation is to free your awareness from its identification with your senses and thoughts. So freed, your awareness permeates everything and clings to nothing. (Ram Dass, 1978)

Mindfulness and meditation are the most important tools employed by Buddhism to facilitate change. They are used not only for exploring the mind, but also to relieve the stress of mental illness and achieve a state of optimal functioning (Ramaswami & Sheikh, 1989). Although most psychotherapy is aimed at helping the individual adjust to society, the scope of meditation extends beyond this to encourage the maximization of one's spiritual potential (Ramaswami & Sheikh, 1989).

Coming back to the discussion on the wholesomeness of one's thoughts, meditation can be thought of as the process of encouraging thoughts that are wholesome, and discouraging those that result in suffering. This is not to be confused with "suppressing" or "pushing away" negative thoughts. It merely means that one invites in thoughts that are wholesome by creating a comfortable abode for them, and does not hold on to thoughts that are harmful. The key is to engage in this process without anger and frustration, and with an attitude of nonjudgmental acceptance. This may seem difficult at first, but becomes easier with continued practice and patience. Traditional Buddhist tales describe this process using the metaphor of a boy walking a water buffalo. As the buffalo begins to get distracted and veers off to the left or right in search of crops, the boy gently taps it with a stick, to bring it back on its path. This tapping is not harsh and hurtful, but tender and compassionate. Similarly, meditation is like a gentle tapping of the mind that simply accepts unwholesome thoughts, while turning one's attention to more wholesome thoughts. Gradually, the mind gets used to this tapping and the mechanism by which it pursues unwholesome thoughts diminishes.

One side-effect of this type of practice and the deepening awareness that it results in, is that it might reveal aspects of one's life that are forbidden, repressed, or generally disquieting (Batchelor, 1997). However, mindful awareness does not deem anything as being unworthy of acceptance (Brach, 2003). Rather, "It accepts all personal experiences (e.g., thoughts, emotions, events) as just 'what is' in the present moment," instead of judging them as 'good or bad, healthy or sick, worthy or unworthy'" (Marlatt & Kristellar, 1999, p. 68). It has been suggested that mindfulness is useful in diffusing and transcending even the most difficult of emotions (Sogyal, 1992). Engaging in the practice of mindfulness meditation also brings about penetrating insight into the true nature of one's experience and enables one to accept all aspects of life—both those that are filled with happiness as well as those that are fraught with suffering—with increasing equanimity and balance.

Although meditation often is viewed as a solitary activity that results in insights of a deep and personal nature, Buddhism also emphasizes the value of group processes in encouraging one's mental and spiritual development. Almost all branches of Buddhism highlight the role of the *sangha* or spiritual community in supporting one's practice. This support can come from a traditional community of monks and nuns, the nurturing environment of a meditation retreat, or simply friends who inspire and influence one in a beneficial way.

COMMON MORAL ISSUES

Whether one believes in religion or not and whether one believes in rebirth or not, there isn't anyone who doesn't appreciate kindness and compassion. (His Holiness The XIV Dalai Lama)

Developing a moral lifestyle is the cornerstone of the Buddhist system and serves as a foundation for the practice of meditation. It involves the threefold training of *sila* or precepts, *Samadhi* or concentration, and *prajna* or insight. Precepts lead to concentration and concentration leads to insight (Hanh, 1995). The Buddha outlined five specific moral precepts that lead to a more conscious existence. The first precept is to refrain from killing and causing harm to any living being. It also may be thought of as a commitment to honoring all life and not acting out of hatred and anger. The second precept is to refrain from stealing and taking what is not given. Stated positively, it means to use things with sensitivity and care and to develop a sense of sharing with others (Goldstein & Kornfield, 1987). The third precept is to refrain from false speech. This involves not lying, being truthful and honest, and using one's words responsibly and wisely.

The fourth precept is to refrain from sexual misconduct and to not use one's sexuality in such a way as to cause harm to another. The fifth precept is to refrain from the harmful and heedless use of intoxicants and to devote one's life to developing clarity and awareness instead (Goldstein & Kornfield, 1987). An essential part of most Buddhist meditation retreats is the taking of the precepts, which are to be kept for the entire duration of the retreat.

It should be noted that the Buddhist ethical system is not a set of commandments that one is expected to follow in a ritualistic or unquestioning manner. Rather, it is described as "a natural sense of morality" that arises out of one's awareness of the suffering of others (Goldstein & Kornfield, 1987). The ultimate purpose of the system is to create an environment of freedom and peace, both within and without. Thus, contrary to misconceptions, Buddhism is not self-centered and passive with regard to being an agent of change. Rather, changes in society are viewed as being dependent on changes at the level of the individual. This is evident in the altruistic aspiration of the *Bodhisattva,* the being who desires enlightenment in order to be of benefit to all other beings.

Certain modern Buddhist groups also take the perspective that "both inner practice and social action are important elements of the spiritual path" (Goldstein & Kornfield, 1987). An organization that is worthy of mention in this context is The Order of Interbeing. The order was founded by the Vietnamese Buddhist monk and peace activist Thich Nhat Hanh as part of a larger movement termed socially engaged Buddhism, and as a direct response to the atrocities of the Vietnam War (Brown, 1997). The order formulated fourteen precepts to replace the original five and express traditional moral values in terms of relevant social issues (Brown, 1997). These precepts were created to guide peaceful action in order to resolve complex problems, and reflect a deep care and concern for society.

COMMON CLINICAL ISSUES

There are a number of areas in which traditional Buddhist values may interfere or conflict with the goals of psychotherapy. For instance, Buddhist clients may hold the belief that meditation and prayer are sufficient to transform their problems (Kornfield, 1993). They may feel that seeking outside help is an indicator of weakness and a failure of their spirituality (Finn & Rubin, 2000). Despite the value of meditation, however, it may not be the answer to every psychological problem, especially those that involve deep-seated issues of trauma, abuse, loneliness, sexuality, and the like (Kornfield, 1993). In order to resolve problems of this nature, one requires "the close, conscious, and ongoing support of a skillful healer"

(Kornfield, 1993, p. 245). In certain cases, meditation may even become an avoidant strategy and a means of escaping the pain inherent in these emotional situations.

In the West in particular, people are attracted to Buddhism, like any other religious or psychological tradition, for a variety of reasons. These reasons may be either healthy and productive or damaging and detrimental. They may range in motive from wanting a sense of connection and fulfillment, and having a greater ability to cope, to creating a rationale for self-punishment, and wanting to block one's awareness of disturbing thoughts and emotions (Finn & Rubin, 2000). As a clinician, it is extremely important to work with a client in assessing the motivation behind their involvement in Buddhism and in understanding if it plays a role that is destructive or beneficial (Finn & Rubin, 2000).

Another area of conflict may involve certain Buddhist beliefs and practices that seem unusual and alien to clinicians from different cultural and spiritual backgrounds. It is important for clinicians not only to be tolerant of these religious and cultural differences, but also to be careful not to immediately judge these behaviors as signs of psychopathology. One example of this might relate to the role of the spiritual teacher in Buddhism. Traditions such as Zen and Tibetan Buddhism see the master–disciple relationship as one that is vital to the student's mental development and one that requires a great deal of respect and devotion. The role of the spiritual teacher is to protect the welfare of students and guide their spiritual awakening with compassion (Kornfield, 1993), and it is strongly recommend that students invest a great deal of time and effort into selecting a teacher who is the embodiment of qualities such as wisdom and morality. However, it is important to be aware that in recent years the misuse of spiritual roles has become a common story. There have been a number of instances in the West where teachers have been corrupted by the temptations of power, money, and sexuality (Kornfield, 1993) and have grossly violated the rights of their students and left them feeling confused and betrayed (Finn & Rubin, 2000). Given these conflicting pieces of information, it is extremely important for a clinician to listen genuinely and objectively for the role of a spiritual teacher in the client's life (Finn & Rubin, 2000) and assess whether the teacher plays a role that is nurturing and compassionate or exploitive and abusive.

Another issue that may be encountered in dealing with American Buddhist clients is the high representation of psychologists in this population. Such clients may be exceptionally discriminating and may engage the therapist in an intellectual debate about the relative merits of meditation and psychotherapy (Finn & Rubin, 2000).

Although there is not much evidence to suggest that patterns of certain disorders may differ in Buddhist communities as compared to other groups, one issue to look out for may be the potentially high rates of post-traumatic stress disorder and depression among Buddhists who have been exposed to war and torture in countries such as Vietnam, Cambodia, Laos, and Tibet (Finn & Rubin, 2000).

In addition to the clinical issues that may be involved in dealing with Buddhist clients, it is also important to discuss the immense impact that Buddhism has had on the field of psychotherapy. In recent years, a larger and larger number of therapeutic orientations are beginning to recognize the beneficial effects of practices such as mindfulness and meditation in promoting healing and health. The recent empirical literature suggests that mindfulness may be of substantial clinical value and is useful in alleviating a number of problems, ranging from pain, stress, and anxiety, to depressive relapse, addictive behavior, and disordered eating (e.g., Kabat-Zinn, 1982; Kabat-Zinn et al., 1992; Kristellar & Hallett, 1999; Marlatt, 1985, 1994, 2002; Marlatt et al., 2004; Tesdale et al., 2000). Interventions that involve training in mindfulness skills are becoming increasingly popular and include such therapies as mindfulness-based stress reduction (Kabat-Zinn, 1990), mindfulness-based cognitive therapy (Teasdale, Seagal, & Williams, 1995), dialectical behavior therapy (Linehan & Heard, 1992), and relapse prevention (Marlatt & Gordon, 1985). These interventions regard mindfulness as more than just a therapeutic technique, and also view it as an attitude that is emitted by the therapist toward the client. Most interventions that involve training in mindfulness skills also emphasize the importance of the therapist's personal practice of meditation. Furthermore, there is an expanding interest in identifying the active ingredients of Buddhist meditative practices so as to better understand and increase their clinical applications.

REFERENCES

Batchelor, S. (1997). *Buddhism without beliefs.* New York: Penguin.

Brach, T. (2003). *Radical acceptance.* New York: Bantam Books.

Brown, P. R. (1997). *Socially engaged Buddhism.*

Dass, R. (1978). *Journey of awakening.* New York: Random House.

Dockett, K. H., Dudley-Grant, G. R., & Bankart, C. P. (2003). *Psychology and Buddhism.* New York: Kluwer Academic/Plenum Publishers.

Epstein, M. (1995). *Thoughts without a thinker.* New York: HarperCollins.

Fields, R. (1981). *How the swans came to the lake.* Boulder, CO: Shambhala.

Finn, M., & Rubin, J. B. (2000). Psychotherapy with Buddhists. In P. S. Richards & A. E. Bergin (Eds.), *Handbook of psychotherapy and religious diversity* (pp. 317–340). Washington, DC: American Psychological Association.

Goldstein, J., & Kornfield, J. (1987). *Seeking the heart of wisdom: The path of insight meditation.* Boston: Shambhala.

Hanh, T. N. (1995). *Living Buddha, living Christ*. New York: Penguin.

Ho, D. Y. F. (1995). Selfhood and identity in Confucianism, Taoism, Buddhism, and Hinduism: Contrasts with the west. *Journal for the Theory of Social Behavior, 25*, 113–139.

Kabat-Zinn, J. (1982). An outpatient program in behavioral medicine for chronic pain patients based on the practice of mindfulness meditation: Theoretical considerations and preliminary results. *General Hospital Psychiatry, 4*, 33–42.

Kabat-Zinn, J. (1990). *Full catastrophe living: Using the wisdom of your body and mind to face stress, pain and illness*. New York: Delacorte.

Kabat-Zinn, J., Massion, A., Kristellar, J., Peterson, L. G., Fletcher, K. E., Pbert, L., et al. (1992). Effectiveness of a mediation-based stress reduction intervention in the treatment of anxiety disorders. *American Journal of Psychiatry, 149*, 936–943.

Kornfield, J. (1993). *A path with heart*. New York: Bantam Books.

Kristellar, J. L., & Hallet, B. (1999). An exploratory study of a meditation based intervention for binge eating disorder. *Journal of Health Psychology, 4*, 357–363.

Levine, M. (2000). *The positive psychology of Buddhism and yoga*. Hillsdale, NJ: LEA.

Linehan, M. M., & Heard, H. L. (1992). Dialectical behavior therapy for borderline personality disorder. In J. F. Clarkin, E. Marziali, & H. Munroe-Blum (Eds.), *Borderline personality disorder: Clinical and empirical perspectives* (pp. 248–267). New York: Guilford Press.

Marlatt, G. A. (1994). Addiction, mindfulness, and acceptance. In S. C. Hayes, N. S. Jacobson, V. M. Follette, & M. J. Dougher (Eds.), *Acceptance and change: Content and context in psychotherapy* (pp. 175–197). Reno, NV: Context Press.

Marlatt, G. A. (2002). Buddhist philosophy and the treatment of bddictive Behavior. *Cognitive and Behavioral Practice, 9*, 42–50.

Marlatt, G. A., & Gordon, J. R. (1985). *Relapse prevention: Maintenance strategies in the treatment of addictive behaviors*. New York: Guilford Press.

Marlatt, G. A., & Kristellar, J. L. (1999). Mindfulness and meditation. In W. R. Miller (Ed.), *Integrating spirituality into treatment* (pp. 67–84). Washington, DC: American Psychological Association.

Marlatt, G. A., Witkiewitz, K., Dillworth, T. M., Bowen, S. W., Parks, G. A., Macpherson, L. M., et al. (2004). Vipassana meditation as a treatment for alcohol and drug use disorders. In S. C. Hayes, V. M. Folette, & M. M. Linehan (Eds.), *Mindfulness and acceptance: Expanding the cognitive behavioral tradition* (pp. 261–287). New York: Guilford Press.

Ramaswami, S., & Sheikh, A. A. (1989). Meditation east and west. In A. A. Sheikh & K. S. Sheikh (Eds.), *Eastern and western approaches to healing* (pp. 427–469). John Wiley & Sons.

Smith, H. (1991). *The world's religions*. New York: HarperCollins.

Sogyal, S. (1992). *The Tibetan book of living and dying*. San Francisco: Harper.

Teasdale, J. D., Segal, Z. V., & Williams, M. G. (1995). How does cognitive therapy prevent depressive relapse and why should attentional control (mindfulness training) help? *Behavior Research and Therapy, 33*, 25–39.

Teasdale, J. D., Williams, M. G., Soulsby, J. M., Segal, Z. V., Ridgeway, V. A., &

Lau, M. A. (2000). Prevention of relapse/recurrence in major depression by mindfulness-based cognitive therapy. *Journal of Consulting and Clinical Psychology, 68,* 615–623.

Thera, N. (1977). *The roots of good and evil: An anthology.* Sri Lanka: The Buddhist Publication Society.

Thera, N. (1993). *The five mental hindrances and their conquest: Selected text from the pali cannon and the commentaries.* Sri Lanka: The Buddhist Publication Society.

Wilber, K. (1998). *One taste: The journals of Ken Wilber.* Boston: Shambhala.

CHAPTER SEVENTEEN

Religion for Psychotherapists: Summary and Commentary

E. Thomas Dowd and Stevan Lars Nielsen

In the last chapter, the authors would like to create a context for the importance of religion in life. First, the definition, restructuring, and shifting meaning of religion and religious or spiritual involvement is examined, especially in light of recent rapid cultural changes. Second, religion is examined as an example of tacit knowledge structures in human cognition, which may account for the variety of religious beliefs throughout history and the changes in those beliefs. Third, possible reasons are discussed why religious expressions have been universal throughout human history. What does religion provide people? Fourth, evidence is presented indicating that religion and religious expressions are usually (although not always) indicative of mental and physical health. Fifth, an overarching analysis of the different chapters is provided.

At the very least, the chapters in this book should convince the reader of the absolutely kaleidoscopic variety of religious expressions. Not only is there great cross-sectional variety at any one time, but different religious groups and religious expressions constantly form, re-form, combine, dissolve, appear, and disappear. Much of this has occurred only slowly over time, so it may not be immediately obvious to the casual observer. However, since the end of World War II, this process has accelerated, especially in the United States, making it more immediately discernible. Beebe (Chapter 2) has well documented this restructuring tendency, as has Wuthnow (1988). Most obviously, from a U.S. point of view, has been the gradual diminution and re-combining of the religious denominations that emerged from the 16th century European reformation. Many of those groups have been in serious numerical decline for decades and some are cautiously merging with others. Against this is the recent rise in the numbers of nondenominational "mega-churches," the increase in the numbers of Muslims in western society, and the increased influence of certain Evangelical Christian groups in the United States.

A DEFINITION OF RELIGION

Surprisingly, the definition of religion is somewhat slippery. If it is defined in strictly theistic terms, it eliminates some Eastern religions such as Buddhism, which tends to be nontheistic. Pargament (1997) has described two fundamental definitional aspects of religion; the substantive tradition (a consideration of the Sacred and the Deity) and the functional tradition (a consideration of issues of ultimate meaning and conditions of existence). He attempts to combine these in this definition: "religion (is) a process, *a search for significance in ways related to the sacred*" (p. 32), which in some ways seems to be psychological in nature. Thus, it can encompass evolving expressions of spirituality as well as traditional structures and expressions. However, it still seems to consign nontheistic religions to a sort of religious limbo.

THE MEANING OF RELIGION

There also have been changes in the very meaning of religion. Beebe (Chapter 2) suggests that there has been a movement away from religion as denoting institutional membership and involvement and toward a more interior attitude (spirituality) that is often divorced from institutional membership. Beebe (2005) also asserts that churches have moved away from previous claims of cornering the market on Truth and the proclamation of moral principles that were expected to find their way into public policy and personal morality, and more toward people experiencing God in their lives and engaging in relevant theology that has an application to their entire lives. Thus, some people can say (and mean), "I'm not religious but I am spiritual." This is perhaps most obviously seen in the various iterations of the Recovery Movement, with its concept of a "Higher Power." Along with this is a shift from religion as a cognitive assent to a series of intellectual propositions and beliefs (which themselves are sometimes unbelievable, leading to the waggish statement, "Religious faith is when you believe something you know perfectly well isn't true") toward a more experiential and transcendental apprehension of the sacred in people's lives. Harris (2004) seems to adopt the former definition when he discusses "faith-based religion" (dogmatically believing in propositions on the basis of insufficient or untestable evidence), which he argues is the origin of much evil in the world. In the process, the very notion of "faith" is in the process of being redefined. Faith in what? And how? Perhaps a more contemporary understanding of faith might be *the security to be insecure*—in other words, a secure trust in God to be present in our life even in the midst of trauma and uncertainty.[1]

Wuthnow (1988) refers to a related restructuring. After discussing the decline of traditional denominationalism in American life, he describes a new division into religious "liberals" and "conservatives," which often cuts through and divides the traditional groups. The latter tend to be the upholders of tradition and institutionalism and view religion as important in shaping and maintaining individual values. Thus, religion may be seen as an important force for social control. The former tend to be much more open to new ideas, including scientific findings and pop psychology, more accepting of diverse lifestyles, and more syncretic. Interestingly, Wuthnow suggests that the religious liberal movement may have been partly fueled by the increasing numbers of people who have completed higher education, leading to an "education gap" in religious commitment. The distrust traditional Christians have often had for secular education may be well founded! Educated people and religious liberals may be more likely to favor "spirituality" over "religion," with the emphasis being on human growth and development rather than on personal and social control of "base" impulses.

Another societal force also may be fueling the religious liberal movement. In another context, Dowd (2005) has referred to the worldwide "clash of cultures" resulting from rapid communication and transportation, as groups previously separated from one another come into close contact. This can be profoundly unsettling and upsetting to people in both cultures, as each argues for its own concepts of goodness, morality, and sometimes attempts to force them and other cultural assumptions on other cultures. The intermingling that results can be gentle or harsh, but both cultures are changed in the process, although not necessarily to the same degree. It is easiest to see this cultural clash between two different religions, such as Christianity and Islam or Buddhism. However, it can also exist within the same broad religion, such as between different Christian or Islamic denominations, religious liberals and conservatives, or the religious and the spiritual. Each group has a vision of the "good and noble" that is not necessarily shared by the other group. By their very nature and beliefs, religious liberals are better equipped to understand and accept this clash and syncretically create new meaning structures than are religious conservatives.

---

[1] E. Thomas Dowd thanks the Rev. Norm Douglas for this insight.

RELIGION AS TACIT KNOWLEDGE

Religious beliefs and other (sub)cultural assumptions can be seen as examples of tacit or implicit knowledge structures that are developed automatically at an early age. This implicit learning occurs through the tacit detection of covariation of features or events in the environment and develop into *encoding algorithms* (Lewicki, Czyzewska, & Hill, 1997). What this means is that neurologically advanced organisms (e.g., humans) notice things that occur together and then tacitly assume that they belong together and represent reality; in other words, they develop into "inferential rules" about the nature of reality and the way it operates. Furthermore, that which occurs first is assumed to be the cause of that which occurs later *(Ad hoc, ergo propter hoc)*. This type of learning can occur very quickly and does not require many repetitions for it to occur. These encoding rules also can be developed from a surprisingly small number of instances of consistent evidence; it does not require much evidence for an inferential rule to develop. Thereafter, these assumptions or "rules for living" become a template or cognitive filter that acts to screen out discrepant data and screen in confirming data, resulting in a self-fulfilling prophecy. Because these tacit cognitions are largely preverbal, they cannot be discussed easily because there are few or no words for them; they are very resistant to change for that reason. This process is especially pronounced in situations that are ambiguous—which most social situations are—and where a variety of explanations might be plausible for a certain event. People often respond, when tacit assumptions are questioned, with: "But that's just the way things are! That's just reality! Everyone knows that!" In other words, people find what they expect and want to find and see what they expect and want to see. Rather than "seeing is believing," a more accurate phrase might be "believing is seeing." Indeed, that phrase may capture the essence of the religious experience as people apply their culturally derived religious encoding algorithms (or inferential rules) to ambiguous situations in an attempt to create structures of ultimate meaning. In the process, "Man creates God in his own image." Because thinking processes and cognitive constructs are deeply embedded in, and derived from, the culture in which people are raised, it could hardly be otherwise; it is the only reference point people have. For from what vantage point does one define the undefinable, comprehend the incomprehensible, or constrain the unconstrainable? Yet many or most religions attempt to place God in their own conceptual box based on their cultural concepts and constraints. As St. Paul said, "Now we see as through a glass darkly . . . ."

THE IMPORTANCE OF RELIGION

Why are religious expressions important to people and why do they appear to be universal throughout human history? There is a general and a specific answer. Humans are fundamentally meaning-makers; their cognitive structures do not easily adapt to ultimate meaninglessness. Indeed, a perceived lack of meaning is deeply frightening to people and they will go to great lengths to find meaning (or create it if necessary) in confusing situations and events. Psychotherapy involves some of the same processes, as people struggle to understand and make psychological sense out of the events in their lives. In that sense, religion and psychotherapy can be seen as competing systems for the creation of meaning, possibly accounting in part for their historical antagonism. However, religion has an ultimate advantage because it enables people to make meaning out of the fact that they will die. Humans are the only creatures aware of their own mortality. Even Harris (2004), who has major concerns about and disagreements with organized religion, agrees the message of all religions is that death is not a problem.

There may be a more specific answer. Genetic researchers recently have found tentative evidence indicating that some individuals are born genetically predisposed to believe in God (a "God gene"?). A recent University of Minnesota study (Koenig, McGue, Krueger, & Bouchard, 2005) suggests that as adolescents become adults, genetic factors become more important in determining how religious they are. This is more true for internal religiousness (e.g., importance of faith, using prayer, reading scripture) than for external religiousness (e.g., attending religious services, observing religious holidays). Over time, the study found that the influence of parents and childhood environmental factors wanes. This could provide a partial answer to the question why some people simply seem more interested in religion, religious activities, and a religious lifestyle than others. It also might provide some comfort to distressed parents who wonder why their children went "religiously astray" and blame themselves.

RELIGIOUS HEALTH AND ITS DISCONTENTS

Is religion psychologically healthy or is it an indicator of neurosis, as Freud, Ellis, and some others have thought? The evidence is not unequivocal, but the preponderance indicates that intrinsically religious people (those who learn about their religion and follow its beliefs) report less anxiety, less worry, less depression, less neurotic guilt (but more healthy guilt), and greater self-esteem and engage less frequently in problematic behaviors, such as substance abuse, divorce, and premarital sex and teen pregnancy, and report greater marital satisfaction (Bergin & Richards, 2000). This is much less true, however, for extrinsic religious people (those who use religion for external ends, such as social status). Sethi and Seligman (1993) found that people who held fundamentalist beliefs were more optimistic, hopeful, and religiously involved than those who held more moderate religious beliefs, who in turn were higher on those attributes that those who held liberal religious beliefs. Many psychologists (and others) hold negative views of Fundamentalists; perhaps those views should be re-evaluated. Koenig (2004) reports that 66% of studies "found a statistically significant relationship between religious involvement and better mental health, greater social support, or less substance abuse" (p. 810). Furthermore, most studies found statistically significant positive correlations between religiousness and variables such as well-being, hope, optimism, social support, and more purpose and meaning in life. Pargament (1997) reported that feelings of spiritual support, congregational support, and benevolent religious reframing (a loving God) were all associated with helpful religious coping. Religious commitment is even related to better physical health. Seybold and Hill (2001) present evidence that religious and spiritual experiences positively affect a variety of health attributes, including heart disease, blood pressure, strokes, cancer mortality, emphysema, chronic pain, kidney failure, and others.

However, there does not appear to be evidence that religions are differentially effective in fostering physical and mental health. Paloutzian, Richardson, and Rambo (1999) found that religious conversion had no appreciable effect on basic personality structure, although it did influence people's goals, strivings, and identity. Ross (1983) found Hare Krishnas to be as normal as the general population on a variety of personality inventories. However, there is evidence that certain lifestyles among different religious groups may lead to better physical health. For example, Enstrom (1989) found that religiously active Mormons in California as a nonsmoking population had an unusually low risk for cancer.

However, religion also can be associated with excessive guilt, obsessions, and anxious ruminations, as well as prejudice and intolerance against other people and other groups who do not share one's belief structure (Koenig, 2004). Regarding the first tendency, Pargament (1997) reported that discontent with one's congregation and with God as well as negative religious reframing (God's punishment) were associated with harmful religious coping. Seybold and Hill (2001) suggest that religion and spirituality can be pathological when individuals believe they have a direct communication or direction from God with little or no accountability or when the use a "leave it all to God" coping strategy. History as well as current events are littered with examples of the latter tendency as different religious groups attempt to force their understandings, beliefs, and practices on others. Those who leave one religion for another (or none) are especially at risk and are often treated more harshly than those who were never insiders. The heretic tends to be viewed more negatively than the unbeliever and is ultimately more threatening to group solidarity and identity. Kimball (2002) has listed five warning signs that suggest a religion may becoming corrupted toward evil ends: (a) absolute claims of truth, (b) blind obedience to charismatic leaders, (c) belief that one's community is bringing in an ideal age, (d) belief that the ends justify the means, and (e) declarations of holy war. Sadly, some of the most hateful and mean-spirited people are those who proclaim their religiosity. Then, they often justify these attitudes and behaviors on religious grounds. Unfortunately, these attitudes are sometimes the first attributes that occur to people when they think of the word "religion." Religion also can fuel feelings of personal inadequacy because one can never live up to the proclaimed ideal.

Why are religious beliefs and practices related to better mental health and fewer injurious behaviors? Koenig (2004) provides some possible reasons. First, as noted, religion can provide meaning and purpose in life through a positive world view that fosters hope. Seybold and Hill (2001) include the beneficial effects religion fosters of other positive emotions, such as forgiveness, contentment, and love. Humans are meaning-makers and those who have a strong sense of meaning are healthier than those who do not, especially about mortality. Second, religion provides a set of rules and guidelines that can help direct people toward better decisions and more prosocial lifestyle activities, which results in a better life structure. Third, religion creates and maintains healthy social connections and social support through strong social networks. Humans are social creatures and are more physically and psychologically healthy if they have strong and lasting support from others. Fourth, religious beliefs provide reinforcers for altruistic behaviors that often do not carry many secular rewards, which in turn benefit the giver as well as the receiver. This can result in a mutually beneficial and reciprocal life reward structure. Bergin and Richards (2000) add another, more explicitly religious, reason: God provides a healing energy toward those who have a devout religious involvement.

THE VARIETIES OF RELIGIOUS EXPERIENCE: REDUX (WITH APOLOGIES TO WILLIAM JAMES)

Finally, the authors would like to examine the chapters that comprise this book. As mentioned in the first chapter, the organizational structure is different than other books that have provided information to mental health professionals about various religious groups. Especially when discussing Christianity, there is an almost unconscious tendency to think primarily in terms of the denominations that arose from the 16th century European Reformation. However, there has been substantial religious restructuring in the United States in recent decades along with the addition of religious groups that were previously inconsequentially small, such as Muslims and Buddhists. The authors wished to examine the current diversity of religious expression rather than the past.

James Beebe's chapter stands outside the framework of the others and in a sense sets the stage for them. Three words seem to describe and summarize the approach to religion and spirituality he describes: choice, consumerism, and postmodernism. Increasingly, Americans, although remaining a highly religious society, are exercising their own choices about the form that their religious expressions will take. As Beebe points out, most young people no longer inherit their parents' faith tradition; rather, their selection involves not only what groups and expressions make them feel personally comfortable, but also reflects family compromises that inevitably occur as separate individuals blend into and create families. Choice is one of the defining characteristics of early 21st century American life, and it is not surprising it has invaded religion as well.

Increased choice is both a reflection and a cause of consumerism or what some have called Commodification. Whereas the consumption of commodities was once restricted to certain areas of life (called the economic sphere), now it has invaded the entirety of U.S. lives. Everything is viewed as a potential commodity to be shopped for and consumed. Thus, people speak of "shopping for a church" and may choose one partly, or even largely, based on the consumer satisfaction it provides. Additionally, people are often all too ready to choose another church, or even another denomination, if the one they have loses its ability to provide gratification. So, if one day your religion does not work for you or involves difficulties and obstacles, "Get a new one!" People also tend to interpret such religious terms as "stewardship" primarily in economic terms; as a request (or demand) to give more money to the church.

Postmodernism makes all this possible because it has reduced "truth" to a relative term. No longer are many people inclined to remain in a religion because they see it as possessing truth others do not have (e.g., "The One True Church"). Truth, if indeed they think of it at all, is seen as specific to the culture, or often the person ("Your truth is not my truth"). In a sense, churches lost the "keys to the kingdom;" the unique road to heaven. Not all religious groups believe this, of course, and attitudes such as these are incomprehensible, even destructive, to those who do not. Postmodernism also has relativized sacred scriptures themselves, because these writings are interpreted in light of the cultures in which they were written. For example, the Book of the Hebrew Bible (Leviticus) that declares homosexuality an abomination also declares eating shellfish an abomination (shrimp eaters, beware!) and prescribes stoning to death as punishment for adultery. This modern–postmodern divide probably accounts for much of the current "culture war" involving religion and politics.

Beebe also discusses both the division between religion and spirituality and the syncretism involved in much contemporary religious life. The former may arise in part from the recent distrust of what are often all-to-human institutions (exemplified by the clergy sexual abuse scandal in the Roman Catholic Church) and a retreat into privatism, which itself may be fostered by technological inventions such as private transportation (cars) and private communications (computers and hundreds of television channels). One can communicate with others without ever having to come into actual contact with them; so why not express that religiously as well? Syncretism can be seen as an inevitable outgrowth of the relativization of truth and church-as-commodity. If no one religious group has everything you want in just the way you want it, create your own! Thus, there are now Jewish Buddhists or Christian Buddhists, who take what they want from each tradition.

The authors now wish to comment on the chapters that describe and analyze psychologically the different faith traditions. Two disclaimers are offered first. Each chapter cannot and should not be described separately. Such an approach would be mindless and mind-numbing and would offer little beyond what the chapter authors themselves have written. It is also wished to emphasize that these comments reflect the authors' own ideas and interpretations as educated laymen and it is quite possible that people within each faith tradition might disagree with certain comments. As mentioned in the first chapter, this volume's very classification scheme may well provoke disagreement. Indeed, individuals might also disagree with some aspects of what the chapter authors in their own faith tradition have written. Such disagreements are inevitable in an area as sensitive and deeply meaningful as religion and readers are asked to understand that the authors, who, like all other humans, have imperfect and limited vision and insight, claim no unique understanding of the Truth.

THE SACRAMENTAL TRADITIONS

Roman Catholicism, Eastern Orthodoxy, and Lutheranism have been placed within this category. The Anglican/Episcopalian tradition also could be included here if there were a separate chapter on it. Although these groups are not the only ones to include a sacramental view of God's action in the world, and they may differ among themselves about how many sacraments there are, they have an especially central view of the sacraments (and sacramentals) operating in their religious lives. The sacraments are seen as intrinsically valuable and grace-producing or -enhancing.

Beyond that, all three groups have a relatively long historical tradition, especially the Roman Catholic and Eastern Orthodox. What is not always appreciated in the United States, however, is how close the Lutheran Church is to the Catholic Church, especially in Europe. Even in the United States, it is possible to hold certain joint Catholic–Lutheran services without offending the beliefs and practices of each faith tradition. The Lutherans and the American Episcopalians have even merged to an extent, now sharing a similar understanding of the episcopate and the sacraments as well as an interchange of clergy.

Like many Christian groups, the sacramental churches are wrestling with the areas of appropriate sexual expression, the understanding of sacred scripture, and the acceptance of modernity and postmodernity, although their answers are somewhat different. The Lutherans appear to have most fully accepted and engaged with the contemporary world, followed by the Orthodox and the Catholics. However, all three have valiantly and sincerely attempted to reconcile themselves to the modern world commensurate with their strong traditions. Significantly changing the religious understandings and practices of centuries-old churches is not easy, nor should it be. Although religious groups, such as other social institutions, must adapt to changing conditions and interpretations, there is much value in a conservative and measured approach, distressing though it might be in the short run to some of its members. These churches also have been somewhat countercultural in ways that are not always appreciated.

Where these churches appear to differ most is in their understanding of the appropriate role of law and rules. The Roman Catholic Church has always placed (and still does) more emphasis on a judicial or rule-governed approach, whereas the Orthodox and Lutheran (as well as the Episcopal) Churches have emphasized more the individual believer's relationship to God as the defining aspect of religion. This is not to say the Catholic Church does not value a relationship with God; only that it arises from and through a different source. In the past, this has led to the phenomenon known as "Catholic Guilt" (a term many contemporary Catholics now treat humorously), as the result of perceived infractions of the rules. All three groups have certain beliefs and practices that they hold sacred but they appear to differ in their acceptance of the immediate individual context in informing them. However, as Gillespie (chapter 3) makes clear, there are signs that even within the Roman Catholic Church, context and contextual understandings are becoming increasingly important. As one Catholic priest recently said to one of the authors (ETD), "Religion is not about following the rules but about establishing a relationship with God." Earlier generations of Catholics might have seen their appropriate role as involving little else *than* following the rules ("Pray, pay, and obey" was the mantra).

THE MAINLINE CHURCHES

The authors admit from the outset that this term is overly and perhaps unduly inclusive. (Are all other churches outside the mainstream?) However, they can be seen as mainstream insofar as they are deeply embedded in current American culture and indeed strongly shaped that culture. They are also a diverse group than nonetheless share many elements in common because they arose out of the 16th century European Reformation. Therefore, to discuss them all separately would involve a high degree of redundancy. The term also illustrates the somewhat artificial nature of the classification system; the Episcopalians and Lutherans, which were placed as sacramental churches, also could be included as mainline churches.

Because they are so diverse, it is difficult to define their central characteristics. At the core, however, several aspects seem to predominate. First is an emphasis on love and compassion, following the life of Jesus as a model. In that sense they are very "Jesus-centered." Second is a dual appreciation of Enlightenment and social justice ideals as informing religious faith and practice. The first aspect may be responsible for the mainline churches' integration into U.S. culture, also heavily influenced by the European Enlightenment. However, the latter aspect has not always been appreciated by all church members, who may be more socially conservative than their leaders. Third is a model of inclusion, at least for many of these groups, that attempts to incorporate people of diverse lifestyles and beliefs into their community. Denominational boundaries are also more fluid here, especially in recent years.

Donald Bubenzer and his colleagues provide a rather different examination than the authors of the other chapters, using a psychocultural approach rather than a strictly psychological view. The approach is heavily metaphorical and narrative (life story)–based and emphasizes living rather than believing. Its members tend to be so integrated into contemporary U.S. culture that religion and religious belief may not be raised at all in therapy.

THE OUTSIDERS

No, this term is not meant pejoratively, but rather as reflecting the way individuals in these groups tend to see themselves in relation to the larger U.S. culture. Although widely disparate in many ways, they have in common distrust (more or less) of the standard culture, which they see as degraded, decadent, and value-less. They differ, however, in how much they engage and attempt to influence that culture or withdraw from it. In recent years, the Evangelicals have moved from the latter to the former, not necessarily with the approval of many elements in the standard culture. In this book, the group is represented by the chapters on Evangelism (Yarhouse & Russell), Conservative Christianity (Belcher), and Fundamentalism (Savage). Members of many of these groups have often been mocked and caricatured by those in the larger culture as uneducated and bigoted louts, especially by those who profess no religion at all. The latter often include psychologists and other mental health professionals, who as a group tend to be less religious than the general population. Hence it is especially important that psychotherapists know more about these individuals and, as a form of cultural competence and sensitivity, attempt as much as possible to understand their world view while not necessarily agreeing with it.

It is extremely difficult to describe similarities and differences among these groups and clusters of groups because there are so many and they are so diverse. Indeed, some may question the classification system of these groups, especially the decision to examine Conservative Christianity separately from Fundamentalism. The Evangelicals are more similar to the mainline church members and some also might be classified in that category. Evangelicals of course proclaim the Good News (of Jesus Christ), so in one sense even members of the sacramental churches might be seen as evangelicals if they proselytize. Their defining characteristics include a personal conversion experience (being "born again"), seeing sacred scripture as the ultimate authority (although not necessarily completely inerrant), and of course sharing the Good News. When they seek psychotherapy, they may tend first (although not exclusively) to seek it among members of their own group.

There are so many different groups within the Conservative and Fundamentalist traditions that it is difficult to describe commonalities without overgeneralizing. In addition, the various groups sometimes do not like each other very much, differing vigorously on points of doctrinal beliefs and practices. However, it is possible to mention some commonalities. They tend to be dualistic thinkers, seeing the world (including other people) as good or bad. They tend to interpret the Bible literally, although of course it is impossible to do this with every passage in every book because some are obviously metaphorical or symbolic. They tend to see members of other Christian groups (most notably the Catholics or mainline Protestants) as "not really Christian." They tend to be profoundly distrustful of "the world" (meaning the larger culture) and see safety only in their closed community. They tend to seek psychotherapy only as a last resort and then check out the therapist carefully to insure that she or he is "a Christian." Nevertheless, psychotherapists see them often enough so that it is helpful to have some knowledge of their ideas and psychological makeup and above all to treat them and their beliefs with respect!

The astute reader may have already asked, "Where are the Baptists?" They are, after all, the second largest religious group in the United States, but the name does not appear in any chapter. The answer is that they are found in several of the previously discussed chapters. There are several groups of Baptists (Belcher, 2005). The American Baptist Church is generally associated with the mainline Protestants. The Fundamental and Independent Baptist churches belong to the Fundamentalist group. The Southern Baptist Convention is not really evangelical, but they certainly are part of the Conservative Christian movement. Exacerbating this division is that the Southern Baptist Convention is split and the denomination is currently experiencing a schism. The more liberal members—the ones who, for example, ordain women or believe that women and men are equal—have considered breaking away and forming their own group. As said earlier, groups are constantly forming and reforming.

THE CHURCH OF JESUS CHRIST OF LATTER-DAY SAINTS

"The Church," commonly known as the Mormons, represents a departure in a number of ways from the other religious groups covered in this book. First, it is the only truly American religion, having been formed in the United States in the 19th century with most of its members still in this country. Second, it is more evangelizing than most of the other groups, and not always well received in an officially secular culture. Third, in common with the Muslims but different from the others, it possesses "extra" books of sacred scriptures. It is sufficiently different from other Christian groups that it has sometimes been accused, despite its full name, of not being "really Christian," much as some Conservative Christian groups might view the Catholics and Mainline Protestants. Thus, there has been a movement to downplay the term "Mormon Church" in favor of its full name. This may be a hard sell, given the tendency of Americans to use shorthand names so that the Society of Friends, for example, is commonly referred to as Quakers.

The Church of Jesus Christ of Latter-day Saints has been viewed by some outsiders as "cultish" and possessing a bizarre theology. Certainly the very strong institutional and interpersonal support system it contains paradoxically can be interpreted as cult-like. However, for those within the religion, it provides much comfort and social support for behavior (especially about marriage and family relations, as the appendix in Nielsen, Judd, & Nielsen, this volume, attests) that these outsiders would likely value. With respect to theology, it should be noted (in line with a theme of this book) that the doctrines and practices of many religions look strange to those outside the group. In its beliefs about the nature of humans, the religion is highly optimistic while expecting the best of people and supporting them in achieving this. Like many religious groups throughout history, Mormons initially were persecuted by those whose views and practices were different but there is no record of them persecuting other groups.

JUDAISM

Although in the United States there are three major Judaic groups (Orthodox, Conservative, and Reform), this is not necessarily true in the rest of the world. In Israel, for example, there are the Orthodox and the ultra-Orthodox, with a very small Reform group that is not officially recognized. The division, used in this book, between Orthodox and Liberal Judaism, was suggested as best representing current broad Judaic groupings. As Halper and Bolton (chapter 11) as well as Savage (chapter 9), point out, however, there are other smaller groups as well as these large ones.

The Reform movement started in Germany with Moses Mendelsohn in the 18th century. The description of Reform Judaism in particular seems to capture well the dilemma faced by many Christian groups as well; how to reconcile ancient texts with modern knowledge. This is nowhere more obvious than the discussion about homosexuality that has wracked many religion groups. However, as Halper and Bolton note, this tradition assumes homosexuality is a matter of (wicked) choice. Modern biological and genetic knowledge, however, tends to indicate that it is innate. The dilemma involves explaining why God would condemn people for being the way they were made.

The description of Orthodox practices (Savage) echoes themes found in several of the more traditional and conservative Christian groups; a strict code of morality (especially sexual), a patriarchal family and societal structure, a strong sense of community, and a certain suspicion of and removal from the secular world. As noted in chapter 1, Judaism illustrates Wuthnow's (1988) division of religious attitudes into liberal and conservative, cutting across traditional religious lines.

ISLAM

No religious tradition in the world has had the bad press of Islam since 9/11. Because those terrorists (as well as others in the news) were and are mostly Muslims, it is easy to assume that, "if all terrorists are Muslims, then all Muslims are terrorists" (at least potentially). However, in doing so, people also equate "Muslims" with "Arabs," forgetting that the country with the largest Muslim population is Indonesia, and the country with second largest Muslim population is India.

Western ignorance of Islam is profound; because of this the authors are especially pleased to include the two chapters on Sunni and Shia Islam in this book. For example, it is often assumed that "Allah" is a separate deity unique to Muslims. However, Allah is simply the Arabic word for God. Therefore, saying that Muslims worship a god named Allah is like saying the French worship a god named Dieu. It is often assumed (especially since 9/11) that Muslims are especially religiously fanatical, zealous, and intolerant. However, historically Islam has been more tolerant and accepting of other faith traditions than Christianity and was scientifically literate long before Christianity. It is often assumed that Islam is very different from Christianity. However, as Ali (chapter 13) points out, Muslims see both Christians and Jews along with themselves as "People of the Book" and revere Jesus as a great prophet. Muslims, Jews, and Christians all share a commitment to social justice, social responsibility, and the care of the marginalized and disenfranchised. The concept of God as merciful and forgiving and encouraging that virtue in others discussed by Ali (chapter 13) has its counterpart in Christian theology.

Islam is one of the fastest growing religions in the world and it is increasingly likely that many psychotherapists will have Muslim clients. Therefore, knowledge of this rich faith tradition is important and will become more so in the future.

THE SPIRITUAL TRADITIONS

The authors have placed the spiritualistic traditions into this category (Murray & M. Nielsen, chapter 15) and Buddhism (Chawla & Marlatt, chapter 16), admittedly somewhat of a *Procrustean Bed*. They are different in many ways. However, as Murray and M. Nielsen note, the former draws syncristically from a variety of eastern faiths, of which Buddhism is an especially prominent example. They share an emphasis on internal and subjective experience and a concomitant rejection of institutional membership and involvement. As Murray and M. Nielsen note, such an emphasis fits well in a postmodern culture, in which all institutional forms and doctrines are seen as culturally derived and -specific and therefore at best approximations to "Truth." One religion is as good (or as bad) as any other and all of us must find our own spiritual way. The concept of a deity can be quite variable, ranging from a belief in a personal God, to the more general "Higher Power" of the Recovery Movement, to the essentially nontheistic approach of Buddhism.

Religion and spirituality overlap of course and many forms of institutional religions have a strong spiritual element in them. The monastics of the Roman Catholic and Eastern Orthodox churches, the Kabbalists of Judaism, and the Sufis of Islam are all predominantly spiritual with a lesser emphasis on the forms and rules of their respective traditions. It is also possible for individuals to be religiously involved with little or no spiritual aspect.

There are a number of reasons for the increased emphasis on spirituality in addition to or in place of organized religion. The influence of the postmodern culture previously discussed has certainly had an impact as previously separated religious groups have come in close contact with each other. With such a multiplicity of religions from which to choose it is easy to assume that none are "correct." Some people may be repelled by what they see as the overly legalistic and rule-bound nature of many formal religions. The U.S. move toward interiority and privatism also has had an effect and many people no longer seek churches for the sense of community they provide. In addition, the spiritual tradition described by Murray and M. Nielsen has been heavily influenced by psychological concepts that have now become embedded in the larger U.S. culture and with which people feel comfortable. Buddhism may have attracted some people initially because of a perceived "exoticism" and trendiness, but its emphasis on the internal and the private also fits in well with important aspects of contemporary U.S. culture. Finally, in some cases calling oneself "spiritual" as opposed to "religious" may simply be a quick and cheap way of providing a religious label for oneself in a culture that demands it.

CONCLUSION

The authors would like to offer a final meta-comment on the material contained in these chapters. Each faith tradition has its similarities with and differences from other groups. The differences can be seen as having arisen from different understandings, different cultures and social conditions, and different time periods. Yet the similarities are greater than the differences. Each tradition, in its own way, has addressed the universal longings and themes of human life over the centuries and millennia. Foremost among these is the nature and attributes of Deity (God) and how people do and should relate to this Deity. The understanding of and the forms and rituals used in relating to this Deity have varied widely across religions and even within the same religion over time but at bottom they are all ways of creating a relationship with God, however, that concept is understood. As discussed, almost by definition no human mind can ever understand the complete nature of God. All people can do is make whatever rough approximations they can based on their understanding and knowledge, encased within the time in which they live. As in the story of the blind men trying to describe an elephant, the danger is in mistaking people's very limited understanding for complete and final Truth.

Religions provide a unique and usually transcendental way of developing meaning in our lives. As discussed, the threat of meaninglessness is deeply distressing to people and they will go to great lengths to find or create meaning in the events of their lives. Religious doctrines and cosmologies help provide this meaning.

All faith traditions have developed principles and guidelines for conducting relations with other people, intimate or more casual. Caring and compassion (although not always by those names) are central themes in all religions. All religious groups appear to share, in some way or another, an especial concern for those who are less fortunate than others. This fundamental attribute can be and often has been clouded and temporarily eclipsed but it can never be extinguished. Furthermore, all religions have emphasized caring and compassion for those who are different from us, not only those who are "like us." The Christian parable of "The Good Samaritan" has echoes everywhere.

Then there is sex. The authors were struck by the extent to which sexuality and concerns about its appropriate expression permeated the moral and clinical issues sections of the various chapters. Some faith traditions have developed more explicit and definitive rules in this area than others. However, all religions, indeed all cultures, must wrestle with the appropriate expression, channeling, and regulation of this most important of human actions. It is interesting that the politico-religious "culture wars" in contemporary U.S. society are largely around sexual issues; including abortion, homosexuality, and premarital and extramarital sex. Few people argue passionately any longer about the nature of God, of Christ, or specific points of doctrines of belief. The only exception seems to be the appropriate place of religious belief and practice (and by implication control) in the larger society, whether it be U.S., Iraqi, Israeli, or Iranian.

The authors hope this book will lead psychotherapists to a greater understanding of and appreciation for the wide diversity of human religious expression. It is not expected that everyone will agree with everything; quite the contrary. Religion involves people's passions because it is passionately important. However, it is hoped that the understanding and acceptance of religious diversity in human life will be deepened among psychologists and other mental health therapists, many of whom historically have been scornful of religious beliefs and those who hold them. It has been well said, "To understand all is to forgive all."

REFERENCES

Beebe, J. R. (2005). *What St. Paul's might look like in 2015*. Post-homiletical discourse, St. Paul's Episcopal Church, Akron, OH.

Belcher, J. (2005). Personal communication.

Bergin, A. E., & Richards, P. S. (2000). Religious values and mental health. In A. E. Kazdin (Ed.), *Encyclopedia of psychology*, (vol. 7). Washington, DC: American Psychological Association.

Dowd, E. T. (2005). *Elements of compassion in cognitive therapy: The role of cultural specifics and universals*. Invited Address, 5th Congress of the International Association for Cognitive Psychotherapy, Gothenburg, Sweden.

Enstrom, J. E. (1989). Health practices and cancer mortality among active California Mormons. *Journal of the National Cancer Institute, 81,* 1807–1814.

Harris, S. (2004). *The end of faith: Religion, terror, and the future of reason*. New York: Norton.

Kimball, C. (2002). *When religion becomes evil*. New York: HarperCollins.

Koenig, H. G. (2004). Religion and mental health. In W. E. Craighead & C. B. Nemeroff (Eds.), *The concise Corsini encyclopedia of psychology and behavioral sciences*. Hoboken, NJ: Wiley.

Koenig, L. B., McGue, M., Krueger, R. F., & Bouchard, T. J. (2005). Genetic and environmental influences on religiousness: Findings for retrospective and current religiousness ratings. *Journal of Personality, 73,* 471–488.

Lewicki, P., Czyzewska, M., & Hill, T. (1997). Nonconscious information processing and personality. In D.C. Berry (Ed.), *How implicit is implicit learning?* Oxford: Oxford University Press.

Paloutzian, R. F., Richardson, J. T., & Rambo, L. R. (1999). Religious conversion and personality change. *Journal of Personality, 67,* 1047–1079.

Pargament, K. I. (1997). *The psychology of religion and coping: Theory, research and practice*. New York: Guilford.

Ross, M. W. (1983). Clinical profiles of Hare Krishna devotees. *American Journal of Psychiatry, 140,* 416–420.

Sethi, S., & Seligman, M. E. P. (1993). Optimism and fundamentalism. *Psychological Science, 2,* 256–259.

Seybold, K. S., & Hill, P. C. (2001). The role of religion and spirituality in mental and physical health. *Current Directions in Psychological Science, 10,* 21–24.

Wuthnow, R. (1988). *The restructuring of American religion.* Princeton, NJ: Princeton University Press.

Index

pre- *vs.* post- Vatican II, and,
32–34, 46
and Conservative Christian
Movement (CCM), 134
Lutherans, and, 78–79
and Mainline Protestants, 93–98, 101
and Mormons, 172, 174–175, 180
'Idioms of distress,' 213
Illness. *See* Psychological illness
Independent thinking
and definition of abnormality, in
CCM, 135
encouragement of, Lutherans, and,
84
Individual
choice/experience
as religious authority, U.S. society
and, 20
focus on (*vs.* in social context)
and mesh with U. S. culture, 152
in moral reasoning, 150
as uniquely American aspect of
Evangelicalism, 114–115
freedom,
importance of
for Liberal Jew, 194, 197–198
for Sunni Muslims, 228
Lutheran church, and presence
of, 84
and sin, synonymous with, 137
relationship to God, direct
and Islam, 227
rights
and over-concern with, in the
"world," 135
Indulgences, 71
Inerrancy
of belief system, 147, 158
of Bible, 132, 145, 147, 150, 158
(*see also* Bible; Verbal
inerrancy (of Bible)
Infallibility
Catholic Pope, and, 36–37
of Imamate, Shiite Muslims, and, 242
Isaiah. *See also* Prophets
commissioning types of religious
experiences, and, 23

Islam. *See also* Meta-narratives;
Religious experiences; Shiite
Muslims; Sunni Muslims
9/11, bad press, and, 301
actions, focus on, 223–224
and commissioning types of
religious experience, 23
continuation, of Judaism and
Christianity, 226, 230, 301
integrated into psychotherapy, 10
Islamic civilization, classical period,
and science, 228
misconceptions regarding, 301
practices of, 225–227
principles of, 223–225
Sufis, spirituality of, 302

Jacob, 179. *See also* Old Testament
James, William, 8
Jesus. *See also* Prophets
as mental health professionals, 134
Jesus Christ. *See also* Altar call
and Catholicism, beliefs regarding,
34–39
and Conservative Christians, beliefs
regarding, 131–132, 134–139
controlling evil, through relationship
with, 135
and Evangelicals, beliefs regarding,
111–115, 117
and example for, Mainline
Protestants, 101, 106
and Fundamentalism, beliefs
regarding, 145–146, 151–152,
154–158, 161
and Islam, beliefs regarding, 226
and Lutherans, beliefs regarding,
69, 75–76
and Mainline churches, 91, 97,
101, 102, 297
and millennial beliefs regarding
second coming of, 131–132,
146 (*see also* Premillennialism)
and Mormons, beliefs regarding,
166–172, 176–178
and Muslims, beliefs regarding, 301
as Prophet, for Muslims, 301